AF841966

THE HEROES OF THE JUDICIAL PERIPHERY

This book assesses the role of court experts, court clerks and court staff, and other actors on the 'judicial periphery' who play an important role and often co-determine the pace, outcome, and tone of the judicial process.

In national civil justice systems, the limelight is all too often cast on the main actors: judges, lawyers, and parties but the court's support staff can sometimes be overlooked. This book explores their role.

The knowledge and skills of experts may be indispensable at times, but it is among the most expensive, complicated and time-consuming means of evidence. The judges adjudicate, but where experts are involved in the process, they have a decisive impact on the outcome of litigation. Therefore, a principal focus of the book is on experts and how they are appointed, managed, and remunerated across Europe and the world.

Other ancillary professions may also be decisive for effective provision of court services. Different jurisdictions have different rules and habits, but inevitably recognise the need of adequate support for judges. Sometimes judges command the whole team of clerks and lawyers; sometimes they share a secretary or a clerk. But in all cases, those who assist judges in their daily work have a significant impact on the effectiveness and quality of the judicial process and its outcome.

The book considers the contribution of different actors including clerks, secretaries, advisors, counsels and reporters. It focuses on cooperation and the interplay between judges and other professional actors in litigation.

The Heroes of the Judicial Periphery

Court Experts, Court Clerks, and Other Actors in the Shadows

Edited by
Alan Uzelac
and
Stefaan Voet

•HART•
OXFORD • LONDON • NEW YORK • NEW DELHI • SYDNEY

HART PUBLISHING
Bloomsbury Publishing Plc
Kemp House, Chawley Park, Cumnor Hill, Oxford, OX2 9PH, UK
1385 Broadway, New York, NY 10018, USA
Bloomsbury Publishing Ireland Limited, 29 Earlsfort Terrace, Dublin 2, D02 AY28, Ireland

HART PUBLISHING, the Hart/Stag logo, BLOOMSBURY and the Diana logo are trademarks of Bloomsbury Publishing Plc
First published in Great Britain 2025

Copyright © The editors and contributors severally 2025
The editors and contributors have asserted their right under the Copyright, Designs and Patents Act 1988 to be identified as Authors of this work.
All rights reserved. No part of this publication may be: i) reproduced or transmitted in any form, electronic or mechanical, including photocopying, recording or by means of any information storage or retrieval system without prior permission in writing from the publishers; or ii) used or reproduced in any way for the training, development or operation of artificial intelligence (AI) technologies, including generative AI technologies. The rights holders expressly reserve this publication from the text and data mining exception as per Article 4(3) of the Digital Single Market Directive (EU) 2019/790.
While every care has been taken to ensure the accuracy of this work, no responsibility for loss or damage occasioned to any person acting or refraining from action as a result of any statement in it can be accepted by the authors, editors or publishers.
All UK Government legislation and other public sector information used in the work is Crown Copyright ©. All House of Lords and House of Commons information used in the work is Parliamentary Copyright ©. This information is reused under the terms of the Open Government Licence v3.0 (http://www.nationalarchives.gov.uk/doc/open-government-licence/version/3) except where otherwise stated.
All Eur-lex material used in the work is © European Union, http://eur-lex.europa.eu/, 1998–2025.

A catalogue record for this book is available from the British Library.
Library of Congress Cataloging-in-Publication data
Names: Uzelac, Alan, editor. | Voet, Stefaan, editor.
Title: The heroes of the judicial periphery : court experts, court clerks, and other actors in the shadows / edited by Alan Uzelac and Stefaan Voet.
Description: Oxford ; New York : Hart Publishing, 2025. | Includes bibliographical references and index. | Summary: "This book assesses the role of court experts, court clerks and court staff, and other actors on the 'judicial periphery' who play an important role and often co-determine the pace, outcome, and tone of the judicial process. In national civil justice systems, the limelight is all too often cast on the main actors: judges, lawyers, and parties but the court's support staff can be overlooked. This book explores their role. The book considers the contribution of different actors including clerks, secretaries, advisors, counsels and reporters. It focuses on cooperation and the interplay between judges and other professional actors in litigation"—Provided by publisher.
Identifiers: LCCN 2024057499 (print) | LCCN 2024057500 (ebook) | ISBN 9781509980529 (hardback) | ISBN 9781509980567 (paperback) | ISBN 9781509980536 (Epub) | ISBN 9781509980543 (pdf)
Subjects: LCSH: Law clerks. | Clerks of court. | Court-appointed experts. | Judicial process.
Classification: LCC K115 .H47 2025 (print) | LCC K115 (ebook) | DDC 347/.016—dc23/eng/20241203
LC record available at https://lccn.loc.gov/2024057499
LC ebook record available at https://lccn.loc.gov/2024057500

ISBN: HB: 978-1-50998-052-9
ePDF: 978-1-50998-054-3
ePub: 978-1-50998-053-6

Typeset by Compuscript Ltd, Shannon

For product safety related questions contact productsafety@bloomsbury.com
To find out more about our authors and books visit www.hartpublishing.co.uk. Here you will find extracts, author information, details of forthcoming events and the option to sign up for our newsletters.

CONTENTS

PART II
COURT EXPERTS

PART III
OTHER ACTORS

LIST OF CONTRIBUTORS

Branka Babović Vuksanović is an assistant Professor at the University of Belgrade, Serbia.

Camilla Bernt is a Professor at the University of Bergen, Norway.

Juraj Brozović is a teaching assistant at the University of Zagreb, Croatia.

Adriani Dori is a postdoctoral researcher at Erasmus School of Law, the Netherlands.

Yulin Fu is a Professor at Peking University Law School, China.

Fernando Gascón Inchausti is a Professor of procedural law at Complutense University of Madrid, Spain.

Gina Gioia is a Professor on civil procedure law at Università degli Studi di Padova, Italy.

Xandra Kramer is a Professor of law Erasmus School of Law, the Netherlands.

Athina Katsiantoni is a lawyer and legal counsel in Cyprus.

Nicolas Kyriakides is an adjunct Professor and the Director of the procedural law unit at the University of Nicosia, Cyprus.

Maurício Magalhães Lamha is a Federal Judge at the 2nd Federal Court Rio de Janeiro, Brazil.

Eduardo Oteiza is a Professor at La Plata National University, Argentina.

Álvaro Pérez Ragone is a Professor for civil justice and procedural law at Pontificia Universidad Católica, Peru.

Seyedeh Sajedeh Salehi is a researcher at the Vrije Universiteit Brussel, Belgium.

Elisabetta Silvestri is an associate Professor at the University of Pavia, Italy.

John Sorabji is an associate Professor of law at University College London, UK.

Magne Strandberg is a Professor at the University of Bergen, Norway.

Michael Stürner is a Professor of civil law, private international law and comparative law at the University of Konstanz, Germany.

Alan Uzelac is a Professor of law at the University of Zagreb, Croatia.

Danie van Loggerenberg is an extraordinary Professor of law at the University of Pretoria, South Africa.

Raf Van Ransbeeck is a Professor of law at KU Leuven, Belgium.

Stefaan Voet is a Professor of law at KU Leuven – UHasselt, Belgium.

Hermes Zaneti Jr is a Professor of civil procedure at the Federal University of Espírito Santo, Brazil.

Tatjana Zoroska Kamilovska is a Professor of civil procedure and arbitration at Ss. Cyril and Methodius University, Macedonia.

1

Unknown is Unloved: The Heroes of Judicial Periphery

STEFAAN VOET AND ALAN UZELAC

I. Introduction

Civil justice is a complex universe, with its central galaxies being national civil justice systems. These systems traditionally revolve around courts as public venues for processing civil matters. In the solar systems of civil courts, the brightest suns are (or at least used to be) those who are ultimately responsible for decision-making: individual judges and their panels. Ulpian's statement, '*iurisdictio est etiam iudicis dandi licentia*', can be freely translated as: dispensing justice is the exclusive licence of judges. It comes as no surprise that in many legal traditions, the 'judge' is synonymous with the 'court', and the 'court' is synonymous with 'justice'. In the exploration of the actors and forces that shape civil litigation, scholarly treatises and doctrinal works on civil procedure have always given the most attention to judges as the central point of research.

However, the solar system of national courts consists of other parts as well. As representatives of the parties involved in the process, lawyers are the planets, bright enough to attract the attention of observers. In a separate, non-contentious space, bailiffs, process servers, notaries, and (court or party appointed) experts have also formed their own galaxies, notable and appreciated in their own right.

Blinded by the light of these prominent figures, other actors in the shadows also deserve attention. Their roles are always significant and sometimes crucial for the effectiveness and quality of the judicial process. To these supporting actors, the heroes of the judicial periphery, we devote this book.

The goal is to focus on cooperation and interplay between judges and other professional actors. We do not wish to address the privatisation of court services or the outsourcing of judicial functions. In the same vein, we would like to focus on court proceedings such as litigation or voluntary jurisdiction, disregarding enforcement and other proceedings transferred to other judicial professionals, such as bailiffs or public notaries. But if such outsourced proceedings have a judicial epilogue (eg, via appeals) and require cooperation, assessing their impact on court proceedings may be a matter of study as well.

II. Court Staff

Even though adjudication is ultimately in the hands of judges, who decide based on submissions from the parties and their lawyers, the processing of civil cases in all national civil justice systems is a collective process requiring teamwork. This teamwork, though varying in form and extent across different systems, involves numerous supporting staff and other peripheral actors who often determine the pace, outcome, and nature of the judicial process. The chapters collected in this book explore these understudied members of the team.

As the following chapters reveal, there is a rich diversity in the roles these shadow actors play within various national justice systems. However, two groups of 'peripheral heroes' stand out, and they correspond to the first two parts of this book.

In Part One, we have gathered insights on higher forms of ancillary court staff. This group encompasses professionals who are typically employed by the court and work in collaboration with, and under the supervision of, judges and/or court administration. The focus here is on staff with legal qualifications. Mere administrative assistants, though important, are generally left aside.

Among higher echelons of court staff, we find a colourful variety. There are generally no uniform titles for such professionals. In this book, we analyse roles such as 'law clerks,' 'judicial advisors,' 'legal officers,' 'judicial secretaries,' 'judicial officers,' 'court registrars,' and 'judicial assistants,' among others. In native languages, they are known as *Rechtspfleger, greffiers des services judiciaires, secretarios judiciales, sudski savjetnici*, and so on. Sometimes, they are on a career track to a judicial position, sometimes not. They might be full-time professionals who work as part of the court staff until retirement with no intention (or prospects) for further promotion, or they might be bright young lawyers employed temporarily before embarking on a different career path in private or public practice. Sometimes, they are associated with judicial chambers, and sometimes they appear in novel organisational forms, such as part of the 'office for judicial proceedings' (*l'ufficio per il processo*) in Italy.

The common element for all 'shadow heroes' in this category is their indispensable role in the preparation of judicial work. It is also important to note that they enjoy some autonomy in handling particular judicial tasks – from drafting judgments to issuing rulings on simpler matters, such as decisions on costs. Nevertheless, their work is typically subject to guidance and revision by judges or administrative authorities to whom they are accountable. Another common aspect is the need for specialist training and education for professional members of the court staff, and such training can be quite substantial, as described in one chapter of this book.

In chapter one, Nicolas Kyriakides and Athina Katsiantoni argue that the use of law clerks in the adjudicative process has gained interest due to the rising caseloads in courts all over the globe, which has led to long judicial delays. These delays are caused, inter alia, by a lack of support staff for judges. Their chapter explores the role of judges and the use of law clerks in different European jurisdictions as well as the United States where they were first used. It then examines whether law clerks may provide relief in reducing delays in jurisdictions in the EU facing severe judicial delays, such as Italy, Greece, and Cyprus. Finally, the chapter explains that to maintain the integrity of the judicial decision-making process and to strike a balance that maximises the benefits of the judge-clerk relationship, judges should bear the final decision and responsibility.

In chapter three, Elisabetta Silvestri argues that among the requirements Italy is supposed to meet in order to have access to the post-pandemic funds known as Next Generation EU, the improvement of the administration of justice is certainly the foremost. For improving the efficiency of the judicial system, a partially new structure of support has been established: the *ufficio del processo*, which can be translated as 'office for the judicial proceeding'. It is a form of judicial clerkship open to young law graduates that offers them the opportunity to work side by side with judges and prosecutors and to engage in a variety of tasks that – ideally – will speed up the pace of Italian justice. But will the addition of these new forces to the outdated logistics of the court system achieve the goal of reducing by 40 per cent the delay of civil cases and by 26 per cent the delay of criminal cases by June 2026 as agreed with the EU Commission?

In chapter four, Juraj Brozović focuses on the role of judicial advisers in Croatia. First introduced as expert associates assisting judges in performing various administrative and preparatory tasks, judicial advisers slowly became an important part of the Croatian judicial system. Although they are formally not judges, not appointed as such, they perform many activities in first-instance cases that are typically considered adjudicative tasks reserved for judges only. The intended career path for judicial advisers is set for them to potentially become judges one day, although most of them spend their careers as advisers, higher advisers, or specialist higher advisers, never living up to a dream. It would not seem as appealing as a choice of career if one did not consider the salaries that, as the advisers climb the ladder, are close to or even higher than the salaries of judges. This chapter aims to compare their positions and status, thus exposing the absurdity of such personnel management within the judicial system, also taking into consideration the goals that such a judicial organisation aims to achieve.

Chapter five, written by Fernando Gascón Inchausti, focuses on the evolving role of judicial secretaries in the Spanish judicial organisation. At first sight, judicial secretaries play a major role, to the point that it can be said that there is a kind of 'bicephaly' between the judge and the judicial secretary. The chapter explains that there is some truth in this, but also that what lies behind it, at least at present, is the story of a collective frustration or, if preferred, the story of the frustration of a collective.

Chapter six shifts the attention to court staff training. Raf Van Ransbeeck states that the training of court staff in Europe seems like an obvious topic that is easy to map out, but that this is only an appearance. Each Member State has its own training structure for court staff, and often the concept of court staff is not always unambiguous either. His chapter touches on some facets that can be inspiring for the definition of the concept of court staff and for the design of court staff training. The training of judicial staff in Belgium and the study on the training needs in EU law of European judicial staff completed by EJTN and EIPA in 2021 are also discussed.

In chapter seven, John Sorabji examines the judicial assistants in England and Wales. The role of judicial assistant was first introduced in the late 1990s in the Court of Appeal. Since its introduction, it has expanded into the High Court and the Supreme Court. The development and nature of this role is explored, primarily by reference to the Supreme Court and Court of Appeal schemes, not least in respect of the provision of Bench Memoranda on matters before the courts, legal research, and discussions with the judiciary on live cases before them.

In chapter eight, Álvaro Pérez Ragone starts with the question: is it possible to measure and to analyse the influence of clerks on the judicial adjudication process? The Latin American answer seems to be complex because most former law assistants avoid giving information about their activities, especially regarding their assistance in the court decision-making process. The chapter begins with an approach to the rational organisation of the courts and a description of the judicial assistant or clerk. Next, attention is paid to the specific tasks of the judicial assistant. Finally, the influence of the judicial assistant on the judicial decision-making process is analysed.

In the final chapter nine of Part One, Yulin Fu starts from the judicial reforms in China in the 1990s. These reforms have promoted the role of litigants and their procedural rights, procedural transparency, and judicial professionalisation. In 2012, Chinese civil procedure was amended once again. These amendments significantly increased the independence and responsibility of judges to exercise trial power on behalf of the courts. One of the aspects was providing for judicial assistants, in the context of a so-called 'judiciary classification'. Court personnel was divided into 'post judges', judicial auxiliaries (including judge assistants, court clerks, and judicial police) and administrative personnel. This reform aimed to release judges from routine and trivial procedural affairs that should be left to judicial auxiliaries. Among the judicial auxiliaries, the role of judge assistants is the most important one.

III. Court Experts

In Part Two, we examine another, apparently more homogeneous group of shadow actors, at least in terms of their name – court experts – which is more or less uniformly accepted. Still, there are numerous differences and variations in the status and use of experts across different national civil justice systems.

The common element among all experts is their role in assisting the court with their specialised knowledge and expertise, which supplements the legal experience and knowledge of judges. Generally, experts possess technical skills and knowledge from non-legal fields, though, as discussed in chapter eleven, they can also be engaged to report on legal issues of foreign law or other specialised legal fields. In any case, experts aid the court by providing persuasive explanations and assessments of issues that will ultimately form the factual (and, sometimes, legal) basis of court decisions.

Unlike court clerks, court experts are not directly subordinate to the court and individual judges. They are rarely, if ever, regular employees of the court. While they are expected to follow judicial instructions regarding their tasks and assignments, experts are independent and autonomous in their analysis of the matters submitted for their assessment. As life becomes increasingly dependent on complex assessments of various technical matters, expert views and assessments become invaluable. They ensure that final decisions are based on appropriate evaluations of factual and legal issues, avoiding unfairness and arbitrariness. However, this comes at a cost: experts are among the most expensive, complicated, and time-consuming means of evidence. Judges adjudicate, but where experts are involved, they have a decisive impact on the outcome of litigation.

The status and role of experts used to depend greatly on legal tradition. In civil law countries, experts are appointed and instructed by the court. They must be independent and impartial, akin to the judges who appoint them. While parties may challenge the expert's view, typically there will be only one expert on each issue, and the court will verify whether the expert has reached a plausible conclusion. In common law jurisdictions, experts are appointed and instructed by the parties, presenting a contradictory picture of two conflicting 'expert witnesses' from which the court should choose the more plausible one.

However, as several chapters of this book illustrate, the binary division between common and civil law experts is increasingly blurred. In civil law countries, experimenting with party-appointed experts is sometimes encountered in unexpected places, such as transition countries in southeast Europe. In England and Wales, the Woolf reforms have limited the number and use of party-appointed experts in cases where they lead to disproportionate costs and expenses. Nonetheless, legal frameworks and specific local rules and practices on the use of experts vary widely across different jurisdictions.

In chapter ten, Eduardo Oteiza argues that experts are closer to the centre than to the periphery. The need for specialised expertise to delve into the technical and scientific complexities is crucial and a great challenge for our procedural culture. After a brief historical overview, the central questions of the chapter are whether the expert witness is an assistant to the judge and how they can and should interact with the parties? Various divergences and convergences between the judge and the expert are analysed. The chapter concludes that it is essential to strike the right balance between the expert appointed by the judge and the one proposed by the party by applying the principles of cooperation and proportionality while ensuring an adequate relationship between the judge and the parties involved.

In chapter eleven, Michael Stürner focuses on experts on foreign law in German civil procedure. The outset of the chapter is that foreign law is law from a German perspective, but is treated as a factual question with regard to the process of establishing its contents. The responsibility for determining foreign law lies entirely with the court. The court is not completely relieved of this responsibility even if the parties agree on the foreign law. Based on a 2018 empirical study, the chapter analyses how this plays out in German civil procedure.

In chapter twelve, Branka Babović Vuksanović analyses the concept of party-appointed experts in Serbian litigation proceedings. The reason for introducing such experts was that, in practice, courts gave insufficient instructions and excessively relied on the expert's opinion when they themselves appointed the expert. To ascertain to what extent party-appointed experts really contribute to the resolution of those problems, the chapter analyses the broader reform of Serbian civil procedure, a part of which was to introduce party-appointed expertise, including the role of court experts.

In chapter thirteen, Tatjana Zoroska Kamilovska states that there has been much debate on the upsides and downsides of party-appointed and court-appointed experts. Macedonian civil procedure underwent major reforms as to expert evidence in 2010 by introducing the adversarial approach to expert evidence, whereby the parties appoint and instruct their respective experts. It has replaced the previous court-centred approach to expertise. The changed position of experts has not lived up to the expected improvement in efficiency and cost cutting, which were the prime reasons for the change. That imposed the need for reconsideration of the concept during the drafting of the new Macedonian Civil Procedure Act (MCPA). The proposal of the new MCPA provides for a mixed model of court-appointed and party-appointed expert evidence as a more promising one.

In chapter fourteen, Magne Strandberg focuses on the appointment of experts in Norway and, more particularly, the role of parties and judges in civil proceedings. The most important question concerns the competence to appoint experts. Is it for the parties to appoint experts, the judge, both parties and the judge, or is it a mix of all these? These questions are important, especially because of the limited capacity of the court to correct or overrule the expert's opinion, which can ultimately determine the outcome of a case. The Norwegian analysis in this chapter may shed light on ongoing comparative tendencies and may provide potential middle-way solutions between more famous and influential procedural traditions or paradigms.

In chapter fifteen, Camilla Bernt states that expert evidence, especially from psychologists, plays an important role in child protection cases and in court disputes between parents on parental responsibility, custody, and contact (custody disputes) in Norway. However, the use of experts in these cases is frequently debated. Considering the great importance of expert evidence, it is a paradox that to this date there is relatively limited research on the use of expert evidence in custody disputes and child protection cases in Norway. There is a pressing need for more systematic knowledge to ensure a suitable use of expert evidence and safeguard the legal rights of children and parents. In this chapter the use of experts in child protection and custody cases is discussed, focusing on the purpose of expert evidence, issues that have been debated, and findings in existing research.

In the final chapter sixsteen of Part Two, Danie Van Loggerenberg looks at the appointment and management of experts in South Africa. The functions of an expert witness are threefold. First, where they have themselves observed relevant facts, that evidence will be evidence of fact and admissible as such. Second, they provide the court with abstract or general knowledge concerning their discipline that is necessary to enable the court to understand the issues arising in the litigation. Third, they give evidence concerning their own inferences and opinions on the issues in the case and the grounds for drawing those inferences and expressing those conclusions. However, at the end of the day, their evidence remains a matter of fact on which the court will have to make factual findings. A novel shadow actor, namely an intermediary, has been introduced in South African civil procedure. An intermediary will, if necessary, be appointed by the court in order to enable a witness who is in need of doing so, to give their evidence through that intermediary if it appears to the court that the proceedings would expose such a witness to undue psychological, mental, or emotional stress, trauma, or suffering if they testify at the proceedings.

IV. Other Actors

Apart from the two large groups of 'heroes of judicial periphery', we wish to attract readers' attention to some further actors who are equally important but are difficult to classify and subsume under a single category. Therefore, under the designation 'other actors', part Three of this book discusses the ever-growing role and impact of Artificial Intelligence (AI) on the role of court staff, the role of psychologists as a special kind of expert in child custody cases and the ever-growing role of third-party funders, especially in the context of collective litigation. Additionally, among the unusual and distinct hidden gems in individual galaxies of specific national civil justice systems, we include a chapter that discusses the role and function of the Brazilian Ministério Público.

In chapter seventeen, Seyedeh Sajedeh Salehi and Gina Gioia look at the integration of AI as an emerging actor into civil proceedings. AI in its analytical capacity has a considerable potential to assist court staff with performing tasks such as evidence analysis and document and case management. This chapter explores the impact of AI implementation – as an assistive analytical tool – on the role of court staff in civil proceedings. It highlights that AI can assist court staff in the automated processing of documents, such as e-filings, natural language processing, and legal research, to reduce their workload and optimise the efficient administration of civil justice. AI can also be utilised by court staff to analyse evidence to, for example, identify relevant information and patterns. Finally, the chapter also examines several challenges in integrating AI into civil proceedings. These challenges include ensuring transparency of data processing methods by court staff while using AI to conduct tasks.

In chapter eighteen, Maurício Magalhães Lamha focuses on the supporting actors of the Brazilian courts, the so-called 'auxiliaries of the Court'. Despite their multiple ordinary daily tasks and activities, regarding in particular international child abduction cases (which are processed exclusively by Federal courts in Brazil), those auxiliaries have a double role that makes their function significant. They are not only important to the due process and the accuracy of the final decision but also support the Court in the most sensitive stage of the proceeding, that is, the possible return of the child to his/her habitual residence in another country (the return order enforcement). The chapter concentrates on three specific supporting actors/auxiliaries – the *Oficial de Justiça*; the Mediator; and the Court Appointed Psychologist Expert.

In chapter nineteen, Hermes Zaneti Jr examines the evolution and current role of the Brazilian *Ministério Público* as both a supervisory and a supportive entity within the governmental framework, essential to the justice system, independent and autonomous from the other branches of power. The chapter explores the Public Prosecutor's Office transformation into a vital pro-accountability agency, especially after the 1988 Constitutional reform, which marked a significant turning point. The analysis delves into the institution's constitutional and legal foundations, highlighting its specialised functions in protecting collective rights and addressing public interest issues. Furthermore, the chapter presents contemporary data, offering a comprehensive portrait of its structure, functions, and pivotal role in safeguarding homogeneous, diffuse, and collective rights in Brazil.

In the final chapter twenty, Adriani Dori and Xandra Kramer discuss the role of commercial funders in light of the development and regulation of Third Party Litigation Funding (TPLF) in Europe, in particular in collective actions and strategic litigation. They also address the concerns about TPLF, including those voiced by the European Parliament that adopted a Resolution on 'Responsible Private Litigation Funding' urging the European Commission to propose a directive, implementing regulation for third-party funders as regards governance, oversight and transparency, and capping of the fees. In particular, they look at the role of funders and debate their role both at the forefront and in the shadow of the procedure.

V. Conclusion

This book is based on the discussions held at the 17th Public and Private Justice Conference, which took place in May 2023 at the Inter-University Centre in

Dubrovnik. On that occasion, legal scholars from Europe, America, Africa, and Asia jointly concluded that different jurisdictions have different rules and habits but inevitably recognise that securing adequate support for judges is essential for the proper functioning of courts. How this support should look is debatable. Sometimes judges command a whole team of clerks and lawyers; sometimes many of them share a secretary or a clerk. But in all cases, the assistance provided to judges in their daily work has a decisive impact on the fairness, effectiveness, and quality of the judicial process. Optimising the use of court staff and other ancillary actors may be the key to successful judicial reforms in the future.

We hope that this book contributes insights that may shed new light on the 'actors in the shadow'. Unknown is unloved; conversely, with new knowledge on the importance of judicial periphery for the quality and speed of judicial proceedings, we hope that supporting actors will obtain their deserved place in scholarly research and policy studies and become proper heroes of judicial reforms in the universe of civil justice.

PART I

Court Staff

2

Law Clerks: A Tool for Reducing Delays in Civil Justice in the EU

NICOLAS KYRIAKIDES AND ATHINA KATSIANTONI

I. Introduction

Due to the rise in the number and complexity of cases in recent years, many jurisdictions worldwide face significant delays, especially in civil litigation. Judicial delays affect the potentially prevailing party by preventing them from claiming their rights, payments, or benefits until a court decision is made. However, the negative impact extends beyond the litigants involved in the cases. Such delays can disrupt the establishment of legal precedent, preclude attorneys from fulfilling their professional obligations, and create a negative perception of an incompetent judiciary, eroding trust in the judicial system and resulting in unfavourable societal outcomes.[1]

The European Court of Human Rights (ECtHR) has developed an extensive body of jurisprudence on Article 6 of the European Convention on Human Rights (ECHR), which guarantees the right to a fair trial, including timely justice delivery. However, delayed justice delivery has become a systemic problem that many countries face. In Greece, for example, an investigation by the Plenary Session of the Council of State concluded that justice is delivered at an extremely slow pace. This delay not only has severe social, economic, and fiscal consequences for both citizens and the state but also undermines the rule of law.[2]

Additionally, the President of the Supreme Court of Cyprus, another EU Member State, recently stated before the national Parliament that long delays in the adjudication of cases are caused by the need for more support staff for judges.[3]

[1] S-S Crichton, 'Justice Delayed is Justice Denied: Jamaica's Duty to Deliver Timely Reserved Judgments and Written Reasons for Judgment' (2016) 44 *Syracuse Journal of International Law and Commerce* 3–5.

[2] KN Sakellaropoulou, MN Pikramenos, I Symeonidis, VP Androulakis, T Nikolaidou, L Tsogas, & P Alikakos, 'Justice in Greece: Suggestions for a modern judicial system' (2019) *diaNEOsis Organization of Research and Analysis* 2, 44–45, Available at: www.dianeosis.org/wp-content/uploads/2019/02/justice_study.pdf.

[3] Presidents of the Constitutional Court and the Supreme Court of Cyprus during the discussion for the 2024 state budget in the Parliament. Available at: www.kathimerini.com.cy/gr/politiki/boyli-to-80-dikastikoy-xronoy-analwnetai-se-mi-dikastikes-ypotheseis.

It is argued that apart from further investment in technology, the support that judges need is mainly one of research assistance. Until technology can provide this, law clerks can be a valuable resource for judges in jurisdictions where they are not yet utilised.[4]

The role and influence of judicial assistants[5] have been the subject of academic discussion in the United States[6] for some time, and it is now gaining more interest in Europe as well.[7] For example, while Llewellyn spoke very highly of the institution of the law clerk, saying that 'the recurring and unceasing impact of a young junior in the task is the best medicine yet discovered by man against the hardening

[4] The caseload has been increasing steadily in the courts of many EU Member States over the last decades, whereas financial resources have become scarce. Therefore, the efficiency of the judiciary has moved into the spotlight of public interest and political discussions. There are different ways to cope with the increasing caseload. First, the number of judges could be increased. Second, the procedural law could be reformed. Third, organisational and management reforms may lead to a more efficient jurisdiction. Last, e-justice has a lot of potential as well. An additional option to cope with the caseload has often been chosen in the recent years: more law clerks can be hired. P Bieri, 'Law Clerks in Switzerland – A Solution to Cope with the Caseload' (2016) 7 *IJCA* 29.

[5] In 1875, Massachusetts Chief Judge Horace Gray hired a law-school graduate to be his secretary. The Chief Judge paid the young man – whom he called a puisne judge – from his own pocket. A few years after the Chief Judge was elevated to the Supreme Court, the United States government decided to pay a clerk for each judge, in order to help them in their work. Most judges hired stenographers, but Judge Gray continued to hire young law graduates. In 1919, after the government decided to pay for typists and a clerk, the other judges began to hire recent law graduates, following in the 'steps' of Judge Gray. Thus, the institution of law clerks was founded in the federal court, which was established in 1936, when district judges were allowed to use law clerks, and its use was widespread since 1959, when certifications of need for district judges were no longer required. G Lebovits, 'Judges' Clerks Play Varied Roles in the Opinion Drafting Process' (2004) 79 *New York State Bar Association Journal* 34.

[6] Although largely invisible to the public, judicial assistants/law clerks frequently play a vital role in the process of adjudication, behind the scenes. Yet, especially outside of the US, little is known about their role and duties in the judicial. N Holvast, 'The Power of the Judicial Assistant/Law Clerk: Looking Behind the Scenes at Courts in the United States, England And Wales, And The Netherlands' (2016) 7 *International Journal For Court Administration* 10. Modern American judging in all courts (federal and state appellate courts) staggers along despite the burden of bloated caseloads and the shortcomings of human judges only by the delegation of a great deal of the labour of judging to law clerks: subordinate, anonymous, but often quite powerful lawyers, who function as the non-commissioned officers in the army of the judiciary. JB Oakley, and RS Thompson, *Law Clerks and the Judicial Process: Perceptions of the Qualities and Functions of Law Clerks in American Courts* (Berkeley, University of California Press, 2018).

[7] Germany: O Massing, 'Chapter 7 Legal Assistants at the German Federal Constitutional Court: A "Black Box" of Research?' [2016] *Constitutional Courts in Comparison* 180–187 and U Kranenpohl, *Hinter dem Schleier des Beratungsgeheimnisses* (VS Verlag für Sozialwissenschaften Wiesbaden, 2010) 126–128, 246–249. UK: T Nesterchuk, 'The View from Behind the Bench: The Role of Judicial Assistants in the UK Supreme Court' (2013) Judge and Jurist: Essays in Memory of Lord Rodger of Earlsferry and A Paterson, *Final Judgment: The Last Law Lords and the Supreme Court* (Oxford, Hart Publishing, 2013). Ireland: G Coonan, 'The Role of Judicial Research Assistants in Supporting the Decision Making Role of the Irish Judiciary' [2006] *Irish Judicial Studies Journal*. Norway and the Nordic Countries: G Grendstad, et al, 'From Backlogs to Quality Assurance, The Development of Law Clerk Units at Norwegian Courts' (2020) 11(3) *International Journal for Court Administration*. Switzerland: A Lienhard, P Bieri, 'Gerichtsschreiberjustiz?' (2017) Justice – *Justiz – Giustizia: die Schweizer Richterzeitung* (4) Weblaw and P Bieri, 'Law Clerks in Switzerland – A Solution to Cope with the Caseload?' (2016) 7(2) *International Journal for Court Administration* 29.

of a senior's mind and imagination',[8] Posner is slightly wary of the increased power of law clerks. He argued that judgments can turn excessively legalistic as clerks lack the authority and experience to look past established case law.[9]

During the past decades of rising caseloads in courts all over the globe, no judge court personnel (law clerks, staff lawyers, judicial assistants, etc) legally trained has been assigned a more prominent role in the adjudicative process. Even though employing judicial assistants is often not novel in these judiciaries, the number of assistants and their duties have increased.[10] This fact leads to a more prominent position in courts for those assistants. Regarding the US, Posner speaks of 'the age of the law clerk',[11] whereas judicial assistants are an unknown concept in some countries.

This chapter seeks to give an overview of the use of law clerks or similar officers in EU Member States,[12] as well as any relevant trends outside the EU (mainly in the US as the jurisdiction where law clerks were first used) regarding the institution of law clerks and whether their use has been successful in tackling caseloads. Moreover, as the boundaries of their role within a legal system can often become blurred, which can sometimes cause them to encroach upon the judicial function,[13] the influence of law clerks in the decision-making process is also examined.[14]

[8] KN Llewellyn, *The Common Law Tradition: Deciding Appeals* (Boston, Legal Legend Series, 1960) 322. For an analysis of Llewellyn's optimism about the role of law clerks, and criticisms of his view, see C Oldfather and TC Peppers, 'Introduction: Judicial Assistants or Junior Judges: The Hiring, Utilization, and Influence of Law Clerks' (2014) 98 *Marquette Law Review* 1.

[9] RA Posner, 'The courthouse mice', *The New Republic* (2006); RA Posner, *How Judges Think* (Cambridge and London, Harvard University Press, 2008) 34. Posner also explains how it is unsatisfactory that judges merely review 'ghost-written' judgments and shoulder the responsibility by putting their name on it – this does not make it their own judgment. Posner, ibid (2006) 34.

[10] See for the US Supreme Court: A Ward & D L Weiden, *Sorcerers' Apprentices: 100 Years of Law Clerks at the United States Supreme Court* (New York, New York University Press, 2006), and on US Federal district courts: TC Peppers, MW Giles & B Tainer-Parkins, 'Inside Judicial Chambers: How Federal District Court Judges Select and Use their Law Clerks' (2008) 7 *Albany Law Review* 353–370. Europe reflects similar movements; see NL Holvast, *In the Shadow of the Judge: The Involvement of Judicial Assistants in Dutch District Courts* (Portland, Eleven International Publishing, 2017).

[11] RA Posner, *How Judges Think* (Cambridge and London, Harvard University Press, 2008) 61.

[12] A study was conducted in 37 Council of Europe Member States on responses to a questionnaire sent out by the CCJE in preparation of Opinion No. 22 (2019) on judicial assistants. rm.coe.int/opinion-22-ccje-en/168098eecb. It is argued that there are different types of judicial assistants: 'seconded judges' as in Germany, who spent limited time at a higher court to gain experience for promotion; potentially permanent 'scribes' as in the Netherlands and Switzerland, and 'interns' fresh from their legal education as in the UK and Ireland. A Sanders, 'Judicial Assistants in Europe – A Comparative Analysis' (2020) 11 *International Journal for Court Administration* 1.

[13] G Coonan, 'The Role of Judicial Research Assistants in supporting the decision-making role of the Irish Judiciary' [2006] *Judicial Studies Institute Journal* 171. See also N Holvast and P Mascini, 'Is the Judge or the Clerk Making the Decision? Measuring the Influence of Judicial International Journal Assistants via an Experimental Survey among Dutch District for Court Administration Court Judges' (2020) 11(3) *International Journal for Court Administration* 1. Sakellaropoulou, Pikramenos, & Symeonidis et al. (n 2) 23 & 45.

[14] The Consultative Council of European Judges (CCJE) approves of the role of law clerks assisting judges in their decision making but cautions against clerks replacing judges. G Grendstad, et al., 'From Backlogs to Quality Assurance. The Development of Law Clerk Units at Norwegian Courts' (2020) 11 *International Journal for Court Administration* 1. Available at: iacajournal.org/articles/10.36745/ijca.352.

II. The Parameters of Being a Judge

Judges hold a unique and vital role in democratic societies. The smooth functioning of the justice system relies on both the state and the judges. While the state is responsible, among others, for organising justice and ensuring judicial independence, judges are responsible for complying with judicial ethics and adhering to legal precedent. The proper functioning of modern democratic states relies heavily on judicial independence, impartiality, and integrity.

For these goals to be achieved, a consensus of judges worldwide gave rise to the Bangalore Principles, a set of standards for the ethical conduct of judges drafted in 2001 by the Judicial Integrity Group.[15] The Principles are based on six core values: independence, impartiality, integrity, equality, propriety, and competence, and diligence. They emphasise the importance of the judiciary's role in upholding the rule of law, and they have been widely accepted and incorporated into national and international codes of judicial conduct. Nihal Jayawickrama, Coordinator of the Judicial Integrity Group, has reported that Bangalore Principles have inspired judicial codes in England and Wales, the Netherlands, Mauritius, Bulgaria, Serbia, Jordan, Belize, the Philippines, and Uzbekistan.[16] At the same time, they serve as a reminder of the critical role that judges play in ensuring justice.[17] By adhering to these principles, judges can remain unbiased when considering a case, ensuring that all parties are given a fair trial and providing clear reasoning for their decisions.

In certain European countries, specialised judicial schools are responsible for selecting, educating, and training individuals who aspire to become judges. These schools provide both initial and ongoing training in 17 Member States. In other countries, training is organised by a judicial council, the ministry of justice, or other court services.[18] In contrast, to become a judge in the US, an individual must meet specific requirements, hold a law degree, gain experience as a lawyer, and pass a rigorous selection process that may include exams, background checks, and interviews.[19] After undergoing training, judges acquire the skills required to produce well-structured, legally grounded, and persuasive opinions throughout their careers. Therefore, most legal systems limit court decision writing to judges,

[15] The cornerstone of democracy and the rule of law is an unwaveringly principled judiciary. It acts as a shield for the public by safeguarding their rights and freedoms against any legal infringements, even if other protective measures have failed. Judicial Integrity Group, 'Commentary on The Bangalore Principles of Judicial Conduct' (2007) *United Nations Office on Drugs and Crime*, 5, available at: www.unodc.org/documents/nigeria/publications/Otherpublications/Commentry_on_the_Bangalore_principles_of_Judicial_Conduct.pdf.

[16] G Mayne, 'Judicial integrity: the accountability gap and the Bangalore Principles' [2007] *Global Corruption Report* 40.

[17] Sakellaropoulou, Pikramenos, &Symeonidis et al. (n 2) 23 & 45.

[18] European e-Justice Portal, Judicial training providers. Available at: e-justice.europa.eu/406/EN/judiciary_training_providers.

[19] Indeed Career Guide, 'How to Become a Judge: A Guide to the Legal Profession'. Available at: www.indeed.com/career-advice/career-development/how-to-become-a-judge.

as their legal expertise and experience enable them to make informed decisions based on legal principles.

However, despite the above, it has been argued by scholars that inexperienced jurists or even non-lawyers could also serve as effective judges, especially, appellate judges. Nevertheless, it is suggested that the primary task of a judge, both first-instance and appellate, is to interpret and apply the law to the facts of the case. This requires a deep understanding of legal doctrine, reasoning, precedent, and familiarity with legal institutions and procedures. These skills are developed through years of training and experience in the law, which non-lawyers will not necessarily undergo. As Kronman puts it: to replace emphasis on judges' 'virtue of practical wisdom' with 'traits such as cleverness and dialectical agility' would cause 'a shift in judicial values, contributing to the decline of the lawyer statesman ideal in the minds of judges themselves by making the beginner in the craft of judging the measure of the master's art'.[20] Moreover, the argument that non-lawyers may be good appellate judges overlooks the importance of judicial virtue. Judges must possess legal reasoning, logical thinking, an understanding of legal institutions and procedures, integrity, impartiality, and a concern for the rule of law. These virtues are developed through legal training and experience, as well as a commitment to and deep understanding of ethical conduct and the values of the legal system, which lawyers are better placed to have developed.[21]

Based on the above, one could argue either for or against the extent to which law clerks are well-equipped to participate significantly in the decision-making process. However, as the answer is not simply binary, the role of law clerks in different legal systems is examined below. Additionally, considering the criteria enabling judges to issue legal decisions, it will be assessed to what extent law clerks can contribute to the process.

III. Law Clerks and their Role in the Judicial System

Clerkship was established in the 1880s[22] as a way for judges to deal with the increasing volume and complexity of legal cases. Over time, the role of law clerks has expanded and evolved to include a wide range of responsibilities, from conducting legal research to drafting opinions and assisting with oral arguments.[23] Many

[20] AT Kronman, *The Lost Lawyer: Failing Ideals of the Legal Profession* (Cambridge, Harvard University Press, 1993) 350–51.

[21] It is argued that 'judicial virtue' refers to what Aristotle called 'phronesis', which is the virtue of practical wisdom. A judge with practical wisdom possesses the ability to identify the goals that are most important in a given case and to select the means that are most effective in achieving those goals. LB Solum, 'The virtues and vices of a Judge: An Aristotelian guide to judicial selection' (1988) 61 *Georgetown Law Faculty Publications and Other Works* 1735, 1753.

[22] See for the US Supreme Court: A Ward & DL Weiden, *Sorcerers' Apprentices: 100 Years of Law Clerks at the United States Supreme Court* (New York, New York University Press, 2006).

[23] ibid.

scholars, such as Holvast and Mascini, mention that judges heavily rely on judicial assistants or clerks, which can alter the decision-making process of judges and negatively affect the quality of their judgments. They suggest that drafting a judgment allows judges to reconsider their initial decision and fully consider all arguments presented by the parties involved. Assisting in the adjudication process raises concerns about judges feeling less personal responsibility for their judgments, which could lead to judgments influenced by policy preferences rather than legal arguments, and result in less comprehensive decision-making.[24]

A. The Role of Law Clerks in the United States

Becoming a law clerk for the United States Supreme Court is a journey that starts early in a lawyer's career. Given the lucrative career paths of Supreme Court clerks who go into private practice,[25] it is no surprise that the application process is incredibly competitive. It typically involves admission to a prestigious law school and remarkable results within the first years. In the final year of law school, students may choose to apply for clerkships with Supreme Court judges. The application process includes the submission of a cover letter briefly describing the applicant's qualifications and any personal connections they may have with the judge. The judges consider various aspects, such as the applicant's class ranking and the law school they attended, as well as letters of recommendation from law school faculty. Other factors include geographic region, prior clerkship experience, personal compatibility, and some controversial factors such as sex, race, sexual orientation, and ideology.[26]

During a panel discussion on judges' perspectives regarding law clerk hiring, utilisation, and influence, several judges shared insights into their selection process.[27] Given the many applications they receive; judges were asked to clarify what they look for in letters of recommendation. One judge mentioned that her selection process has evolved and involves reviewing every submission holistically before deciding whom to invite for an interview. Another judge seeks applicants who share his philosophy of faithfully applying the law. Additionally, he hires clerks from diverse ideological backgrounds, including libertarians, conservatives, liberals, and moderates, and places relatively less emphasis on writing samples. Interestingly, Baum has noted that many American Supreme Court justices tend to hire clerks who have previously served lower-court judges with similar political beliefs to the justice. He attributes this to ideological polarisation in American

[24] N Holvast and P Mascini, 'Is the Judge or the Clerk Making the Decision? Measuring the Influence of Judicial Assistants via an Experimental Survey among Dutch District Court Judges' (2020) 11 *International Journal for Court Administration* 1, 2.

[25] A Ward, C Dwyer & K Gill, 'Bonus Babies Escape Golden Handcuffs: How Money and Politics Has Transformed the Career Paths of Supreme Court Law Clerks' (2014) 98 *Marquette Law Review* 228.

[26] Ward and Weiden (n 22).

[27] DR Stras, DS Sykes and JA Wynn Jr, 'Panel Discussion: Judges' Perspectives on Law Clerk Hiring, Utilization, and Influence' (2014) 98 *Marquette Law Review* 441.

society.[28] By contrast, other judges prioritise intellectually curious candidates with vital academic records, emphasising the importance of law review, experience and grades, and do not take political beliefs into account when selecting clerks. They also consider diversity a valuable asset, yet the number of minority clerks is not rising.[29]

It was further emphasised that one of the most challenging issues when working with a law clerk is the need for more persistence in thoroughly researching and understanding cases. While briefs serve as a starting point, judges expect clerks to go beyond the provided materials and seek additional information, as required. Clerks must also be willing to engage in discussions and not hesitate to share their thoughts. The panel also discussed the utilisation of law clerks in drafting opinions and noted that judges rely on their legal staff to some extent due to the high volume of cases.[30] According to academic research, law clerks are essential to decision-making, working closely with judges and offering unique perspectives and insights. In an older piece, David Crump, referring to an interview with a trial judge, points out how each clerk may be assigned half of the judge's docket.[31]

While clerks have historically provided research assistance, verifying citations and researching points of law, their responsibilities have expanded over time. Historically, clerks were occasionally tasked with drafting opinions, but this was primarily as a learning exercise rather than for the judge's use. However, over time, clerks have been given more significant responsibilities by an increasing number of judges. Posner amusingly notes that 'in some instances, it is to be feared, [clerks] are indeed invisible judges, for there are appellate judges whose literary style appears to change annually'.[32] Although clerks' footnote contributions have sparked controversy, their role in opinion writing has become increasingly important, with some clerks serving as primary opinion drafters.[33]

The opinion-writing process can be conducted using three different methods: delegation, retention, or collaboration. The most commonly used method is delegation, where a judge assigns the first draft to a clerk, who then revises it. In contrast, retention involves judges drafting their opinions and using clerks for editing, citations, and footnotes. Collaboration involves both, the judge and their clerks, working together on the opinion. Historically, judges preferred the retention approach and viewed opinion drafting as solely their responsibility, while clerks worked on an advanced apprenticeship in the law. However, it is argued that this shift in clerk involvement has led to clerks attempting to draft opinions that their judges found satisfactory, resulting in some judges issuing wholly clerk-written opinions under their names. This increase in clerk involvement has also

[28] L Baum, 'Hiring Supreme Court Law Clerks: Probing the Ideological Linkage Between Judges and Justices' (2014) 98 *Marquette Law Review* 333.

[29] T Mauro, 'Diversity and Supreme Court Law Clerks' (2014) 98 *Marquette Law Review* 361.

[30] ibid.

[31] D Crump, 'Law Clerks: their roles and relationships with their judges' (1985) 69 *Judicature* 236.

[32] RA Posner, *The federal courts: crisis and reform* (Cambridge, Harvard University Press, 1985).

[33] Ward and Weiden (n 22).

contributed to a potential loss of quality. Judicial opinions have become longer, less clear, and filled with arguments and citations, making them difficult to interpret.[34] It is supported that even though clerks constitute an extension of the judge, the judge should remain responsible for their work, and the final decision-making. On the contrary, many agree that involving multiple people in the creation of judgments can lead to better outcomes since, although judges are expected to control their core functions, clerks can assist them in becoming better judges.[35]

Last, it is accepted that the ultimate responsibility for the adjudicative function and decision-making process must remain exclusively with the judge, regardless of who writes the initial drafts. The judge should carefully review and approve every word of the opinion to ensure that litigants' rights are protected, and public confidence in the judiciary is maintained. Specifically, while collaborative writing between law clerks and judges is an effective way to produce high-quality opinions, the judge must retain control over the process and make the final decision. Law clerks lack the training, qualifications and institutional safeguards (eg, life tenure) that judges have, and if their role was not in some way limited, this would breed worrying questions about the legitimacy of the judicial process.[36] It is, therefore, crucial to recognise that the judge is the leader in the judgment writing process and since legal writing is critical, clerks must take every opportunity to improve and learn from their judge's feedback.[37]

B. Diverse Approaches to Law Clerks across Europe

Law clerks increasingly assist judges in numerous EU jurisdictions. While there may be initial differences in the role of judicial assistants based on the legal

[34] Ward and Weiden (n 22).

[35] C Oldfather and TC Peppers, 'Judicial Assistants or Junior Judges: The Hiring, Utilization, and Influence of Law Clerks' (2014) 98 *Marquette Law Review* 1. In Norway, the use of law clerks has undergone significant changes, with their role shifting from addressing the backlog problem to focusing on quality assurance. The clerks assist judges in identifying issues more efficiently, leading to a more comprehensive understanding of cases. Furthermore, Norway's Supreme Court, Borgarting, and Gulating Court strive to attract high-quality clerks. The hiring criteria for clerks at the Borgarting and Gulating Courts are primarily focused on the candidates' legal competence, as measured by their grades on their law degree. However, relevant legal experience, personal qualities, and diversity are also necessary. Clerks from private law firms, for example, are valued for their efficiency, while those with experience as deputy Judges have a better understanding of the overall function of the court. Overall, candidates with a solid legal background, relevant experience, and a range of skills that can contribute to the efficiency and effectiveness of the court are more valued. It is also worth noting that research commissioned by the Norwegian Court Administration demonstrated that clerks could replace judges in specific tasks, resulting in greater efficiency and cost-effectiveness. The study has also shown that clerks' advice influences judges' decisions, contributing to more excellent decisional quality and minimising potential mistakes. However, clerks do not yet have the final say, as the responsibility falls on the judges. Grendstad et al. (n 14).

[36] Holvast (n 6).

[37] G Lebovits, 'Judges' Clerks Play Varied Roles in the Opinion Drafting Process' (2004) 76 *New York State Bar Journal* 34, 35–39.

system in which they work, many similarities can also be identified. According to the Consultative Council of European Judges (CCJE), the primary rationale for employing judicial assistants is to support the administration of justice in the interest of society. Competent judicial assistants can provide valuable support to judges and improve the quality of judicial decisions. Another reason for employing judicial assistants is to educate young lawyers, especially those interested in becoming judges. Serving as a judicial assistant can provide a valuable understanding of the work of courts. In some Member States, supporting a judge is mandatory in legal education before practice. Even in regions where it is not mandatory, as some academics have asserted, 'for the law clerk, the experience is likely to be a high point in his legal career'.[38] Therefore, the work of judicial assistants can also serve educational purposes.

Efficiency is another essential rationale for employing judicial assistants. By unburdening judges from non-judicial tasks, judicial assistants can help speed up the work of courts, reduce backlogs, and help judges prepare decisions of higher quality.[39] Moreover, trial judges interviewed, explain how more than 90 per cent of cases are usually settled, and so judges can save copious amounts of time and energy by assigning clerks to motion practice.[40]

The judicial personnel of European courts can be classified into four categories. Of particular interest is the first category, which draws inspiration from the German system of '*Rechtspfleger*' (judicial officers) and is responsible for carrying out judicial duties. However, due to constitutional provisions, such as in the case of Greece, this category cannot be implemented in some European countries, where the administration of justice is exclusively entrusted to regular judges, who are granted guarantees of independence. The second category comprises individuals who assist judges in their judicial work, including record-keeping, case preparation, and drafting judicial decisions. The third category consists of individuals who manage court administration and handle administrative tasks outside judicial work, such as case registration, archiving, and accounting. The fourth and final category involves individuals responsible for technical aspects of court management, such as building maintenance and cleanliness.[41]

In several European countries, including Germany, Denmark, Austria, Iceland, Georgia, Hungary, Croatia, and the Czech Republic, the *Rechtspfleger* institution is recognised as the 'second pillar of the third power'. This group of civil servants possesses judicial and administrative competencies, primarily in land registry cases,

[38] Crump (n 30).

[39] Consultative Council of European Judges (CCJE), CCJE Opinion No. 22 (2019), The Role of Judicial Assistants, CCJE(2019) 6, Strasbourg, 7 November 2019, 1–4. Available at: rm.coe.int/opinion-22-ccje-en/168098eecb. Sanders (n 12).

[40] Crump (n 30).

[41] M-P Toli, 'The status of judicial clerks in view of the constitutional guarantees they enjoy – Comparison with the status of civil servants' (2022). Available at: polynoe.lib.uniwa.gr/xmlui/bitstream/handle/11400/3636/Toli_1809.pdf?sequence=1&isAllowed=y. See also, Sanders (n 12).

issuing payment orders, legal assistance, compulsory execution, and other areas. Similar to judges, *Rechtspfleger* officials enjoy judicial independence. In France, however, the '*greffiers des services judiciaires*' (court registrars) institution serves a different purpose: supporting judges in processing legal documents, conducting legal research,[42] preparing drafts of decisions, and training their colleagues. '*Greffiers des services judiciaire*' are permanent civil servants who receive eighteen months of training at the School of Judicial Officials.[43]

In Greece, one of the countries facing severe judicial delays, judicial personnel provide essential administrative and secretarial support as indirect and supportive organs of justice. Operating under judicial power rather than the executive, their independence from the other two powers of government strengthens the rule of law. Additionally, their role as the link between citizens and justice is crucial. They communicate with interested parties daily, providing information and essential guidance to litigants and lawyers and representing the external image of court and prosecution offices. To enhance the efficiency of the judicial system and ensure it adapts to the demands of the modern era, the Ministry of Justice in Greece invests in the education and training of judicial staff. The National School of the Judiciary and the Hellenic Institute of International and Foreign Law offer training programs for judicial officers, focussing on promoting legal research and knowledge dissemination among law students and the general public.[44]

The administrative staff of the courts of Cyprus, another EU country facing acute delays, includes fixed positions for judicial support posts, such as the Chief Registrar, the Assistant Chief Registrar, Legal Officers, Registrars, Stenographers, and Bailiffs. In addition to the judicial support staff, the court system has clerical staff, hourly paid staff – such as messengers and cleaners – and other staff (such as

[42] In England, the Judicial Research Office (JRO) is a department staffed by judicial assistants that provide research assistance to the judiciary in all jurisdictions. The office is responsible for conducting research for judges, preparing material for publication on the judges' intranet, creating and updating handbooks for all court jurisdictions, and proofreading judgments and other documents. The JRO also manages a database of research materials. Judicial assistants are assigned to judges of various court jurisdictions and aid judges in preparing for court, escort them to court, conduct legal research, draft judgments, and proofread completed judgments before publication. Another group of judicial assistants is assigned to support the work of the Supreme Court, Court of Appeal, and High Court. For judicial training, the Judicial College delivers courses to approximately judges, Magistrates, and independent Legal Advisors. The training includes online courses, e-learning materials, social and diversity issues, and cross-jurisdictional support for case management and judgment writing. Judicial assistants are not commonly employed, especially in lower courts where judges do not receive assistance from non-judicial staff. See, Functional Review of the Courts System of Cyprus, Technical Assistance Project 2017/2018, IPA, Ireland, supported by the Structural Reform Support Service (SRSS) of the European Commission, March 2018, 106–107. Holvast (n 6) 10–25.

[43] H Albanou, 'The human resources of the courts: Exploring the educational needs and evaluation criteria of court officials, Master's program in Public Administration thesis, 2021'. Available at: dspace.lib.uom.gr/handle/2159/27127.

[44] ibid.

librarians and technical assistants).[45] A report on the review of the court system in Cyprus[46] in 2018 indicated that the Supreme Court in Cyprus has a range of support options to assist judges[47] in finalising cases.[48] In particular, the registry offers day-to-day operational support, ensuring that cases are well-prepared, parties are informed, court lists are published, and trained stenographers and support staff are available during hearings.[49] Legal officers, who are qualified lawyers, support Supreme Court judges[50] in preparing judgments, conducting legal research and other necessary tasks, while having access to the judges' library in the Supreme Court building and legal databases for conducting legal research, as well.

[45] Institute of Public Administration Ireland, 'Functional Review of The Courts System Of Cyprus' (2018). Available at: at www.cyprusbarassociation.org/files/publications/Functional_Review_of_Courts_System_of_Cyprus_IPA_Ireland_-_Final_Report.pdf.

[46] The judicial system in Cyprus now operates on a three-tier system with one level for trial jurisdiction and two levels for appellate jurisdiction. This is a result of the recent establishment of a new Court of Appeal as an intermediate step between trial and an appeal to the Supreme Court (or to the Supreme Constitutional Court in the case of administrative and constitutional matters). The primary trial court is the District Court, which deals with most civil and criminal matters. Cases are judged by a single judge, excluding serious crimes for which the Assize Court is competent. Specialised tribunals consisting of one professional and two lay judges adjudicate rent-control claims and employment disputes, and family law matters fall under the Family Court's jurisdiction. Administration of Justice (Miscellaneous Provisions) Law of 1964 (Law 33/1964), Article 3A. See also AK Emilianides, 'The Judicial Reform until now', economytoday.sigmalive.com/oikonomia/kypros/71844_i-mehri-simera-poreia-tis-dikastiriakis-metarrythmisis.

[47] The EU Justice Scoreboard has persistently highlighted the need for more training for the judiciary in Cyprus. This has ultimately materialised in the enactment of the Law on the Establishment and Operation of a School for Training Judges, establishing a formal training program including the creation of a School for Judicial Training. See Law on the Establishment and Operation of the School of Judges of 2020 (Law 101(I)/2020). International Organization for Judicial Training, 'Declaration of Judicial Training Principles' (2017), Available at: ncfsc-web.squiz.cloud/__data/assets/pdf_file/0014/6152/2017-principles.pdf, as quoted in N Mouttotos, *The impact of Europeanization in Cyprus Contract Law and the spill-over to matters of civil procedure: more pieces on the mosaic?* (Maastricht University, Eleven International Publishing, 2021).

[48] Institute of Public Administration Ireland (n 44).

[49] ibid 43 & 145.

[50] Before the reform of the Cyprus Courts system, as Hatzimihail explained, the Supreme Court of Cyprus had no discretionary power to choose its caseload, and all civil and criminal judgments from trial courts were subject to appeal. Furthermore, Hatzimihail noted that the Supreme Court of Cyprus was burdened with a heavy workload due to its trial-level jurisdiction over administrative law cases under Article 146 of the Constitution. As a result, Supreme Court judges spent more than half of their time dealing with administrative matters individually, while three-member panels examined civil and criminal appeals. This situation posed challenges for senior judges, who had spent years reaching the appellate level, and for those who had never studied administrative law before ascending to the Supreme Court bench. Therefore, the court's legal officers, who were holding permanent positions as assistants to individual judges, played a vital role. NE Hatzimihail, 'Cyprus as a Mixed Legal System' (2013) 6 *Journal of Civil Law Studies* 38, 60–69. Available at: digitalcommons.law.lsu.edu/cgi/viewcontent.cgi?article=1087&context=jcls. Some registrars in Cyprus have legal backgrounds and may handle various tasks such as reviewing appeals and petitions, editing and publishing Supreme Court jurisprudence, etc. The Courts (Composition of the Secretariat, Powers and Duties of Officials) Procedural Regulation of 2002 (27/2002), Arts 2 and 9, www.cylaw.org/nomoi/kanon/non-ind/2002_27/index.html.

IV. Defining How Law Clerks Could be Utilised in Countries Facing Delays

A. Backlog and the Need for Reform

While some countries are still debating whether to expand the role of judicial assistants, other countries embrace the use of AI in the decision-making process. The Federal Judicial Center has recently published a guide on AI for Federal judges in the US, stressing the importance of judges having a comprehensive understanding of AI, its implications for fact-finding, and the potential risks involved. The guide outlines several key questions judges should be able to answer, such as how AI is being used in court or judicial decisions and whether they understand the strengths and limitations of AI and its potential biases.[51] In the United Kingdom, Sir Geoffrey Vos, Master of the Rolls and Head of Civil Justice in England and Wales, confirmed the future introduction of an Early Legal Services and Advice portal featuring AI-based elements.[52] Most notably, he identified the judiciary's need to keep up with technological advancement, precisely to honour the interests of justice and of citizens who have 'a right to live in a democratic society governed by the rule of law where the ability to vindicate legal rights quickly and effectively is central to that rule of law'.[53] Nations thus recognise the importance of modernisation in order to uphold the rule of law and the efficiency of justice.

In contrast, certain jurisdictions in the EU like Greece and Cyprus experience severe problems in the administration of justice, caused mainly by the resistance to change for many years and limited familiarity with legal technology. The 2023 EU Justice Scoreboard, among others, highlighted the complexities of managing case backlogs. While some Member States successfully maintained stable backlogs despite an increase in the number of pending cases, others encountered significant challenges. This difference highlights the importance of implementing strategies to resolve backlog issues in the justice systems of various Member States. The estimated time required for the judicial resolution of civil, commercial, administrative, and other cases during the years 2012, 2019–21 in countries such as Italy has exceeded 400 days, about 450 days in Greece, whereas Cyprus has surpassed 1,000 days.[54]

[51] Federal Judicial Center, 'An Introduction to Artificial Intelligence for Federal Judges' (2023). Available at: www.linkedin.com/posts/martin-ebers-4984444b_fdc-introduction-to-ai-for-federal-judges-activity-7049650729342410752-JNCO/?originalSubdomain=zw.

[52] Sir G Vos, 'Speech by the Master of the Rolls to the Bar Council of England and Wales' (20th Annual Law Reform Lecture, London, Lincolns Inn, 21 June 2023). Available at: www.barcouncil.org.uk/static/789f134c-38d7-4ff5-9e2fba6c541eec8d/20230611-Bar-Council-Law-Reform-Lecture-2023-AI-Digital.pdf.

[53] ibid 2.

[54] EU Justice Scoreboard, Publications Office of the European Union (2023) 11 & 56. Available at: commission.europa.eu/strategy-and-policy/policies/justice-and-fundamental-rights/upholding-rule-law/eu-justice-scoreboard_en; J-P Jean & H Jorry, 'Analyse des systèmes judiciaires des Etats

Italy's judicial system is considered one of the less efficient in Europe. Italy's judicial system has a bad reputation for a number of reasons, including delayed court proceedings.[55] In the same context, Greece encounters significant delays in the resolution of legal cases. The Greek justice system, particularly in civil proceedings, is burdened by substantial delays due to the high volume of actions, legal remedies and aids submitted to civil courts. As a result, these factors have prolonged the timeframes for issuing court decisions.[56]

Marta Cartabia, a former Minister of Justice in Italy, suggested that the introduction of law clerks could be a solution to reduce the caseload burden on judges. She supported that this would expedite proceedings, but also that it could provide valuable experience to a new generation of lawyers who could acquire significant knowledge of the justice system early in their careers.[57]

Similarly, Cypriot courts confront the same long-standing challenge, the growing backlog of pending cases. The consequences of judicial delays have been highlighted in numerous reports, and a significant factor contributing to this issue is the absence of a well-defined management and structure.[58] In January 2023, the Ministry of Justice and Public Order of Cyprus reiterated that the large backlog of cases pending before the courts has prompted the government to launch a comprehensive courts' reform plan aimed at building a modern, accessible, and efficient system for administering justice.[59] One of the most significant reforms was the revision of the Civil Procedure Rules by promoting the use of technology. The new Civil Procedure Rules, which are very similar to the English CPR, were approved by the Supreme Court in May 2021 and entered into force this past September 2023.[60] On the other hand, an e-justice system was only very recently introduced, since 21 July 2021, providing for digital filing and administration of courts' cases.[61] The reform plan aims to recruit more judges and closely monitor

membres de l'Union européenne (European Commission for the Efficiency of Justice (CEPEJ), Council of Europe' (2013). Available at: rm.coe.int/judicial-systems-of-the-european-union-countries-analysis-of-data-by-t/1680788280.

[55] See G Esposito, S Lanau, and S Pompe, 'Judicial System Reform in Italy – A Key to Growth' (2014) *International Monetary Fund* 3. Available at: www.imf.org/external/pubs/ft/wp/2014/wp1432.pdf.

[56] SG Alexandris & C Agathos, 'Litigation & Dispute Resolution Laws and Regulations' (2023) *Greece, Global Legal Insights*, www.globallegalinsights.com/practice-areas/litigation-and-dispute-resolution-laws-and-regulations/greece#:~:text=The%20Greek%20justice%20administration%20system,delays%20in%20delivering%20court%20judgments.

[57] D Ghiglione, 'Foreign investors hindered by Italy's sluggish legal system' (2021) *Financial Times*, www.ft.com/content/0b0fae37-13a8-496a-a9b5-1dcc6a7992a3.

[58] EU-CoE Joint Project on the Establishment of an Independent Court Service and Re-engineering of Court Registries, Full Set of Reports (2023) 54.

[59] Ministry of Justice and Public Order of the Republic of Cyprus, Courts' Reform – Strengthening the Justice System. Available at: www.mjpo.gov.cy/mjpo/mjpo.nsf/All/8DBA33CF2CEE8EEEC225861400467FAB?OpenDocument.

[60] YN Yiasemis, 'The Philosophy Behind the New Civil Procedure Rules and the Main Changes' (Final Conference regarding the Modernizing the Civil Procedure Rules in Cyprus, Nicosia, 8 December 2021) Available at: www.supremecourt.gov.cy/judicial/sc.nsf/All/007465EBDC14AC41C22587AA0031E2C7/$file/ATTCK376.pdf.

[61] European Commission, 'I.Justice System' (1 July 2023) commission.europa.eu/system/files/2023-07/86_1_52801_input_mem_cyprus_en.pdf.

the project to handle the backlog of cases.[62] The government established a training school for judges to provide ongoing and regular training, ensuring they remain up-to-date on new laws and procedures.[63] In general, the court reform programme includes several initiatives to increase efficiency and reduce the backlog, while significant changes in how courts are managed and operated are being proposed.[64]

Regarding law clerks, in a proposal presented recently in a joint project by the EU Commission and the Council of Europe in reforming the justice system of Cyprus, it has been suggested that to improve case management, particularly in situations of limited judicial capacity, one option is to delegate administrative or quasi-judicial case management responsibilities to staff members who work under the supervision of the judiciary. Court registrars could assist judges with administrative tasks, potentially reducing the administrative workload of judges. Specifically, expanding the role of registrars to encompass greater judicial management responsibilities, including case prioritisation, and supporting judges in preparing for hearings, will potentially be advantageous for the judiciary.[65] The more time registrars devote to administrative case preparation, including communication with involved parties, the more time judges would dedicate to legal preparation and adjudication.[66] It has been suggested that officers could be beneficial in drafting judgments, providing research support, and managing judicial calendars. Additionally, registrars can take on a broader range of duties, such as handling requests for adjournments and extensions of time. With the appropriate training and educational structures put in place, these measures could optimise the use of judicial time without compromising the decision-making authority of the judiciary[67] or the rigour and quality of judicial decisions.

Paul R. Baier, speaking from an American legal perspective, emphasised that 'the research required for the job will expose the clerk to wide areas of substantive law'.[68] The deployment of law clerks has, as seen above, been embraced (or, at least, considered) in the wider European context as a measure for more efficient justice. But other, less conventional arguments may be (and have in fact been) advanced: clerkship is both a solution to expedite judicial processes, but also an educational element in legal systems, providing for more long-term changes in the judiciary with regard to the competence of its members. The introduction or expansion of the role of law clerks and officers is thus not merely a remedy for a general issue in legal systems, but also valuable in itself.

It is argued that, to address judicial delays, EU countries such as Italy, Greece, and Cyprus could consider introducing or expand the usage and responsibilities of law clerks across all tiers of justice.

[62] Ministry of Justice and Public Order of the Republic of Cyprus (n 58).

[63] Law on the Establishment and Operation of the School of Judges (n 46).

[64] Ministry of Justice and Public Order of the Republic of Cyprus (n 58).

[65] EU-CoE Joint Project on the Establishment of an Independent Court Service and Re-engineering of Court Registries (n 57) 74–75.

[66] ibid 316.

[67] Institute of Public Administration Ireland (n 44).

[68] PR Baier, 'The Law Clerks: Profile of an Institution' (1973) 26 *Vanderbilt Law Review* 1125, 1161.

B. Balancing the Role of Law Clerks

There are concerns about the extent of duties assigned to law clerks and their participation in court decision-making. Judges are the only ones authorised to write court decisions for several reasons. Judges are appointed for their legal expertise and experience, which allows them to make informed decisions grounded in legal principles. Furthermore, judges must remain impartial and unbiased when making decisions. Allowing them to write court decisions ensures that their opinions are based solely on the facts and legal arguments presented in the case. Additionally, judges receive training to effectively communicate their legal findings by utilising accurate legal terminology and citing precedents to justify their reasoning. This ensures that court decisions are easily understandable by the parties involved in the case and the public.[69] Therefore, balancing the need for a speedy judicial process with the parties' right to an independent and impartial court is crucial. While law clerks can provide valuable support to the judicial system, this should not come at the expense of appointing an adequate number of judges.[70]

In any case, when hiring law clerks, it is essential to consider the specific courts and cases where they will be utilised, how to organise their workload to enhance the quality and efficiency of the judicial system, and how to assess their impact to ensure that their employment aligns with the intended objectives. In the US, the duties of law clerks vary depending on factors such as the number of clerks and their legal experience. Typically, clerks handle most daily civil case management tasks for most judges, including reviewing docket activity reports for new filings, tracking deadlines in pending cases, scheduling conferences, and flagging urgent matters. They also conduct legal research, prepare draft orders and opinions, and assist with trials.[71]

Furthermore, in the US, the amount of time a judge spends supervising law clerks varies depending on their experience level, familiarity with federal civil litigation, and knowledge of the court's local rules and practices. New law clerks or those without experience as law clerks may have limited experience with case management, discovery disputes, or drafting orders and opinions. In such cases, judges should provide detailed instructions on their tasks, set clear deadlines, and discuss when and how they should seek guidance. On the other hand, law clerks, who have prior experience, may be familiar with litigation and local rules but they still need to learn the judge's chambers' procedures and writing style. While the judge should always supervise their work, the level of supervision required

[69] EW Thomas, *The Judicial Process: Realism, Pragmatism, Practical Reasoning and Principles* (Cambridge, Cambridge University Press, 2005). Available at: books.google.com.cy/books?hl=en&lr=&id=Sn6fBTLwV9IC&oi=fnd&pg=PR15&dq=judicial+principles&ots=9MAgFijsVn&sig=CSDeZxBe1RqWYtZjHmEtdjztYrM&redir_esc=y#v=onepage&q=judicial%20principles&f=false.

[70] Grendstad et al. (n 14) 3.

[71] The Judicial Conference of the United States Committee on Court Administration and Case Management, Civil Litigation Management Manual Third Edition (2022), 147–150. Available at: www.fjc.gov/sites/default/files/materials/29/Civil_Litigation_Management_Manual_Third_Edition.pdf.

decreases as the law clerks become more familiar with the judge's judicial style and chambers' operating procedures. After hiring a law clerk, the judge should stress the importance of confidentiality when discussing pending cases and instruct them to act professionally in the courtroom, as well as when dealing with court staff, attorneys, and the public.[72]

The role of the judge as supervisor of the clerk's operation is significant also to the content of said clerk's function. As per the Law Clerk Handbook for the US Federal legal system, '[t]he primary function of an appellate court law clerk is to research and write about the issues presented on appeal, while law clerks for district, bankruptcy, and magistrate judges may be involved in the many decisions made at every stage of each case'.[73] At first glance, this appears to be a vague description of the duties of clerkship. It is logical that concerns should raise as to whether 'research' and 'writing' about legal issues or decisions can potentially encroach on the functions traditionally expected of the actual judge. If this were the case, it is problematic that staff who has obtained some form of legal education, but who 'lack[s] the practical experience that a seasoned judge is likely to have',[74] will effectively be making binding decisions concerning the legal rights of citizens. It is therefore submitted that the function of a clerk or registrar, as explained above, should always be directed by the relevant judge: delegation, and thus expeditiousness, must be qualified by judges' understanding of what the specific duties of their clerks are and how far they extend. This is necessary in order to avoid an undue level of involvement of clerks in judicial decisions and, provided the appropriate supervision and guidance is in place, not an argument against the use of clerks altogether.

In light of the above, law clerks can be assigned important tasks in the judicial system. However, it is essential to acknowledge that they cannot substitute the expertise of judges. Instead, the role of law clerks could be regarded as auxiliary. Ultimately, it is the responsibility of judges to make decisions based on legal principles and uphold public trust in the judicial system.

C. Final Approaches

The involvement of law clerks in the adjudication process is a topic of debate. The cognitive differences between law clerks and judges are central to this discussion. Judges' education and experience qualify them with the necessary skills to carry out their duties effectively. Although many law clerks possess legal knowledge, this is not enough to be considered sufficient and competent to penetrate the judicial decision-making process to the same degree as judges, especially in cases where law clerks are law graduates. However, the gap between judges and

[72] ibid.
[73] AB Leo & A DiLeo, *Law Clerk Handbook*, 4th edn (Federal Judicial Center, 2020).
[74] JD Mahoney, 'Law Clerks: For Better or For Worse' (1988) 54 *Brook Law Review* 321, 338.

law clerks may be bridged if law clerks undergo training similar to judges and gain significant experience in the field. Moreover, the unique characteristics of the various judicial systems worldwide make it challenging to adopt a uniform stance. In some countries, judicial independence requires judges' personal and operational independence. Thus, concerns arise that law clerks may influence judges in the decision-making process.

Like the adoption of new technologies, expanding the responsibilities of legal officers could be critical in achieving a more efficient judicial system. Based on the experience in various jurisdictions, increased utilisation of law clerks can enhance judges' efficiency. Their duties can entail legal research, editing judgments, preparing indexes and summaries, gathering and categorising essential elements of evidence and handle simple procedural issues.

In countries where the use of law clerks is yet to be implemented or is in its initial stages, the practices of other countries that have established codes of conduct and ethical standards for law clerks to uphold public trust in the judiciary system can be considered. Typically, these codes require law clerks to maintain the independence and integrity of the judiciary. Additionally, they are expected to avoid any behaviour that may appear improper or lead to conflicts of interest. This includes adhering to appropriate standards while performing their duties, refraining from inappropriate political activities, and avoiding conflicts between office responsibilities and outside activities. Law clerks should also have ethical obligations to comply with. These obligations include maintaining confidentiality, avoiding conflicts of interest, and exercising caution in online activities and gifts. Law clerks should also be expected to engage in community and other social activities responsibly and ethically. When facing an ethics question, law clerks should consult the relevant codes and seek advice from supervisors, if necessary.[75] Therefore, if law clerks maintain high ethical standards, the public trust in their contribution to the judiciary system may be upheld, and fairness and impartiality in the administration of justice could be promoted.

Bearing all these points in mind, law clerks may play a crucial role, providing valuable assistance in legal research and case management. However, it is essential to balance law clerks' appropriate level of influence on the judges' decision-making process. Judges must retain control over their core functions of deciding cases and ensure they fulfil their duties in the best interest of justice. While law clerks can enhance the judges' decision-making process and contribute to their professional development, judges should also be mindful of their clerks' expertise limitations and their own biases. To maintain the integrity of the judicial decision-making process and strike a balance that maximises the benefits of the judge-clerk relationship, judges should bear the final decision and responsibility.

[75] Judicial Conference Committee on Codes of Conduct, *Maintaining the Public Trust Ethics for Federal Judicial Law Clerks 2019*, revised 4th edn (Federal Judicial Centre, 2019).

3

The Italian Path to Judicial Clerkship

ELISABETTA SILVESTRI

I. Introduction

In a book on the deplorable state of Italian civil justice,[1] a book that unfortunately did not receive the attention it deserves, the author emphasised a fundamental mistake made by the Italian legislators, namely, the countless changes to the rules governing the development of litigation that from the 1990s on have altered the Code of Civil Procedure overlooking the obvious need to pay attention to the organisational aspects of civil justice. The metaphor suggested by the author is particularly appropriate: it is as if a building is about to collapse due to a structural failure, and its owner decides to fix the roof first and not the foundations.[2]

Years have gone by since the publication of that book, and the legislators seem to continue to ignore the notorious problems affecting the 'back office' of Italian courts: lack of administrative personnel, outdated IT systems, dilapidated buildings, messy and dusty archives, and similar facilities to the despair of litigants, attorneys, and judges.

Fortunately, the latest reforms enacted by the Italian government seem to have changed the trend. Even though the legislators have not given up the old habit of reshuffling again the rules designing the landscape of adjudication, new regulations have been set with a view to improving the efficiency of the justice system, establishing – inter alia – new organisational units supposedly aimed at helping the judges in the performance of their traditional tasks. The main goal to be reached is to reduce the length of civil proceedings, which is essential to increase the trust of the stakeholders in the administration of justice and, in the long run, promote the economic growth of the country at large. This essay describes the newly established organisational units and their operation.

[1] M Modena, *Giustizia civile. Le ragioni di una crisi* (Canterano (RM), Aracne editrice, 2019).
[2] ibid 42.

II. The Background

Before elaborating on the organisational measures mentioned above and concentrating on the specific measure on which the legislators seem to have high expectations, it is necessary to offer some background, meaning a bit of information that may help the reader understand the reasons why the establishment of a new structure of support for the Italian judiciary and its operation has the potential to be of paramount importance. This new structure is called *ufficio per il processo*, which can be roughly translated as the 'office for the judicial proceeding'. Henceforth, this author will refer to it simply as UPP, for it seems acceptable to take advantage of the abbreviation widely used in the official Italian documents and literature on the subject.

Here then is the background, which hopefully will give the reader a better understanding of the current state of affairs.

The European Union responded to the economic crisis resulting from the Covid-19 pandemic with a huge recovery plan known as Next Generation EU. Italy is the primary beneficiary of the funding granted through two specific forms of financial support: the Recovery and Resilience Facility and the Recovery Assistance for Cohesion and the Territories of Europe. Both programs consist of large-scale financial support offered to the Italian government through grants (ie, non-repayable funds) and loans. Within the Recovery and Resilience Facility, Italy is supposed to receive a total of €191.5 billion to be utilised between 2021 and 2026. Of this amount, €68.9 billion are non-repayable funds and €122.6 billion are technically loans to be repaid.

In order to gain access to these funds, Italy had to present to the EU institutions a detailed plan of investments and reforms in six specific sectors, one of which is the administration of justice at large. The plan is commonly known as PNRR, which is the abbreviation of the official denomination of the plan, namely, the National Recovery and Resilience Plan.[3]

Over the years, different country-specific recommendations issued by the European Commission constantly emphasised the problem of the excessive delays associated with judicial proceedings in Italy, even though in 2019 and 2020 a few minor improvements could be acknowledged. In order to meet the requirements set by the Commission, an extensive reform of both civil and criminal procedure was devised and adopted by the Italian Parliament in 2021 and 2022. In evaluating what was done already between 2020 and 2022, in May 2023 the Commission stated, 'The (*Italian*) justice system still records among the longest times in the EU to reach decisions. It has a large backlog of cases,

[3] The plan can be read (in English) on the website of the Italian Ministry of Economy and Finances www.mef.gov.it/en/focus/The-National-Recovery-and-Resilience-Plan-NRRP/.

which undermines the overall effectiveness of rules and curbs investment.'[4] In this regard, it seems relevant to point out that according to the latest available data collected by the Ministry of Justice, Italian civil proceedings last on average three years before the courts of first instance; two years before the appellate courts; and one year before the Court of last resort, meaning the Court of Cassation.[5] These data are partially different from those offered by the CEPEJ 2022 Evaluation Report that lists the average length of Italian civil proceedings as follows: 674 days (one year and eight months) before the courts of first instance; 1,026 days (two years and eight months) before the appellate courts; and 1,526 days (over four years) before the Court of last resort.[6] Considering the differences and keeping in mind that the data collected by CEPEJ concern the year 2020, it is difficult to determine to what extent the improvement in court delays, if any, has taken place.

The budget allocated to the sector 'Justice' within the National Recovery and Resilience Plan is approximately €3 billion in total, out of which the largest portion is assigned to increasing the 'human capital' applied to the court organisation. More precisely, the estimate is to allot €2.26 billion to the recruitment of 21,910 judicial clerks (ie, staff members of UPPs); the remaining part of the budget will be used for the recruitment of general administrative personnel.

The objectives pursued by the PNRR in the administration of civil justice are the following:

- By the end of 2024, a reduction of 65 per cent in the backlog of civil and commercial cases pending before the courts of first instance and 55 per cent in the cases pending before the courts of appeal.
- By mid-2026, a reduction of 90 per cent in the backlog of civil and commercial cases pending before all courts (including the cases pending before the Court of Cassation).
- By mid-2026, a reduction of 40 per cent in the length of civil and commercial proceedings.

Clearly, these objectives are not only very ambitious, but also realistically unattainable, at least in this author's opinion. Be that as it may, a variety of measures have been adopted alongside an extensive rewriting of civil procedure and the

[4] Commission Staff Working Document 2023 Country Report – Italy accompanying the document Recommendation for a COUNCIL RECOMMENDATION on the 2023 National Reform Programme of Italy and delivering a Council opinion on the 2023 Stability Programme of Italy (COM(2023) 612 final) (Brussels, 24.5.2023) data.consilium.europa.eu/doc/document/ST-9777-2023-ADD-1/en/pdf, 5.

[5] Monitoraggi della giustizia civile e penale www.giustizia.it/giustizia/page/it/monitoraggi_giustizia_civile_e_penale#:~:text=3%20anni%20per%20i%20procedimenti,per%20i%20procedimenti%20in%20Cassazione (updated on 3 August 2023).

[6] European judicial systems CEPEJ Evaluation Report 2022, Evaluation cycle (2020 data), Part 2 Country profiles rm.coe.int/cepej-fiche-pays-2020-22-e-web/1680a86276, 73.

strengthening of ADR methods with the goal of reducing the intake of new cases.[7]

III. Why an 'Office for the Judicial Proceeding' (*Ufficio per il Processo*)?

Since the sole reform of judicial procedures and the diversion of disputes towards out-of-court avenues for their resolution cannot guarantee adequate results, a variety of organisational measures have been adopted. One of these measures is the institution of the UPP: the goal pursued is to support the activities performed by the judiciary so as to improve the performance of the courts in the disposition of cases, with a view to reducing the delays in civil and commercial cases. Incidentally, the UPP operates with regard to the criminal side of the courts as well, but here no reference will be made to the measures in force for the improvement of criminal justice.

Up until now, the administrative organisation of Italian courts has included registrars, clerks, and bailiffs. They all perform different tasks; they are all public servants, and, as such, they enjoy permanent employment. Notoriously, most Italian courts lack an adequate administrative staff; in particular, they lack employees who are able to manage the new digitalised procedures that degree by degree are replacing the traditional paper trail of civil proceedings. When we consider that the average age of Italian public servants is 50, we may understand why so many individuals are not proficient in managing IT. At the same time, it is undeniable that what we call the PCT (*Processo Civile Telematico*, meaning digitalised civil proceeding) suffers from technology that is simply not up to the task. But the widely held view that the number of judges is insufficient is certainly disputable when one notes that other EU countries with a comparable number of judges in relation to the number of inhabitants do not share the same problems as Italy in the area of backlog of cases and excessive delays in the disposition of cases.

IV. The 'Office for the Judicial Proceeding': Some Basic Information

It is time to disclose just what the UPP, this 'office for the judicial proceeding', is.[8] According to the latest legislative text on the matter (ie, article 2 of

[7] For an overview of the strategies pursued by the Italian government within the PNRR to increase the performance of the justice system, see M Fabri, 'The Italian National Recovery and Resilience Plan to Decrease the Length of Judicial Proceedings' (2022) 184(4) *Revue française d'administration publique* 1015–28.

[8] The literature on the subject is exclusively in Italian: see, for instance, ML Guarnieri, 'La morfologia dell'Ufficio per il processo e il ruolo dell'addetto Upp nelle dinamiche del giudizio di cognizione

legislative decree number 151 of 2022), UPPs are the structures established with a view to 'guaranteeing the reasonable length of judicial procedures through the innovation of organisational models and a more efficient use of information and communication technologies' (this author's translation). The head of each judicial office (meaning the judge presiding over the court) is in charge of determining how the UPP is supposed to be organised and which tasks its staff is expected to perform, taking into account the flux of cases and the critical issues brought about by the need to manage the court's workload. UPPs are established within the courts of first instance, the courts of appeal and the Court of Cassation, and there are separate UPPs for the civil side and the criminal side of the courts just mentioned.

In reality, the UPP is not a new structure. It was established on a trial basis in 2014 as an organisational structure that included lay judges (as the justices of the peace), law graduates involved in special forms of internship, and administrative staff. The experiment was quite unsuccessful, essentially due to the fact that in many judicial districts it was impossible to recruit prospective members of the UPP.

It would be pointless to list the numerous normative texts that were issued with a view to revitalising the UPP in the years that followed its establishment. One major problem – and it is a persistent problem that is likely to affect the fate of UPPs even in the future – is the fact that all the members of the structure were recruited and are still recruited with fixed-term contracts (on average, contracts with a duration of approximately two years). In this regard, the reader should keep in mind that Italians are obsessed with the holy grail of permanent job positions, especially, if possible, within the public administration at large. So, rightly or wrongly, obtaining a position as a member of a UPP was and still is considered not very attractive.

In any event, in light of the goals to be achieved as regards the improvement of the justice system by 2026, Italian legislators thought that miraculous results could be attained via reviving UPPs by extending the roles played by their members, so as to free the judges from routine tasks and preparatory chores, and by having as a 'guiding light' the disposal of the backlog of cases and the reduction of court delays. In fact, it was decided to hire no fewer than 16,500 new staff posts for UPPs at Italian courts. Between 2021 and 2022, the recruitment procedures for 8,000 posts took place; it was expected that by the end of 2023 the remaining vacancies would be filled.

The UPP recruitment procedure consists of a multiple-choice examination with a time limit of one hour. Candidates are presented with 40 multiple-choice questions concerning, first of all, public law at large. One may ask why the questions are not specifically related to the branches of law that members of UPPs, working in civil or criminal courts, are expected to know inside out. It is a reasonable question, but unfortunately no logical answer can be provided. A few questions also deal with the structure of judicial organisation and others are aimed at testing the candidates' knowledge of the English language, as if the use of English were common practice in Italian courts, which it is not.

In light of the tasks that prospective members of UPPs are supposed to perform, one is inclined to presume that applicants must hold a law degree, but a law degree is not mandatory since applicants can also hold a degree in Economics or Political Science. There are a number of factors that can help candidates receive higher points when it is time to rank those who gave correct answers to the questions: for instance, those who are already qualified as lawyers, as well as those who hold a PhD, receive additional points.

The candidates who pass the selection process are hired for two years and seven months (why seven months, and not, say, six months, is unknown), but recently their contracts have been extended to three years. The gross salary is €1,700 on average, a salary that is in line with the salary a low-level public servant receives according to official statistics.[9]

Hopefully, the information offered above will help the reader understand why the effort to improve the machinery of justice through the establishment of a strong, well-organised support structure designed to attract young, competent, and motivated graduates is bound to fail. As a matter of fact, out of the initial 8,000 posts for which a call for candidates was issued, only 7,000 were filled. This author interviewed a number of her former law students to find out whether they were attracted by this new employment opportunity, and invariably the answer was 'No', followed by the question: What am I going to do when the contract expires? This is a reasonable question: the Italian market for the legal professions is not very dynamic, for a variety of reasons that cannot be explored in this chapter due to their complexity. The reality is that UPPs are destined to become a sort of 'parking lot' for individuals (many of whom come from the southern part of Italy, meaning the part of the country experiencing the highest rate of unemployment) who are unable to find any other decent job after the completion of their university education.

riformato' (2023) judicium.it; V Capuozzo, 'Il nuovo ufficio per il processo e l'efficienza dell'attività giurisdizionale' (2023) treccani.it; C Castelli, 'Le sfide da affrontare nella giustizia: PNRR, Ufficio per il processo, digitalizzazione' (2022) questionegiustizia.it; G Vecchi, 'Uffici per il processo e modelli organizzativi nelle sezioni della Corte d'Appello di Milano. Una prima analisi a seguito dell'inserimento degli addetti finanziati dal PNRR' (2022) questionegiustizia.it; A Di Florio, 'La riforma del processo civile e l'ufficio per il processo (art. 1 co. 18 e 19 l. 26 novembre 2021, n. 206)' questionegiustizia.it; F Farri, 'Gli uffici per il processo: un'analisi di (in)efficienza economica' (2022) L-Jus; I Pagni, 'L'Ufficio per il processo: l'occasione per una (ulteriore) osmosi virtuosa tra teoria e pratica, con uno sguardo alle riforme processuali in cantiere' (2021) questionegiustizia.it; R Caponi, 'Un orizzonte aperto su una nuova forma di vita giudiziaria: l'ufficio per il processo' (2021) questionegiustizia.it; D Cavallini, 'L'ufficio per il processo' (2021) *Rivista trimestrale di diritto e procedura civile* 981–92; MG Civinini, 'Il "nuovo ufficio per il processo" tra riforma della giustizia e PNRR. Che sia la volta buona!' (2021) questionegiustizia.it.

[9] See dati.istat.it/Index.aspx?DataSetCode=DCSC_RETRCASSCOMPPA.

V. The 'Office for the Judicial Proceeding': How it is Supposed to Work

Let us move on now to the list of tasks that the staff members of UPPs are supposed to perform as far as civil and commercial cases are concerned. These tasks are explained in detail by a statutory instrument issued towards the end of 2022[10] together with a few normative texts providing for the reform of civil procedure. Here are the tasks:

1. UPPs should undertake preparatory activities that are aimed at supporting the court's duties, such as the study of pleadings; the drafting of memoranda and briefs with information on specific cases; the preparation of hearings; the evaluation of individual cases so as to determine which cases are suitable for court-ordered mediation. Furthermore, law clerks Italian-style are expected to conduct extensive legal research and compile case materials; to attend court sessions in order to record the minutes; and to draft orders and opinions.
2. Each UPP should act as the interface between the judges and the administrative staff, and support the efficient use of IT.
3. Staff members of each UPP are also in charge of creating databases of the judgments and orders issued by the court. They are also expected to prepare statistical analyses of the case flow, so as to monitor the court's performance.
4. Last but not least, UPPs are expected to devise and implement new organisational models with a view to improving the 'productive capacity' of the court and reducing the backlog of cases.

It is worth emphasising that the statutory instrument mentioned above clarifies the goal pursued by the establishment of the UPPs: they aim at 'guaranteeing the reasonable length of judicial proceedings by the implementation of new organisational models and a more efficient use of IT technology'.[11] Simply put, the legislators thought that it was time to improve the 'productivity' of the courts by increasing the human resources devoted to the administration of justice. The problem is that the factors affecting court delays are many, as shown by an interesting study on timeliness in civil justice in which the factor 'Judicial structures and resources' is definitely an important one, but not in the least is it the only one.[12]

[10] Legislative decree n 151 of 10 October 2022 that implemented the rules laid down by a statute enabling the government to adopt measures to promote the efficiency of civil justice and reorganise the ADR methods (statute n 206 of 26 November 2021).

[11] Art 2 of legislative decree n 151 of 10 October 2022 – the translation is the sole responsibility of this author.

[12] For the study mentioned, see K Economides, AA Haugh and J McIntyre, 'Toward Timeliness in Civil Justice' (2015) 41(2) *Monash University Law Review* 414–44.

VI. Conclusion

When looking at the long list of tasks UPPs are supposed to perform, one may think that thanks to the formidable help the new staff members will provide to the courts, the efficiency of Italian courts is bound to skyrocket. This is indeed the general hope, but it will take time to verify whether the reform will turn the Italian justice system around. As mentioned earlier, the first wave of recruitment for UPP members took place between 2021 and 2022. According to the latest available statistics, in the first semester of 2022, the average length of civil proceedings recorded a meagre reduction in delays of 11.8 per cent. For all of 2022, the backlog of cases was reduced only by 9.3 per cent in the courts of first instance and by 28.3 per cent in the appellate courts. At this pace, it will be virtually impossible to attain the objectives of the PNRR.

In closing, one may wonder whether this author is overly dubious about the virtues of UPPs and the possibility that their operation could be a key factor in the improvement of civil justice. Again, it is worth emphasising that court infrastructure and, in particular, the availability of appropriate staff in support of the judges and their specific tasks are important, but many other factors are essential for the swift, modern, and effective disposition of the claims brought to the courts. The establishment of the 'office for the judicial proceeding' is indeed a first step, but one that will have to be followed by many others if the Italian legislators want to give meaning to the constitutional rule according to which 'The law provides for the reasonable duration of trials.'[13]

[13] Art 111, s 2, of the Italian Constitution, available (in its official English translation) at www.senato.it/documenti/repository/istituzione/costituzione_inglese.pdf.

4

If She Acts as a Judge, Earns as a Judge, then She Must Be a Judge! The Case of Judicial Advisers in Croatia

JURAJ BROZOVIĆ

I. Introduction

In its Opinion No. 22 (2019), the Consultative Council of European Judges (CCJE) defined judicial assistants as law graduates who support 'judges or panels of judges in their adjudicative work'.[1] Such support can range from legal research and administrative tasks to supporting preparatory activities in the decision-making process.[2] By hiring judicial assistants, the judicial system can benefit both in terms of efficiency and quality, and such instant benefits may also pay off in the future, as many judicial assistants later become judges.[3] Croatian *sudski savjetnici* were also assessed in the report, based on the national questionnaire. The careful reader will curiously note that the title of this chapter speaks of judicial 'advisers' and not 'assistants'.

The notion 'judicial adviser' is by no means a perfect translation of the original *sudski savjetnik*. Another possible translation would be 'judicial counsellor' since the stem *savjet* could both be translated as 'advice' and 'counsel'. The use of the literal translation is intended to warn the reader about the non-adequacy of using the notion 'judicial assistant', which was unfortunately the case in the CCJE Opinion. As will be demonstrated in this contribution, only the judicial advisers at the second instance courts and the Supreme Court can truly fit in the definition of judicial assistants offered by the CCJE.

This chapter portrays the special features of Croatian judicial advisers, by explaining the historical context of their integration into the judicial system and by comparing them to the status of judges. After providing a short empirical analysis,

[1] CCJE Opinion No. 22 (2019), para 4.
[2] CCJE Opinion No. 22 (2019), paras 21–34.
[3] CCJE Opinion No. 22 (2019), paras 11–16.

it ends in a critical assessment of the role of judicial advisers, exposing the procedural concessions that were made in favour of their growing engagement. The text may righteously seem critical, but its purpose is not to criticise the labour of many hard-working judicial advisers. In assessing whether they can be considered the 'heroes of the judicial periphery', the principal aim of this chapter is to demonstrate that many of them can hardly be considered a part of the 'periphery', and that their growing engagement represents an erroneous method for tackling court backlogs.

II. Judicial Advisers: History in Brief

A. From Expert Associates to Judicial Advisers

The notion of legal adviser is a rather new one, introduced in the Courts Act (CA) after Croatia gained independence. The CA solely changed the terminology, as the tasks of legal advisers completely corresponded to the tasks of former expert associates (*stručni suradnici*).

The task of the expert associates, as defined both by the Regular Courts Acts of 1977 (RCA 77') and 1988 (CA 88') in the Former Yugoslavia and in the first CA (CA 94') in independent Croatia, was to assist judges in their work, prepare drafts of court decisions, take down minutes of hearings, record the statements of claims and other submissions of the parties made in oral form, and perform other professional tasks as provided by law and the court rules, either independently or under the supervision or guidance of the judge (cp arts 108 RCA 77', 110 RCA 88' and 76 CA 94'). It soon became customary for expert associates to support and assist judges in various additional tasks like legal research, reporting judicial statistics, or providing legal aid to citizens.[4]

Our research confirmed that many judges already in the 1990s effectively started to use the assistance of judicial advisers rather extensively.[5] Especially in enforcement proceedings, it was not unusual that they secretly conduct part of the proceedings in judge's chambers. In the largest court in Croatia – Civil Municipal Court in Zagreb – some judicial advisers even already had their own cabinets, which they previously only shared with (mentoring) judges.

First considerable legislative change of the role of judicial advisers happened in 2003. First, they were mentioned in the new Inheritance Act (IA) as persons in charge of inheritance proceedings (art 176 para 2 IA), and two months later in the biggest amendments to the Civil Procedure Act (CPA) as persons conducting certain types of litigation under the limited supervision of judge. The latter became

[4] M Kovačević, *Komentar Zakona o redovnim sudovima: saveznog zakona, SR Srbije i SR Bosne i Hercegovine* (Beograd, Privredna štampa, 1975) comment to art 110.

[5] This was confirmed by several judges, with decades-long experience in the judiciary.

a model for wider use of first-instance judicial advisers, although the motivation for their mentioning in the CPA seems to be completely coincidental.

Namely, when the single judge was introduced in litigation instead of the judging panel, the working group decided to fill in the void due to the deleted provision and to simultaneously give a more prominent role to judicial advisers which in a way reflected the tendencies already present at some courts. The idea was supported by the general goal of fighting the court backlogs.[6] In civil cases initiated upon payment or damages claim, with the disputed value up to 50,000 HRK (ca €6,500) and in commercial cases up to 500,000 HRK (ca €65,000), judicial advisers were authorised to hold hearings, conduct the (evidentiary) proceedings, and propose the contents of the decisions (art 13 paras 1 and 3 CPA). The mentoring judges, who were supposed to sign the decision, got the obligation to conduct the proceedings themselves and render their own decision, should they not be satisfied with the adviser's proposal (art 13 para 4 CPA). The role of legal advisers in the appellate proceedings and before the Supreme Court was reduced to judicial support, entitling the judicial advisers to report on the status of cases and to draft the decisions (art 13 para 2 CPA).

The amendments to the CA in 2004 (CA 04') basically copy-pasted the same provision but expanded the role of judicial advisers, entrusting them the conduct of other types of proceedings: inheritance proceedings, enforcement proceedings, land registry proceedings, some non-contentious proceedings (voluntary jurisdiction), and misdemeanour proceedings (art 76.a CA 04'). Simultaneously, the title of higher judicial adviser was introduced (art 76 CA 04'), to enable better career opportunities for advisers who were not appointed as judges.

The new CA in 2013 (CA 13') added additional proceedings to the list: some labour disputes, administrative disputes with value lower than 100,000 HRK (ca €13,000), business registry disputes, summary insolvency proceedings, and decision on costs. The value of the disputes in which the advisers already could have participated in municipal courts was also raised to 100,000 HRK (ca €13,000). They were also authorised to publish the decisions signed by judges and to decide on the costs of proceedings (art 110 CA 13'). The current version of the CA, after the amendments in 2018, only differs in the new career opportunities because now there is also an even higher position of specialised higher advisers (art 109 para 1 CA) and the appointment requirements (discussed more thoroughly later in 3.1). Another important amendment in the CA 13' was also enabling special laws to regulate the position of judicial advisers differently, in other words, to give them an even more prominent role (art 110 CA).

Such opportunity was indeed very soon used in land registry cases (art 109.a Land Registry Act 13), business registry cases (art 13 Business Registry Act 13), and later in summary insolvency proceedings (art 435 Insolvency Act), where the

[6] I Crnić, 'Sudski savjetnici kao pomoćnici sudaca' in V Belajec et al. (eds), *Novine u parničnom postupku* (Zagreb, Inženjerski biro, 2003) 86–87.

judicial advisers were authorised not only to conduct the proceedings and propose the contents of the decisions but to render their own decisions. In these proceedings, this to a large degree made them comparable to German and Austrian *Rechtspfleger*.[7]

B. The Issue of Constitutionality Resolved?

One of the issues with growing engagement of judicial advisers arose from the fact that the very provisions of the Croatian Constitution (CC) entrusted the judicial tasks to judges personally, while only lay judges were mentioned as persons taking part in the judging (art 117 CC). There was no mention of the judicial advisers as a special category of non-judicial staff.[8] Instead, a general provision merely envisaged that the establishment, jurisdiction, and organisation of courts, as well as the court procedure, are regulated by law (art 116 para 3 CC). This issue was solved in 2010 during the amendments to the CC when judicial advisers were added to the above-mentioned provision which regulates who can take part in judging.

In the meantime, the participation of judicial advisers in court proceedings had to be assessed in accordance with the applicable statutory rules. When the judicial advisers were officially mentioned as persons more directly involved in certain types of court proceedings, actually conducting the proceedings, first in the CPA, and later in the CA, the dilemma seems to have been resolved. These provisions were unsuccessfully subject to constitutional review.[9] Despite all these legislative amendments, the case law throughout the years proves that there was a high degree of confusion regarding the involvement of judicial advisers in court proceedings and the elements of 'judging' which are reserved for judges only.

In litigation, the dilemma existed because one of the absolute manifest errors of procedure exists if the judgment was rendered by 'a person who is not a judge' (art 354 para 2 subpar 1 CPA). There were numerous cases where the appellants sought annulment of the first instance decision because the hearings were held, evidentiary proceedings conducted, and the contents of the decision proposed by judicial advisers. In many of them the appellate courts and – in some occasions – even the Supreme Court and Constitutional Court upheld such decisions as long as the judge was the one reviewing and signing the judgment.[10] The situation

[7] For comparison and a critique see A Maganić and L Hraste, 'Različiti oblici rasterećenja u pravosuđu u Republici Hrvatskoj – trebaju li Hrvatskoj *Rechtspflegeri*' (2013) 46 *Pravnik: časopis za pravna i društvena pitanja* 31, esp 45–51.

[8] S Triva and M Dika, *Građansko parnično procesno pravo* (Zagreb, Narodne novine, 2004) 188.

[9] Constitutional Court U-I/2191/2005 of 13 December 2016.

[10] County Court Varaždin Gž-320/09-2 of 15 April 2009; County Court Zagreb Gž Ovr 1901/2020-2 of 29 December 2020; Supreme Court Rev x 876/2014-2 of 18 November 2014; Constitutional Court U-III/869/2021 of 16 November 2022.

was somewhat different in cases where the judicial advisers have indeed merely conducted the proceedings and proposed the contents of the decision, but in types of proceedings that are not expressly placed under the jurisdiction of judicial advisers.[11]

The case law is by no means uniform here, and sometimes vague provisions allow for different interpretations.[12] There are even some decisions of the Constitutional Court that did not see anything wrong with judicial advisers conducting the proceedings in cases that are indeed outside their jurisdiction. One of such cases ended up being reviewed by the European Court of Human Rights (ECtHR). In *Egzeta v. Croatia*, the ECtHR concluded that proceedings conducted by the judicial adviser in such cases cannot be considered handled by 'the court established by law', as required by the fair hearing principle.[13]

In my doctoral research, I was fortunate enough to gain access to detailed information on solved cases from 2015 to 2019, accessible in the integrated case management system (ICMS) named *eSpis*, which I expanded in the following years (up to 2022). This not only allowed me to analyse the efficiency of judges and judicial advisers in litigious cases at municipal and commercial courts, which will be discussed in more detail later (3.3 Numbers compared), but also to observe the type of cases that were assigned to the judicial advisers.

In 35,078 cases that were resolved by judicial advisers in municipal courts from 2015 to 2022, the vast majority of cases in municipal courts were indeed proceedings initiated as a result of payment (91.15 per cent) and damages claims (7.34 per cent), but at least 1.31 per cent of cases most likely fall out of the jurisdiction of judicial advisers (eg, unlawful enforcement, divorce and other marital proceedings, maternal/paternal disputes, non-validity of contracts, unlawful dismissal, ownership disputes, etc), which is possibly also the case for 0.20 per cent of them (eg, 'other' family disputes, 'other' employment disputes, etc). Simultaneously, in commercial courts the number of cases that most likely (0.21 per cent) or possibly (2.58 per cent) fall outside the jurisdiction of judicial advisers is lower, but still proves that some cases that should be assigned to judges are instead assigned to judicial advisers.

In practice, the issue of constitutionality is thus far from being resolved. The allure of engaging legal advisers appears to overshadow concerns regarding potential risks.

[11] Supreme Court Rev 1355/2015-2 of 7 October 2015 (absolute manifest error because adviser conducted the proceedings for the annulment of contract); Supreme Court Rev 1883/2013-3 of 18 May 2016 (absolute manifest error due to payment claim exceeding the statutory threshold for participation of judicial advisers).

[12] Jurisdiction in litigation is conditioned by the value of the dispute, but it is not expressly prescribed for enforcement proceedings. The dilemma was solved in case law, confirming that for enforcement proceedings the value of the claim is irrelevant (see, eg, USRH U-III/20/2013 of 28 January 2016).

[13] Judgment of 07 September 2017, Application no. 40562/12, paras 41–45.

III. Judges and Judicial Advisers Compared

A. Appointment

The appointment of judges is mentioned in the CC. The CC introduces the State Judiciary Council (SJC), the independent body consisting of seven judges, two law professors, and two members of the Parliament, who are in charge of appointing, removing, or sanctioning judges in disciplinary proceedings (art 121 CC). More detailed and rather complex provisions on the judicial appointment are contained in the State Judiciary Council Act (SJCA).

Any candidate satisfying the minimum requirements is eligible to apply for a judicial position. The requirements depend on the court level (Table 4.1).

Table 4.1 Appointment requirements for judges

Judges	Appointment requirements
At municipal, commercial, and administrative courts	Judicial Academy final exam
At county courts	10 years of holding judicial office (judge or state attorney)
At higher specialised courts	12 years of holding judicial office (judge or state attorney)
At Supreme Court	15 years of holding judicial office (judge or state attorney) / 15 years of practicing law as an attorney, notary public, or law professor (after passing bar exam) / 20 years for other esteemed lawyers (after passing bar exam)

On the first level, the main prerequisite is the successfully passed final exam at Judicial Academy. The candidates are ranked (art 56 SJCA) considering:

- the success in the final exam at the Judicial Academy – total points;
- how the candidate performed as judicial/state attorney adviser, if they were previously hired on that position – up to 100 points;
- the impression during the interview with the SJC, assessing their sense of justice, motivation, and capability for carrying out judicial duties – up to 20 points.

The chosen candidates are also referred to psychological testing and basic security clearance before the Security Intelligence Agency (art 56.a SJCA).

Slightly different grading system exists in the case of appointments at higher courts (art 55 SJCA), where the ranking is based on:

- the assessment of the performance at the current judicial position or special examination of the candidates who are not already judicial officers – up to 150 points;

- the impression during the interview with the SJC, assessing their sense of justice, motivation, and capability for carrying out judicial duties – up to 20 points.

On the other hand, judicial advisers are appointed as any public servant, in accordance with the Public Servants Act (PSA) and Regulation on Public Tenders and Internal Job Postings in the Civil Service (Regulation). The minimum appointment requirements are defined in the CA.

The appointment of judicial advisers at the first and second instance courts solely depend on the bar exam, while the appointments at higher or specialised adviser positions, or adviser positions at the Supreme Court, require either a certain period of employment within the judiciary (as adviser, judge, state attorney, attorney, or notary public) or slightly longer period of time for the qualified candidates working outside the judiciary (Table 4.2). No formal education is needed, even for the judicial advisers whose position is comparable to the German and Austrian *Rechtspfleger*.[14] From 2009 to 2022, only the judicial advisers which were on a judicial career path were obliged to do the training at the Judicial Academy, but such training is currently completely optional.[15]

Table 4.2 Appointment requirements for judicial advisers

Advisers	Appointment requirements
Judicial adviser (municipal, commercial, administrative, county courts, and higher specialised courts)	bar exam
Higher judicial adviser (municipal, commercial, administrative, county courts, and higher specialised courts) and judicial adviser (at Supreme Court)	two years in judiciary or five years of other qualified practice (incl. bar exam)
Specialised judicial adviser (municipal, commercial, administrative, county courts, and higher specialised courts) and higher judicial adviser (at Supreme Court)	four years in judiciary or eight years of other qualified practice (incl. bar exam)
Specialised judicial adviser (at Supreme Court)	six years in judiciary or 10 years of other qualified practice (incl. bar exam)

There has to be a public tender announcing the job opening, after the Ministry of Justice (Ministry) has confirmed that the funds for such an appointment were secured in the state budget (art 108 CA). The candidates are selected by the president of the court and at least two other employees, usually also judges (art 160 PSA and art 8 Regulation).

14 Maganić and Hraste (n 7) 53.

15 These judicial advisers had employment conditioned upon successful passing of the final exam before the Judicial academy (former art 109 paras 5–6 CA 13'). This obligation was abolished in 2022, since it was considered ineffective (Final proposal for the amendments to the Judicial Academy Act in 2022, 7).

There are two important conclusions to be drawn from this comparison. It is obvious that, like in many other countries, a judicial adviser position is a ticket to enter the judiciary.[16] It is also obvious that the appointment requirements for the judicial advisers are much less stringent than the requirements for judicial positions, not requiring any special professional development or training. This can either affect the quality of the candidates that apply for the positions (attracting the less ambitious candidates) or their career prospects. In such circumstances, the only two incentives for the quality candidates are the promise of becoming a judge one day or advancing to a better paid higher/specialised position or positions at higher courts.

B. Status and Remuneration

Unlike judicial advisers, judges are considered state officials ('*državni dužnosnici*'), which is a status usually reserved for the highest political functions in the country.[17] They are appointed in a special procedure and have different material rights defined in a special Judicial State Act. Judicial advisers, on the other hand, are public servants *(državni službenici)* who are remunerated as any other public servant, by way of special government regulation.[18] The technique for calculating their income is similar, consisting of the base and the coefficient, but they use different variables. Their gross salary depends on multiple factors.

While the salaries of judges are significantly affected solely by their advancement to higher courts (Table 4.3), the salaries of judicial advisers depend both on the level of court where they are appointed and their own ranking (Table 4.4). Even within the same court, they can be ranked as advisers, higher advisers, and specialised higher advisers which affects their salaries. Of course, being appointed at the higher specialised courts or Supreme Court, automatically puts them in a higher salary range.

Table 4.3 Average gross salaries of judges (April 2023)

Judges	**Average gross salary (April 2023)**
Municipal, commercial, and administrative courts	€2,223.39
County courts	€2,857.75
Higher specialised courts	€3,580.04
Supreme court	€4,932.26

[16] CCJE Opinion No. 22 (2019), para 12.

[17] I Borković, *Upravno pravo* (Zagreb, Narodne novine, 2002) 277. See also arts 43–45 Law on Organization of Administration.

[18] Since recently, Regulation on Job Titles, Conditions for Assignment, and Coefficients for Salary Calculation in the Civil Service.

Table 4.4 Average gross salaries of judicial advisers (April 2023)

	Average gross salary (April 2023)
Judicial adviser (municipal, commercial, administrative, and county courts)	€1,400.02
Higher Judicial Adviser (municipal, commercial, administrative, and county courts)	€1,652.53
Specialist Judicial Adviser (municipal, commercial, administrative, and county courts)	€2,031.48
Judicial Adviser (higher specialised courts)	€1,750.03
Higher Judicial Adviser (higher specialised courts)	€1,968.33
Specialist Judicial Adviser (higher specialised courts)	€2,404.94
Judicial Adviser (Supreme Court)	€2,202.09
Higher Judicial Adviser (Supreme Court)	€2,625.05
Specialist Judicial Adviser (Supreme Court)	€3,157.28

Exactly such a disparity in the pay grade was the reason for growing dissatisfaction in the judiciary in recent years. The position of judicial advisers at the Supreme Court is the best example of such inconsistencies. Although judicial advisers are public servants of lower status and require basically no training except for their working experience and bar exam (compare Table 4.2), if they are hired at the Supreme Court, they will receive basically the same salary as the judges at the first instance courts.

Growing dissatisfaction with judicial salaries, which have – according to some calculations – grown six times slower than the average gross salary (observed in a twenty-year period),[19] seems to have resulted in multiple judges leaving their office in recent years.[20] In May 2023, such dissatisfaction culminated in the first official

[19] Association of Croatian Judges, *Od ponedjeljka sudačke mjere upozorenja: Tražimo minimum kako bi se status sudaca vratio na stanje otprije 24 godine*, 7 May 2023 (uhs.hr/archives/39961).

[20] 2023 Rule of Law Report Country Chapter on the rule of law situation in Croatia, SWD(2023) 811 final, Brussels 5 July 2023, 9 (commission.europa.eu/system/files/2023-07/27_1_52610_coun_chap_croatia_en.pdf).

(white) strike of the judiciary in Croatian history. Organised by the Association of Croatian Judges (ACJ), the 'precautionary measures', which lasted two weeks, consisted in the postponement of all hearings in the first instance hearings (except in urgent cases) and suspension of dispatch (albeit not rendering) of all second-instance decisions. Although such a collective action was a matter of controversy,[21] the concern was also raised within the European institutions.[22] The opposition to raising salaries stemmed from Croatia's abundance of courts and excessive (judicial and non-judicial) staff.[23] Nonetheless, the pressure seems to have paid off. The legislative amendments in June 2023 resulted in a 13 per cent increase, and the Ministry promised to propose further adjustments by the end of the year.[24]

Meanwhile, non-judicial staff was facing similar problems: multiple resignations of administrative staff, as well as dissatisfaction with salaries, especially in comparison to other civil servants. Encouraged by the judicial white strike, in early June 2023, non-judicial staff started their own, this time the official one, organised by the Public Servants Union, which effectively disabled access to courts in non-urgent cases.[25] The legality of such a strike was challenged, but it was confirmed both by the County Court in Zagreb and later Supreme Court.[26] This turned out to be one of the longest strikes that ended in August 2023, with a slight raise for servants with the lowest salary and renewed promises of a better position in the upcoming collective negotiations after the new Public Servants Remuneration Act is passed.[27]

Both of these promises seem to have been broken, which resulted in new 'precautionary measures' in January 2024, this time by the order of the President of the Supreme Court.[28]

[21] On the one hand, it was a matter of interpretation of procedural rules: Have judges postponed hearings in accordance with the statutory rules that the hearing is to be postponed only if there are 'valid reasons' for doing so (art 116 Civil Procedure Act)? The ACJ seems to have invoked judicial independence as the valid reason (uhs.hr/archives/39969), although the opinion was not shared by everyone (see, eg, www.telegram.hr/politika-kriminal/ugledni-profesori-pravnih-fakulteta-tvrde-da-je-strajk-sudaca-posve-nezakonit-ovo-sto-rade-je-nakaradno/). On the other hand, it is questionable whether state officials are at all entitled to any kind of industrial action (www.tportal.hr/vijesti/clanak/bijeli-strajk-sto-suci-zele-i-koji-su-to-hitni-slucajevi-koji-ce-se-ipak-rjesavati-20230508).

[22] Except for the already cited Rule of Law Report, see European Association of Judges, Statement of 2 June 2023 (uhs.hr/wp-content/uploads/2023/06/EAJ-resolution-on-salaries-of-judges-in-Croatia-approved.docx).

[23] For the overall analysis of organisational disarray in Croatian judiciary, see (unfortunately) still relevant A Uzelac, 'Current situation, causes of crisis and possible reform measures. Discussion material', 2020 (www.alanuzelac.from.hr/pubs/C04_Judiciary_in_Croatia_preprint.pdf).

[24] Rule of Law Report 2023, 10.

[25] Union of Civil Servants, Štrajk u tijelima sudbene vlasti i državnom odvjetništvu počinje 5. lipnja, 29 May 2023 (www.sdlsn.hr/strajk-u-tijelima-sudbene-vlasti-i-drzavnom-odvjetnistvu-pocinje-5-lipnja/).

[26] County Court in Zagreb, P-10/2023-8 of 5 June 2023 and Supreme Court, Gž 6/2023-2 of 19 June 2023.

[27] Union of Civil Servants, Zapisničarke više nisu beznačajne u igrama moći javnog sektora, 1 August 2023 (www.sdlsn.hr/zapisnicarke-vise-nisu-beznacajne-u-igrama-moci-javnog-sektora/).

[28] Instruction of 22 January 2024, Su-V-9/2024-1.

The repercussions of any type of strike in the judiciary cannot be discussed here. The growing dissatisfaction, on the other hand, can be a symptom that there are systemic issues in human resources management within the judiciary. This happens in the country where judges have salaries that are 1.9 (at the start of the career) or 3.6 times (at the end of the career) greater than the national gross average.[29] Although this is below the European median (2.3 and 4.5), it is far from being the lowest pay grade in Europe[30] and gross salaries still make 81.47 per cent of the implemented court budget (116.39 per cent of the European median).[31]

C. Numbers Compared

In European comparisons, Croatia is already known to be one of the champions when it comes to the average number of judicial and non-judicial staff. In recent CEPEJ data, Croatia was the fourth top employer of professional judges, hiring as many as 40.71 judges per 100,000 inhabitants (131.31 per cent of the European median)[32] and the third top employer of non-judicial staff, hiring as many as 145,82 employees of that category per 100,000 inhabitants (159.79 per cent of the European median).[33] It has to be noted, though, that both the number of judicial and non-judicial staff on one the hand and the ratio of non-judicial staff per judge on the other hand have dropped in a ten-year period (10 per cent decrease).[34]

The official data confirms these trends.[35] However, it would seem that the drop in the numbers of non-judicial staff can be attributed to decreased numbers of administrative staff, while the number of judicial advisers has slightly increased (Graph 4.1).

The growing numbers of judicial advisers are more visible in data provided for municipal (Graph 4.2) and commercial courts (Graph 4.3), where judicial advisers have a quasi-judicial role.

It would be interesting to analyse whether such an increase had any influence on the increase of judicial efficiency. After all, one of the reasons why the judicial advisers were given a more prominent role was to fight the court backlogs. Self-assessment, carried out by the national reporters in the CCJE questionnaire, seems to confirm that the courts that hire judicial advisers 'have better performance

[29] CEPEJ Country Profiles 2022, 35.

[30] CEPEJ Report 2022, 80.

[31] CEPEJ STAT: public.tableau.com/app/profile/cepej/viz/QuantitativeDataEN/Tables?publish=yes. Compare CEPEJ Report 2022, 27.

[32] CEPEJ Report 2022, 48. See also CEPEJ Country Profiles 2022, 35.

[33] CEPEJ Report 2022, 55. See also CEPEJ Country Profiles 2022, 35.

[34] CEPEJ Report 2022, 56.

[35] Data is available at www.vsrh.hr/izvjesca-o-stanju-sudbene-vlasti.aspx and mpu.gov.hr/statisticki-pregled-o-radu-sudova/26209.

Graph 4.1 Total number of judges and judicial advisers in courts (2006–22)

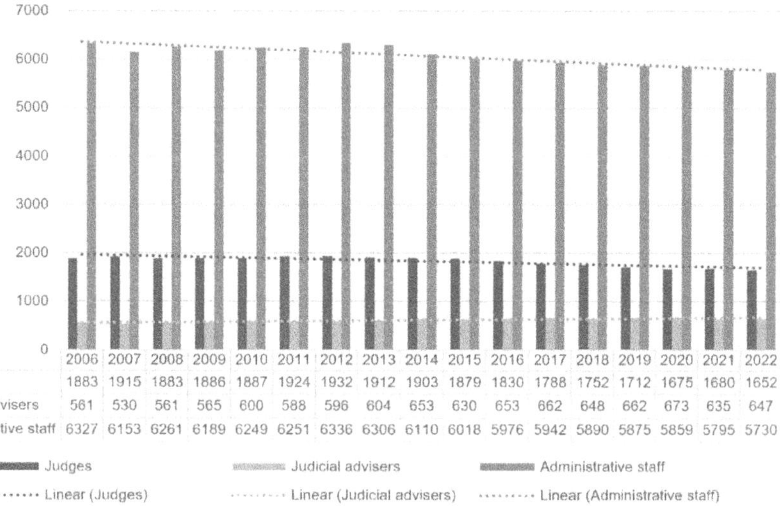

	2006	2007	2008	2009	2010	2011	2012	2013	2014	2015	2016	2017	2018	2019	2020	2021	2022
Judges	1883	1915	1883	1886	1887	1924	1932	1912	1903	1879	1830	1788	1752	1712	1675	1680	1652
Judicial advisers	561	530	561	565	600	588	596	604	653	630	653	662	648	662	673	635	647
Administrative staff	6327	6153	6261	6189	6249	6251	6336	6306	6110	6018	5976	5942	5890	5875	5859	5795	5730

Graph 4.2 Number of judges and judicial advisers at municipal courts (2006–18)[36]

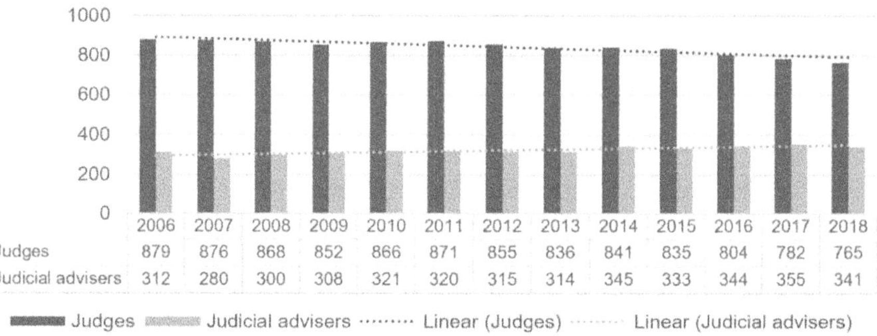

	2006	2007	2008	2009	2010	2011	2012	2013	2014	2015	2016	2017	2018
Judges	879	876	868	852	866	871	855	836	841	835	804	782	765
Judicial advisers	312	280	300	308	321	320	315	314	345	333	344	355	341

Graph 4.3 Number of judges and judicial advisers at commercial courts (2006–22)

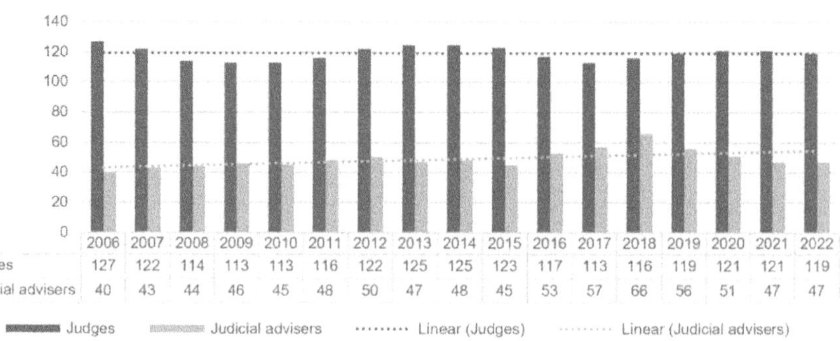

	2006	2007	2008	2009	2010	2011	2012	2013	2014	2015	2016	2017	2018	2019	2020	2021	2022
Judges	127	122	114	113	113	116	122	125	125	123	117	113	116	119	121	121	119
Judicial advisers	40	43	44	46	45	48	50	47	48	45	53	57	66	56	51	47	47

[36] Unfortunately, in 2019 misdemeanour courts which have jurisdiction to decide on small offences were merged with municipal courts, so the data published after 2018 is not comparable to prior years.

rate that those courts and judges who do not [hire them]'.[37] Since such analyses have not been published, the methodology used remains unclear, and their conclusion cannot be verified. In fact, a comprehensive empirical analysis would require deep scanning of the official data accessible in the ICMS. The data acquired during my doctoral research and in the following years provides useful pieces of information for this subchapter.

The first step was to compare the ratio of cases that were solved by judges and judicial advisers to the employment trends discussed earlier. If the data is to be trusted, it should not yield illogical or protruding results strongly opposing the officially available data. In that regard, it would seem the data from the ICMS corresponds to the official data. The ratio of the cases solved by the judicial advisers was higher in the years where there was a greater number of the judicial advisers hired at courts, which is true both for municipal (compare Graphs 4.2 and 4.4) and (even more so) for commercial courts (compare Graphs 4.3 and 4.5).

Graph 4.4 Distribution of solved cases at municipal courts (2015–22)

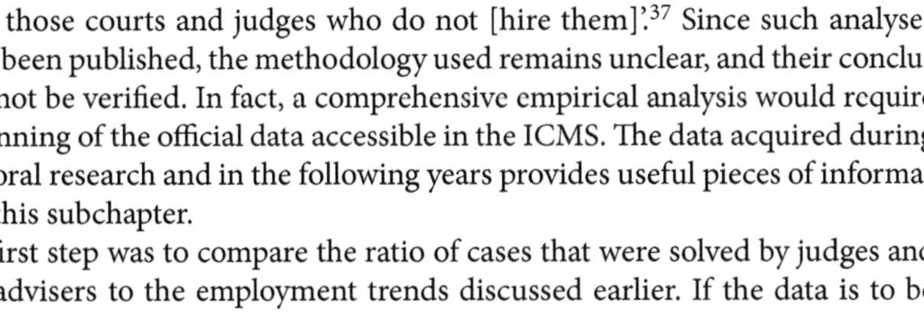

	2015	2016	2017	2018	2019	2020	2021	2022
Judicial advisers	15.61%	15.92%	15.15%	16.66%	15.25%	12.45%	20.91%	19.41%
Judges	84.39%	84.08%	84.85%	83.34%	84.75%	87.55%	79.09%	80.59%

Graph 4.5 Distribution of solved cases at commercial courts (2015–22)

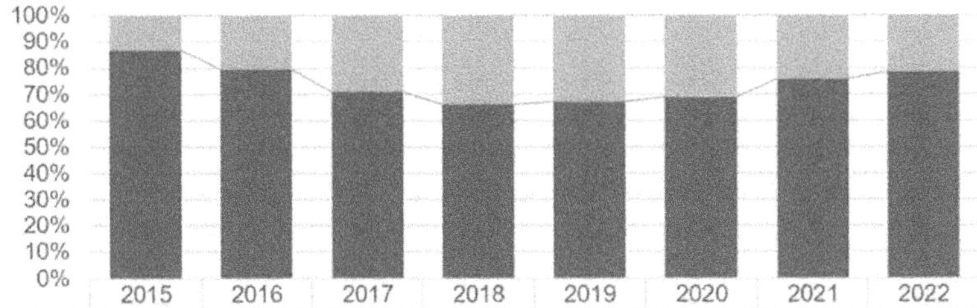

	2015	2016	2017	2018	2019	2020	2021	2022
Judicial advisers	13.46%	20.37%	28.97%	33.90%	32.80%	31.07%	24.45%	21.68%
Judges	86.54%	79.63%	71.03%	66.10%	67.20%	68.93%	75.55%	78.32%

Whatever is concluded about the efficiency of judicial advisers and judges in our sample is thus relevant for the overall conclusions.

Proceeding with the analysis, our data shows the average and median time for disposing of cases by way of contradictory judgment, which was rendered after full

[37] CCJE Questionnaire – Croatia, q 10.

hearing and evidentiary proceedings. The average duration is much lower for the cases handled by judicial advisers than the ones handled by judges. Median values are also lower, although the difference is more significant in commercial courts (compare Tables 4.5 and 4.6).

Table 4.5 Duration of proceedings at municipal courts in years (2015–22)

Municipal courts		2015	2016	2017	2018	2019	2020	2021	2022
Judges	Mean	2.72	3.02	3.31	3.24	3.06	2.97	2.33	2.60
	Median	1.51	1.67	1.77	1.70	1.63	1.64	1.23	1.64
Judicial advisers	Mean	2.57	2.30	2.36	2.43	2.74	2.78	1.27	1.59
	Median	1.41	1.42	1.81	2.12	2.40	2.28	0.74	1.23

Table 4.6 Duration of proceedings at commercial courts in years (2015–22)

Commercial courts		2015	2016	2017	2018	2019	2020	2021	2022
Judges	Mean	2.50	2.58	2.65	2.59	2.70	3.09	3.28	3.41
	Median	1.86	1.81	1.79	1.63	1.64	1.86	2.20	2.31
Judicial advisers	Mean	1.84	1.82	1.97	2.22	2.20	2.14	2.66	2.82
	Median	1.34	1.25	1.44	1.66	1.52	1.48	1.83	1.83

It would seem that the cases assigned to judicial advisers are processed remarkably faster than the cases assigned to judges. Admittedly, it may be a consequence of the fact that judicial advisers deal mostly with small claims. Our data supports such an opinion because the judicial advisers are in charge of cases whose value does not fall within the threshold for small claims in 16.66 per cent of cases at municipal courts and in 2.24 per cent of cases at commercial courts. However, one should be careful in drawing conclusions here.

First, it should be noted that not all small claims are assigned to judicial advisers. Our data shows that the indicated value of the dispute is below the small claims threshold in 58.59 per cent of cases in municipal courts and in 67.72 per cent of cases in commercial courts. If the indicated value of the dispute can be considered a valid indication of potentially complex cases, only one third of the cases fit that description. This means that average cases, many of which are simple, are also assigned to judges, which should then reflect in their efficiency.

Second, not all cases assigned to judicial advisers really fit the description of proceedings upon payment and damages claims not exceeding the threshold. As was shown before (see II.B.), smaller number of cases of municipal and commercial courts cannot be considered cases which, according to the statutory rules, are supposed to be assigned to judicial advisers. Having the serious procedural and constitutional implications of such assignment aside here, these numbers again show that not all cases assigned to judicial advisers can automatically be considered 'simple'.

Both of these circumstances indeed justify the conclusion that judicial advisers do dispose of cases faster than judges and that their integration into the system may have some benefits for the court efficiency. Of course, the question remains: at what cost?

IV. Critical Assessment

Hiring judicial assistants has its merit. There is an obvious appeal to using judicial assistants, which may lead to a gradual expansion of their role, ranging from mere assistance to quality assurance.[38] However, granting them a more prominent role and erasing the significant differences from the role of judges, with the intention of addressing the court backlogs, has been rightfully marked as a dangerous road to take.[39]

In Croatia, the judicial advisers at the second instance courts and the Supreme Court do not seem to be problematic. They can truly fit in the definition of 'judicial assistants', as they only provide useful support to judges. The first instance judicial advisers, on the other hand, can be considered quasi-judges of lower status and lower income who are not compelled to undertake any form of professional training, unless they intend to apply for judicial office in the future. They do not merely participate in the judging, as envisaged by the CC. Instead, they play a significant role in the judging process,[40] despite early warnings from foreign experts.[41]

This extent of delegation poses a significant threat to the concept of judicial independence, while simultaneously obfuscating accountability for the final outcome. Regrettably, there have been several other procedural concessions along the way.

Officially, the judges sign the decisions, merely indicating that they were based on the proposal of judicial advisers. They determine the final contents of the decisions and correct any inaccuracies in factual conclusions or misinterpretations of substantive law made by the judicial advisers. Even if judicial advisers do not agree with such revisions, they cannot influence the outcome. The judicial independence does not seem to be affected here.

[38] G Grendstad, WR Shaffer, JØ Sunde and EN Waltenburg, 'From Backlogs to Quality Assurance. The Development of Law Clerk Units at Norwegian Courts' (2020) 11 *International Journal For Court Administration* 1, 12–13.

[39] CCJE Opinion No. 22 (2019), para 14.

[40] As was highlighted in one decision of the High Commercial Court, to judge means 'to hold hearing, render, and announce the decisions'. High Commercial Court, Pž 3631/05-5 of 2 July 2008. Croatia has been marked as a country with the highest level of involvement of judicial assistants. A Sanders, 'Judicial Assistants in Europe – A Comparative Analysis' (2020) 11(3) *International Journal for Court Administration* 12, 15.

[41] CG Martínez and JB Delgado, Fefiniranje nove uloge savjetnika u pravosudnim tijelima i unapređenje njihova statusa, Twinning project: 'Professional Development of Judicial Advisors and Future Judges and State Attorneys through Establishment of Self Sustainable Training System', (pak.hr/cke/ipa%202009/hr/Res.1.2.%20DEFINIRANJE%20NOVE%20ULOGE%20SAVJETNIKA.pdf), esp. 6–8.

However, a lot of psychology research suggests that heuristics and mental biases condition our conclusions even when we are not aware of it. People tend to heavily rely on the first piece of information that has been available to them (the so-called anchoring effect).[42] Seriousness of this issue was also raised by the CCJE.[43] Empirical research has proven that the activities of judicial assistants can considerably influence the outcome of court proceedings,[44] especially if they outnumber the judges or if they are highly qualified and experienced.[45]

Unfortunately, this is not where the story of conclusion errors ends. Since judges do not conduct the evidentiary proceedings themselves, there could be other subtle cognitive biases at play. Useful tools such as previous experience can unexpectedly lead to erroneous conclusions.[46] Croatian Judicial Academy has only recently included workshops teaching judges the most important findings on cognitive biases.[47] This means that a considerable number of judges are still not aware that many of their conclusions may be subconsciously affected by different factors, including the conclusions previously drawn by judicial advisers. The sense of independence and impartiality that we have may thus only be an illusion.[48]

Even if we were sufficiently convinced that the judges' final word in deciding the case is enough to uphold judicial independence and impartiality, another issue arises from the fact that they are not formally accountable for the decision they sign. They literally do not participate in the proceedings until a decision on merits or certain procedural issues is needed.[49]

Unlike in neighbouring Slovenia, where judicial advisers carry out evidentiary proceedings under the supervision of judges,[50] the judges in Croatia simply are not present in the courtroom when the proceedings are conducted by the judicial advisers.[51] In the literature, such a solution has long ago been marked as a serious departure from the principle of immediacy, as the person in charge of conducting and evaluating evidence is different from the person deciding the case.[52] However, the problem goes even further.

[42] D Kahneman, *Thinking fast and slow* (New York, Farrar, Straus and Giroux, 2013) 249.

[43] CCJE Opinion No. 22 (2019), para 26.

[44] N Holvast and P Mascini, 'Is the Judge or the Clerk Making the Decision? Measuring the Influence of Judicial Assistants via an Experimental Survey among Dutch District Court Judges' (2020) 11 *International Journal for Court Administration* 4, 9–15.

[45] N Holvast, 'The power of the judicial assistant/law clerk: Looking behind the scenes at courts in the United States, England and Wales, and the Netherlands' (2016) 7 *International Journal for Court Administration* 10, 24.

[46] Á Pérez Ragone and E Vitorelli, 'Judicial Independence, Impartiality, and Judicial Decision-Making' in E Oteiza and GP Posada (eds), *Judicial Independence in the Third Millenium. XVII World Congress of Procedural Law. General Reports* (Lima, Palestra, 2023) 360–371.

[47] ibid 372–373.

[48] The research is actually only starting, Ragone and Vitorelli (n 46) 385.

[49] Judicial advisers are authorised to decide independently on the costs of the proceedings after withdrawal of claim or appeal (art 164 CPA) and on securing evidence (arts 186.a para 10 and 273 CPA).

[50] Art 52 para 2 Slovenian Courts Act. The instructions and supervision of the judges is required to preserve the principle of immediacy. High Court in Ljubljana, Cpg 947/2007 of 15 May 2008.

[51] This is clearly demonstrated in case law. See *Egzeta v Croatia* (cited in 13) and also County Court Rijeka, Gž Ovr-302/2022-2 of 25 May 2022. The information provided in the CCJE Summary Report was thus mispresented. CCJE Summary Report 2021, fn 90.

[52] Triva and Dika 2004, 188.

There has always been an opportunity to revive the principle of immediacy if judges, unsatisfied with the draft, take over the case from judicial advisers, conduct proceedings, and render their own decision. However, these provisions seem to have been a dead letter from the very beginning. Instead, the judges get involved only informally, providing less time-consuming mentoring advice and suggesting the necessary adjustments.[53]

It is not only the proceedings that the judges are not accountable for. They do not even have the accountability for the outcome. The case is not formally assigned to them. Unlike in their own cases,[54] overturning of the decision by the appellate court would not influence their evaluation and possible career advancements. And for their limited mentoring activities they are exempted from up to 12 per cent of their obligations, as defined in art 6 of General benchmarks ('Norm').

Simultaneously, the evaluation of the first instance judicial advisers, who do not enjoy the same level of (substantial) independence, generally depends on the quality of their decisions. Except in land registry cases,[55] satisfying the Norm is not officially an evaluation criterion, however, it is generally considered in the evaluation process.[56]

One could argue, though, that judicial intervention in the decision-making process can only reduce the rates of overturning or overriding decisions of the appellate courts, in other words, increase the quality of the court decisions. Our empirical data seems to support that. The number of overriding decisions is slightly lower for judicial advisers when compared to the same data for judges (Table 4.7) or overall official numbers (Table 4.8).

Table 4.7 Official overall percentage of remittals in courts (2015–19)

Year	Percentage of remittals
2015	26.33%
2016	28.88%
2017	30.71%
2018	27.60%
2019	29.15%
Average	**28.53%**

[53] This is not only based on anecdotal information from experienced colleagues in judiciary, but on the efforts to collect concrete empirical data of cases which were reassigned from judicial advisers to judges. There was simply no data to collect, which probably explains the amount of surprise in the Ministry when the query was made.

[54] Methodology for Evaluation of Judges was developed by the State Judiciary Council.

[55] Regulation on the general benchmarks for official in land registry judicial units.

[56] See Methodology for Evaluation of Judicial and State-Attorney Advisers. The reports, filled in in accordance with Regulation on evaluation of public servants, usually take into account the number of overturning and overriding decisions of the appellate courts.

Table 4.8 Percentage of remittals per responsible persons (2015–19)

2015–2019	Percentage of remittals
Judge	28.62%
Judicial adviser	21.73%

However, this may also be the consequence of the type of cases that judicial advisers handle. They mostly deal with small claims, where appeal is not available in cases of factual errors (art 467 para 1 CPA). There is simply no opportunity to review the unintentional factual errors that may be the result of such a division of work in the first-instance proceedings.

In my view, the issue surpasses only the considerable constraint of the principle of immediacy. It essentially influences the parties' right to a fair hearing. Appellate limitations may be justified on the basis of procedural proportionality ('the benefit of expediting small claims proceedings outweighs the risk'). In fact, the appeal may completely be excluded in such cases.[57] However, when combined with (possibly) less qualified and trained individuals handling the case, and more qualified ones refusing, without any consequence, to handle it personally, such procedural concessions appear to push the boundaries a bit too far.[58]

Another whole set of issues arises from the fact that many of those small claims cases arise out of contested payment orders. Namely, in order to certify and collect simple (often small) money claims, there is a complex combination of enforcement and payment order proceedings, involving both the courts and public notaries, which – if the debtor objected to the order – ultimately end up in courts.[59] If the value of the debt is low enough (and it very often is), such cases will be assigned to judicial advisers. Our overall data, analysing the activities of judicial advisers from 2015 to 2022, shows that there were 76.38 per cent of such cases in municipal courts and 54.32 per cent in commercial courts that were resolved by judicial advisers.

The fact that such simple cases did not overburden the judges, leaving them the opportunity to handle more complex ones, is certainly commendable. Nonetheless, hiring judicial advisers to manage the overwhelming influx of cases, many of which ideally should have been resolved outside of the courtroom, highlights that the issue of court backlogs is not being addressed at its source. It actually suggests the implementation of a 'patching up' strategy, dealing with symptoms, instead of fighting the disease.

[57] A Uzelac, 'Features and Shortcomings of Appellate Review in Civil and Administrative Cases in Croatia' in A Uzelac and C H van Rhee (eds), *Nobody's Perfect. Comparative Essays on Appeals and other Means of Recourse against Judicial Decisions in Civil Matters* (Cambridge – Antwerp – Portland, Intersentia, 2014) 252–253.

[58] This is especially true after 2022 with the introduction of the possibility to decide on the small claim case without holding a hearing (art 461.a paras 3–4 CPA).

[59] M Bratković, 'In Search of Efficiency: Court Structure and Case Management in Croatia' in P Chan, and CH van Rhee (eds), *Civil Case Management in the Twenty-First Century: Court Structures Still Matter* (Singapore, Springer, 2021) 172–174.

Fighting it would presuppose stronger incentives to encourage the amicable dispute resolution. Such incentives are apparently lacking as both Consumer Alternative Dispute Resolution Act and recent Amicable Dispute Resolution Act do not seem to yield any serious results.[60]

V. Conclusion

It is obvious from the comparisons made in this chapter that the tasks of many judicial advisers in Croatia exceed what is usually considered to be the task of judicial assistants. It is also clear that many of them do not enjoy all the benefits of being a judge. There are some training opportunities for them, should they wish to pursue a judicial career, and they get some mentoring advice along the way. But it is far from being a well thought-through career path.

Their growing engagement comes with a great price. On the brink of constitutionality, fundamental procedural principles were sacrificed to assist judges in fighting the court backlogs. Despite such a solution drew criticism from both scholars in the field and foreign experts, all subsequent reforms appear to have merely exacerbated the issue.

The judiciary, which does not filter the cases entering courts, is condemned to perpetually revisit the same struggles. Addressing these issues through staff management may superficially scratch the surface but will not effectively resolve the underlying issues. Instead, it is likely to cultivate dissatisfaction within the judiciary, also affecting the quality of provided services.

So, can judicial advisers be considered 'heroes of the judicial periphery'? In a way, many of them can be deemed heroic as they bolster court efficiency, persisting for years despite lower status and compensation, uncertain if they will ever be appointed as judges. Nonetheless, their tasks in the first-instance proceedings are an important part of the judging process, which places them at the very core of judicial activities.

Such a solution should be reconsidered, although it entails making difficult decisions in the restructuring of the judiciary. After boosting, more efficiently, the alternative dispute resolution methods and reassessing the types of cases that enter the courts, addressing the issue of a large workforce becomes imperative, while also considering regional disparities. This approach could lead to improved efficiency, salary raises, and increased satisfaction among court personnel. Finally, it would create a more meaningful career path for judicial advisers, making these young legal professionals true heroes in the making.

[60] A Uzelac, 'Izazovi novog uređenja izvansudskog rješavanja potrošačkih sporova' in G Mihelčić et al. (eds), *Liber amicorum Aldo Radolović* (Rijeka, Sveučilište u Rijeci, Pravni Fakultet, 2018) 145–165 (for consumer ADR) and A Uzelac and J Brozović, 'Zakon o mirnom rješavanju sporova: Korak unaprijed ili još jedna propuštena prilika?' *Portal IUSINFO*, 14 June 2023, www.iusinfo.hr/strucni-clanci/zakon-o-mirnom-rjesavanju-sporova-korak-unaprijed-ili-jos-jedna-propustena-prilika (for new Amicable Dispute Resolution Act).

5

The Role of Judicial Secretaries in Spain: The Story of a Collective Frustration?

FERNANDO GASCÓN INCHAUSTI

1. The starting point: the evolving role of judicial secretaries in the Spanish judicial organisation. – 2. Claiming a more prominent position. – 3. Recent developments and current state of affairs

If one reads the Spanish general legislation on the judiciary (the so-called *Ley Orgánica del Poder Judicial*)[1] and the specific legal bodies regulating each type of proceedings – ie, civil,[2] criminal,[3] administrative[4] and social[5] proceedings – a first impression can be drawn: judicial secretaries play a major role, to the point that it can be said that there is a kind of 'bicephaly' between the judge and the judicial secretary, even if on the first instance the landscape is composed of single judge courts.

In the following pages I will try to explain that there is some truth in this, but also that what lies behind it, at least at present, is the story of a collective frustration or, if preferred, the story of the frustration of a collective. The focus will be put on civil justice, although the situation is similar elsewhere – except, maybe, in criminal proceedings, where the role of the judge is clearly more prominent.

[1] *Ley Orgánica* 6/1985, of July 1. It is the general act that establishes the structure of the Spanish judiciary, the status of judges, judicial secretaries and other court officers and the common rules on judicial activity.

[2] Civil proceedings are ruled by the Code of civil procedure (*Ley de Enjuiciamiento Civil*, Ley 1/2000, of January 7).

[3] Criminal proceedings are ruled by the Code of criminal procedure (*Ley de Enjuiciamiento Criminal*, passed in 1882 and still in force, although strongly amended).

[4] Administrative proceedings are ruled by a specific Code of administrative procedure (*Ley reguladora de la Jurisdicción contencioso-administrativa*, Ley 29/1998, of July 13): in Spain administrative courts belong to the ordinary judiciary, although the proceedings are different to civil ones.

[5] Proceedings in labour and social matters are also ruled by a specific Code of social procedure (*Ley reguladora de la jurisdicción social*, Ley 36/2011, of October 10).

I. The Starting Point: The Evolving Role of Judicial Secretaries in the Spanish Judicial Organisation

Let us start with a short explanation of the way in which the Spanish judicial organisation is structured in the first instance. In many neighbouring jurisdictions, following the French model, there is a 'court of first instance' – whatever name it may be given – in each judicial district, in which several judges – depending on the population and the number of cases – carry out their functions under the coordination or supervision of a president. In a different way, the Spanish judicial organisation has traditionally been atomised in the first instance. In each judicial district there is at least one single-judge-court of first instance, which has a fixed structure: a judge, a judicial secretary, and several court officers, in principle self-sufficient for everything that a procedure requires, from the beginning to the enforcement of the judgment. In districts such as Madrid, this structure is reproduced or replicated as many times as necessary to meet the 'judicial needs': there are not just one, but 105 courts of first instance. But, to a large extent, they function as islands disconnected from each other.

What is the role of the judicial secretary in such a structure? Initially, the existence of a judicial secretary within the court is due to the need to provide judicial activity with 'authenticity', ie, to provide irrefutable evidence of the conduct of the proceedings. Closely linked to this underpinning, judicial secretaries have been traditionally entrusted with the documentation function, which involves them in the drafting of the minutes of every hearing and in the management of all the procedural files, with the help of the rest of the court officers. In fact, during the nineteenth and part of the twentieth century, judicial offices resembled notary's offices, although run by judicial secretaries, who were responsible for selecting officers and for ensuring the productivity and functioning of the administrative or bureaucratic part of the court proceedings.[6] These judicial offices were at that time primarily financed by 'tariffs' (*aranceles*), ie, by fees that were to be paid by the litigants, and which depended on the value of the claims.[7] From an external point of view – which is precisely that of the litigants – judicial secretaries at that time earned much more money than the judges – who were 'mere' state servants – an anomalous situation often criticised by academicians and many practitioners. Although in 1947 all court officers had become civil servants – and not just mere employees of the judicial office – judicial secretaries continued to collect their fees. The situation only ended in 1986, when court fees were abolished[8] and judicial secretaries started to be exclusively paid by the state – in many cases this entailed a clear reduction of their revenues.

[6] For a very detailed explanation of the historical evolution, see M de Benito Llopis-Llombart, *Justicia o Burocracia* (Madrid, Civitas, 2017).

[7] The press article published by *El País* on 21 October 1984 describes some of the corrupt practices triggered by this structure (elpais.com/diario/1984/10/21/sociedad/467161205_850215.html).

[8] Court fees were reintroduced in the Spanish legal system later on (with a first act in 2002 and another one in 2012), but on a radically different basis, since they are collected directly by the state, not by the judicial secretary.

From that point in time onwards, the figure of the judicial secretary changes its focus because they fully become civil servants. They are required to be law graduates, and they need to pass a difficult national competitive exam, not much lower than that established for judges and prosecutors. However, from an organisational point of view, they are not part of the judiciary: they do not have jurisdictional powers and, above all, they are not independent; on the contrary, they have a hierarchical organisation that, in the end, makes them depend on the Ministry of Justice.

However, their high legal qualifications mean that de facto they begin to take on the role of collaborators with the judge in the management of proceedings, beyond the mere administration of the workload inside the judicial office. One could say that they start to be perceived as a qualified collaborator of the judge and, for some purposes, even their delegate.

This situation is, in fact, the result of several converging trends:

a) In 1985, the so-called 'decision proposal' (*propuesta de resolución*) is created:[9] it is a draft of a procedural decision that is prepared by the judicial secretary and submitted to the judge, who should give it and who, indeed, may limit herself to ratifying it as such, without further ado. For most decisions that affect the conduct of the proceedings and that the judge must issue, it is foreseen that the judicial secretary can make a proposal, which the judge can simply confirm. This is one way of lightening the judges' workload, which is complemented by another: the judicial secretary is reserved certain areas of the proceedings in which the decision is his or her own; in other words, some procedural decisions shall be taken by the judicial secretary, not by the judge. This highlights the value of the judicial secretary as a legal professional. In 2000, however, a completely new Code of Civil Procedure (*Ley de Enjuiciamiento Civil*) is approved and decision proposals disappear, as they were considered unnecessary and confusing;[10] but, in return, the list of procedural matters that must be resolved directly and in their own name by the judicial secretaries is increased.
b) Enforcement is called for more efficiency. In Spain, unlike in other countries, enforcement is the responsibility of the courts (Article 117 of the Spanish Constitution so requires) and this, obviously, increases the workload of courts: enforcement proceedings rest on the court that dealt with the case in the first instance, and their management encumbers their daily lives. According to the law, as enacted in 2000, the most important acts of enforcement are entrusted

[9] See Arts 246 and 290 of the Organic Act of the Judiciary in their initial wording.
[10] The preamble of the Code of Civil Procedure states in its Section IX the following on this issue:

> The decision proposals, introduced by the Organic Law of the Judiciary in 1985, have not in fact served to take advantage of the undoubted technical knowledge of the judicial secretaries, but rather to increase the confusion between their attributions and those of the courts, and to give rise to different criteria for action in the different courts and tribunals, frequently giving rise to insecurity and dissatisfaction. For this reason, it has not been considered appropriate to maintain their existence, but rather to propose alternative formulas that would result in a better functioning of the judicial bodies.

to the judges; in practice, they tend to delegate enforcement as a whole to judicial secretaries. Although the law at the time determined, for instance, that the judge should organise and direct the conduct of the public auction to sell the debtor's seized assets, this work was in practice always carried out by the judicial secretary.

c) Since the entry into force of the new Code of Civil Procedure, which took place in January 2001, oral hearings are recorded; the preparation of minutes is no longer necessary since extensive minutes are replaced by the videorecording of the hearing. The time that had been until then needed to draft the minutes is now available for the judicial secretary to devote it to other tasks and activities, including, as mentioned, enforcement proceedings.

d) From the 1990s onwards, so-called 'common structures' (*servicios communes*) began to be created in judicial districts with several single-judge courts in order to rationalise the work of court officers: 'notification common structures' (*servicios comunes de notificaciones*) or 'enforcement common structures' (*servicios comunes de ejecución*) were organised, at the disposal of all the courts of the district; these – sometimes very big – administrative structures are headed by judicial secretaries, disconnected to any specific court and judge: there are judicial secretaries – those in charge of the common structures – that do not work *in* nor *for* a court, but still they manage relevant procedural activities independently of the judges, ie, without being under their direct supervision. These common and shared structures begin to break with the traditionally atomised vision of the Spanish courts of first instance, albeit only in a very tenuous form.

II. Claiming a More Prominent Position

As a consequence of the trends described above, a progressive increase in the importance of the judicial secretary within the justice system has been consolidated. This, in turn, has led to a collective demand for greater prominence, both in formal and material terms.

From a 'formal' point of view, judicial secretaries demand that the work they do be recognised in law, so that they are officially attributed the powers to do what they are de facto doing. The suppression of 'decision proposals', in the view of many judicial secretaries, led to *invisibilising* or *ghosting* their work, and what is being sought is just the opposite. This claim is clearly justified: the real activity of judicial secretaries should be backed by the law and not just by practice.

From a 'material' point of view, judicial secretaries also aspire to extend their scope of competence in procedural matters and to be entrusted with the handling of more affairs on their own behalf, especially in enforcement and non-contentious proceedings (also known as 'voluntary jurisdiction'). In support of this claim, the argument of efficiency is used: i) judges are overloaded and eager to use any help they can get; ii) judicial secretaries aspire to assume a decisional power on tasks that do not form part of the hard core of the judicial function, ie, they are not deciding on the merits of the case, nor limiting access to justice, but rather addressing 'merely procedural matters' or being involved in situations where no real conflict is to be solved and where the function of courts is more similar to that of notaries (non-contentious divorces of couples without children, for instance); and iii) judicial secretaries are highly qualified professionals, with a good knowledge of the law, but they are being 'underused', ie, their lack of activity may be regarded as a waste of resources.

Regardless of their grounds – very controversial as far as ii) above is concerned – these demands serve to channel several aspirations, which are undoubtedly legitimate: On the one hand, there is a clear economic claim: it is presumed that the assumption of additional functions and tasks, together with the official recognition of those that had been performed unofficially, should be accompanied by a salary increase.

On the other hand, there is a demand for a new and higher status within the Administration of Justice: judicial secretaries aspire to be seen/perceived as an authority 'from outside' – ie, by lawyers and by society – and not only 'from inside' – ie, inside the judicial office. It is common to say that they aspire to become the 'judges of the procedure'. And this, in the end, could be, in the eyes of many, the springboard from which to aspire to join the judicial career – to become judges de jure, even if only judges of the procedure.

As I have already pointed out, the major reform of civil procedure in 2000 did not satisfy these aspirations; on the other hand, the disappearance of the decision proposals led to a return to a certain invisibility, to an assumption of the role of 'secondary actors' by the judicial secretaries. Perhaps this is why the efforts of vindication got intensified since then, crystallising in three major moments: 2003, 2009, and 2015.

a) In *2003*, a big legal reform laid the foundations for restructuring the Spanish judicial organisation, especially in the first instance, under the slogan of creating a 'New Judicial Office'.[11] The aim was to put an end to the atomisation of the single judge courts and to reinforce and generalise an organisation based on common structures. In this new scheme, each court will continue to have its own judicial secretary and some officers, but there will be many judicial secretaries, detached from specific single judge courts, in charge of the organisation and functioning of the new common structures, at the service of the single judge courts of the district.

The act also did something that had not been done before: it identifies and categorises the functions of the judicial secretaries, which are no longer more or less implicit in the legislation. Specifically, the following functions are identified:

- judicial secretaries keep being the holders of judicial authentication powers;
- they are main responsible for the documentation of the proceedings, ie, they are in charge of setting each case's judicial file;

[11] Organic Law 19/2003, of December 23, amending the *Ley Orgánica del Poder Judicial*.

- judicial secretaries are responsible of driving and organising the proceedings;
- judicial secretaries become the directors of the judicial office, both from a technical and a procedural perspective – and this means that the judges are deprived of this function, which was strongly criticised;
- judicial secretaries are entrusted with the collaboration and cooperation with other public bodies and administrations.

And, above all, the figure of the judicial secretary is legally reformulated: they are defined as members of a single, national, senior legal body, at the service of the Administration of Justice and dependent on the Ministry of Justice; at the same time, they are hierarchically organised, with the aim of ensuring greater efficiency in the performance of their function.[12]

Immediately above each judicial secretary there will be a so-called 'Provincial Coordinating Secretary' (*Secretario Coordinador Provincial*) – note that Spain is currently divided into 50 provinces. Above them, at the regional level, on the next rung, there are the so-called 'Executive Secretaries' (*Secretarios de Gobierno*) – Spain is currently divided into 17 regions (*Comunidades Autónomas*). At the top of the pyramid of hierarchy, the Secretary General of the Administration of Justice (*Secretario General de la Administración de Justicia*), appointed by the Minister of Justice, is in charge of the direction and coordination of all judicial secretaries.[13]

Within their sphere, each of these 'superiors' can issue practical directions and general instructions to the judicial secretaries of their territory concerning the handling of proceedings, although, in principle, they may not give particular instructions for specific cases.[14] The only area of activity in which the judicial secretary remains truly independent is that of authentication,[15] but this role is being reduced as new technologies are introduced: minutes of the hearings are no longer drafted (the videorecording serves this function) and the presence of judicial secretaries is no longer even necessary in oral hearings.

b) In *2009*, a major procedural reform took place, with the aim of specifying in the procedural laws the consequences of the organic changes adopted in 2003 and,

[12] The legal status of judicial secretaries is regulated in Royal Decree 1608/2005, of December 30).

[13] Article 13 of Royal Decree 1608/2005 clearly states in its first section the following: 'Under the superior dependence of the Ministry of Justice, the Body of judicial secretaries will be organised hierarchically'. The rest of the provision identifies the different steps of the hierarchy.

[14] Pursuant to Article 3(3) of Royal Decree 1608/2005:

> In the exercise of the functions of technical-procedural management of the Judicial Office, as well as in all those entrusted to them [...], they shall act under the principles of unity of action and hierarchical dependence, providing the necessary means for the Judicial Office to act under the criteria of effectiveness, efficiency, agility, responsibility for management, rationalisation of work, coordination and cooperation with the competent administrations in matters of justice, so that the citizens obtain a service that is close to them and of quality, with respect for the principles set out in the Charter of Citizens' Rights before Justice.

[15] According to Article 3(2) of Royal Decree 1608/2005, 'In the exercise of their authentication function they shall act autonomously and independently'.

above all, to give precise content to the functions of the judicial secretaries as drivers and managers of the proceedings.[16] The reform was impressive, as it affected a very high percentage of the Spanish procedural codes (civil, criminal, administrative, and social), in which the aim was to write down in complete detail and precision what was to be decided by the judge and what, on the other hand, was to be decided by the judicial secretary: where previously the law said generically that something had to be done by the *court*, it now goes on to detail whether the *judge* or the *judicial secretary* will do it and, furthermore, whether or not it will have to be done through a reasoned decision – a so-called 'decree' (*decreto*).

In order to achieve this distribution of functions, at least in theory, a criterion hitherto unknown in Spain was made up: the distinction between 'merely procedural' decisions and 'jurisdictional' decisions. According to this criterion, jurisdictional decisions can only be adopted by the judge. However, until then, judges had also been adopting 'procedural' decisions, which are those that, due to their content and impact, could also be taken by other officers and which, in fact, are those that supposedly are formally entrusted to the judicial secretaries. What distinguishes 'procedural' from 'jurisdictional' matters? The 2009 Act fails to explain it clearly in a straightforward manner: it states that any decision to be taken in the course of proceedings that is not 'strictly jurisdictional' in nature shall be attributed to the judicial secretaries. And what is the meaning of 'strictly jurisdictional'? According to Article 117 of the Spanish Constitution, jurisdiction consists in 'judging and enforcing what has been judged', which does not help to clarify the problem either, especially if one considers another provision of the Constitution, Article 24, which enshrines the right to effective judicial protection – in line with Article 6 of the European Convention on Human Rights or Article 47 of the European Charter of Fundamental Rights.

Judicial secretaries can be – and are – clearly entrusted with functions relating to the organisation and the progress of proceedings, such as the scheduling of hearings or the implementation of enforcement activities (eg, the conduct of the public auction to sell seized assets). But there are many other decisions whose nature – as merely procedural or jurisdictional – is debatable[17] and has been, indeed, strongly criticised.[18]

[16] Law 13/2009, of November 3, amending procedural legislation to implement the new Judicial office.

[17] On the difficulties to trace a clear line see I Díez-Picazo Giménez, 'Jurisdicción y resoluciones de los secretarios judiciales. Breves reflexiones a propósito de la sentencia del Tribunal de Conflictos de Jurisdicción de 28 de septiembre de 2011' in JL Gómez Colomer, S Barona Vilar and P Calderón Cuadrado (eds), *El Derecho procesal español del siglo XX a golpe de tango. Liber amicorum Juan Montero Aroca* (Valencia, Tirant lo Blanch, 2012) 309–318.

[18] For a very critical assessment, see J Banacloche Palao, 'Algunas consideraciones sobre la potestad jurisdiccional al hilo de las últimas reformas procesales' in JL Gómez Colomer, S Barona Vilar and P Calderón Cuadrado (eds), *El Derecho procesal español del siglo XX a golpe de tango. Liber amicorum Juan Montero Aroca* (Valencia, Tirant lo Blanch, 2012) 173–192. In this author's view the distinction is impossible to delineate, since procedural decisions serve to prepare decisions on the merits and, thus, precondition them (189); the legal situation leads, therefore, to a partial 'dejudicialisation of proceedings' (185).

In this vein, for instance, the judicial secretary is empowered to decide that a statement of claim – the plaintiff's document to be filed in order to institute proceedings – be admitted for processing without the judge even seeing it nor being aware of its submission; in such a case, the judicial secretary himself will serve the defendant with the claim and grant them the time limit provided by law to submit their statement of defence; only then will the judge receive the whole file, which she must study before the first oral hearing with the parties – at which point she may, paradoxically, consider that the claim should not have been admitted. Conversely, if the judicial secretary considers that the statement of claim is not admissible due to some procedural defect, they cannot itself reject it, but must refer the matter to the judge for a ruling on admissibility: according to the Spanish constitutional scheme, the non-admission of a claim entails a restriction on the fundamental right of access to the courts, which can only be established by a judicial decision. The same structure is replicated in the specific order for payment proceedings (*proceso monitorio*), which can be fully processed by judicial secretaries without the intervention of the judge in case the initial claim is considered admissible and the debtor, summoned to pay by the judicial secretary, ends up paying what is claimed.

To continue with the examples of what are, or are not merely procedural decisions, it is worth mentioning that the judicial secretary is empowered to terminate formally the proceedings: (i) if the plaintiff waives their claim or withdraws from the proceedings, (ii) if the defendant acquiesces to the plaintiff's claim, or (iii) if the parties reach a settlement. In these situations, there is nothing to decide; it is just a question of 'certifying' the free decision of one or both parties; the judge's intervention is, therefore, not necessary.

In enforcement matters, the judge is only responsible for issuing the general enforcement order, which provides for the formal commencement of enforcement proceedings and specifies its objective and subjective scope: from that point onwards, decisions are taken by the judicial secretary, unless the debtor or a third party lodges an opposition to enforcement. However, if several creditors concur to receive the proceeds after the sale at auction and payment to the creditor, the distribution also corresponds to the judicial secretary, although this is a decision that, in my opinion, goes far beyond the notion of what one should consider 'merely procedural'.

The scheme of division of functions between judges and judicial secretaries was complemented in the 2009 reform with a somewhat complicated system of appeals, which can be summarised as follows:

- If the judicial secretary takes a decision that puts an end to the proceedings or prevents their continuation, that decision may be appealed directly before the judge (*recurso de revisión*): there is an immediate judicial control over the judicial secretary's actions.
- On the other hand, if the decision taken by the judicial secretary is not one that terminates the proceedings or prevents their continuation, it is only possible to

make a motion for reconsideration to the judicial secretary themself (*recurso de reposición*), which they will decide by means of a decision that, as regulated in 2009, cannot be appealed directly before the judge; if anything, the party concerned may raise this issue again at the first hearing before the judge, or, if there is to be no hearing, it will be formulated in writing to the judge so that they can take it into account when deciding the dispute. In these cases, therefore, there is no direct and immediate judicial control, something that has been identified as dangerous since the reform was passed in 2009. I will get back to this later.

c) This redefinition culminates in *2015*, when a change of name takes place by means of a new legal reform: they cease to be called 'judicial secretaries' and become 'Attorneys of the Administration of Justice' (*Letrados de la Administración de Justicia*, usually mentioned by their acronym, LAJ); it is also made explicitly clearer that they are the directors of the judicial office.[19] It is a change located, therefore, in the realm of 'symbolism' and 'social message'.[20] That same year, a new Act on Non-contentious Proceedings (*Ley de Jurisdicción Voluntaria*) was passed,[21] in which a clear commitment was made to entrust the judicial secretaries with the complete management of the vast majority of non-contentious proceedings,[22] including non-contentious separations and divorces when there are no minor children. Only non-contentious proceedings affecting the civil status and capacity of persons should be resolved by judges, but not the others.

III. Recent Developments and Current State of Affairs

The panorama described above allows to sustain, to a large extent, the idea of the Spanish civil procedural system's bi-cephaly in the first instance of civil proceedings, given the major role played by the judicial secretary in the development of declaratory proceedings and its almost exclusive management of enforcement

[19] Organic Law 7/2015, of July 21, amending the *Ley Orgánica del Poder Judicial* (see Additional Provision 1, section 2.a).

[20] The Preamble of the Act states the following:

> The Body of judicial secretaries is renamed the Body of Attorneys of the Administration of Justice. This is in response to a historical demand of the Body, which considers that the name of judicial secretaries leads to misunderstandings about the function actually carried out.
>
> In this sense of adaptation to the current functions carried out by this Body, an express reference is included to the fact that its members are responsible for the direction of the Judicial Office; new competences are added such as mediation and the processing and, where appropriate, the resolution of payment order proceedings, all within the framework of what is provided for in the procedural rules; decrees are included as a type of resolution specific to these civil servants and it is provided that the Ministry of Justice will approve their list on an annual basis. Likewise, it establishes the system of rights and duties of the Attorneys of the Administration of Justice, thus clarifying their status as civil servants […].

[21] Ley 15/2015, de 2 de julio, *de la Jurisdicción Voluntaria*.

[22] In many matters, also Notaries and Land Registrars are competent to deal with the proceedings.

and non-contentious proceedings. The situation does not differ that much in the appeal phase; nevertheless, judicial secretaries are less visible, since oral hearings are not the rule, and the written structure of proceedings leaves less leeway for relevant procedural decisions.

Be it as it may, in court practice, lawyers and parties have to deal not only with judges but also with judicial secretaries along the whole development of proceedings. Many decisions during the proceedings are directly taken by judicial secretaries, even if, from a theoretical point of view, it should have been appropriate that they rest on the hands of the judges. The court, in the eyes of the lawyers and of the parties, is as much composed by the judge as by the judicial secretary; it all depends on the specific activity at hand.

However, if one looks at the reality, the balance may also be partially perceived in a different manner.

On the one hand, successive legal changes have led to a greater workload, but also to a progressive mutation of the function and role of judicial secretaries.

As regards the management of declaratory proceedings, of enforcement and of non-contentious proceedings, judicial secretaries have now greater powers, but also greater responsibilities, which put them more and more directly in the spotlight of disciplinary bodies and public opinion.

As for their role as heads of the new judicial office, they assume non-legal competences and are subject to a much greater hierarchy. The judge is no longer their chief, but this may be worse because they are now clearly inserted in a 'chain of command' that culminates in the Ministry of Justice and in which they feel more subject to political and corporative pressures. In fact, their legal qualification is gradually losing its meaning: to run a judicial office well, one needs to have skills in management and human resources organisation, not that much in procedural law … To perform that kind of function, in the end, top-level legal experts are not as suitable as persons with other professional profiles.

However, this increased workload and the greater pressure resulting from the assumption of functions for which judicial secretaries are not specifically qualified have not been accompanied by an improvement in salary until very recently. Judicial secretaries demanded and assumed, as a collective, this extension of functions and responsibilities, thinking that, somehow, the salary improvement would 'fall under its own weight'. The truth is that it was only after a strike lasting several months at the beginning of 2023 that they achieved this goal, with a salary increase of around €450 per month in linear terms. But the consequences of the strike were paradoxical: they took place in an election year and took thus advantage of the consequent weakness of the Ministry of Justice to impose itself. So, just after the ending of the judicial secretaries strike, the judges took over and also threatened to strike in order to obtain better salaries; and, simultaneously, the rest of the court officers 'below judicial secretaries' started to strike, also demanding better salaries, with the argument that, in practice, it was them who carried out the majority of the functions attributed to the judicial secretaries and for which the latter have obtained their salary improvement. On the other hand, the strikes of the judicial secretaries led to an accumulation of suspended proceedings and hearings, which weighed down the efficiency of the judicial system for months.

If the remuneration battle has been partially won, what has happened to the status battle? In my view, judicial secretaries may have lost it, and, probably, the situation in the long run can only get worse. Judicial secretaries have not managed to become 'the judges of the procedure', nor to be perceived as such, for a very simple and compelling reason: they are not independent, and independence is the clearest landmark for anyone to be a judge. In this connection, judicial secretaries have received two major 'setbacks', one at the national level and the other at the European level.

At the national level, the Constitutional Court has reminded them several times that they are not judges. As explained earlier, the system of appeals against the decisions of the judicial secretary established that decisions that were not final could only be challenged by means of a motion for reconsideration before the judicial secretary themself, but could not be challenged directly before the judge. Well, the Constitutional Court has declared that this scheme is unconstitutional, because, in practice, it means leaving the decisions of the judicial secretary devoid of judicial control in matters in which the jurisdictional function may be compromised, which in practice means recognising their status as administrative bodies.[23] A very recent procedural reform, passed in December 2023,[24] has amended the Spanish procedural legislation in order to comply with the Constitutional Court's rulings; it has been established that the decisions of judicial secretaries solving a motion for reconsideration may always be subject of a direct appeal before the judge (*recurso de revisión*).

At the European level, it was the Court of Justice of the European Union that found and declared that Spanish judicial secretaries are not independent.[25] The question arose in the context of one of the special proceedings which are entirely in the hands of the judicial secretaries, the privileged proceedings for lawyers to collect from their clients the fees associated with their defence at trial. The judicial secretary hearing one of those proceedings considered whether, in compliance with Directive 93/13 on unfair contract terms, he had the power to assess of his own motion the unfairness of one of the terms of the contract on which the lawyer based his claim against his client, and to that end referred a question to the Luxembourg court for a preliminary ruling. In doing so, however, he raised the question – and asked the Court – whether, as a judicial secretary, he could qualify as a 'court or tribunal' for the purposes of Article 267 TFEU, that is to say, for the purposes of being able to refer the question itself for a preliminary ruling, given that, under domestic law, he is merely a civil servant in the administration of

[23] See, at least, the following judgments of the Constitutional Court: judgment 58/2016 of March 17 ECLI:ES:TC:2016:58; judgment 72/2018 of June 21 ECLI:ES:TC:2018:72; judgment 34/2019 of March 14 ECLI:ES:TC:2019:34; and judgment 15/2020 of January 28 ECLI:ES:TC:2020:15.

[24] Royal Decree-law 6/2023, of December 19.

[25] Case C-503/15 Ramón Margarit Panicello v Pilar Hernández Martínez ECLI:EU:C:2017:126.

justice, attached to the Ministry of Justice. The Court found (at paragraph 40) that when he examines actions for the recovery of fees, the judicial secretary does not satisfy the requirement of independence, 'which requires there to be no hierarchical constraint or subordination to any other body that could give him orders or instructions'. On that basis, the Court of Justice considered that he is not a 'court or tribunal within the meaning of Article 267 TFEU' and that he does not have the power to refer a question for a preliminary ruling.

The result is great dissatisfaction and collective frustration, which has crystallised in the 2023 strike. Once the failure to claim a higher status was assumed, the judicial secretaries, as a collective, seem to have realised that only the salary demands made sense.

But, as I said before, the bicephaly is unstable. The functions that originally justified the existence of the judicial secretaries are increasingly becoming secondary and can be delegated to technology: hearings are recorded and no minutes are taken; AI programs transcribe the hearings more and more accurately; the management of the proceedings may, to some extent, be automated, so that the role of the judicial secretary as a procedural manager will also be reduced. In this vein, the reform passed in December 2023, regulating the use of ITC in the justice system, has admitted making recourse to AI technology and distinguishes between automated, proactive, and assisted activities, covering the most usual fields of activity of judicial secretaries.[26]

There will remain, of course, the function of directing the judicial office; but, as I have said before, it is far away from that which is proper to a lawyer and, of course, to someone who aspires to be seen as a 'judge', even a 'judge of the procedure'.

Although I am not prone to predictions, it is to fear that the status of judicial secretaries in Spain is not finally settled and that changes may contribute to vanish and diminish their role.

[26] Articles 56 to 58 of Royal Decree-law 6/2023. Automated activities are defined as procedural activities carried out by a computer system without the need for human intervention. They are foreseen for the management of the electronic court file (numbering or paging documents, generating copies or certificates, declaring that a decision is final because it has not been appealed within the legal time limit). Automated actions are labelled as proactive when they are self-initiated by the system, without human intervention, taking advantage of the information in a file for a specific purpose, such as generating a notice. In relation to these automated and proactive actions, the law imposes three requirements:

a) They must all be identifiable as such, traceable and justifiable.
b) It must be possible to carry out the same actions in a non-automated form.
c) It must be possible to disable, revert or render ineffective the automated actions that have already taken place.

The third category is assisted activities and decisions: in these, the computer system generates a full or partial draft of a complex data-driven document, which may be produced by algorithms, and may form the basis or support for a court decision. For these actions the law imposes stronger safeguards:

a) In no case shall the documentary draft in itself constitute a decision, but shall require validation by the competent authority.
b) The draft document is only generated at the will of the user and can be freely and completely modified by the user.

6

A Brief Overview of Some Aspects of Court Staff Training from a Belgian and European Perspective

RAF VAN RANSBEECK

I. Introduction

The training of court staff in Europe seems like an obvious topic that is easy to map out, but unfortunately this is only an appearance.

Indeed, each Member State of the European Union has its own training structure for court staff, and often the concept of court staff is not always unambiguous either. In France and Romania, for example, there are specific schools for court clerks (registrars), while in other countries, such as Italy and Portugal, the Ministry of Justice is responsible for this training. Some countries such as Belgium and the Netherlands, have an independent national umbrella institute for training magistrates and judicial staff. In addition, there are then many other variants where the training of court staff is assigned to or split between the public prosecutor's office, specific courts, training institutes, or other bodies and/or the ministry of justice.

Beside this, at European level, it is not always clear what is exactly meant by the term 'court staff'. In some countries, for example, certain positions, such as 'bailiffs' are liberal professions while in other countries they are part of the court staff.

This chapter has no ambition whatsoever to provide a comprehensive overview of the concept of court staff in Europe, nor does it intend to give an overview of the possible training systems for court staff. This chapter wants to touch very briefly on some facets that can be inspiring for the definition of the concept of 'court staff' and for the design of court staff training. Therefore, it will discuss the training of judicial staff in Belgium and the study on the training needs in European law of European judicial staff completed by EJTN and EIPA in 2021. Finally, a brief overview will be given of the training offer for court staff delivered by EJTN as a result of the aforementioned study.

II. Training of Court Staff in Belgium

A. Concept of 'Court Staff' in Belgium

Belgium has a classic 'civil law' system, inspired by the French system. As such, everyone in Belgium is considered court staff who is not a magistrate (judge or public prosecutor).

Indeed, in Belgium, both judges and public prosecutors belong to the 'judiciary' or 'judicial order' ('*Corps Judiciaire*'). Staff working in support of the public prosecutor's office are therefore considered to be full members of the Belgian Court staff.[1]

If it is assumed that all non-magistrates in the judicial order are to be considered 'Court Staff', there were 9,011 staff members active in the Belgian judicial order in 2022 (see Figure 6.1).[2]

Figure 6.1 Belgian judiciary

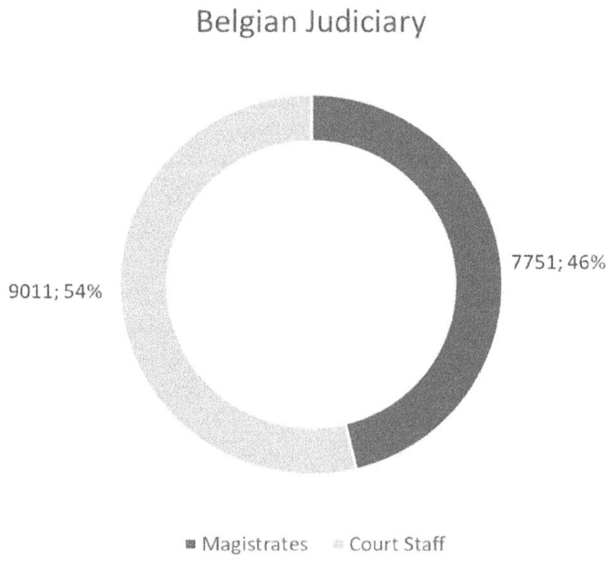

The designations and grades of court staff are therefore different according to what they work on. For example, clerks/registrars will work in the courts, while their counterparts in the public ministries (also known as prosecutors' offices), are called prosecutors' secretaries (see Figure 6.2).

[1] In Common Law systems, Public Prosecutors are not considered members of the judiciary.

[2] The large number of magistrates (7,779) is due to the fact that this also included the non-professional judges of the Labour Courts, Company Courts, Labour Courts and courts controlling the execution of penalties, as well as deputy judges. There are about 2,600 professional magistrates in Belgium (about 1,000 Public Prosecutors and 1,600 judges in the Courts and Tribunals).

Figure 6.2 Court staff

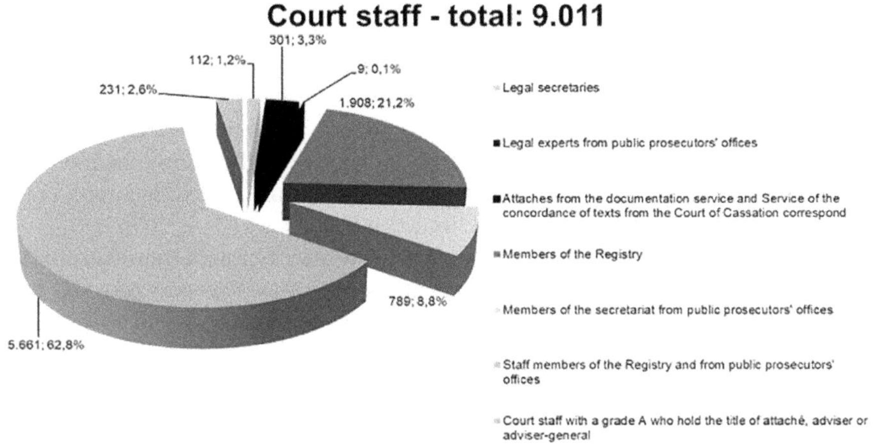

B. Training of Court Staff

All members of the court staff have the right to follow training courses. This principle is laid down in Article 6 juncto 2 of the Act of 31 January 2007 establishing the Belgian Institute for Judicial Training (hereinafter referred to as the IGO-Act).[3] The practical implementation of this legal article can be found in the Royal Decree of 18 May 2009. Article 2 of this Decree repeats that court staff are entitled to receive the training they need for their functioning in the Judiciary.[4]

Previously, as such, there was no system of training for the entire court staff. However, the Ministry of Justice did provide training to become a court clerk and prosecutor's secretary spread over an entire year and concluded with an examination. This training focused on the various aspects and legislation that clerks and prosecutor's secretaries faced.

This modus operandi changed dramatically in 2008. In that year, sweeping reform took place. Court staff lost their specific status in the judicial order. Until then, court clerks and prosecutor's secretaries had a different status from other federal civil servants. These differences were eliminated so that court staff were all considered federal civil servants.[5] This reform was put in place by the Law of

[3] La loi du 31 janvier 2007 sur la formation judiciaire et la gestion des connaissances et portant création de l'Institut de formation judiciaire, *Belgian official gazette*, 2 February 2007, 5481: www.ejustice.just.fgov.be/cgi_loi/change_lg.pl?language=fr&la=F&cn=2007013130&table_name=loi.

[4] Arrêté Royal du 18 Mai 2009 fixant les droits et obligations en matière de formation judiciaire, ainsi que le modalités d'exécution des formations pour les personnes visées à l'article 2, 4° à 10° de la loi du 31 janvier 2007 sur la formation judiciaire et portant création de l' Institut de formation judiciaire, *Belgian official gazette*, 4 June 2009, p. 39942 www.ejustice.just.fgov.be/cgi_loi/change_lg.pl?language=fr&la=F&cn=2009051805&table_name=loi.

[5] See the audit of the court staff made by the Belgian 'Cour des Comptes' of the 20 April 2015: COUR DES COMPTES, *Audit du personnel judiciaire:* Audit du personnel judiciaire (ccrek.be).

the 10 June 2006,[6] the Royal Decree of the 10 November 2006[7] and the Law of the 25 April 2007.[8]

Since then, greater mobility among civil servants in the federal government has been sought. The former examination specifically geared to the role of secretary and court clerk fell away and was replaced by a generic mailbox test to enable other public servants of other federal services to become court clerk or secretary without any legal or judicial background. As a result, new court staff entering the judiciary is less prepared for the job since the reform. It should also be noted that a real brain drain has occurred due to the many retirements.

There is also no longer any general obligation to attend certain training courses. Article 11 of the before mentioned Royal Decree of 18 May 2009 only provides that the hierarchical superior can oblige a member of the judiciary's staff to undergo certain training. However, there is an internal 'Circular Letter' No 187 from the Minister of Justice dated 9 November 2011 stating that the initial training organised by the IGO-IFJ for new court clerks and secretaries of the Public Prosecutor's offices is nevertheless mandatory in nature and a service exemption should be given to the participants for it.

Article 3 of the aforementioned Royal Decree of 18 May 2009 provides for the creation of a '*guidance committee*' to assist the Minister of Justice in preparing and formulating guidelines regarding training programs, but this committee has not been active for several years. As such, therefore, only the Belgian Judicial Training Institute (IGO-IFJ) is de facto responsible for examining training needs, developing and organising training for judicial staff.

C. The Belgian Judicial Training Institute (IGO-IFJ)

The Belgian Judicial Training Institute was established by the aforementioned IGO-Act of 31 January 2007 and became operational in 2009.

The Belgian Judicial Training Institute[9] is an independent training institute with its own legal personality. As such, it is not dependent of the Minister and the Ministry of Justice, the High Council of Justice, the Communities and, more specifically, the administrations in charge of education, the College of the Courts

[6] Loi du 10 juin 2006 portant réforme des carrières et de rémunération du personnel des greffes et des secrétariats de parquets, *Belgian official gazette*, 24 Novembre 2006, 65523 www.ejustice.just.fgov.be/cgi_loi/change_lg.pl?language=fr&la=F&cn=2006061068&table_name=loi.

[7] Arrêté Royal du 10 novembre 2006 portant statut, carrière et statut pécuniaire du personnel judiciaire, *Belgian official Gazette* 24 November 2006, 65535 www.ejustice.just.fgov.be/cgi_loi/change_lg.pl?language=fr&la=F&cn=2006111040&table_name=loi.

[8] Loi du 25 avril 2007 modifiant le code judiciaire, notamment les dispositions relatives au personnel judiciaire de niveau A, aux greffiers et aux secrétaires ainsi que les dispositions relatives à l'organisation judiciaire, *Belgian official Gazette*, 1 June 2007, 29680 www.ejustice.just.fgov.be/cgi_loi/change_lg.pl?language=fr&la=F&cn=2007042564&table_name=loi.

[9] See: www.igo-ifj.be.

and Tribunals, the College of the Public Prosecution Service, and the managing authority of the Belgian Supreme Court (Court of Cassation, Cour de Cassation, Hof van Cassatie). Of course, these bodies are represented in the governing board of the Belgian Judicial Training Institute and therefore play an important role. In addition, the Belgian Judicial Training Institute receives an annual allocation from the overall Justice budget envelope.

As such, the Belgian Judicial Training Institute is responsible for national and international training (the initial training as well as the permanent training) and this for both magistrates and court staff. However, in the first operational years of the IGO, the offer was mainly focused on the training of magistrates. Besides some specific training courses for court staff, they could also join some training courses for magistrates.[10]

Meanwhile, the Belgian Judicial Training Institute is also actively examining on a yearly basis the training needs of the Belgian court staff and this is the reason why more attention is paid to training courses for court staff in national and international trainings. Already in 2015, IGO-IFJ was a partner in the EU project '*European Judicial Training for Court Staff and Bailiffs'(JUST/2014/JTRA/AG/EJTR/6869)* where the training has been organised in different EU countries together with all the partners. This project was very much appreciated by the court staff, so the partners again applied for EU funding, which was selected. and continued their cooperation in the second part of this project from 2017 on.

The offered trainings at IGO-IFJ are divided into three axes: Technical-Judicial trainings, Managerial and organisational trainings, and Socio-communicative trainings. Different methodologies are used for these trainings. Thus, the Belgian Judicial Training Institute not only organises face-to-face trainings but also creates digital webinars, hybrid trainings[11] or e-learnings.[12] In addition to the traditional training courses on its own premises, it sometimes resorts to a residential formula in seminar centres or decentralises certain courses.[13]

Within the judiciary, there are different challenges. For example, there is a great need for digitalisation. There is also a certain brain drain because of the many retirements. Therefore, IGO-IFJ continuously adapts its program according to the real needs of the target group.

For several years, the flagship training program for court staff has been an initial training program for clerks and public prosecutor's secretaries consisting

[10] For a full overview of the function of the Belgian Training Institute, see the annual reports (Dutch and French versions) as well as the 'annual reports light' (in English, German, French and Dutch): www.igo-ifj.be/fr/content/rapport-annuel.

[11] Hybrid training is training that is delivered face-to-face but is also simultaneously broadcast so that it can also be followed remotely.

[12] For example: Introduction to the Belgian Judicial System, Introduction to Civil Law, e-learnings of the Council of Europe (HELP) on different topics.

[13] For the full catalogue with all the trainings of IGO-IFJ (in French), see: www.igo-ifj.be/fr/content/igo-online.

of nine face-to-face modules delivered over six months, twice a year. These are the following training modules:

1) The role and ethics for Members of the Registry and the secretariat from public prosecutor's offices (1 day).
2) Public Law (2 days).
3) Civil Law (3 days).
4) Civil procedural Law (4 days).
5) Criminal Law (2 days).
6) Criminal Procedural Law (7 days).
7) Social Law and Social Security Law (2 days).
8) Accountancy of the Registry and secretariat from public prosecutor's offices (1 day).
9) Methodology of Law (1 day).

This initial training program is currently being re-evaluated. It is observed that the training offered is not always of a nature to counteract the consequences of the aforementioned brain drain. Presumably, this will result in further intensification of private procedural law and criminal procedural law. The desirability of focussing more on the specific function of each participant will also be examined.

III. European Aspects of Judicial Staff Training

A. The Study on the Training Needs of Judicial Staff in European Law

The European Commission has long been interested in the training needs of court staff. A first study on the so-called 'lot 3 partners' was delivered by EIPA[14] in 2014.[15]

A second study conducted by EJTN[16] and EIPA followed in 2021. This study is also freely available for consultation on the European Commission's website[17]

[14] European Institute of Public Administration (= EIPA) is a training provider to all professionals related to EU public affairs: www.eipa.eu/.

[15] See: Study of the State of Play of Court Staff Training in EU Law and Promotion of Cooperation between Court Staff Training Providers at EU Level, JUST/2012/JUTR/R/0064/A4, published in 2014: eur-lex.europa.eu/legal-content/EN/TXT/PDF/?uri=CELLAR:a70f8e68-40f5-4232-bf9f-755643f15fea; eur-lex.europa.eu/resource.html?uri=cellar:a70f8e68-40f5-4232-bf9f-755643f15fea.0001.01/DOC_1&format=PDF and also: eur-lex.europa.eu/resource.html?uri=cellar:a70f8e68-40f5-4232-bf9f-755643f15fea.0001.02/DOC_1&format=PDF.

[16] European Judicial Training Network (= EJTN) is a network of different Judicial Training Institutions of the European Union: ejtn.eu/.

[17] See: Study on the Training Needs of Court Staff on EU Law in the EU (June 2021) commission.europa.eu/system/files/2021-06/2021-06-14_just2018jaccprcrim0131_study_report_final.pdf; For the annexes, see: commission.europa.eu/system/files/2021-06/2021-06-14_just2018jaccprcrim0131_study_annexes_final.pdf.

and provides in its annexes a very interesting overview of the existing categories of court staff in each country as well as an insight into how court staff training is organised in the different Member States.

The starting point of this study involved data collection by a team of national coordinators appointed by court staff training providers from each of the 27 EU Member States. Three different questionnaires were submitted in all these countries.

The first questionnaire focused on updating the inventory from the Lot 3 Study on the State of Play of Court Staff Training in EU Law and Promotion of Cooperation between Court Staff Training Providers at EU Level of 2014,[18] eg, on the different categories of court staff, their functions and the extent to which they apply EU law.

The second questionnaire focused on the state of the training activities on EU law for court staff and finally, the last questionnaire focused on the training capacities and future European networking needs and capacities.

This Study used the following classification:

- Type 1: Staff members performing tasks that require the application of EU law.
- Type 2: Staff members performing tasks that might require the application of EU law.
- Type 3: Staff members not performing tasks that require the application of EU Law.

In a first phase, therefore, it was checked exactly how many court staff were active in the European Union and how many of those court staff ultimately also needed European law and training in European law. This revealed that 280,292 court staff were active in the European Union. Some 180,471 court staff (ie, 64 per cent of 280,292) need or might need training in EU law to carry out the tasks associated with their job.[19] It is clear that the training needs for court staff in EU law cannot be underestimated.

The next step was the creation by the researchers, with the involvement of the Experts Committee of the project, of four additional descriptors of court staff, based not simply on title and tasks, but more broadly on their key functions. The experts in judicial training in the project assigned each aforementioned Type 1 and 2 category of court staff to the relevant group function(s) (one or several). The researchers and the experts group upheld four group functions:

1) Court staff with functions primarily related to the administration and management of the courts (Group F1).

[18] See before: eur-lex.europa.eu/resource.html?uri=cellar:a70f8e68-40f5-4232-bf9f-755643f15fea.0001.01/DOC_1&format=PDF, and also: eur-lex.europa.eu/resource.html?uri=cellar:a70f8e68-40f5-4232-bf9f-755643f15fea.0001.02/DOC_1&format=PDF.

[19] According to this study 45% of the European court staff were staff members performing tasks that require the application of EU law and 19% are staff members that might require the application of EU law. So, 36% of the court staff does not perform tasks that require the application of EU law.

2) Court staff whose functions include providing assistance to judges and prosecutors in case preparation and research (Group F2).
3) Court staff whose tasks include some judicial functions (Group F3).
4) Court staff whose tasks include procedural functions of a cross-border nature (F4).

On the basis of the above mentioned typology of court staff and the results of the questionnaires, the research team came to different recommendations. We cannot go deep into all these recommendations but it is interesting to recall three of them:

First of all, the research team encouraged the use and update of the 'Type' and 'Function' classifications as a way of identifying the court staff who needs or might need training in EU law and to help identify the nature of the training.

Second, the study showed clearly that there is a need for a pan-European training Program to support the training of court staff (Types 1 and 2) and to facilitate further networking opportunities.

Third, the study stressed the importance of development of the training for court staff trainers as well as the development of transnational mentorship schemes or cross-border apprenticeships schemes.

B. The Reaction of EJTN

Because of its methodology, research findings and recommendations, the forementioned study is a particularly interesting document for the training of court staff in a European context.

Based on these results of the aforementioned study, the European Commission formulated in its '*European Judicial training strategy for 2021-2024*' a very clear objective:[20]

> *Court and prosecution office staff* are essential for the smooth functioning of justice systems. Some are involved in drafting and enforcing court decisions, the cross-border service of documents, European payment orders, European arrest warrants and other cross-border procedures. This requires a wide range of training on EU law, which should be precisely tailored to identified needs. The Commission encourages the networking of all national and EU-level court staff training providers to share best practices and strengthen national training offers.

The European Commission expressed a clear action for all stakeholders. By 2024, continuous training on EU law should each year reach 15 per cent of court and prosecution office staff who would need EU law competence. The Commission also explicitly urged EJTN to establish a network of all court staff training providers to exchange expertise and best practices.[21]

[20] See European Commission, Document 52020DC0713, 'Communication from the commission to the European Parliament, the Council, the European Economic and Social Committee and the Committee of the Regions – Ensuring justice in de EU – a European judicial training strategy for 2021–2024 (COM/2020/713 final), 7: eur-lex.europa.eu/legal-content/EN/TXT/?uri=CELEX:52020DC0713.

[21] ibid 8 and 9.

This call to pay more attention to the (European) training of judicial staff was immediately picked up by EJTN, the 'European Judicial Training Network.'

As already mentioned before, EJTN is a network of most of the Judicial Training providers in the European Union. It is a non-profit organisation under Belgian law and has been very successful in boosting Judicial Training in Europe with the financial support of the European Commission. EJTN receives annually an operating grant of the European Commission.

EJTN was created in 2000 and focused especially on the training and exchanges of European judges and prosecutors. The training of court staff was previously not covered. Even more, according to the Statutory Rules of EJTN, court staff was not considered as the target audience of EJTN.

To comply with the forementioned strategy of the European Commission, EJTN has adapted his Statutory Rules to create activities and a training and exchange offer for court staff.

Therefore, the study and the typology formulated therein have helped EJTN, in their strategic plan 2021-2027, to identify the categories of court staff and its members it wants to focus on. This definition reads as follows:

> Persons working in courts and prosecution authorities where they form part of the 'corps judiciaire', who are not judges or prosecutors, and who have legal training and who either:
>
> (a) Help prepare judgements or prosecutorial decisions
> (b) Make judicial or prosecutorial decisions at least at a preliminary phase, or
> (c) Play a significant role in cross border cooperation[22]

In 2021, EJTN amended its Statutory Rules in this respect. A new category of members was created: the associate members. The associate membership is open to all national institutions of the Member States of the European Union specifically responsible for the training of court staff[23] and which are not eligible for full membership.[24] All associate members have the right to attend the meetings of the General Assembly but are not entitled to vote. They can also participate at the meetings of the different working- and sub-working groups.[25]

With these changes, EJTN wanted to create a genuine platform for court staff and Magistrates to facilitate network opportunities among court staff and the court staff training providers.

Meanwhile, EJTN's training and exchange offer was actually opened to a significant extent to European court staff.

[22] See: ejtn.eu/wp-content/uploads/2022/08/EJTN-Strategic-Plan-2021-2027_FREN.pdf, more specifically 15, nr. 61.

[23] So, they are not responsible for the training of magistrates (the former target audience of EJTN).

[24] The actual associate members are: ENG (France), National School of Clerks (Romania), Ministry of Justice (Italy), Court Service Agency (Malta) and the Directorate-General of Justice Administration (Portugal).

[25] See more detailed the annual report of EJTN 2021: ejtn.eu/wp-content/uploads/2022/12/EJTN-Annual-Report-2021.pdf; see also the website of EJTN: ejtn.eu/.

C. Training Offer of EJTN for Court Staff

Before going deeper into the EJTN training offer, it should first be underlined again that EJTN is a network of the various European training institutes. It is therefore not a training institute itself, but the EJTN secretariat coordinates and supports cooperation between the various members, associated members and partners.

This manifests itself in a range of training courses and exchange programs developed in the various working groups of EJTN.

EJTN has several permanent working groups: Working group Exchange Programmes, Working Group Programmes with a number of permanent sub-working groups on administrative law, criminal justice, civil law, human rights and fundamental freedoms. There are also the working groups on 'Linguistics', 'Judicial Training Methods' and 'Digitalisation'. Every three years, all members and associate members can apply to become members of one or more of these working groups and sub-working groups.

Below, a brief overview of the organisation of the exchange programs and the courses offered through EJTN will be given.

i. Training Courses Organised by EJTN

In the aforementioned Working Group Programmes (incl. the sub-working groups), Working Group Linguistics, Working Group Judicial Training methods and Working Group Digitalisation, not only manuals and tools are developed,[26] but also webinars and conferences. This leads to a nice range of training and exchange programs.[27]

For each of these training programs, the target audience for these courses is determined. In some training courses, court staff are allowed in addition to magistrates. In 2024, a number of training courses would also be specifically open only to court staff.[28]

In addition, EJTN is also a partner with ERA[29] under a separate European project for certain training courses for court staff on civil and criminal law, including certain legal language courses on this topic.[30]

[26] See: ejtn.eu/publications/.

[27] For an overview of the complete offer for 2024, see: ejtn.eu/wp-content/uploads/2023/12/EJTN_catalogue_training_activities_2024.pdf en; catalogue.ejtn.eu/.

[28] See, eg, the training '*The Role of Court Staff in Justice – Deontology and Ethics (AD/2024/10)*', 35 in de EJTN catalogue ejtn.eu/wp-content/uploads/2023/12/EJTN_catalogue_training_activities_2024.pdf.

[29] ERA or the Academy of European Law is a training Institute based in Trier (Germany) and is also a member of EJTN, see www.era.int/cgi-bin/cms?_SID=1cd37fae2997ea849fee45a09e9fd3f5a1146aca01046780763994&_sprache=en&_bereich=ansicht&_aktion=detail&schluessel=era.

[30] See: ejtn.eu/news/ejtn-and-era-to-work-together-for-training-court-staff-and-bailiffs-in-european-civil-and-criminal-law/; see also: csab.legaltraining.eu/.

Finally, it is also possible to take certain training courses with the members or 'associated members' of EJTN through the so-called 'Catalogue' and 'Catalogue+' trainings. Here the members themselves open part of their own offer to European colleagues.[31]

ii. Exchange Programs and Study Visits

In addition to training courses and webinars, EJTN also organises various exchange programs and study visits through the Working Group Exchange Programmes. An important part of these exchanges are also open to court staff.

The Exchange Programme was created to enhance the European judiciary's practical knowledge of other judicial systems as well as European and human rights law through direct contacts, exchange of views and experiences between judges, prosecutors, court staff and trainers from different EU Member States. This program also aims to develop a European judicial culture based on mutual trust between judicial authorities in the common European judicial area.[32]

For court staff, the following exchanges were opened: general exchanges, specialised exchanges, judicial leaders exchanges and trainer exchanges. These exchange programs have a duration of at least three days for the Judicial Leaders exchanges (maximum five days) and five days for the other programs. For the general exchanges and the trainer exchanges, the duration is a maximum of 10 days. These programs are organised either individually or in groups.[33]

In addition, a significant part of the project-based exchanges are also open to court staff. This is the case for the bilateral exchanges, regional exchanges and the Judiciary Learning Grant Programme.[34]

In contrast, the exchange with CEPOL[35,36] and the Long Term Exchanges (Eurojust,[37] Court of Justice of the EU (ECJEU),[38] European Court of Human Rights (ECHR)[39] and European Public Prosecutor's Office (EPPO)[40] are not open to court staff.[41]

Finally, EJTN also organises study visits to the EPPO, Eurojust, FRA[42]/UNODC,[43] EU Institutions, ECJEU, ECHR and the Hague Conference on Private International

[31] See: ejtn.eu/seminars/.
[32] See: portal.ejtn.eu/en/Exchange-Programme/.
[33] For an overview, see: ejtn.eu/activity/exchanges/.
[34] For an overview, see: ejtn.eu/activity/project-based-exchanges/.
[35] European Union Agency for Law Enforcement Training: www.cepol.europa.eu/.
[36] Seeejtn.eu/activity/project-based-exchanges/.
[37] European Union Agency for Criminal Justice Cooperation: www.eurojust.europa.eu/.
[38] European Court of Justice of the European Union: curia.europa.eu/jcms/jcms/j_6/en/.
[39] European Court of Human Rights: www.echr.coe.int/.
[40] European Public Prosecutor's Office: www.eppo.europa.eu/en.
[41] See: ejtn.eu/activity/long-term-training-periods/.
[42] European Union Agency for Fundamental Rights: fra.europa.eu/en.
[43] United Nations Office on Drugs and Crime: www.unodc.org/.

Law (HCCH).[44] For court staff, a study visit at EPPO is only possible if it is a general visit together with a visit to the European institutions. A more specialised study visit is not open to them but only to magistrates.

There is also a study visit at the Max Planck Institute for Social Anthropology (Halle, Germany).[45] This last study visit provides a deeper knowledge and comparative perspectives on how to address cultural and religious diversity in the courtroom.[46]

IV. Judicial Training for Court Staff: International Principles

The practicalities of training court staff in Belgium and Europe were discussed in more detail above.

In this context, however, it should be noted that the training initiatives of both the Belgian Judicial Training Institute (IGO-IFJ) and the EJTN for the European Union, follow a number of European and International principles.

For instance, the EJTN General Assembly, held on 10 June 2016 in Amsterdam, adopted nine principles of Judicial Training:

> Judicial training is a multidisciplinary and practical type of training, essentially intended for the transmission of professional techniques and values complementary to legal education.
>
> 1. All judges and prosecutors should receive initial training before or on their appointment.
> 2. All judges and prosecutors should have the right to regular continuous training after appointment and throughout their careers and it is their responsibility to undertake it. Every Member State should put in place systems that ensure judges and prosecutors are able to exercise this right and responsibility.
> 3. Training is part of the normal working life of a judge and a prosecutor. All judges and prosecutors should have time to undertake training as part of the normal working time, unless it exceptionally jeopardises the service of justice.
> 4. In accordance with the principles of judicial independence the design, content and delivery of judicial training are exclusively for national institutions responsible for judicial training to determine.
> 5. Training should primarily be delivered by judges and prosecutors who have been previously trained for this purpose.
> 6. Active and modern educational techniques should be given primacy in judicial training.

[44] Hague Conference on Private International Law: www.hcch.net/en/home.
[45] Max Planck Institute for Social Anthropology: www.mpg.de/153644/social-anthropology.
[46] For all these study visits, see: ejtn.eu/activity/study-visits/.

7. Member States should provide national institutions responsible for judicial training with sufficient funding and other resources to achieve their aims and objectives.
8. The highest judicial authorities should support judicial training.[47]

The same principles were adopted by the European Network of Councils for the Judiciary (ENCJ).[48] The European Commission also makes explicit reference to these principles. They wrote in their strategy explicitly, 'Its nine 'judicial training principles' are becoming a global reference for good judicial training.'[49] It follows that these principles undoubtedly enjoy significant authority in the field of judicial training in Europe and beyond.

Importantly, however, these principles contain no reference to 'court staff' as such. Yet their influence cannot be underestimated on that front too. After all, these EJTN 'Principles for Judicial Training' precede the 'Declaration of Judicial Training Principles'[50] that IOJT (International Organisation for Judicial Training)[51] finally adopted in 2017. These principles can also be found on the UNODC website[52] and they are as follows:

> PRINCIPLES
>
> 1. Judicial training is essential to ensure high standards of competence and performance. Judicial training is fundamental to judicial independence, the rule of law, and the protection of the rights of all people.
>
> INSTITUTIONAL FRAMEWORK
>
> 2. To preserve judicial independence, the judiciary and judicial training institutions should be responsible for the design, content, and delivery of judicial training.
>
> 3. Judicial leaders and the senior judiciary should support judicial training.
>
> 4. All states should:
>
> (i) Provide their institutions responsible for judicial training with sufficient funding and other resources to achieve their aims and objectives;
> and

[47] See EJTN, 'Judicial Training principles' (2016), 3: portal.ejtn.eu/PageFiles/15756/Judicial%20Training%20Principles_EN.pdf.

[48] See EJTN, 'Judicial Training principles' (2016), 2: portal.ejtn.eu/PageFiles/15756/Judicial%20Training%20Principles_EN.pdf.

[49] See European Commission, 'Communication from the Commission to the European Parliament, the Council, the European Economic and Social Committee of the Regions – Ensuring justice in the EU – a European judicial training strategy for 2021–2024' (2020), COM (2020) 713 final, 12: commission.europa.eu/document/download/f782dbde-f970-430a-847d-a77ff3e428a5_en?filename=2_en_act_part1_v4.pdf.

[50] See: ncfsc-web.squiz.cloud/__data/assets/pdf_file/0014/6152/2017-principles.pdf; for the brochure on the IOJT Judicial Training Principles. See: ncfsc-web.squiz.cloud/__data/assets/pdf_file/0027/8865/english-declaration-of-judicial-training-principles.pdf.

[51] For IOJT of 'International Organisation for Judicial Training', see: www.iojt.org/.

[52] UNODC = United Nations Office on Drugs and Crime; the IOJT principles on judicial training can be found on the website of the UNODC, see: www.unodc.org/ji/en/resdb/data/2017/declaration_of_judicial_training_principles.html.

(ii) Establish systems to ensure that all members of the judiciary are enabled to undertake training.

5. Any support provided to judicial training should be utilized in accordance with these principles, and in coordination with institutions responsible for judicial training.

TRAINING AS PART OF THE JUDICIAL ROLE

6. It is the right and the responsibility of all members of the judiciary to undertake training. Each member of the judiciary should have time to be involved in training as part of their judicial work.

7. All members of the judiciary should receive training before or upon their appointment, and should also receive regular training throughout their careers.

TRAINING CONTENT AND METHODOLOGY

8. Acknowledging the complexity of the judicial role, judicial training should be multidisciplinary and include training in law, non-legal knowledge, skills, social context, values and ethics.

9. Training should be judge-led and delivered primarily by members of the judiciary who have been trained for this purpose. Training delivery may involve non-judicial experts where appropriate.

10. Judicial training should reflect best practices in professional and adult training program design. It should employ a wide range of up-to-date methodologies.

It cannot be denied that these IOJT principles are quite close to the EJTN principles on the matter. What is important in this context, however, is that the IOJT brochure on these principles does refer explicitly to court staff. So, the preamble to the IOJT brochure on the 'Declaration of Judicial Training Principles' states the following:

> The term 'judiciary' as used in this document may include prosecutors, defenders/defence counsel, *court staff*[53] and others, depending on the justice system.
>
> The term 'judicial training' is used in this document to accord with the name of the organization. It is recognized that the expression used may vary, including 'judicial education', 'judicial development', 'judicial cultivation'.
>
> The term 'state' in this document encompasses national political entities, but also federate states or any regional public entity, according to the national context.[54]

It therefore follows that these principles should also be considered applicable to training institutions that focus on the training of court staff and that it should be assumed that court staff also have the right to proper initial and continuous training of a high quality and that governments should provide sufficient institutional guarantees and funding to this end.

[53] Emphasis added by the author.

[54] See IOJT 'Declaration of Judicial Training Principles' (2017), 3: ncfsc-web.squiz.cloud/__data/assets/pdf_file/0027/8865/english-declaration-of-judicial-training-principles.pdf.

V. Conclusions

It is clear that the training of court staff is not as simple as it seems. The aforementioned European study shows that it involves a particularly large number of people and that court staff can then be divided into different job groups. Measuring and monitoring training needs require a good definition. The aforementioned study on the training needs of European court staff as regards EU law can in any case be an inspiration for this.

It seems that, both in Belgium and at the European level, the training of court staff has too often not received enough attention compared to the training of magistrates (judges and prosecutors). The large numbers and diversity of functions of court staff certainly do not make this easy. Consequently, if very specialised attention is paid to court staff at all, it is often limited to specific groups of court staff, such as clerks, for example. Nevertheless, it may be inferred from the existing international principles on judicial training that due attention should be given to this.

It is therefore to be welcomed that there currently seems to be a greater focus on court staff training. It is important to be able to identify and respond to the needs of each category, however specific it may be, from the moment it comes under the definition of court staff. The European focus on this is therefore stimulating, not only for European actors in the field of court staff training, but also for national training bodies. After all, justice continues to face major challenges. An organisation is only as strong as its weakest link. Well-trained court staff is therefore necessary to keep the workload for magistrates workable and to cope with the various challenges of justice also in the future. This is therefore an issue that will continue to gain importance.

7

Judicial Assistance in England and Wales

JOHN SORABJI

I. Introduction

The classic picture of the English and Welsh (English) judiciary is that of an impartial, umpire, a point most famously illustrated by Pollock and Maitland in the 1890s. As they put it,

> The judges sit in Court, not in order that they may discover the truth, but in order that they may answer the question, 'How's that?' The English judge will, if he can, play the umpire rather than the inquisitor.[1]

Inherent in this picture is the idea that the judge, as part of England and Wales' adversarial system, was a passive figure, one who simply reacted to what was presented in court by parties to litigation. Unlike in other jurisdictions where judges adopted a more active role, particularly in respect of case management, the English judge did not involve themselves in any aspect of case preparation. Not for them, a role in proactively setting a case management timetable, identifying relevant evidence or issues of law. And not for them, legal research. There is little that remains of that picture now. The caricature suggested English judges were indifferent to the truth. That they were not involved in its discovery was perhaps taken to suggest they were unconcerned with determining the truth. That, of course, was incorrect. It was to conflate their lack of responsibility for identifying and securing probative evidence, which is and remains a matter for the parties, with their duty to determine right fact on the balance of probabilities based on the evidence adduced before them.[2] And in terms of its other features, they were all swept away

[1] F Pollock & F Maitland, *History of English Law* (1895) cited in J. Jacobs, *The Fabric of English Civil Justice*, (Stevens & Sons, 1987) 11.

[2] *Harmony Shipping Co SA v Davies* [1979] 3 ALL ER 177 at 181; *Air Canada v Secretary of State for Trade* [1983] 2 AC 394 at 410–411.

by the Woolf reforms of the late 1990s.[3] They are now responsible for active case and costs management, for setting procedural time tables and taking positive steps to secure compliance with court orders, for oversight and management of party evidence-gathering, amongst other things.[4] In so far as the English judge might once have been a passive bystander to the litigation process, they are now an active and energetic director of it.

One particular area where this shift in nature of the judicial role has changed has been the development of various forms of assistance to members of the judiciary. Members of the court administration, specifically those who are qualified and practicing lawyers, can, for instance, be authorised to exercise a prescribed range of judicial functions. In the Court of Appeal (Civil Division) such lawyers,[5] amongst other things, may approve consent orders, dismiss appeals by consent, grant or refuse extensions of time to seek permission to appeal, and determine applications for security for costs.[6] Their decisions are subject to review by a judge of the court in the event of challenge by a party. Such lawyers are also appointed on a full-time basis in the Court of Appeal (Criminal Division), where their primary responsibility is to prepare memoranda for the court for challenges to criminal convictions and sentencing appeals before that court. Similarly, legal advisers in the County Court can also be authorised to exercise judicial functions, particularly in respect of procedural matters concerning the management of low-value claims.[7] This development does not, however, provide assistance to judges directly. What assistance it provides is by way of diverting routine, procedural work away from judges, thus enabling them to deal with more significant and contentious matters.

A more direct form of assistance has, however, also developed since the late 1990s. That is the introduction of judicial assistants (JAs) in a number of courts.[8] They work directly with specific judges and provide them with a range of help relating to their case load and, in some cases, their extra-judicial

[3] H Woolf, *Access to Justice: Interim Report to the Lord Chancellor on the Civil Justice System in England and Wales* (HMSO, 1995) (Woolf (1995)); H Woolf, *Access to Justice: Final Report to the Lord Chancellor on the Civil Justice System in England and Wales* (HMSO, 1996) (Woolf (1996)).

[4] CPR Pts 1, 3, 31, 32, 33, 34, 35.

[5] Lawyers have been appointed to this role since 1989. For a history of the introduction and early development of this role see, J Bowman, *Report to the Lord Chancellor, Review of the Court of Appeal (Civil Division)*, (September 2007) 207–210.

[6] CPR r.52.24. The statutory basis for the jurisdiction is contained in the Courts and Tribunals (Judiciary and Functions of Staff) Act 2018 and, particularly, the Courts and Tribunals (Judiciary and Functions of Staff) Act 2018 (Consequential, Transitional and Saving Provision) Regulations 2020 (SI 2020/100). The extent to which they are authorised to exercise the court's powers is set out in Judicial authority of court officers in the Court of Appeal (Civil Division), dated 2 August 2023 www.judiciary.uk/guidance-and-resources/judicial-authority-of-court-officers-in-the-court-of-appeal-civil-division/. Also see CPR r.54.1A in respect of the authorisation of court staff to exercise judicial functions in the High Court.

[7] CPR r.2.4(2) and PD 2E.

[8] As Sanders rightly notes, this role is distinct from that members of the court administration who take on judicial functions, see A Sanders, 'Judicial Assistants in Europe – A Comparative Analysis' (2020) 11(3) *IJCA* 1, 4.

workload. Separately from JAs, additional assistance is provided to the senior judiciary of England and Wales; specifically, the Lord Chief Justice, Master of the Rolls, President of the King's Bench Division, President of the Family Division, Chancellor of the High Court, and the Senior President of Tribunals. This assistance is provided by practicing lawyers appointed either as Legal Secretary or as Legal Adviser to these various judges. These lawyers, who have either been appointed under a statutory power contained in the Senior Courts Act 1981 or appointed as civil servants, are not engaged in work relating to proceedings before the courts. They are primarily employed, and are civil servants within the Judicial Office for England and Wales, to provide assistance to the senior judge to whom they are assigned in respect of matters concerning the administration of the judiciary. Specifically and primarily, they provide legal advice and assistance to the senior judiciary on matters that arise under the Lady Chief Justice's and Senior President of Tribunal's statutory responsibilities as head of the courts and tribunals judiciary, respectively.[9]

This chapter examines the nature and development of JAs, as their work focuses on the judiciary's primary responsibility of dealing with proceedings.

II. Judicial Assistants – Their Introduction

Initial consideration for the introduction of JAs was given in the Woolf Reports in the late 1990s. The original intention was to appoint recently qualified solicitors or barristers as 'law clerks', who would assist judges in the High Court. Their role would have been to assist individual judges, who they were to be assigned to work with, in dealing with, ie, case managing, complex litigation. To this end the Interim Woolf Report recommended their introduction on a pilot basis, whereby several law clerks would be appointed, assigned to work for several judges, and embedded in case management teams. Case management teams, which were another recommendation in that report, were to consist of High Court judges and procedural judges, with the latter specifically responsible for the effective management of cases within specific courts.[10] As Lord Woolf explained it,

> High Court judges would benefit from the secondment of recently qualified barristers or solicitors as law clerks to assist in the management of heavy litigation. For the role of a law clerk to be effective, it is desirable to attach the post to an individual judge rather than to pool resources. I appreciate that to move straight to a situation where each High Court judge has his own law clerk would be asking too much. As a pilot scheme, I would suggest instead that there should be one law clerk attached to some of the

[9] Constitutional Reform Act 2005, s 7; Tribunals, Courts and Enforcement Act 2007, s 2, Sch 1, Part 4. For a discussion of those responsibilities, see G Gee, R Hazell, K Malleson, & P O'Brien, *The Politics of Judicial Independence in the UK' Changing Constitution* (Cambridge, CUP, 2015) ch 6.

[10] Woolf (1995) (n 3) 66–67.

> [case management] teams. The teams are small enough to ensure that the necessary relationship exists between the judges constituting the team and the law clerk.[11]

Following that recommendation, informal trials of the approach were carried out, with the law clerks carrying out legal research and document summary exercises for a small number of High Court judges.[12] Based on that experience, particularly positive feedback from the Commercial Court Users Group concerning their utility in so far as assistance for Commercial Court judges was concerned, and information obtained by Lord Woolf concerning the use of law clerks in the courts in the United States of America, Australia, Canada, and New Zealand, their formal introduction in both the High Court and Court of Appeal was recommended in the Final Woolf Report.[13]

Ultimately, the recommendation to introduce legal clerks in the High Court was not taken forward following the publication of the Woolf Reports. However, renamed JAs, they were introduced on the initiative of Lord Justice Otton on a trial basis in January 1997 into the Court of Appeal.[14] The immediate impetus for their introduction was to assist the court in reducing a backlog of applications for permission to appeal, not least those brought by litigants-in-person.[15] The scheme was initially limited to the appointment of twelve part-time JAs, each seconded from their law firms or Chambers for up to a year.[16] As with the recommendation from the Interim Woolf Report, the scheme was limited to practicing solicitors and barristers 'of the highest calibre'[17] who were towards the start of their careers. As Jamieson notes, the basis for this approach was to ensure that the JAs had had some litigation experience prior to appointment, and they could thus be of use to the Court 'from day one'.[18] Again, consistent with the recommendation from the Interim Woolf Report, the JAs were initially pooled. Rather than being appointed to assist a specific Lord or Lady Justice of Appeal, they were assigned to work for at least two judges.[19] The scheme became permanent after 1998, with JAs subsequently being assigned to a single Lord or Lady Justice of Appeal, with

[11] ibid 68.

[12] P Jamieson, *Of judges, judgments and judicial assistants* [1998] *CJQ* 395, fn 3, noting that these initial experiments were carried out in the Commercial Court, which forms part of the High Court's King's Bench Division.

[13] Woolf (1996) (n 3) 100, 102.

[14] G Drewry, L Blom-Cooper, & C Blake, *The Court of Appeal* (Oxford, Hart Publishing, 2007) 93.

[15] Bowman (n 5) 211, 'They were part of a plan to reduce the backlog of applications for leave to appeal and waiting times in the [Court of Appeal].' Also see Jamieson (n 12) 395; N Holvast, 'The Power of the Judicial Assistant/Law Clerk: Looking behind the scenes at Courts in the United States, England and Wales, and The Netherlands' (2016) 7(2) *IJCA* 10, 19.

[16] Bowman (n 5) 211. Although note that Holvast states that initially there were sixteen part-time JAs; Holvast (n 15) 19.

[17] *Parker v Law Society (No. 1)* [1999] C.O.D. 183; *The Times* (December 8) 1998; [1998] 12 WLUK 101.

[18] Jamieson (n 12), fn 10, noting J Ames, *Judges Scout for US-style Clerks*, Law Gazette, (13 November 1996).

[19] Jamieson (n 12) 396.

16 appointments being made over each twelve-month period; some appointments were for a full-twelve months, others for shorter periods.[20] It currently sees 24 to 25 full-time appointments made each year for a ten-month period from a broader pool of applicants. Furthermore, JAs now no longer need to be practising solicitors or barristers. The minimum current appointment requirement is that they have completed an undergraduate degree and gained some practical experience in legal research.[21]

JAs were introduced in the House of Lords to assist the Law Lords in 2001. Their introduction was facilitated by Lord Bingham, the Senior Law Lord, due to his experience of their utility in the Court of Appeal, of which he had previously been the President as Lord Chief Justice.[22] Originally, there were four appointments who were assigned to assist the four most senior Law Lords on an annual basis. With the transfer of the House of Lords' appellate jurisdiction to the UK Supreme Court in 2009, their number was expanded to eight.[23] Their expansion owed much to the rather mundane reason that the transfer of jurisdiction to the Supreme Court meant that there was more space to accommodate them in the court's premises than there was when the Law Lords were based in the House of Lords. More substantively, their expansion has also been reported to have owed something to the recognition of their value to the, by then, Supreme Court justices and lobbying by the more junior justices to have JAs assigned to them.[24] There are now currently eleven JAs appointed annually and one permanent JA. Appointment criteria are similar to those applied to recruitment of JAs in the Court of Appeal, albeit greater weight is placed on their demonstrating that they are qualified lawyers.[25] The permanent JA, who is JA to the President of the UK Supreme Court, is a senior lawyer who manages the annually recruited JAs.[26]

Finally, in 2019, following a successful pilot scheme, JAs were introduced in the High Court. The pilot scheme ran the previous year and was focused on providing JAs for the Commercial Court, which forms part of the High Court's King's Bench

[20] Holvast (n 15) 19. Bowman (n 5) 211 notes the '*strong support*' for the scheme becoming permanent shortly after its introduction as a pilot.

[21] Judicial Assistants to the Court of Appeal 2024-2025, Recruitment Advert, 'There is no fixed profile for a successful candidate, but the post of judicial assistant is intended to provide entrants to the legal profession with a unique opportunity to work at close quarters with judicial members of the court. As a minimum candidates will have graduated with an excellent degree (2:1 or better) and have practical experience in legal research. Please note that candidates must have graduated at the time of application. Experience gained in the early years of practice or in a paralegal role is valued although not essential. As well as high intellectual ability a judicial assistant must demonstrate incisiveness and an ability to work well under pressure. Excellent IT and written skills are also essential.' Copy on file with the author.

[22] A Paterson, *Final Judgment – The Last Law Lords and The Supreme Court* (Oxford, Hart Publishing, 2013) 247.

[23] Holvast (n 15) 19.

[24] A detailed history of the introduction and development of JAs in the UK Supreme Court is set out in Paterson (n 22) 247–248.

[25] UKSC Judicial Assistant Specification 2024 www.supremecourt.uk/docs/ja-person-specification-2024.pdf.

[26] See 'Head Judicial Assistant', UKSC Executive Team www.supremecourt.uk/about/executive-team.html.

Division. Unlike previous schemes, the pilot was run by the court with the assistance of, and particularly funding provided by, the Commercial Bar Association. Thus, unlike other JA schemes, it was, in its pilot phase, limited to barristers at the beginning of their practice, ie, within the first years of completing pupillage, at the Commercial Bar.[27] Unlike the pilot scheme and like the Court of Appeal and UK Supreme Court JA schemes, the High Court JA scheme is operated by the court itself; assistance from the Commercial Bar Association was not retained following the scheme's formal adoption. Again, unlike the pilot scheme, High Court JAs are assigned to judges across all three of the High Court's Divisions (King's Bench Division, Family Division, and Chancery Division). To facilitate assignment, applicants are required to specify in which part of the High Court they wish to work.[28] In contrast to the other two JA schemes, up to 26 High Court JAs may be appointed each year. The number of appointments differs, as the JAs may be appointed for two judicial terms or up to four judicial terms, ie, for six or twelve months, respectively. In 2024, additionally, one JA with Ukrainian legal experience was to be appointed for three months from January 2025. It was intended that they would be assigned to work for a judge in the High Court's Chancery Division.[29]

Across the three schemes, it is apparent (save for one exception) that, as Sanders rightly notes, the UK Supreme Court and Courts of England and Wales have adopted the 'internship' model in appointing JAs.[30] That is to say, while the JAs provide a specific benefit to the courts and judges to whom they work, the positions are time-limited and intended to provide the JA with 'insights "from behind the bench"'.[31] Hence the positions are educative and 'serve as a springboard to another job rather than [being] a career on [their] own.'[32] The one exception, where the UK Supreme Court adopts the 'scribe' model of JAs is that of the Head Judicial Assistant in the UK Supreme Court.[33] That position did not, however, exist prior to Lord Phillips' appointment as President of the UK Supreme Court. As Paterson notes the initial Head Judicial Assistant was appointed at that time, having previously been Lord Phillips' JA when he was first Master of the Rolls and Lord Chief Justice, ie, when he was a judge in the Court of Appeal. The position was thus not part of the original Supreme Court JA scheme.[34]

[27] Notes for Applicants for Commercial Court Judicial Assistant Pilot Scheme Phase 2, July 2018.

[28] The choice in the 2024–25 competition was: Chancery Division (Business and Property Courts); Family Division; King's Bench Division (Commercial Court (Business and Property Courts); Technology and Construction Court (Business and Property Courts); Administrative Court; and, KB Civil. See High Court Judicial Assistants Job Advert 2024 (copy on file with the author).

[29] High Court Judicial Assistants Job Advert 2024.

[30] Sanders (n 8) 4. This model has significant advantages to the JA as intern; see T Nesterchuk, 'The View from Behind the Bench', in A Burrows, D Johnston, & R Zimmermann (eds), *Judge and Jurist: Essays in Memory of Lord Rodger of Earlsferry* (Oxford, OUP, 2013) 105–110, concerning the UK Supreme JAs. And see J Semakula, *Day in the life … of a judicial assistant*, Counsel, 29 June 2018 www.counselmagazine.co.uk/articles/day-the-life ….

[31] Sanders (n 8) 4.

[32] ibid.

[33] ibid 5.

[34] Paterson (n 22) fn 213; And see Nesterchuk (n 30) 102.

III. Judicial Assistants – Employment and Assignment

JAs are not appointed by the judiciary. The appointment process is run for the Court of Appeal by His Majesty's Courts and Tribunals Service (HMCTS) and for the UK Supreme Court by the court's administration. Once appointed, these JAs are employed as civil servants by HMCTS and the UK Supreme Court's administration, respectively. While employed in this capacity, they are required to ensure that they do not engage in activity that is likely to give rise to a conflict of interest. JAs in the Supreme Court are, for instance, specifically prohibited from engaging in a range of activities for the duration of their appointment. These are specified in the terms and conditions of their appointment, as follows,

> Judicial Assistants will be civil servants for the duration of the fixed term appointment and expected to abide by the Civil Service Code of Conduct. This includes acting with integrity, impartiality and honesty at all times. Judicial Assistants must not publish anything without permission (including e-publishing), or allowed to continue either acting or advising on any case connected to the UKSC, or any case likely to be heard at UKSC in the foreseeable future. In addition, Judicial Assistants must not act as a Solicitor or Barrister in their own name for the duration of the appointment. In addition, if you work in a voluntary capacity for another organisation you may have to apply for permission to continue to ensure there is no conflict of interest with the role of Judicial Assistant at The Supreme Court.[35]

As civil servants, similar restrictions will apply to those JAs appointed in the Court of Appeal; in particular, they will be bound by the terms of the Civil Service Code.[36] That such restrictions apply, and particularly that JAs are not permitted to undertake outside work or act or advise in proceedings that are before the courts to which they are appointed, obviates a potential problem that was identified in the initial phase of their introduction. When JAs were initially appointed to the Court of Appeal, which was on a part-time basis, the potential existed for conflicts of interest to arise. As Jamieson argued at the time when JAs were first introduced,

> Under [the original part-time JA scheme], there would appear to be a potential for conflicts of interest to arise with other aspects of an appointee's legal professional work. The potential for a judge's impartiality to be then called into question has arisen in the United States in the context of law clerks' negotiations for post-clerkship employment. How much stronger may this concern be where the potential for conflict of interest arises in respect of a judicial assistant's current employment outside the Court?[37]

[35] Terms and Conditions of Appointment – Judicial Assistants to the Justices at www.supremecourt.uk/docs/terms-and-conditions-ja-recruitment-2024.pdf.

[36] Esp., see the Civil Service Code's express prohibition on civil services misusing their 'official position, for example by using information acquired in the course of your official duties to further your private interests or those of others': see Civil Service Code at www.gov.uk/government/publications/civil-service-code/the-civil-service-code.

[37] Jamieson (n 12) 407.

That concern may have been capable of being raised when the JA scheme was first introduced, with barrister and solicitor appointees continuing to work for part of the week outside the Court of Appeal. Even then, it is noteworthy that no instances of concern were ever raised. Moreover, at the time and, particularly during the time when the Court of Appeal JA scheme was overseen by Lord Justice Buxton, clear guidance, in similar terms to that now explicitly in place in the UK Supreme Court, was given to JAs that they were to avoid any potential conflicts of interest. When the Court of Appeal scheme moved to one where the appointments were full-time similarly explicit instruction was given not to take on outside work and to inform the judge to whom they were assigned or the Master in the Court of Appeal (Civil Division) who had oversight of the scheme of potential conflicts of interest that might arise in proceedings before the Court.[38]

While such risks cannot, of course, be eliminated completely as there is always the possibility that an appeal may be pursued on a matter that a JA was instructed in some capacity when it was determined at first instance, the prospect of potential conflicts arising has been greatly minimised given the move to full-time appointments and explicit prohibitions on outside working. The greatest care to police potential conflicts will, of necessity, take place where the High Court JA scheme is concerned. The High Court scheme is not run by HMCTS. On the contrary, that scheme is run by the Judicial Office for England and Wales, which is the body of civil servants who provide administrative support to the senior judiciary to enable them to carry out the statutory responsibilities that are placed on the Lady Chief Justice as head of the judiciary in England and Wales.[39] The appointment process involves the judiciary, who along with a civil servant, interview applicants. Appointees, who are employed by the Judicial Office, are either paid a monthly salary by HMCTS or HMCTS pays their employer (if they are in employment) an equivalent monthly fee as a 'secondment fee'. Unlike in the Court of Appeal and UK Supreme Court, the JAs will be working specifically in their own practice area and will be dealing with a range of proceedings at first instance. There will thus be an increased likelihood that they will potentially be exposed to working on proceedings that, for instance, their law firm or Chambers will be advising or representing the parties or in respect of which they have been instructed. Again, however, there have been no reported instances of conflicts of interest arising under the High Court scheme, a point that is strongly suggestive of the efficacy of the measures implemented to minimise the potential for such problems arising. And, again, High Court JAs will be subject to the Civil Service Code.

Once appointed, JAs are assigned to work for a specified judge. In the UK Supreme Court originally, this was done by trying to match the JAs with the

[38] The author was a JA in the early years of the 21st century. The guidance was made very clear to incoming JAs. On occasion, potential conflicts were reported to the Master and measures were put in place to ensure that the relevant JA had no dealings with the proceedings that could have given rise to a conflict of interest.

[39] High Court Judicial Assistants Job Advert 2024; Constitutional Reform Act 2005, s 7.

personality of the judge to whom they were to be assigned. As Paterson explained, the approach operated by Lord Hope, who originally oversaw the appointment process, focused on the JA's 'personality and background'. Assignment was not based on an attempt to match the JA's 'specialism' with that of the judge.[40] It is unclear if that approach has been maintained under his successors managing the Supreme Court scheme. Equally, it is unclear on what basis JAs are assigned to judges in the Court of Appeal. As with the Supreme Court no criteria are publicly available to explain the approach taken. By way of contrast, express guidance is provided to applicants for the High Court scheme. There JAs, 'will be placed with a judge or judges working in their chosen specialisation or one of their chosen specialisations'.[41] It is to be assumed that, given the large number of JAs appointed each year to the Court of Appeal a similar approach is taken to its JAs; a matching scheme such as that operated by Lord Hope in the Supreme Court would not seem to be tenable. Matching individual JAs in the Court of Appeal to one of over 40 judges based on personality and background does not appear to be a tenable objective, albeit where allocation of a JA to one of the six senior judges in the Court of Appeal (the Lady Chief Justice, Master of the Rolls, President of the King's Bench Division, President of the Family Division, Chancellor of the High Court, and Senior President of Tribunals) may involve some greater degree of consideration of their background.

IV. Judicial Assistants – Their Role

The JAs' role across the three courts is broadly similar. The UK Supreme Court JAs' role is concisely summarised in the application materials for appointment:

> The Judicial Assistants support the Justices of the Supreme Court and JCPC by:
>
> 1. Conducting research in connection with appeals and applications for permission to appeal;
> 2. Drafting bench memos summarising applications for permission to appeal;
> 3. Attending appeal hearings and discussing the legal issues arising therefrom with the Justices;
> 4. Drafting plain English summaries of judgments for publication on the Supreme Court and JCPC websites;
> 5. Preparing responses on behalf of the UKSC to requests for information from international judicial and comparative law networks;
> 6. Generally assisting the Justices in their work, including with extra-judicial speeches, articles and other publications;
> 7. Assisting the Registrar with regards to applications for permission to appeal and appeals; and

[40] Paterson (n 22) 248. And see Nesterchuk (n 30) 102–103.
[41] High Court Judicial Assistants Job Advert 2024.

8. Supporting educational and outreach activity, such as student mooting competitions and debate days.[42]

A similar, albeit less detailed set of criteria is set out for the Court of Appeal. Its JAs are specified as having to provide Court of Appeal judges will assistance in terms of 'analysis of appeal papers and legal research clarifying issues in advance of an appeal as well as sorting out the shape and nature of appeals in less well-presented cases'.[43] The last point refers specifically to the assistance these JAs are required to do go through permission to appeal applications and appeals, and their assorted document, provided by litigants-in-person. A key skill for Court of Appeal JAs is helping to order such material and, through the preparation of Bench Memoranda for the judiciary, an effective road map through that material for the court. Unsurprisingly, the role of High Court JAs seems to require them to carry out similar tasks, albeit with a greater focus on summarising case materials and particularly party submissions.[44] The three key areas of the work of each of the three types of JA are: drafting Bench Memoranda; carrying out research; and discussing legal issues with the judiciary.

V. Bench Memoranda

In each of the three courts, a JA's primary responsibility is to prepare Bench Memoranda.[45] These are primarily prepared in the Court of Appeal and UK Supreme Court for applications for permission to appeal or, as they are known in the latter, petitions for leave to appeal. They are also prepared in the Court of Appeal for appeals by JAs whose judge is assigned as the lead judge hearing the appeal. The nature of these memos was helpfully summarised in the first judgment, which dealt with the status: *Parker v The Law Society*, as follows

> The bench memoranda which judicial assistants prepare normally consist of a summary of the facts involved in a particular appeal, a history of the proceedings in the lower

[42] Person Specification – UKSC Judicial Assistants 2024–25, www.supremecourt.uk/docs/ja-person-specification-2024.pdf.

[43] Judicial Assistants to the Court of Appeal 2024–25, Recruitment Advert.

[44] High Court Judicial Assistants Job Advert 2024 'JAs will assist the judge(s) to whom they are allocated, for example by carrying out research, marking up and summarising case documents and transcripts, summarising submissions, discussing cases and hearings and providing general support for the judge(s) in the organisation of their work and hearings. The role will require candidates to manage involvement in multiple cases, some of them very large and involving extensive evidence. JAs will also be expected to aid their assigned judge(s) to meet tight deadlines.' In *Infinity Treasures Pte Ltd v Global Currency Exchange Network Limited* [2023] EWHC 2945 (Comm) at [16], Foxton J acknowledged the work carried out by his JA summarising and tabulating material submitted by the parties.

[45] *Parker v Law Society (No. 1)* [1999] C.O.D. 183; *The Times* (December 8) 1998; [1998] 12 WLUK 101, JAs' 'primary responsibility is to prepare bench memoranda and conduct research for members of this Court'.

courts, an indication of the issues on appeal and any opinion which the judicial assistant has on the merits of the appeal.[46]

Within the memoranda, JAs will, ordinarily, be expected to cross-reference to the appellant's documents, so that the judge dealing with the permission application or appeal can cross-reference easily.[47] Thus assisting the court to deal with the matters before them more efficiently. While such memoranda, for leave petitions, in the UK Supreme Court are generally required to be no more than three to four pages long.[48] While concision is also important in the Court of Appeal, there is, however, no similar approach, not least because of the differential nature of applications to that court where appellants are likely to raise a much greater number and range of grounds of appeal. As Nesterchuk, a former JA in the UK Supreme Court notes, and the point is equally applicable to the Court of Appeal, work carried out on leave petitions in the UK Supreme Court by JAs plays an important contribution to the smooth running of the court.[49]

While Bench Memoranda are provided to the judges dealing with the proceedings in the relevant court, they are not disclosed to the parties. In this they differ from similar memoranda that are prepared by lawyers employed by the Court of Appeal (Criminal Division) for criminal appeals; such disclosure is mandated.[50] The fact that they are not disclosed has been subject to review by the courts. In *Parker v The Law Society*, a bench memorandum for an appeal before the Court of Appeal was inadvertently disclosed by the court administration to the appellant. The appellant complained that the memorandum was 'one-sided' and contained factual errors. The basis of his complaint, which was set out as an additional ground of appeal in his case before the Court of Appeal, was that its non-disclosure before the hearing of his application for permission to appeal had prejudiced that hearing. The Court of Appeal concluded that with Bench Memoranda their non-disclosure did not place parties, and particularly appellants, at a disadvantage. Non-disclosure did not create any procedural unfairness, nor would that approach prejudice any party. Should a Bench Memoranda alert a judge to a specific issue that needed to be brought to the attention of a party, the judge could be expected to bring that matter to the parties' attention.[51] If, for instance, a memorandum

[46] *Parker v Law Society (No. 1)* [1999] C.O.D. 183; *The Times* (December 8) 1998; [1998] 12 WLUK 101.

[47] Paterson (n 22) 249, where he notes how bench memoranda are to provide a 'road map linking the [appellant's] documents and their key arguments to the petition'.

[48] Paterson (n 22) 249.

[49] Nesterchuk (n 30) 104. She also notes how assisting the Registrar of the UK Supreme Court and its press office deal with queries from public and the press assists in this as well. Their assistance thus contributes not just to the efficient use of the Supreme Court justices' time through reducing the time taken on their dealing with leave petitions, but equally it contributes to the efficient use of the Court's administrative time and resources. Similar points can be made in respect of the Court of Appeal and High Court JAs in respect of the assistance they provide.

[50] Practice Direction (CA (Crim Div): Criminal Appeal Office Summaries) (No.1) [1992] 1 WLR 938.

[51] For a short discussion of *Parker v The Law Society*, see, R White, 'Disclosure of Bench Memoranda prepared by Judicial Assistants' (2001) 2(1) *Judicial Studies Institute Journal* 153.

highlighted a point of authority or precedent that the Court considered to be relevant and which the parties had not referred to in their submissions, then the Court would be expected to bring that matter to the parties' attention so that they could make appropriate submissions on it. The Court specifically justified non-disclosure on four grounds:

(i) disclosure would be inconsistent with the relationship between judicial assistants and members of the Court and would inhibit judicial assistants from expressing their opinions.
(ii) disclosure would result in unnecessary argument before the court as to whether the bench memorandums were accurate or the opinions which they expressed correct when they are only used by the members of the Court as an aide to their preparations and regularly members of the Court take a different view of the facts or as to the outcome of the appeal from that of the judicial assistants.
(iii) the Court in any event would draw to the attention of the parties any matter which they were proposing to take into account of which the parties would not already be aware. They do this when their own research reveals information of this character and the same course would be adopted with regard to information provided by the judicial assistants.
(iv) it would be impractical to provide the parties with details of oral discussions between the judicial assistant and members of the Court (especially if the discussions were immediately prior to the hearing) and to provide only written communications could be misleading.[52]

Additionally, the Court was satisfied by considering the approach taken to non-disclosure of comparable materials by law clerks and similar judicial assistants in other jurisdictions, such as the United States of America, Canada, Australia, New Zealand, the European Court of Justice and the European Court of Human Rights, that the approach taken was not problematic. When non-disclosure was further challenged following the enactment of the Human Rights Act 1998, on the ground that it was incompatible with Article 6 of the European Convention on Human Rights, the Court of Appeal affirmed that non-disclosure was not problematic.[53]

One particular concern that has been raised about JAs is the extent to which they are involved in drafting judgments. Bench memoranda could, in principle, for instance, be utilised for this purpose. No doubt, in some cases, judges do adopt summaries of the background set out in bench memoranda in their judgments. This is, however, not their purpose and where judges do so, they will be doing so for two principal reasons: first, because having examined the material placed before the court by the appellant on a permission to appeal application

[52] *Parker v Law Society (No. 1)* [1999] C.O.D. 183; The Times (December 8) 1998; [1998] 12 WLUK 101.

[53] *Attorney-General v Barnes* [2003] EWCA Civ 975 at [43]–[44]. Also see *Attorney-General v Covey* [2001] EWCA Civ 254, where Lord Woolf CJ affirmed the practice of non-disclosure on the basis that bench memoranda did not form part of appeal documentation, but were private documents, the aim of which was to assist the judiciary; on which see Drewry, Blom-Cooper, & Blake (n 14) 93. There have been no further challenges to non-disclosure or the status of bench memoranda since 2003.

or the parties on an appeal, they are satisfied that the summary is accurate; and, secondly, adopting the summary is a means to promote the efficient use of the court's resources, particularly judicial time.[54] Where judgment drafting is specifically concerned, Sanders notes how this is viewed in England and Wales as being 'objectionable'. She does so based on a response by the English and Welsh judiciary to a survey carried out by the Consultative Council of Judges of the Council of Europe (CCJE).[55] Interestingly, the survey response by the English judiciary under-emphasises the issue. It is not just that such delegation, as it could properly be called, of the judicial function is viewed as objectionable, it is prohibited. While Lord Justice Otton may have been keen to stress the point that this should not happen when the Court of Appeal's JA scheme was first introduced,[56] the Court of Appeal in *Parker v The Law Society* was clear that this was not something that could properly be done. As Lord Woolf CJ stated in his judgment in that case, with which Hutchinson and Tuckey LJJ agreed, 'I would emphasise that in this court there is no question of the judicial assistants being engaged in the drafting of any judgments.'[57] As with the delegation of judicial functions generally, such delegation to JAs is as impermissible as it is objectionable.

It could be said that the provision, as part of Bench Memoranda, of the JA's opinion on how the matter should be resolved might lead to concerns regarding judgment-drafting or delegation of judicial functions. As Sanders notes where this type of function is carried out by JAs or their equivalent, they 'become more involved in the decision making process'.[58] Again, the responses to the CCJE survey suggested that JAs in the UK are 'not always' permitted to provide such opinions.[59] This may well be true in the UK Supreme Court, where Bench Memoranda for leave petitions are required to be neutral.[60] However, in the Court of Appeal, the provision of an opinion on the merits is a standard feature of a Bench Memoranda, as was noted by Lord Woolf CJ in *Parker v The Law Society*.[61] And, even in the UK

[54] Nesterchuk (n 30) 105 'A well-written petition memo should save the Justices time and be used as a route map through the often voluminous appeal papers.'

[55] Sanders (n 8) 10.

[56] Jamieson (n 12) 400.

[57] *Parker v Law Society (No. 1)* [1999] C.O.D. 183; *The Times* (December 8) 1998; [1998] 12 WLUK 101.

[58] Sanders (n 8) 9.

[59] ibid. As Semakula (n 30) explains the process where Court of Appeal JAs are invited into pre-hearing discussions, '... the other judges will attend my judge's office for the pre-court meeting. This is their time to discuss the bench memo, their initial views of the case and raise any pertinent issues. Being in the room for these meetings is one of my favourite parts of the role because it involves witnessing a legal discussion between some of the greatest legal minds in the country. It is also rewarding when a Lord or Lady Justice of appeal agrees with my analysis of the case (this can all change once they hear the oral arguments).'

[60] Paterson (n 22) 249; Nesterchuk (n 30) 106 '... the petition memos never include a judicial assistant's recommendation as to whether or not the leave to appeal should be granted ...' She also notes at 105 that 'The memo specifically does not contain any advice on the merits of the application; its aim is to summarize the case objectively without advocating a particular answer.'

[61] *Parker v Law Society (No. 1)* [1999] C.O.D. 183; *The Times* (December 8) 1998; [1998] 12 WLUK 101. In the author's experience as a JA in the Court of Appeal, Bench Memoranda always included an opinion on the merits.

Supreme Court, Nesterchuk notes a growing trend for justices to ask their JA to prepare separate notes (additionally to the Bench Memoranda) in which they set out their opinion on the merits of leave petitions.[62]

Again though, in the Court of Appeal such opinions are simply there to assist the judiciary in their preparation for dealing with an application for permission to appeal or an appeal. They set out one view, which has to be placed in the context of the judiciary also considering the parties' written and oral submissions, as well as the judges who deal with any application or appeal considering the views of the other judges dealing with the matter. And, importantly, it has to be put in the context of the opinion being that of an intern, albeit a highly-qualified one. It is noteworthy in this latter respect that Nesterchuk highlights how on one or two occasions when a JA in the Supreme Court was invited to give their opinion on the merits after a hearing for leave to appeal, and after the judges dealing with the matter expressing their views on the merits, were able to persuade them to grant leave to appeal.[63] First, this highlights how UK Supreme Court JAs are restricted in when and how they may proffer their opinions, not least that it is restricted to petitions for leave and not done after full appeals. Secondly, it highlights how rare are such instances of JA influence on decision-making. It could, in fact be queried if it occurs at all: Nesterchuk identifies these instances as 'legendary',[64] which given an absence of first-hand experience of them might also suggest that legendary might be better read as 'apocryphal'. Thirdly, and perhaps most importantly and consistently with the Court of Appeal's approach in *Parker v The Law Society*, were a JA's opinion on the merits to be one which a judge considered to raise valid points, they would have to be put to the parties, just as if the point was one which they had alighted upon without any assistance.[65]

This is not to say that JAs have no proper involvement in judgment drafting, in a broader sense. What involvement they do have is more administrative than could properly be described as judicial. In both the Court of Appeal and UK Supreme Court, they will be involved in proofreading draft judgments. Thus helping the court to identify drafting errors so they can be considered, and if necessary, corrected by a judge before the judgment is handed down. Moreover, in the UK Supreme Court JAs are required to provide summaries, as press releases, of the court's judgments. While these, explicitly,[66] do not form part of the court's judgment, they are an important means by which the court communicates the nature of

[62] Nesterchuk (n 30), 107 '… sometimes, and separately from the general petition memo prepared by a judicial assistant, the Justice's own judicial assistant will be asked to record his or her thoughts in a short written note containing concisely stated facts and a conclusion as to whether leave should be granted.'

[63] Nesterchuk (n 30) 106.

[64] Nesterchuk (n 30) 106.

[65] See the third ground on which Lord Woolf CJ justified non-disclosure of Bench Memoranda in *Parker v The Law Society*, noted in n 52, above.

[66] See, for instance, the standard disclaimer on, *Hassam v Rabot* [2024] UKSC 11, Press Summary, 26 March 2024 www.supremecourt.uk/cases/docs/uksc-2023-0025-press-summary.pdf.

its decision-making to the public. Such summaries being written in plain English and made available at the time the court's judgment is handed down and thereafter made available on the court's website. Increasingly, this role is also being taken by JAs in the Court of Appeal.

VI. Legal Research and Case Discussions

The second major aspect of the JAs role is conducting legal research. As with the provision of Bench Memoranda to help guide judges through material submitted by parties to proceedings, this marks a significant departure from the classical common law stereotype of the passive judge, who simply receives the law and submissions on it from the parties. In both the UK Supreme Court and Court of Appeal, it is well-established that JAs are required to conduct this type of research to assist judges. Paterson, for instance, notes how Lord Saville in the UK Supreme Court would generally expect his JA to conduct research that would encompass academic literature as well as case law authorities. Moreover, he notes how Lord Collins, also in the UK Supreme Court, would rely on his JAs to conduct case law research, and particularly do so in respect of US authorities.[67]

The fruit of any research is sometimes acknowledged publicly with reference to it being made in judgments. By way of example, Lord Justice Sedley acknowledged research conducted by his JA on the development of legislation concerning provision for special educational needs in *Slough Borough Council v Special Educational Needs and Disability Tribunal*.[68] As was acknowledged by the UK Supreme Court, such research may not only take place before a hearing, it may also do so after a hearing has concluded. In this latter circumstance, were such research to raise matters that were germane to an appeal and, potentially, its determination, the court would – consistently with the approach taken to points raised in Bench Memoranda – raise them with the parties. As Lord Carnwath put it in *R (Newhaven Port & Properties Ltd) v East Sussex County Council*,

> At the end of the hearing in the present case, the court offered Mr George QC the opportunity to provide information about the practice in other common law jurisdictions. He did not take up that invitation, perhaps in the understandable fear of opening up a Pandora's box. Some comparative material can, however, be found in the appendix to the Scottish Law Commission's 2001 Discussion Paper. That has been supplemented since the hearing in this case by some further work by our own judicial assistants, particularly relating to the United States of America. This research is far from exhaustive, and, since it is not material to our conclusion in the present case, it has not been thought

[67] Paterson (n 22) 250.

[68] *Slough Borough Council v Special Educational Needs and Disability Tribunal* [2010] EWCA Civ 668 at [20]; also see, for instance, *Pritchard v Co-operative Group Ltd* [2011] EWCA Civ 329; [2012] Q.B. 320 at [32].

> necessary to invite comments from the parties. However, as it may be of relevance to future cases, it seems desirable to make a brief reference to some of the main points.[69]

The summary set out in his judgment encompasses some eleven paragraphs and discusses the approach taken to the substantive point before the court in France, Germany, Norway, Spain, Canada, England & Wales, New Zealand, as well as the United States. Two points arise here.

First, the provision of such research is of significant benefit to the development of precedent in the UK. An important feature of the common law has been its ability to both draw on the experience of other jurisdictions as it has developed, even if it has not always done so explicitly. Historically, this occurred, for instance, through the influence of the civil law, and particularly Roman law, as well as through judicial familiarity with academic treatise by, for instance, Pothier.[70] The ability of the Court of Appeal and UK Supreme Court to draw on JAs to provide them with comparative research materials thus better enables such matters to be taken account of by those courts in developing the law. It helps to ensure, for instance, that legal developments do not take place in ignorance of approaches taken in other jurisdictions, even if the courts do not adopt those approaches. It also helps to ensure that the court can obtain effective argument on such developments from the parties in appeals before them; parties who may not, for good reason, not have engaged in such comparative research and not put such materials before the court as part of their submissions.

Secondly, it plays into the approach that judges take to their JAs. An increasingly important aspect of the JAs' role is to act as a 'sounding board'[71] for the judge to whom they are assigned. Paterson in his examination of the Supreme Court JAs' role particularly highlights how Supreme Court justices emphasise the importance of this.[72] He notes how discussions between JA and the judge to whom they are assigned variously enable the justices to test their own views, to consider different perspectives – perhaps ones they themselves or the parties had not alighted upon – or simply, as Lord Dyson put it to help them 'sharpen [their] own thinking'.[73] That this can take place before and after hearings and do so in either or both a general way or in respect of individual issues or points in the case under consideration,

[69] *R (Newhaven Port & Properties Ltd) v East Sussex County Council* [2015] UKSC 7; [2015] A.C. 1547 at [119]. Also see *Ghaidan v Godin-Mendoza* [2004] 2 A.C 557 at [39].

[70] For an historical survey of this influence see, Lord Toulson, *International Influence on the Common Law* (2014) www.supremecourt.uk/docs/speech-141111.pdf.

[71] Paterson (n 22) 252.

[72] This role is to a certain extent less important in the Court of Appeal. JAs will not always engage with the judge dealing with a permission to appeal application for which they prepared a Bench Memoranda. Discussions with judges, including the one to whom they are assigned, in respect of appeals are generally prior to any hearing. As Sanders notes JAs, who are not routinely invited into post-hearing discussions, only participate in them asked. Participation is not the general rule; Sanders (n 8) 12. Discussions generally with the judge to whom they are assigned will very much depend on the judge and the approach they take.

[73] Paterson (n 22) 252–254.

provides the justices with the opportunity to enhance the decision-making process. It could be said, that this also provides the JA with the opportunity to shape the decision through discursive influence. It could do so, where discussions take place before hearings, by enabling the justices to raise matters with the parties. As Paterson put it, discursive success for a JA in such a circumstance could be to see their points put to counsel for the parties at the hearing.[74] Where it occurs after the hearing, consistent with Lord Carnwath's observation noted earlier, it could be raised with the parties so that they could respond to it by putting in written submissions on the point to the court. That would particularly be the case where the discussion raises matters not put to or canvassed by the parties at the hearing or where the discussion focusses on research that raises comparative materials, not dealt with at the hearing, again as noted above.

Care does have to be taken in this regard. As beneficial as this might be for the judges concerned, this form of engagement can lead to a subtle influence on the judicial decision-making process. Where, for instance, pre-hearing discussions help to confirm a judicial view on an issue, it might reduce the prospect that that judge would or could approach the issue with an open-mind at the hearing.[75] Where they challenge preliminary views formed after a hearing,[76] it may see the JA influence the decision-making process in a subtle way, that is, in a way in which the parties themselves are unable to respond to, not least because they are unaware of it. Judges who work with JAs ought properly to be mindful of this. It is not necessarily the case, as Paterson notes Lord Kerr suggested, that discussion with a JA is a discussion where 'neither party has an agenda', with the JA, unlike counsel, not seeking to 'persuade [the judge] to a particular point of view'.[77] As Nesterchuk's account of JA success, which was noted earlier, in persuading Supreme Court justices to come round to their view of the merits of granting or not leave to petition the court makes clear, JAs have their own views too. They are not necessarily or always the neutral interlocutors that Lord Kerr's comment might be taken to suggest. As the JA role continues to develop, as it undoubtedly will, the judiciary will need to continue to be mindful of the JA remaining an individual who provides them with assistance, and is not someone whose role is one that tacitly or otherwise becomes one that exerts influence over the decision-making process, other than influence in respect of which the parties are made aware and have an opportunity to respond to as is required to be the case in the Court of Appeal and High Court given Lord Woolf CJ's guidance in *Parker v The Law Society* and as is

[74] Paterson (n 22) 252.

[75] Lord Kerr noted how such discussions could help confirm views as well as challenge them; Paterson (n 22) 251.

[76] As Semakula (n 30) puts it concerning his experience in the Court of Appeal, the judge to whom he was assigned would use the pre-hearing discussion to 'ask me clarification questions, challenge my legal opinion and give helpful feedback on my work.' The pre-hearing discussion thus has more of an educative, in different ways, role for both judge and JA.

[77] Paterson (n 22) 251–252.

evident through the approach taken in the UK Supreme Court to legal research conducted by JAs.

VII. Conclusion

The introduction of JAs across the UK Supreme Court, Court of Appeal and, most recently, High Court is one instance of the broader shift away from the concept of the English judge as a passive judge. It is a means by which judges in those courts are assisted in the effective case management of proceedings. Whether through drafting Bench Memoranda, which reduce the time taken by judges to deal with permission to appeal applications or through the provision of legal research, which can both reduce the time taken to deal with appeals and also improve the quality of decision-making, JAs now play an important role in the administration of justice. Care has, so far, been taken to minimise the prospect that their appointment could undermine either the quality of justice or bring the administration of justice into question. JAs are required to avoid conflicts of interest. Judges are required to disclose matters to the parties that may be relevant to their decision-making, which have been brought to their attention by JAs, not least through the provision of Bench Memoranda and legal research. And, JAs have been kept away from the drafting of judgments, and decision-making generally. While the possibility remains that future developments may, in principle, see the JAs' role develop in ways similar to that in other jurisdictions, particularly those where law clerks have some role in judgment-drafting. It is a possibility that is highly unlikely to be realised. Two decades of development is strongly suggestive that the JAs' role is now clearly defined and confined to providing assistance and not to acting as a judge's delegate.

8

Judicial Assistants and Courts as a Teamwork – The Clerkship: A Vision from Latin America

ÁLVARO PÉREZ RAGONE

I. General Overview

The courts are work spaces governed by principles of the state bureaucracy and they are complex organisations. In this sense, with this work it has been possible to verify that they are not 'static' spaces with guaranteed 'mobility routes' and 'careers at work': judge's assistants have a special role in the adjudication: preparation, organisation and also in the decision-making of cases. At the same time, approaches from organisational or managerial analysis that omit constitutive aspects of the state bureaucracy cannot be used either, because they are the pillars that structure work in the public sphere, as well as the particularities of the administration of justice as part of state power.[1]

There are a number of different approaches to the status, task, and organisation of clerks. In most Member States, judicial assistants work at all courts and instances. In some states, they are only engaged at the higher courts and constitutional court, or only the constitutional court, or at specialised courts. Judicial assistants can be civil servants or employees, for a limited time or with long-term contracts. The tasks and responsibilities of judicial assistants vary between jurisdictions (for example, differences can be noted regarding common law versus civil law jurisdictions), court levels, and legal domains.[2] Universal duties can be distinguished that judicial assistants share in all these contexts: independence, impartiality, confidentiality, and ethical and professional standards.

[1] P Todd and A Ward, *In Chambers: Stories of Supreme Court Law Clerks and Their Justices*, (Charlottesville, University of Virginia Press, 2012) 25–50.

[2] A Ward, 'Law Clerks', in L Epstein & SA Lindquist (eds) *The Oxford Handbook of U.S. Judicial Behavior* (Oxford, Oxford University Press, 2017) 100–125.

I would like to put out the following question: Is it possible to measure and to analyse as reliable the influence of clerks on judge adjudication tasks? The answer seems to be complex because most former law assistants under confidentiality, avoid giving information about their activity, especially regarding the assistance by the court in decision-making. Qualitative data collected from interviewing seems to be not enough: as said in the confidentiality, among other things, the current and former legal assistants do not like to discuss their experiences.[3]

This chapter begins with an approach to the rational organisation of the courts (II). Next it describes the role of the judicial assistant or clerk (III). The following section explores the role of judicial assistants and their tasks (IV). The two final sections (V–VI) analyses the influence of the judicial assistant on the judicial decision, departing from the difficult research of the subject because of confidentiality and judge-clerks loyalty. Section VII concludes.

II. An Approach that Seeks to Understand the Organisation of Work in the Administration of Justice

An approach that seeks to understand the organisation of work in the administration of justice has to consider three areas of study in an articulated way: (i) the principles of state bureaucracy to explain the structure of the judiciary and hierarchical subordination relationships; (ii) the particularities of the judiciary as part of the state (where judges with jurisdictional power carry out their dispute resolution function independently of other hierarchies, with no other obedience than to the legal order); and (iii) the analysis of the organisation of work that is carried out daily in the courts, to know the distribution and content of the tasks, the mobility mechanisms, the distance between the prescribed work and real work, the material conditions in which agents perform the work and the availability of work resources.[4]

The judicial field is strongly influenced by the socio-political context; that is, the courts are far from being 'static' work spaces but rather have to respond to diverse and growing demands and are 'sounding boards' for conflict and crisis. These demands translate into adaptations in the distribution of tasks, intensification of work, and length of the day. Mobility, that is, the possibilities for ascending in a judicial career, is not guaranteed according to the qualification and professionalism that the agents acquire through formal training and experience and learning

[3] WE Nelson, H Rishikof, LS Messinger & M Jo, 'The Liberal Tradition of the Supreme Court Clerkship: Its Rise, Fall, and Reincarnation?' (2009) 62 *Vanderbilt. Law Review* 1749–1806.

[4] M Fabri, 'Comparing the number of judges and court staff across European countries' (2019) 26(1) *International Journal of the Legal Profession* 5–19.

on the job, but rather due to the limited positions that may remain, vacancies due to the retirement or resignation of senior officers.[5]

On the other hand, from the exploration and analysis of the judicial reform proposals whose purpose is to carry out interventions in the operation and organisation of work in the courts, it has been possible to observe that their design and perspective correspond to a procedure by hearings (orality and written procedure mixed) with managerial approaches: indicators and goals designed to achieve profitability and increase the flow of production with cost savings (decrease in downtime, increase in productivity).[6]

Towards the second half of the 1990s, the reforms promoted by multilateral credit and development agencies such as the World Bank and IDB focused on the institutional reorganisation, which is considered part of the 'unfinished subjects' of the countries 'in the road of development'. The states of Latin American countries should be adapted to the new global contexts. In this context the Judicial Reform's projects have been encouraged with the granting of foreign loans aimed at transforming the management and application of new technologies in the areas of judicial work.[7]

The (neo) liberal and 'development' conceptions promoted and disseminated by multilateral credit agencies are going to be translated into plans to reform the organisation of work in Latin American courts through new management models from the private field, proposing to impose functional specialisation and quantitative standards of efficiency. The method of case study research marks limits of the analysis of the Judicial Reform to a particular case: the 'Model Court Project' in a civil trial. This delves into 'how' the implementation proceeded and what were the conditions of that process. The judge assistants were included in this model as direct supporting of the judge/court in different levels. The division of adjudicative and administrative task is a main point. From this point, the clerks have different names and functions in Latin-America. The common points are linked in different grades and forms with the adjudicative face or the legal decision-making.

III. A Tomography of the Clerkship

The classical and romantic clerkship history of the US Supreme Court is usually referred to in Latin America, disregarding the big and deep differences within the

[5] J Wilner, 'To Be or Not to Be?: Some Legal Ethics for Judicial Law Clerks' (2011) 89(3) *Canadian Bar Review* 611.

[6] P Mascini and NL Holvast, 'Explaining Judicial Assistants' Influence on Adjudication with Principal-Agent Theory and Contextual Factors' (2020) 11(3) *International Journal for Court Administration* 1–18.

[7] F Fariello, LB de Chazournes, & KE Davis, *World Bank: New Directions in Justice Reform: A Companion Piece to the Updated Strategy and Implementation Plan on Strengthening Governance, Tackling Corruption* (Washington, DC, World Bank, 2016) *passim*.

world of legal assistance in the Supreme, Constitutional or lower courts. The situation of clerks at the US Supreme Court was and is the same: (i) the legal assistants are almost always recent law school graduates from the best law schools, and they will spend one year at the US Supreme Court; (ii) they have spent a year usually on one of the US Courts of Appeals.[8]

In the other model, in France, the clerk (*greffier)* is present at all stages of the procedure. He records the cases, compiles files, notifies the parties of hearing and closing dates, draws up minutes, drafts documents, and formats decisions. He assists the judge at the hearing. Its role is essential since any formality or act carried out in its absence could be void. The clerk is a middle management agent, his mission is to coordinate the activities of the agents who collaborate with him on a service. He may also serve as head of the case files registry. Finally, the clerk welcomes and informs the public. Privileged interlocutor of the litigant, he provides information on the procedures and on the creation of a file. Access to the corps of clerks is by competitive examination.[9] There is both an external and internal competition for the selection. Initial training, on the principle of work-study, offers theoretical and practical components in courts. It aims to prepare the future clerk for the different aspects of the function. Provided by the National School of Grafts (E.N.G.), in Dijon, the training lasts 18 months. It is supplemented by compulsory continuing training of 10 days per year for five years following the end of their initial training.[10]

The reality in Latin America with reformed civil proceedings or still (more complex) written proceedings is different. The clerks are usually law graduates, many postgraduates with master or Ph.D. degrees, permanent court staff, and judiciary employees. As an example, you can find at the Supreme Court in Argentina (an overloaded Supreme Court) a legion of clerks (over 200) for only five supreme justices and suprema judges. The delegation and teamwork to make a Supreme Court judgment are not clear and '*soto voce*' not challenged; the main real authors of the final judgment are the clerks (as memos or legal opinions), but assigned by the justices.

At the highest level (Supreme and Constitutional Courts) the factual discussion is not the main task, but the legal matters are the pivot and centre. The general and more complex task of a legal assistant usually involves drafting legal opinions and judgment on cases, preparing questions and organising for hearings, to organising and following the acts and other additional tasks, which I will discuss in detail in this chapter. There are also in courts, organised in chambers, an informal cooperation with other judges and their legal assistants regarding the facts and the law relevant information of different cases.

[8] Todd and Ward (n 1) 75–90.

[9] C Fleuriot, 'Le greffier n'est pas là pour prendre la place du magistrat' [2015] *Dalloz Actualité*, 4 june.

[10] L Belfanti, 'La création des juristes assistants: entre utilité et questionnements' (2018) 20 *Gazette du Palais*, no. 323k7, 10ss.

A very important key point is the following: serving as a law clerk for a justice of the Supreme or Constitutional Courts could open many doors for a leader law office, the scholar career, or to become a future judge. Because in many Latin American countries the clerks at the highest level are: (i) well paid and are permanent public justice employees, with a salary in some cases better than that of a first instance judge, could be an incentive to stay in the clerk position; and (ii) as a plus point, in all cases the legal assistance will not appear as the authors of a judgment for public scrutiny, but only the justice who assigns the decision (final outcome), is an additional incentive to stay and conserve the judicial assistance position.

Simultaneously, it can be appreciated from the teamwork of the judicial assistant that law clerks are not autonomous political actors. From the first day of the clerkship, the law clerk is bound by formal and informal institutional rules and norms imposed by the court, as well as the individual judges. Observers must clearly understand the interplay of those rules, norms, and preferences before reaching a final verdict on the extent or desirability of clerk influence.[11]

From the view of the assistance supporting task, there is not one kind of judicial assistance in comparative perspective. The work of judges can be supported by different kinds of assistants and court staff. The judicial assistants have a legal education and support judges or panels of judges in their adjudicative work. The tasks, as said, undertake a wide range from legal research to preparing memos and drafting judgments. Such persons may have many different names or titles, including judicial assistants, law clerks, legal officers, secretaries, *Referendare, Wissenschaftliche Mitarbeiter, Gerichtsschreiber, référendaires* or *greffiers*.[12]

The clerkship supports the administration of justice in the interest of society as the main rationale task. Their contribution provides valuable support to judges and, in this way, improves the quality of judicial decisions. The work of judicial assistants with specialised legal knowledge can be particularly useful. 'Nevertheless, the appointment of qualified judges and adequate training opportunities for judges should not be neglected in favour of hiring judicial assistants'.[13] The (CCJE) Opinion No. 22 (7 November 2019) remarks additional positive contributions of the legal assistant: educating young lawyers, especially (future) judges and efficiency. The recommendation Nr. 16 is clear: 'While all member States using judicial assistants agree that they provide valuable assistance and save judges' time, only very few member States collect data on how

[11] P Todd amd C Zorn, 'Law Clerk Influence on Supreme Court Decision Making: An Empirical Assessment' (2008) 58 *DePaul Law Review* 51, 51–78.
[12] Consultative Opinion of Council European Judges No. 22 of The Role of Judicial Assistants [2019].
[13] ibid Nr. 11; comp. Fabri (n 4) 5–19.

useful judicial assistants actually are. It is therefore recommended that member States evaluate the contribution of judicial assistants'. And also Nr. 19:

> The role of the judicial assistant follows from the role of the judge. Judicial assistants must support judges in their role, not replace them. Whatever their duties are, they must be supervised by the judge or judges who remain responsible for the decision-making in all aspects. However, by supporting judges in their adjudicative process, judicial assistants are involved in the exercise of judicial tasks. Therefore, they must comply with the highest professional and ethical standards and thereby help to build high public trust in judicial institutions.

IV. Judicial Assistants and their Tasks

The differences in Latin American justice begin with the appeal and first instance court. In some appeals courts, clerks have to finish an abstract of each case before the hearings. Others court of appeals and many first instance courts use the clerks directly to write the full final draft of a judgments under the justification that the clerks need to be trained and under the over case loaded.

Here it is interesting to note a non-formal data collection from many scholars and justices in Latin America that were given a single question: In your civil justice system in the first instance, who makes and writes the final judgments? The answers were very interesting. First only in Uruguay, Chile and Costa Rica the answer was: only the trial judge. There is no assistant to delegate this exclusive task. Second, in countries with new civil and criminal procedures with hearings like Bolivia, Ecuador, and Colombia, the answers were a little different: it depends on the tribunal and as a personal choice to delegate to the clerks the task, and in a court with overload cutting, they have to delegate; in other words it is impossible. Regarding the hearings and the immediacy of the evidence, they do not consider a key question to delegate the final decision-making as a draft to a clerk. The assessment of the evidence and the judgment supporting reasoning could be assigned with a better outcome to the clerks. In this case we have in fact one court before the parties, lawyers, and for the publicity principles, but behind another unknown decision-maker with the main task, the main outcome (as a draft may be token by the judge as a judgment). The interactions of judicial assistance and judges should be limited: *Clear instructions, mutual respect, exchange and clear workgroup rules.*

A. Organising Papers and Researching Facts

Judicial assistants may help researching facts, for example, by organising and sifting through large documents under the guidance and supervision of the judge. However, since judicial decision-making builds on the facts, the establishment and evaluation of facts remain the sole responsibility of the judge. Consequently, an assistant's role should remain limited in this respect.

B. Screening

The first approach to the case is the screening duty to select procedural managerial options or the more important task, to leave the review of the case to a higher court. Many Supreme and/or Constitutional courts have systems of discretionary criteria review, granting only small percentages of requests for review. The process of selecting cases for judicial review at the appeal and second appeal level could differ in civil (more open and overload with many distinctions from system to system) and common law countries (more closed). The examination of the 'filters' (*summa gravaminis*, certiorari (negative and positive) and other forms of selection has been studied extensively). Different tasks are supposed to be had by a clerk in the first instance to follow the right procedure to the final decision. Many lower courts (and also some highest courts) do not have a system of discretionary review.[14] Supreme and constitutional courts have a valuable role in the unification of case law, often with a large number of cases.

The clerks who serve at supreme and constitutional courts often have the task of summarising the facts of cases and the relevant applicable law in order to make suggestions as to whether a case should be admitted for appeal or constitutional review. Here the European recommendation is also clear:

> Such help in the 'sifting' of applications can help judges to focus on important cases while assistants help to deal more quickly with routine cases. However, there is a risk that judicial assistants gain influence on the selection of cases. Member States must be aware of such risks and ensure that judges remain in control of deciding and selecting cases themselves.[15]

Hence, judicial assistants in these courts do not participate in selecting cases for review in order to leave the case to be reviewed. Disregarding this point would be important other screening factors as: decisions by a specialised court, single judge or judicial panel and jury constitution. Through these screenings, however, the judicial assistants can also have an (indirect) influence within the case management: time, costs and also future interim and final decisions.

C. Sound Board of Decision Making

In many courts, it is common for judges to discuss the merits of a case with judicial assistants. In this way, it could also be emphasised the role of judicial assistants as advisors to judges, presenting both qualitative facts and law questions and possible answers. The discussion between judges and their assistants

[14] See also: SL Wasby 'Clerking for an Appellate Judge: A Close Look' (2008) 5(1) *Seton Hall Circuit Review* 54–55.

[15] (CCJE) Opinion (n 12) Nr. 28.

may be informally, or with an institutionalised deliberation. The latter occurs when assistants are present at the hearings and their role as cases law and doctrinal contribution is ruled.[16]

D. The Clerk's Memos

The memos drafted by the judicial assistant are one of the most important tasks: the law and factual findings with their personal point of view. Some of them summarise the legal and factual key points of a case; others include suggestions for questions to ask during a hearing; also, the case management advice is important, and the main kind of memos are those regarding possible advice on how to decide a case.[17] Research on cognitive heuristics and biases in (judicial) decision-making evidences the influence on the judge by information that is presented prior to a hearing, which is relevant and which is irrelevant. This could be the same as what happens with the memo, although it depends on each judge's leadership to use the memos directly for the decision-making or only as ancillary support and guidance. Let me continue with this point in the next section.

E. Decision and Legal Opinion Drafts

The most controversial task of judicial assistants is to draft the judicial decisions and legal opinions. It has become common practice for judges in different jurisdictions to delegate to their judicial assistants this duty. And it is some not closing evidence regarding the writing style from which it is possible to identify in a final judgment of a Supreme and Constitutional Court a mix of opinions from multiple authors. That suggests that judges delegate at least parts of the drafting decision to their clerks. However, the fact that judicial assistants prepare a first draft of a judgment does not automatically imply that they also influence the outcome of cases.[18] Many questions arise, like: Do judges, for instance, provide detailed instructions for writing the draft? And/or do they drastically revise the first draft of an assistant, turning it truly into their own judgment?

Regarding the European Standard (Nrs. 25 and 26):[19]

> If judicial assistants are involved in the drafting process, they should work under the close supervision and with the guidance of the judge. Therefore, the member States

[16] P Todd, *Courtiers of the Marble Palace: The Rise and Influence of the Supreme Court Law Clerk* (Stanford, Stanford University Press, 2006) 10–25.

[17] CD Kromphardt, 'Fielding an Excellent Team: Law Clerk Selection and Chambers Structure at the U.S. Supreme Court' (2014) 98(1) *Marquette Law Review* 289–311.

[18] W Artemus & DL Weiden, *Sorcerers' Apprentices: 100 Years of Law Clerks at the United States Supreme Court* (New York, New York University Press, 2006) 20–35.

[19] (CCJE) Opinion (n 12).

should consider whether and to what extent it is appropriate to allow the presence and participation of judicial assistants at deliberations of cases. If judicial assistants prepare complete drafts, there is a risk that the assistant's suggestions steer the judge's thinking (anchoring effect). Such an effect is also possible, however, if a judicial assistant just prepares a memo on how a case should be decided.

V. The Micro Level Legal Assistant View

A complex task is to try to analyse the weight of the clerk's influence at the court organisation and their secretive institution character that reveres confidentiality and loyalty. In fact, like other employees, new clerks must be confident. In addition, the clerk's network within the chambers is a difficult point. This is not only a private matter -the orientation of a court regarding one case - but also the data protection of the parties and the third within each case. The proceeding and real court (judges and judicial assistants) behind the formal court is secretive insofar as it is difficult to find a whole written code of professional conduct for law clerks. Maybe because it could be limited to the discretionary task delegated to the judge's assistant. In the same way, the written unformal or formal rule on confidentiality agreements remains unclear.[20]

The European Convention on Human Rights (ECHR) guarantees the right to an independent and impartial tribunal established by law. Judges' independence and impartiality are protected both during their appointment and in the exercise of their duties so that they can adjudicate according to these guarantees. When judges are supported in the adjudicative process by assistants, the quality and efficiency of their work can further be improved in the interests of society and the parties to the proceedings. However, this must be done in a way not endangering the parties' rights under Article 6 of the ECHR. Insofar as the protection of judicial independence is a pre-requirement to the rule of law, judicial assistants are not judges, and in their role as judicial assistance are not independent of the judges they support.[21]

The clerks' influence on court outcomes is a very important and unclear point. With influence, I could mean somewhat oddly, certainly narrowly, as the skills of a law assistant to persuade the judge to make decisions in ways other than usual. With judicial assistance, having different policy preferences and goals than his chief judge, it could be a valuable contribution from another point of view. And at this point it is important to persuade the judge to abandon his own preferences and therefore change to the clerks' preferred decisional outcomes. With the

[20] T Kappl, 'Strong Justice for a Strong Europe: A European *Rechtspfleger*' (2016) 8(1) *International Journal for Court Administration* 1.

[21] N Holvast and P Mascini, 'Is the Judge or the Clerk Making the Decision? Measuring the Influence of Judicial Assistants via an Experimental Survey among Dutch District Court Judges' (2020) 11(3) *International Journal for Court Administration* 2–19.

word 'influence', I am not suggesting manipulation nor control. Legal assistance is viewed as valuable input, despite the judge who will finally decide.[22]

At the Supreme or Constitutional Courts, we have an additional component: a clerks' group and a network. Clerks regularly talk to each other about their justices' as well as their own views and positions on cases and issues and then relay that information to their justices. Clerks informally mine the network during the coalition-forming stage as votes are cast, opinions joined, and requests for changes are made from chambers to chambers.

VI. The Judicial Assistance Advice: Between Loyalty, Self-Policy Determination and the Correct Outcome

The justices and other personnel employed by the many courts used to be isolated from the scholarly or media attention world. Judicial assistants do not like to talk about 'their' chambers inside, and they don't know what happened inside other chambers. The confidence universe of the clerks and their strong adherence to the judge could overstate the importance of the work they do. The judicial assistant has a duty of diligence, loyalty, and confidentiality both to the judge who appoints him and to the other justices. He also has a duty of loyalty to his fellow clerks and to other court employees.[23]

The judicial assistance at the Supreme and Constitutional Courts has especially received a great deal of media and scholarly attention for another issue, the lack of express opinion diversity among the judicial assistance under a judge. It seems to be that the clerks under the same justice were selected regarding some homogeneous criteria.[24]

Because of the rising caseloads in the courts all over the world, the legally trained, non-judge court judicial assistants are assigned a more prominent role in the adjudicative process. Today, judicial assistants have an important role in the judicial decision-making process. Although the legitimacy and the limits regarding the due and fair process of law of their role could be questioned. The main point is to evaluate and determine how long the judicial assistants could be actively involved in adjudication and influence the judicial decisions.[25]

In order to have a plausible answer on the legitimacy of the judicial assistants' contribution, we can begin with the reality: they are actively involved in adjudication and influence the outcome of judicial decisions. However, these pressing questions remain largely unanswered because of loyalty and confidentiality. The

[22] J Wilner, 'To Be or Not to Be?: Some Legal Ethics for Judicial Law Clerks' (2011) 89(3) *Canadian Bar Review* 611.

[23] A Bonica, AS Chilton, J Goldin, K Rozema, & M Sen, 'Measuring Judicial Ideology Using Law Clerk Hiring' (2017) 19(1) *American Law and Economics Review* 129–161.

[24] ibid.

[25] A Bonica, AS Chilton, J Goldin, K Rozema, & M Sen, 'The Political Ideologies of Law Clerks' (2017) 19(1) *American Law and Economics Review* 96–128.

role and influence of judicial assistants remain in a 'grey zone' to achieve an empirically acceptable answer.[26] The confidentiality agreements between judges and judicial assistants make it difficult to pursue research on the decisional influence of judicial assistants. The determination of the involvement and influence of judicial assistants is thereby exclusively based on judges' and assistants' self-reported research interviews.[27]

VII. Closing Remarks

Let me come back to the questions posed at the beginning of this chapter. What is the measure of the influence of clerks on judges' decision-making? Should scholars trust the information obtained from former clerks as reliable and verifiable? The answer seems to be that, while most former clerks remain quite reluctant to talk about their role at the court, when they do choose to share what they've learned with scholars, they can provide valuable information.

Nevertheless, for a variety of reasons explained throughout this chapter, scholars must approach these data with a healthy scepticism. (i) In part because of confidentiality issues, former clerks appear to be more willing to discuss their experiences after the death or retirement of the judge who hired them. (ii) Clerks can be an important source of information for judges, and these recent or experimented law graduates can help judges become acquainted with current legal theories taught in law schools. (iii) Clerks also seem to act as ambassadors or liaisons for their judges, helping them to learn about the views of their colleagues and perhaps helping them to negotiate indirectly with other judges through the clerical network.

However, an uncomfortable question could be raised: is the assistance of the judiciary more influential and more tolerated than that of congressional staff or presidential advisors? It seems unlikely that the judges of the Supreme Court and Constitutional Court do not make their own independent decisions. Clerks may be a useful source of assistance to judges, but it is unlikely that clerks would somehow manipulate the decisions of individual judges. Clerks are temporary employees, severely limited by their youth and inexperience.

Clerks may also exaggerate their own importance. Only the justices themselves know the influence of the clerks on the Supreme Court. And the justices generally refuse to discuss the issue. To be sure, there are institutional realities that may prevent scholars from examining in depth the question of how much influence or control the clerks have over the justices whom they hire.

However, the value of a comprehensive study of the clerks: the decision-making court 'behind' the institutional court, is not diminished by these obstacles.

[26] ibid.
[27] Fabri (n 4) 5–19.

9

The Missed Assistant Judges and the Lost Judge Assistants: A Reflection of the Judiciary Classification in China

YULIN FU

I. Introduction

The judicial reforms, which began in the 1990s, started first with procedural reform, gradually deepened into the reform of judicial mechanisms, partially touched on institutional reform, and finally launched the reform of court personnel. The procedural reforms have indeed promoted the litigants' role and procedural rights vs. the court; the reform of judicial mechanism aimed to promote the judges' role and independence vs. the 'monitors' and 'supervisors' in the courts (such as the President and the Judicial Supervision Committee of the court); the institutional reform tried (but failed) to promote the courts' roles and independence vs. the administrative departments and the local governments; and the personnel reform aimed to promote the judges' role in contrast to the civil servants inside and outside the court. Meanwhile, the series of reforms have generally and significantly promoted procedural transparency and judicial professionalisation.

As the result of the judicial reforms since the 1990s, the Civil Procedural Law was amended in 2012. As outcomes of the reforms of trial mechanism and court personnel system, the substantial amendments of the Organic Law of the Courts ('the OLC') and the Judges Law ('the JL') were successively promulgated in 2018 and 2019. The amendments significantly increased the independence and responsibility of the judges to exercise trial power on behalf of the courts by: (i) releasing the judges from their supervisors on the one hand; and (ii) providing judicial assistants on the other hand. The reform I is mentioned as 'de-bureaucratisation', while the reform II is named as 'judiciary classification' or 'personnel quota system'. The latter will be the key topic of this chapter.

The reform of 'judiciary classification' separates the court personnel into three classes: 'post judges', the class of judicial auxiliaries, and the class of administrative personnel. The post judges are the 'judges' who are regulated by the JL; and the administrative personnel are the general civil servants who are regulated by the Civil Servants Law. By classifying the judges from auxiliary judicial personnel and administrative staff, the reform aimed to release the judges from routine and trivial procedural affairs that should be left to the auxiliary judiciary. However, the judicial auxiliaries are neither judges nor ordinary 'civil servants'. The OLC only briefly provides the judicial auxiliaries, including judge assistants (Art 48), court clerks (Art 49), judicial policemen (Art 50, but meanwhile provides 'Judicial policemen shall be administered in accordance with the People's Police Law'), and judicial technicians in some specific fields (Art 51) like intellectual property. Among the judicial auxiliaries, the roles of judge assistants are most important but least-defined.

II. From 'Assistant Judge' to 'Judge Assistant'

Before the reform of 'judiciary classification', under the OLC 2006,

> the courts may, according to their needs, be staffed with assistant judges, who shall be appointed or removed by the people's courts themselves. Assistant judges help the judges in their work. Upon the recommendation of the president of the court and with the approval of the judicial committee, an assistant judge may provisionally exercise the functions of a judge. (Article 36)

Under the JL 2001 (revised in 2017 but no touch on this issue), 'Judges are the judicial personnel who exercise the judicial authority of the State according to law, including presidents, vice presidents, members of judicial committees, chief judges and associate chief judges of divisions, judges and assistant judges' (Article 2). Accordingly, the associate judges were clearly in the scope of the judges under the JL before 2018.

After 2018, the former 'assistant judge' (zhu li fa guan, 助理法官) was informed to be 'judge assistant' (fa guan zhu li, 法官助理). Under Article 48 of the OLC 2018, 'Judge assistants of a people's court shall, under the direction of judges, be responsible for reviewing case files, drafting legal documents and other assistant affairs. Judge assistants who are qualified for the post of judge may be selected and appointed as judges according to the procedures for appointment and removal of judges.' While the OLC 2018 renamed the 'assistant judges' to be 'judge assistants', it leaves 'the duties, management and quality guarantee of judges (shall) be subject to the provisions of the Judges Law' (Art 47).

Then, the Judges Law 2019 clearly defines the term 'judge' narrowly and applies only to the 'judges in posts', so it logically removes the 'judge assistants' from the scope of the 'judges'. By now, there's no sign or any mention of some law on judge assistants. Such a legislative omission has not only led to the disappearance of associate judges and the loss of judges' assistants, but has also created a model of full responsibility for judges in posts.

To read their roles before vs. after the reform, 'assistant' is the definite word of assistant judge while 'judge' is the status, so an assistant judge is also a judge; in contrast, as a judge's assistant, 'judge' is the definite word while 'assistant' is the status, so a judge assistant is an assistant.

As to the future of the assistant judges and the judge assistants, they are both in the pool of potential judges, but most of the assistant judges will become judges sooner or later, with few exceptions, while less than half of the judge assistants will have such opportunities since the reform limit quota of judges in a percentage of 30 per cent of the court staff.

III. The Problems of the Assistant Judges before the Reform

The main problem of the assistant judges was that their roles were extended beyond their qualifications and almost equal to the judges in the practice, mainly in that their powers, functions and duties didn't match the procedures of their appointment and the way they gained them.

Under the OLC 2006, the judges were appointed and removed by the standing committees of the congresses at corresponding levels. And the qualifications of a judge are very clearly provided in the OLC and the JL.[1] In contrast, the assistant judges were appointed and authorised by the court in a summary manner, as mentioned above (Article 36).

In general trial practice, however, an assistant judge was almost exactly the same as a judge, the only difference being that he or she was signed as 'Acting Judge' on the judgment document. And the difference between the two in terms of trial competence was that, when the panel includes a judge, the judge is always the presiding judge, even if the actual. The law did not, however, prohibit the full composition of the panel, say, the law did not prohibit collegiate courts from being composed entirely of assistant judges, nor did it exclude assistant judges from acting as single judges; on the contrary, the Supreme People's Court confirmed in its 1983 approval that 'assistant judges, when temporarily acting as judges, shall enjoy the same rights as judges in their work, in accordance with the law, and may either sit alone or be members of a collegiate court, appointed by the president or

[1] For the detailed introductions and discussion of the judge's qualifications, see Y Fu, 'Court Management in Transformation', in L Cadiet, & Y Fu (eds), *On Judicial Management from Comparative Perspective. Contemporary Chinese Civil and Commercial Law* (Singapore, Springer, 2023) 191–213.

the chairman of the court. President or the President's designation may also act as presiding judge of the panel.'[2]

The problem is clear when the associate judges generally exercise almost exactly the same powers as judges without the formal appointment process of judges, even without considering the question of individual competence, in terms of institutional legality, legitimacy, and the professional security of judges. In terms of competence, associate judges are generally used as single judges in simple proceedings, especially as skilled workers in the speedy court or in the summary adjudication of certain types of cases. On the one hand, their professional strengths from the legal profession are not brought into play and do not grow, and on the other hand, due to their youth and lack of social experience and exposure, they make unorthodox judgements and responses when dealing with complex social issues alone and without the guidance of senior judges. In recent years, the media have reported cases such as the 'Peng Yu case' and the 'sky- high toll case', in which assistant judges were the presiding judges, which have caused irreparable damage to the personal growth of these young judges and the reputation of the court as a whole. These problems, in turn, often serve as a justification or excuse to reinforce the administrative leadership of trials by presidents, deans, and trial committees. In fact, the root cause of these problems is the overstepping of the authority of assistant trial judges, which is beyond their own capacity and contrary to the law of training judicial talent.[3]

IV. The New Problems of the Judge Assistants

The main problems of the judge assistants as the judicial reform newly introduced into Chinese law in 2019 to replace the associate judge are twofold. The most important defect is that the role of the judicial assistants is open to be defined by the post judges. When Article 48 of the OLC 2018 provides 'judge assistants of a court' shall be responsible for reviewing case files, drafting legal documents and other assistant affairs 'under the direction of judges', in the context that there are no laws to provide their functions, duties and professional rights, the judge assistants 'of a court' are becoming the private assistants 'of a judge in a court' in the judicial practice. This omission of legislation for such an important judiciary

[2] See '*Reply from the Supreme People's Court on the Issue of Whether an Assistant Judge Can Serve as a Member of a Collegial Panel and Act as the Presiding Judge*', May 25, 1983, No.12 [1983] of the Supreme People's Court.

[3] In many jurisdictions like Japan, there are two (or more) levels of judgeship before becoming a full judge, and what is most important, different qualifications are required for appointment as a judge depending on the level of the court. Those appointed to the bench after their judicial training are usually assigned to the larger district courts in Tokyo and Osaka for the first two years, mainly as puisne judges in collegial cases. See Y Fu, 'Classification of Court Personnel Based on the Definition of Function and Duty' [2015] *Modern Law Review* 12–30.

who shares judicial powers with the judge, not only leads to the disappearance of associate judges and loss of judge assistants, but also creates a model of full responsibility for judges in posts. In the context of the situation of 'too many cases and too few ad judicators', lack of legal definition of the role of the judicial assistants has resulted in a new pattern of trial mechanism that 'those who try do not judge, and those who judge do not try', which was exact the defects to be removed by the judicial mechanism reform. This is getting to be true in practice. I will discuss this in more detail as follows.

Under the OLC, 'The judging staff of the people's courts shall consist of the president, vice-presidents, members of the judging committees and judges.' (Article 40) 'Judges, trial auxiliaries and judicial administrative personnel of the people's courts shall be managed in a categorical manner.' (Article 45) By reading the two articles, does the term 'trial personnel' in Article 40 include only the 'judges' in Article 40, or does it include judges and (some) trial assistants? The answer will determine whether trial assistants can exercise a limited trial power as distinct from judges. The two legal provisions themselves do not provide a direct answer.

Then turning to Article 48 of the OLC, 'Judges' assistants in the people's courts are responsible for reviewing case materials, drafting legal documents and other trial support matters under the guidance of judges. A judge's assistant who meets the requirements for appointment as a judge may be appointed as a judge after selection in accordance with the procedures for appointment and removal of judges.' This provision can be interpreted as follows: Firstly, a judge's assistant is a judge's assistant 'of the people's court', a public official with a specific position and specific duties in the people's court, and not a 'judge's assistant' as a law clerk in the US. Secondly, the duties of a judge's assistant are prescribed by law, including the review of case materials, drafting of legal documents and other ancillary matters, although these duties should be performed 'under the direction of the judge'. Thirdly, a judge's assistant is a reserve judge candidate. The judges' assistants are reserve candidates for appointment as judges, and those who 'meet the requirements for appointment as judges' may become judges after being selected and appointed by judges.

Logically reading, the statutory role of the judge's assistant may be further defined: firstly, although not a judge, the judge's assistant is also a trial professional, otherwise, how could he or she take on such a central role as drafting legal documents? If it is a matter of personal competence, why is it that clerks, who are also responsible for trial support (Article 49), do not enjoy such a statutory opportunity? Secondly, the duties of a judge's assistant are clearly defined by law, not arbitrarily assigned by a judge, and a judge's assistant cannot exceed his or her own statutory duties, or even act in the place of a judge; thirdly, the law clearly defines the relatively independent duties of a judge's assistant, so it is logical that in order for a judge's assistant to perform his or her statutory duties, the law should also clearly define his or her corresponding powers and rights, as well as the manner in which his or her powers are exercised and the corresponding responsibilities.

Thirdly, the law clearly stipulates the relative independence of judges' assistants, so it is logical that in order to perform their statutory duties, the law should also clearly stipulate their respective powers and rights, as well as the manner in which their powers are exercised and their corresponding responsibilities, rather than being as vague and general as 'under the direction of a judge'.

V. Some Reflections on the Roles of Auxiliary Judiciary and the Logic Base of Judiciary Classification

From a comparative perspective, the roles of auxiliary judiciary in different jurisdictions largely depend on the definition of 'judge' that is either limited to 'judges in post' or broken through to include judges with limited authority. China has just illustrated this issue by transferring 'assistant judge' (as junior judge) to judge assistant (auxiliary judiciary) but this is resulting in a worse allocation of judicial power among the judicial classes.

Generally, the concept of 'judicial power' has never been packaged and cannot be dismantled. On the contrary, the logical base of judiciary classification is the possibility of classification and sharing of judicial power. The specific methods are diverse against multiple judicial systems where there are diverse ways to allocate powers for the sake of trial patterns, judicial structures, and legal cultures, etc. And all these factors influence or even decide the models of the cases, the types of procedures, and accordingly classification of judiciary personnel.

A. The Ways of Judiciary Classification According to a Relative Logic Bases

One way of judiciary classification is by case categories based on various criteria. For example, to type the cases and proceedings by value orientation. (1) Only for money or with multiple values, only private interests or related to the third or public interests? Thus separate the proceedings into small claims (cf. peace justice in the UK) from ordinary proceedings, and the judges with limited judicial power may be entitled to decide these cases in completely independent power. In other words, we may say, that junior judges like assistant judges or some auxiliary judiciary like judge assistants exercise 'full power' to decide such types of cases with no monitoring, supervision or 'under the judge's guidance'. The same logic is also sound under the criteria two, (2) to type a proceeding by 'dispute or non-contest'? The type of non-contest proceedings are disposed by the clerks (auxiliary judiciary) in Japan, but by the full power judges in China – the same ways under the laws before and after the reform of 'judiciary classification'.

There are other criteria to type the case categories to allocate judicial power to the auxiliary judiciary (as named in some jurisdictions) or junior judges (as named in some other jurisdictions). For example, a Chinese judge assistant or assistant judge may be authorised to dispose independently of such proceeding of (1) Payment Order (cf. Dunning Procedure in Germany) that is only for the money claims with no or minor contest/dispute; (2) Mediation of dispute lawsuits and if failed, transferring to the judges to exercise trial power (cf. practice in some local courts in China).

B. Judiciary Classification Based on Case Categories

The second way of judiciary classification is based on issue categories, where the auxiliary judiciary exercises limited power in ordinary cases under the supervision of a full-power judge. This is more complicated and less justified. Hereafter some logic seems to be reasonable to be based.

Criterion 1: by the nature of the objective to be dealt with, for example, 'merits' or 'formal matter', or substantive matter or procedural matter? Criterion 2: by nature of the power to be excised, the power of management or power of decision? Criterion 3: by combining fact-finding, law application and reading, claim grant or dismiss? Criterion 4: by conclusion or reasoning in draft judgment (as a duty of a judge assistant provided in the OLC). When considering issue categories, some important factors or tests should be taken into account, A1, anticipatable and public authorisation (by legislation and legal procedure); A2, transparency of the specific matters and shared power; A3, procedure for checking/examining and challenging by the related litigants; A4, effect of and accountability for the alternative 'decisions' or behaviours; A5, relief for the alternative decisions or behaviours not meeting A3 and/or A4.

VI. Conclusion

As an achievement of the reform of the judiciary classification, the OLC, in addition to stipulating the judicial competence and duties of judges, confers limited judicial duties on judges' assistants. Given the heavy reliance on the professionalism and ethical behaviour of judges' assistants in relation to these duties and competencies, the professionalisation of judges' assistants forms an important part of the professionalisation of the judiciary. In particular, the law has explicitly delegated some of the judicial duties to judges' assistants, the powers, norms of conduct and responsibilities required for the performance of these duties should also be shared by the assistants, otherwise the current state of disorder will emerge. However, the Judges Law excludes such an important judiciary role who shares part of the judicial power by a narrow definition of 'judge' on the one hand, and, some ideas of the Law of Judicial Assistants have never entered the legislator's mind, on the other hand. Thus the role and behaviours as well as rights and responsibilities of the judges' assistants will remain in a vacuum for a long time. Unless further reforms stress a logical base of the personnel classification by separating cases and typing procedures in a reasonable way, the judiciary classification can never succeed only by changing a name from 'assistant judge' to 'judge assistant' or by transferring their class from junior judges to auxiliary. The span from a status of 'associate judge' to 'judge assistant' involves a reconfiguration of the core position, authority and responsibility of trial power, and will therefore face more complex issues and more serious challenges than the previous round.

In addition, the roles and duties of judges and other adjudicator should be regulated by the OLC other than the JL, in terms of the scope of legal regulation in the Chinese legal system. This is because the duties of judges are not the duties of individual judges, but rather the duties of judges in a specific trial organisation structure. To have the law of judges regulate the duties of judges would, on the one hand, partially duplicate the content of the Organic Law of Courts and, on the other hand, not exhaust the duties of judges in different organisational structures and the specific structure of competence on which they are based, as well as the relationship between the allocation of competence and duties of the relevant subjects. Even if the OLC explicitly provides that 'the duties, management and protection of judges shall be in accordance with the provisions of the Law of the People's Republic of China of Judges', it can at most solve the problem of duplication of content, but not the problem of the specific context of judges' duties and the matching of competences.

PART II

Court Experts

10

Expert Knowledge: Closer to the Centre than to the Periphery

EDUARDO OTEIZA

I. Knowledge and Decision

To assume that the person responsible for assessing the effective occurrence of an event and its scope in judicial proceedings is a professional or lay judge,[1] overlooks the need for specialised expertise to delve into the technical and scientific complexities crucial for resolving such issues. This is a great challenge for our procedural culture. The speed of development in the different areas of technology compounded by scientific advances is such that no one is capable of keeping pace with the expertise and knowledge required to cover all the relevant details of judicial cases when these contain facts that are difficult to unravel. No judge can fully master the knowledge necessary to understand the technical and scientific matters of the complex litigation of our times.

To entertain the idea that those entrusted with managing and resolving conflicts within the sphere of state power lack the conceptual tools to fully grasp the intricacies of the conflict raises concerns that, for numerous reasons, are best left unexplored. Exposing this weakness to some extent undermines confidence in the capacity of state justice and, fundamentally, in its legitimacy. The idea that knowledge is restricted, typical for a person with a general education in areas of law but whose knowledge of other spheres is limited, undermines the symbol of a judge capable of correctly weighing up all the facts to be evaluated during the proceedings and at the moment of passing sentence. Hence the reason for Damaška's[2] question:

> But is the average trial judge not similarly baffled by complex mathematics and perplexed by arcane scientific insights? Modern science increasingly confronts all

[1] I will use the expression judge to talk about male and female judges, also understanding, with this expression, those who manage and decide judicial cases on behalf of the state, whether or not they have legal training.

[2] RM Damaška, *Evidence Law Adrift* (New Haven, Yale University Press, 1997) 33.

generalist adjudicators – whether legally trained or not – with information that only experts have no difficulty understanding.

The tension between the impossibility of knowing everything and the legal restriction weighing on the judge to delegate the attribution of adjudication is inescapable.

Tackling this dilemma means resolving a considerable number of issues and adopting a strategy involving procedural design whose aim is to overcome it. This leads to speculation about the difficulties intrinsic to the relationship between the person possessing that specific knowledge and the one in control of the processes that lead certain conclusions to be drawn about the facts. The notion of centre (a body that makes decisions during and at the end of the procedural debate) and periphery (those participating in the judicial structure or who are incorporated into the process by the judge's or the parties' choice), was central to our debates during the seminar on *Public and Private Justice: Dispute Resolution in Modern Societies* (Dubrovnik, May 2023). This requires us to question the essential or marginal place that can be assigned to experts, as well as the consequences of the role assigned in the process. The title of our meeting was *The Heroes of Judicial Periphery Court Experts, Court Clerks and other Actors in the Shadow* and it focused on the degree of influence that certain participants have on the response provided by justice. Among these is the expert, a prominent figure, since they contribute significantly to explaining what happened. The usual tendency to place the expert in orbit around the judge however affects the design of the rules implemented to regulate their participation.

The Latin *expertus* refers to someone with special knowledge on a specific subject, linked to his experience in a singular area that is thus not part of the judge's training, a 'typically average man from a cultural point of view', according to Taruffo.[3] Denti maintained that the real fundamental problem of scientificity occurs when the judge, in order to appreciate the evidence, must use notions that transcend the knowledge of an average person.[4] The impact of the expert's knowledge prompted Stein to state that the judge makes the expert the co-recipient of the evidence for two reasons. The first is to convert the expert's technical explanation into the judge's own perception. The second is to be able to control, inasmuch as is possible, the expert opinion that the judge must evaluate.[5] It is interesting to note that Stein says 'inasmuch as is possible' since nothing can guarantee that the judge possesses the ability to understand issues in their correct dimension when these

[3] M Taruffo, 'La prova dei fatti giuridici: nozioni generali', in *La prueba de los hechos* (Bloomington, Trotta Publishing House, 1992), translated into Spanish by Jordi Ferrer Beltran, 2002, 333 et seq.

[4] V Denti, *Cientificidad de la prueba y libre valoración del juzgador*, general report made at the 1st World Congress of the International Association of Procedural Law, published in the Boletín Mexicano de Derecho Procesal, Nueva Serie, Year V, Number 13-14, UNAM, 1972, 9. It may also be consulted at revistas.juridicas.unam.mx/index.php/derecho-comparado/article/view/890/1150.

[5] F Stein, *Das private Wissen des Richters Untersuchungen z. Beweisrecht beider Prozesse* (1893). Spanish translation by A de la Oliva, *El conocimiento privado del juez* (Madrid, Centro de Estudios Ramón Areces, 1990) 62.

exceed his training. Using a similar line of reasoning, Tapper[6] considers that the law recognizes that, with respect to matters requiring special knowledge or skills, judges and juries are not necessarily qualified to draw true inferences from the facts stated. Jolowicz agrees with respect to this kind of limitation by noting that:

> It is axiomatic that no judge is omniscient. We do not – and we cannot – in reality demand of a judge a universal knowledge even of the rules of law in force in his jurisdiction … As regards the facts, since we cannot demand of the judge that they have knowledge of every branch of science, of every art and of the mysteries of every profession, we cannot demand either that they resolve questions of fact requiring such knowledge unless they have help from suitable qualified experts.[7]

The European Court of Human Rights followed suit when it held in *CB v. Austria*,[8] that 'an expert in general assists in solving a question or problem raised in the proceedings that a judge is unable to solve by him or herself'. This is inexorably linked to Damaška's observation that:[9]

> If justice were to shut the door to newly emerging methods and instruments likely to mushroom in this century, forensic fact-finding would soon become vulnerable to charges of exhibiting quasi-Luddite attitudes and being obscurantist. And when the mind-set favoring the use of science and technology establishes itself in the administration of justice, an increasing number of rules are likely to appear requiring expert corroboration of ordinary witness testimony, despite the likely encroachments of these rules on the adjudicators' legally unconstrained evaluation of evidence. In other words, the number of cases is likely to decrease in which judges will be able to find facts solely on their subjective or untutored assessment of evidence.

The mythical know-it-all judge is a serious temptation for justice administration systems, as he tends to sweep uncertainties aside. This is a convenient chimera, which silences the epistemological weaknesses of both judge and procedural design. Disguising systemic vulnerability seems to be intrinsic to the veil of security intended to safeguard the power to resolve disputes fairly. Underestimating these weaknesses explains why the lack of capacity to understand the scope of certain situations has been relegated to the back burner, particularly when there is no other remedy other than to resort to knowledge that the judge lacks. This situation is compounded by the fact that obtaining help from someone with knowledge of an area for which the judge lacks equivalent training is tantamount to recognising a weakness. This is undeniably irksome for a state power whose purpose is to seek a decision that is as correct as possible.

It should be added that incorporating expert knowledge in the form of an assistant to the judge also entails economic costs that the institution would prefer

[6] C Tapper, & R Cross, *Cross and Tapper on evidence*, 12th edn (Oxford, Oxford University Press, 2010) 530.

[7] JA Jolowicz, *On civil procedure* (Cambridge, Cambridge University Press, 2000) 225.

[8] 30465/06, 4 April 2013, § 40, hudoc.echr.coe.int/eng#{%22itemid%22:[%22001-118044%22].

[9] M Damaška, *Evaluation of Evidence: Pre-modern and Modern Approaches* (Cambridge, Cambridge University Press, 2018) 146.

to avoid, given the meagre contents of public coffers. On the contrary, requiring those seeking access to justice to cover the costs of expert knowledge can represent an effective barrier to due process as well as to equality of arms.

The scientific and technical conclusions contributed by experts to the proceedings are subject to the control of the parties and evaluated by the judge. At all events, the degree of error with respect to the facts to be proven can be difficult to determine and contrast, particularly when the judge lacks the training needed to fully understand them – and must turn to someone in a position to properly evaluate them. Taruffo[10] points out that traditionally, the judge has been considered a *peritum peritorum* and thus able to assess the expert's conclusions. However, this only makes sense in theory; in practice, the judge lacks the knowledge or training necessary to oversee an expert's work. Hence, the judge's free evaluation of expert evidence may contain an 'epistemic deference' to the expert and then the judgment may actually be determined by the expert. Although the expert does not have the power to decide on the scope of certain facts, the weight of their opinion may, in practice, be the key to resolving the substance of the issue. This is particularly the case when we find complex evidence for which a full understanding of the scientific or technical aspects is crucial, meaning that the provisions of accessibility, equality and neutrality are relevant. Thus, Taruffo sustains that, 'in any case, the product of expert evidence, persuasive as it may be, never binds the trier of fact: actually, expert evidence is always left to the discretionary evaluation of the court'.[11]

Another risk that must be avoided is falling into trial by experts. Lack of capacity can lead to an unsupported adherence to the experts' opinion, due to the judge's inability to assess their opinion and his lack of conceptual tools to investigate its fallibility. The Supreme Court of Canada, in the case *White Burgess Langille Inman v. Abbott and Haliburton*,[12] considered that:

> The point is to preserve trial by judge and jury, not devolve to trial by expert. There is a risk that the jury 'will be unable to make an effective and critical assessment of the evidence.' The trier of fact must be able to use its 'informed judgment', not simply decide on the basis of an 'act of faith' in the expert's opinion. The risk of 'attornment to the opinion of the expert' is also exacerbated by the fact that expert evidence is resistant to effective cross-examination by counsel who are not experts in that field.

Faced with these difficulties, it is interesting to note that efforts have largely focused on establishing the pros and cons between having an expert act as an assistant to the judge and the expert designated by the parties. Insufficient attention has been paid to the fact that both models, based on historical and cultural reasons, may be

[10] M Taruffo, 'Evidence', in M Cappelletti (ed), *International Encyclopedia of Comparative Law* (Mohr Siebvech, Martinus Nijhoff Publishers, Tubigen, Dordrecht, 2010) V. XVI, 47.

[11] Taruffo (n 10) 47.

[12] Criterion expressly followed by the Supreme Court of Canada in *White Burgess Langille Inman v. Abbott and Haliburton Co.*, 2015 SCC 23 (CanLII), scc-csc.lexum.com/scc-csc/scc-csc/en/item/15328/index.do 30 April 2015, not. 5, [18].

used by procedural systems if space is given to the principles of cooperation and proportionality. The focus should be on the neutrality of the expert, the quality of his work, and the greater access that both judges and parties have to knowledge that will enable reliable information to be incorporated into the proceedings.

II. Echoes of the Past

I will briefly refer to a medieval regulation from the Roman-canonical tradition that testifies to the judge's position in those times, as it reveals the guidelines provided for use when the judge encountered difficulties in appreciating the veracity of certain facts. I mention it because, although from a distant era when social customs were very different to today's, it incorporates the concept of expertise by assuming the difficulties of the judge in appreciating truthfulness and imposes the requirement for an oath to protect neutrality. It establishes that the judge must receive assistance and requires the expert to declare that they have no bearing on the interests discussed.

The amalgamation of Roman-canonical judicial procedures (*ordo iudiciarius*) promoted by the work of Bolognese jurists in the twelfth and thirteenth centuries[13] finds eloquent expression in the adoption by Alfonso X the Learned, King of Castile, of the *Book of Laws*, known as the *Seven Partidas*.[14] This text had a far-reaching influence on the Iberian Peninsula and Latin America with varying degrees of intensity, according to evolving relationships between kingdoms, empires and states from the twelfth to the nineteenth centuries. *Partida* III was the result of the pragmatism characterising this legislation that attempted to provide answers to the daily problems besetting what was variously a kingdom, an empire, and a nation-state.[15] With little margin for generality and abstraction, the text proffered guidelines on how to resolve one of the central issues of that period where social relations gave immense importance to the handwritten documentation of the events on which legal relations of various kinds were based. The fidelity and authorship of letters presented in a trial when their authenticity was questioned was a crucial issue in those times. Which of the parties should the judge believe when faced with documents (letters) whose authenticity was in dispute? Whom should he trust? What evidence prevailed in a situation when the issue at

[13] An original explanation of the importance of scholasticism in the evolution of law can be found in T Herzog, *A Short History of European Law, The last two and a half millennia* (Cambridge, Harvard University Press, 2018) ch 5.

[14] RC Van Caenegem, 'History of European Civil Procedure', in *International Encyclopedia of Comparative Law, Volume XVI, Civil Procedure* (Mohr, Tuebingen, 1973–2014) ch 2, 63 et seq.

[15] The Ordinances of the Court of Santo Domingo, of October 5, 1511, introduced the law of the Kingdom of Castile that would govern the Indies as common law. From that moment on, the *Partidas* take on radical importance, since they are part of Castilian law according to the Ordinance of Alcalá of 1348, and were reiterated in 1505 by the first Law of Toro. They had third preference for the application of laws, after royal legislation and municipal jurisdictions.

stake rested on the veracity of a document? What was a judge who lacked knowledge to do in order to determine whether a person's handwriting and signature were authentic? What knowledge should someone advising on the authorship of a document have? What should be required of the person entrusted with such a task? The answers are to be found in Law 118, Title XVIII, of *Partida* III.[16] Law 118 contains a detailed description of how a judge should act if the authenticity of a document was questioned. The standard established the guidelines to be followed in such circumstances and took as a starting point the judge's inability to verify whether the document was authentic. It pointed out that it was incumbent upon the judge to call men who, because of their knowledge (called *sahidores et entendudos*) could unravel (*escodriñar*) the meaning of the shapes and figures of the letters and their ensuing variations. It was not enough for them to examine the documents, as this had to be done correctly: 'well and faithfully'. Furthermore, they were required 'to not desist from saying the truth of what they understood, whether this be pursuant to a request, out of fear or love, or out of a lack of love, nor for any other reason whatsoever'.[17]

The premises of this legislation were the following: (i) the judge, if he lacked the knowledge essential to his task, had to seek the advice of people able to help him determine the veracity of the facts, (ii) those who collaborated with the judge had to be qualified for the task, (iii) the Advice had to be fair and without bias, and (iv) they were required to take an oath of impartiality. In summary, Law 118 tried to strike a balance between the judge's ignorance and the search for qualified experts to assist him after swearing to their impartiality in the matter.

This rule provides the main features of a procedural scheme that conceived of the expert as an assistant to the judge, taking part in the proceedings to alleviate the difficulties arising from the lack of knowledge that would enable the judge to determine the truth of a fact. It is an example that shows the influence of the relationship between expert and judge on continental European and Latin American

[16] The 1807 edition of *Partida* III can be consulted at www.boe.es/biblioteca_juridica/publicacion.php?id=PUB-LH-2021-217.

[17] LAW CXVIII … 'Qué dehe facer el judgador quando alguna de las partes quiliere duechar la carta que mm.stran en juicio contra él, diciendo que la letra de aquella carta non fue escripta por mano de aquel cuyo nombre está escripto en ella … debe el judgador tomar amas las cartas, et haber homes sahidores et entendudos consigo que sepan bien conoscer et entender las formas, et las fegnras de las letras et los variamientos dellas, et débeles facer jurar que esto caten et escodriñen bien et lealmente, et que non dexen de decir verdat de lo que entendieren por ruego, nin por miedo, nin por amor, nin por desamor nin por otra razon ninguna'. See *Las siete partidas del Rey Don Alfonso el Sabio, cotejadas con varios códices antiguos por la Real Academia de la Historia*, 2nd vol. Madrid. Order and expenses of S.M. Imprenta Real, Madrid, 1807, 2nd vol, 629. Available at: www.cervantesvirtual.com/obra-visor/las-siete-partidas-del-rey-don-alfonso-el-sabio-cotejadas-con-varios-codices-antiguos-por-la-real-academia-of-history-volume-2-partida-second-and-third--0/html/01f12004-82b2-11df-acc7-002185ce6064.htm. This is the facsimile edition of the Royal Printing Press of 1807, made under the validity of the Old Regime, a year before its collapse due to the crisis arising from the Aranjuez events and the Napoleonic invasion. With the restoration of absolutism, in 1818, Fernando VII declared this to be the only official version.

procedural culture. It is also a historical testimony revealing the deeply rooted view that the expert witness is there to assist the judge.[18]

III. Is the Expert Witness an Assistant to the Judge? How do they Interact with the Parties?

There are different objectives and options governing the rules used by a system to incorporate the information provided by a third party to the proceedings, which determines the effective occurrence of an event as well as the scope that should be assigned to these rules when resolving a conflict. These are weighed up alongside social conceptions about the role of the judge and that of the parties during the course of judicial proceedings. However, the simplicity of the generalisation that merely separates those proceedings under the control of the judge from those dependent on the activity of the parties, is not enough to understand the reasons why certain normative options and related practices were adopted and upheld. The range of nuances and the variety of responses to this challenge make it clear that it is not a case of some versus others; the divisions between one model and another merely provide a superficial view of the characteristics of a system with a past on both sides of the English Channel. However, it presents deficiencies when attempting to explain the various phenomena whose evolution has placed the United States at a distance from that geographical and cultural milestone in terms of the original abstract positioning.

As Damaška recalls,[19] the dichotomy distinguishing a process that required the impulse of one party to get going (*processus per accusationem*), from one that could commence in his absence (*processus per inquisitionem*), acquired various technical meanings. In fact, it has been used to express the contrast between Anglo-American and continental European justice. Seen from a perspective based on a significant degree of abstraction, the 'adversarial' procedural model arises from a dispute that develops as the compromise between two 'adversaries' before a passive judge, whose primary duty is to adjudicate. The 'non-adversarial' model privileges the judge's control over the development of proceedings. In the first model, the 'adversaries' take charge of the judicial activity, whereas in the second, most of the actions are performed by the officials in charge of administering justice, without

[18] According to D Dwyer, *The Judicial Assessment of Expert Evidence* (Cambridge, Cambridge University Press, 2009), the earliest history of the use of the parties' expert witness relates to the ecclesiastical courts in 1570 to help measure the amount of claims and the first civil cases a century later (246). Regarding the use of expert witnesses appointed by the court, there are very few antecedents before the 19th century. The first precedent was the use of translators of the meaning of Latin terms to help the judge specify their meaning (269). A Precedent Book from circa 1575 and a Formulary from circa 1630 refer to such inspections, which were to result in written reports.

[19] RM Damaška, *The Faces of Justice and State Authority. A Comparative Approach to the Legal Process* (New Haven, Yale University Press, 1995) 3 et seq.

preventing either strategy from responding to the rivalry and antagonism between the 'adversaries'. The basic meaning of this opposition provides some insight into visions that are deeply rooted in the traditions and culture underlying procedural regulations and the conceptualisation of their institutes.

Damaška, among other categorisations, separates procedural systems into hierarchical and coordinated ones. His analysis is more rounded than an observance of the simple difference based on the judge's powers, commonly used to differentiate the models known as 'civil law and common law'. Among the various implications of the hierarchical model of civil process, Damaška appeals to the idea of the exclusivity of public action. He says it is not surprising that private parties rarely call in expert witnesses, even when normatively entitled to do so. '"Experts" are treated as judicial assistants, and it seems normal that they be appointed by the judge, preferably from among persons accustomed to bureaucratic court routine – hence, Continental "permanent" or professional court experts.'[20] The expert witness forms part of the structure that the judge relies on for his rulings as it helps him to understand issues for which he was not prepared by his legal education.

The incorporation of expert knowledge in civil law systems may come from the judicial organisation itself, if it has its own corpus of experts, or from lists of experts drawn up to help the judge with the selection process. The first option presents the difficulty of the costs associated with running an internal bureaucracy financed by the state, made up of a growing number of spheres of technical knowledge required to assist the judge. The second option, although it makes selection easier, requires an exhaustive examination of suitability and control over time, which is not easy to implement and whose practice exhibits shortcomings in a good number of jurisdictions. The problem lies in the inconvenience of supervising the suitability of experts with sufficient regularity, which is a serious practical obstacle. The mere registration and its associated controls are a relative guarantee of an expert's essential suitability.

The cost issue and the organisational difficulties involved in selecting judicial experts have prompted a search for other options that would enable the necessary special knowledge to be incorporated. As an alternative, drawing up lists of professionals whose responsibility is certified by the state itself and their random selection has the disadvantage of presenting an imperfect form of control of reliability. This is compounded by the fact that such experts have scant incentives for intervening in cases that do not offer a significant economic incentive.

Although the difficulties regarding the official option and the list option are problems to be solved, the adoption of party expert witnesses as a general way of adding expert knowledge produces two negative consequences. On the one hand, it fosters suspicion as to their partiality of origin and, on the other, there are problems of access to justice when one of the parties lacks the means to be assisted by an expert.

[20] ibid 54.

When the participation of an expert depends on the decision of one party, it raises doubts about his neutrality. There is no reliable information about the reasons for the selection or about the various conditions implicit in the decision to propose a specific individual. In any case, it is reasonable to assume, at least, that the party will not propose any experts who could jeopardise their case during proceedings. It could be understood that their indifference with respect to the interests at stake is only relative and weak. The decision to choose a given expert arises from the need to corroborate a defensive position. This leads to the situation whereby it may be thought that there is a possible bias of the expert in favour of one of the parties. Furthermore, the party expert needs to overcome the bias that the proponent may expect from him. Vázquez Rojas[21] calls this initial situation 'structural partiality' because of the relationship with the party hiring the expert, as otherwise, the party would not have proposed said expert to support his claims. Haack points out[22] that expert witnesses are unlikely to voluntarily provide information that could be detrimental to whoever hired them, even if this information were useful to the judge. The Woolf Report[23] contains a forceful statement regarding the party's selection of the expert. It says that, 'There is widespread agreement with the criticisms I made in the interim report of the way in which expert evidence is used at present, especially the point that experts sometimes take on the role of partisan advocates instead of neutral fact finders or opinion givers.'

Additionally, the cost of hiring an expert can represent a serious financial obstacle. The expense of alleviating the judge's specific lack of knowledge can become a barrier to access to justice. In societies where equality is a mere formality and the vulnerability of broad sectors of the population is widespread, addressing the problem of the cost of expert knowledge should be a priority. The notion of equality of arms is called into question when the parties face difficulties in contracting the assistance of those who must contribute their knowledge in order to clarify the facts.

The question about whether the expert is an assistant to the judge cannot be answered assertively without clarifying that his contribution also benefits the parties. The expert helps the judge understand a situation for which he or she lacks sufficient knowledge, and helps the parties when the procedural model is able to strike a fair balance with the notion of disagreement. The two most influential procedural systems have a strong inclination towards contention, antagonism, competition, rivalry, enmity, opposition, competition, rivalry, enmity, and opposition. Terms are all used to underline the logic of the confrontation. The use of the

[21] C Vázquez Rojas, *De la prueba científica a la prueba pericial* (Madrid, Marcial Pons, 2015) 72 et seq. See also C Vázquez Rojas, 'La imparcialidad pericial y otras cuestiones afines. Confiabilidad, desacuerdos y sesgos de los expertos' (2018) 48 *Isonomía* 69–107.

[22] S Haack, 'The Expert Witness: Lessons from the U.S. Experience, Humana Mente' (2015) 28 *Journal of Philosophical Studies* 45.

[23] HK Woolf, *Access to Justice. Final Report* (Lord Chancellor's Department, 1996) 137.

word 'adversary' denotes a recurring feature of these systems. It qualifies as 'adversaries' those who seek an answer to the lack of agreement on how a situation in which the positions of the parties differ should be legally resolved. The systems of 'civil law' respond to a similar logic of conflict, despite assigning different powers to the judge. The use of the term 'non-adversarial' to refer to the process of 'civil law' is not particularly precise, as it only purports to indicate that the judge has a greater role reserved for him, one of mythical proportions. However, this is more correct than the inquisitorial proceedings reminiscent of the medieval inquisition of the twelfth century designed to combat heresy. These have no relationship at all with the civil proceedings in use from the eighteenth century onwards, a product of the Enlightenment, in many of which the judge is as passive as he is in 'adversarial' proceedings.

These views about confrontation as the main paradigm of proceedings clash with the social transformations of recent decades, including the tendency towards horizontality and the desire to achieve sustainable human development in conditions of greater equality. There is greater emphasis placed on the virtues of open dialogue as an essential means of reaching individual and collective consensus, and greater attention to cooperative ideals. The phenomenon of 'cross-fertilisation' has arisen, due to greater access to information on the advantages and disadvantages of institutional arrangements, as well as the emergence of virtuality and its effects on the administration of human resources and product assets on a global scale. There is an increasing demand for speed, efficiency, and expediency, and the demand for the adequate administration of funds received by justice and new perceptions of its role as a venue for the discussion of collective conflicts. These are all factors that, added to the permeability of the diffuse borders between the public and private, constitute a strong stimulus to abandon the stigmatising notion of struggle or confrontation as the great backdrop to judicial proceedings.

In contemporary democratic states, civil process must foster cooperation between free and equal parties. The idea of collaboration takes on a moderating role between availability, equality and the exercise of state authority. It is thus wrong to start from the standpoint of irreducible rivalry between the parties. Although they may strive for different solutions, they are still bound by a framework that places emphasis on loyalty, good faith and cooperation. If a party proposes a specific solution for the case, this does not justify any subsequent lack of collaboration to achieve the correct resolution of the dispute. It is largely about reconciling the public sphere where rights are determined, with the interests of the parties, without creating an unfounded stereotype of rivalry. Procedural designs have begun to give greater importance to the principle of collaboration between the parties and the judge, an option that endows the organisation of the different procedural steps with greater flexibility. This, added to the principle of proportionality that involves examining and justifying the material, economic and time efforts required by judicial proceedings, is bringing about a radical change compared to systems historically considered expressions of disparate cultures. These changes and crossovers make it easier to choose expert witnesses from an efficient combination of the experts suggested by the parties and those selected by the judge.

IV. Divergences and Convergences

The conflict that judges must address presents varying degrees of complexity. They need to interact with the parties in straightforward cases as well as in more complex ones where specialised knowledge is necessary to solve specific problems. It is true that there have always been issues that went beyond a judge's expertise, but it is also true that today's society is characterised by the value of knowledge, which has become a determining factor in human relationships.[24] The guidelines for including knowledge must be both secure and flexible, since there is a risk of issuing incorrect legal decisions because the facts are either misunderstood or incorrectly weighed up. The historical and cultural reasons for this cannot be more fully gone into here. However, there are common denominators that can help us identify basic components of the public policy chosen for regulating the integration of expert knowledge.

The approach I use mainly takes the role assigned to the expert witness in national systems and the guidelines established for employing his or her opinion, as well as the inherent drawbacks and contradictions to this situation. The matrix of my methodology is connected to functionalism and contains notes that tie it to the notion of tradition. For instance, I will illustrate this by comparing the choices made by countries following civil law and common law systems, along with the variations presented by procedural regulations in countries of both traditions. The focus on Latin American countries, with their unique characteristics bridging both legal traditions without squarely belonging to either, highlights the inadequacy of a centrist or dominant perspective associated with the effects of colonisation. To this should be added the fact that levels of economic inequality are much higher. The reference to soft law projects that I will discuss in the next section allows us to observe that some dichotomies should be transcended.

In terms of the main lines, I will begin by taking four countries from Continental Europe: France, Germany, Italy and Spain, and four from Latin America: Uruguay, Argentina, Brazil and Colombia. The solutions they provide in their main guidelines present differences and similarities with the options taken by the United States and England, as I will show later. Once the key components of each system have been identified, which help us to identify these differences and similarities in certain solutions, I will compare these findings with the framework outlined by the principles of cooperation and proportionality. These serve

[24] See JL Mateo, *Sociedad del conocimiento*, ARBOR Ciencia, Pensamiento y Cultura, CLXXXII, 718 March-April (2006), 145–151, scholar.google.en/scholar_url?url=https://arbor.journals.csic.en/index.php/arbor/article/download/18/18Reference&hl=es&sa=X&ei=Kx_iZf34O8bKy9YPoOa0kAM&scisig=AFWwaeZbnHPvHw0_YUDn9wC-BAGz&oi = scholar.

as balancing factors in judicial activity, which are evident in some regulatory experiences and in projects proposing solutions that aim to reconcile disparities.

There is a tendency to label the expert as an assistant to the judge in several European and Latin American states, which is far from being a uniform trend.

In France, the expert witness acts as an assistant to the judge. In the *Code de procédure civile*, the expert (*technicien*) is chosen by the judge to illuminate him, whether through verifications, consultations or by drawing up a report, about a given fact.[25] The *technicien* is invested with his powers by the judge because of his special qualifications. Judges typically select experts from lists published by appellate courts or the *Cour de Cassation*, and they can only be appointed exceptionally if their name is not on these lists. In addition to being able to be challenged, the expert must fulfil his duty with *conscience, objectivité et impartialité*.[26] In referring to the use of a technician as a friendly method of conflict resolution, Article 1548 of the *Code de procédure civile* indicates that it is up to the technician, before accepting his mission, to reveal any circumstance that may affect his independence so that both parties may benefit from it.

In Germany, the expert is an advisor to the judge in charge of providing information derived from his special knowledge, as established by the *Zivilprozessordnung* (ZPO). The legal regulation on expert evidence refers to the rules governing testimonial evidence but also contains specific regulations that take into account the fact that an expert, according to the ZPO, is an assistant to the judge.[27] The choice of expert is up to the judge, unless the parties have come to a prior agreement, in which case the court must respect it. Regardless of this, the court has the power to reduce the number of experts, and even limit the choice to only one of those proposed jointly by the parties. At all events, this selection requires a prior hearing with the parties. The decisive question is to find the expert who really has sufficient expertise and experience to be able to carry out his task. To ensure a certain level of expertise, the preference is primarily for publicly-appointed and certified experts. These individuals have undergone a rigorous selection process and are subject to oversight by a public entity. They must take an oath with regard to their impartiality and ability to perform their activity according to their best knowledge and conscience.[28] The opinions presented by the parties are not considered evidence themselves; instead, they are specific aspects of their claims that the judge must assess carefully.[29] Expert opinions presented by the parties in German procedural culture are considered suspect and are generally not accepted as evidence of a certain fact.[30]

[25] Arts 233–234. See L Cadiet, *Code de Procédure Civile* (Paris, LexisNexis, 2023) 246–255.

[26] Art 237. A Jacquin, *L'impartialité objective de l'expert judiciaire et sa récusation*, 31 Gazette du Palais, 1 February 2003, 3–8.

[27] §§ 402–414 of the ZPO.

[28] § 410 ZPO.

[29] B Hess, & O Jauernig, *Zivilprozessrecht* (Verlag CH München, 2011), consulting the translation by ER Molés, *Manual de Derecho Procesal* (Mexico, Marcial Pons, 2015) 328–331.

[30] PL Murray, & R Stürner, *German Civil Justice* (Durham, Carolina Express, 2004) 280–290.

In Italy, the *Codice di Procedura Civile* establishes that, when necessary, the judge may be assisted by one or more *consulenti*, of particular technical competence, whenever necessary.[31] It also contemplates the participation of the *consulente tecnico di parte*.[32] Carpi and Taruffo[33] maintain that *la consulenza tecnica d'ufficcio* was incorporated into the scope of the *ausiliari del giudice*, as a functional, and sometimes substantially, jurisdictional activity. The notions of impartiality applicable to la *consulenza tecnica d'ufficcio* do not differ from those provided for the judge, and may be challenged.[34] The *consulenza tecnica d'ufficio*, in Ansanelli's opinion,[35] is characterised by a kind of regulatory duplicity. From a subjective point of view, the figure of the *consulente tecnico* is included among the judge's assistants. And precisely because of this position is featured as an auxiliary one, the *consulente tecnico* shares with the judge the assurance of impartiality, which stems from the rules governing reasons for abstention and disqualification. At a functional and dynamic level, the *consulenza tecnica d'ufficio* is framed in the context of evidentiary instruction, but is regulated separately from typical evidentiary methods. The choice of *consulente tecnico* must be made by the judge from the members on these special lists, and his reasons for doing so duly justified, after dispensing with those registered to perform the task. With respect to the *consulenza tecnica di parti*, Carpi and Taruffo understand that this does not constitute a means of proof but merely defensive allegations.[36]

In Spain, the *Ley de Enjuiciamiento Civil* (LEC) establishes that when suing or answering, the parties may provide the expert opinions that they deem necessary or convenient for the defence of their rights.[37] There is an exception to this duty whenever any of the parties has the right to free legal assistance, in which case, the expert is appointed by the court.[38] When issuing an opinion, each expert must swear to tell the truth and that he has acted and, where appropriate, will act with the greatest possible objectivity, taking into consideration both what may favour and what may cause harm to any of the parties. He is also required to state that he understands the criminal sanctions that could be incurred if he fails to fulfil his duty as an expert.[39] Furthermore, the opposing party has the

[31] Art 61.

[32] Art 201.

[33] F Carpi, & M Taruffo, *Commentario Breve al Codice di Procedura* (Padova, Wolters Kluwer CEDAM, 2023) 280–281.

[34] Art 148.

[35] V Ansanelli, 'El modelo italiano de la consulenza técnica d'ufficio', in J Picó i Junoy (ed), *La prueba pericial a examen propuestas de "lege ferenda"* (Barcelona, J.M. Bosch Editor, 2020) 241–254.

[36] Carpi & Taruffo (n 33). See also V Ansanelli, *La consulenza tecnica nel processo civile – Problemi e funzionalità* (Milan, Giuffrè, 2011) 157–202.

[37] Arts 265.4 and 336.1.

[38] Art 339, s 1. In s 339, the LEC also contemplates that the plaintiff or the defendant, although they do not have the benefit of this being free of charge, may request in their respective initial briefs that the judicial appointment of an expert be carried out, if they consider the issuance of an expert report convenient or necessary for their interests.

[39] Art 335, para 2.

right to mark a *tacha* against another party's expert if they consider, for example, that said expert has a direct interest in this or another similar matter.[40] Also, court-appointed experts may be disqualified,[41] providing a legal reason for dismissing a witness' statement in a lawsuit. The expression *tacha*[42] means lack or defect and derives from the French *tache* and from the Latin *tacca*, both referring to the idea of stain. The word *tacha* is also used by the LEC to question the reliability of a witness.[43] Picó i Junoy, shortly after the approval of the LEC, heavily criticised the regulation of expert evidence, arguing that it was one of the worst regulated matters as it gave one party full control over introducing expert opinions.[44] To which it should be noted that the exception to the expert witness based on an inability to afford legal fees is an inadequate solution as it does not take into account the challenges faced by large segments of the population who are required to hire an expert as part of proving certain facts. The regulation of the LEC has had an impact on procedural regulations in Latin America, as I will mention later.

Of the four countries taken as an example, only Spain chose to trust the expert proposed by the party and limit the judge's power to appoint him. The system chosen by Spain does not solve the issue of bias, nor does it alleviate the restrictions faced by individuals needing to access the system, as the mechanism of free justice does not mitigate these challenges.

In Uruguay, the General Process Code[45] (1989) provides for the appointment by the judge of a single expert, who may also, depending on the circumstances, request the opinion of institutes, academies, colleges, or other organisations whose speciality allows the analysis of the disputed facts. If the parties agree on the expert, the judge will appoint him or her except for well-founded reasons. The expert can be challenged for the same reasons as the judges.[46]

In Argentina, the Civil and Commercial Procedure Code (1967)[47] contemplates the appointment of an expert by the judge, who acts as his assistant, and can

[40] Art 343, 1.

[41] Arts 343, paras 1 and 124.

[42] J Corominas, & JA Pascual, *Diccionario Crítico etimológico castellano e hispánico*, (Editorial Gredos, 1983) T. V, 370.

[43] Art 377.

[44] In J Picó i Junoy, *La prueba pericial en el proceso civil español. Ley 1/2000, de Enjuiciamiento Civil* (Barcelona, J.M. Bosch Editor, 2003) 1. He explains that one of the confusions regarding the conceptualisation of expert activity stems from considering it evidence instead of treating it as an auxiliary mechanism for the judge (42–48). See also J Picó i Junoy, 'La dinámica de la prueba pericial', in AX Lluch (ed), *Tratado Pericial Judicial* (Madrid, Wolters Kluwer Spain, 2014) 79–153.

[45] Art 177, according to the reform of Law 19,990. See S Pereira Campos, *Código General del Proceso. Reformas de la Ley 19.990. Comentado y Anotado* (Montevideo, University of Montevideo, 2013) 262–265.

[46] Art 179. The original text of the Chilean Procedural Code is from 1902.

[47] I am referring to the Civil and Commercial Procedure Code of 1967 applied in cases processed before national and federal judges. Argentina is a federal country and each of the 24 provinces or jurisdictions has the power to dictate its own code. However, there are no major differences between the Codes of the different provinces in expert matters. See R Berizonce, & E Oteiza, 'Argentina Civil Procedure', in *International Encyclopaedia of Laws series* (The Netherlands, Kluwer Law International B.B., 2021) 174–176.

be challenged for the same reasons as him.[48] Although the legislation establishes that even before the judge exercises the power to appoint the expert, the parties can propose him,[49] this never happens. The judge may request an opinion from universities, academies, corporations, institutes and public or private entities of a scientific or technical nature, when the expert opinion requires highly specialised operations or knowledge.[50] The Civil and Commercial Procedural Code Reform Bill presented by the Executive Branch in 2019, still pending consideration by Congress, upholds the role of the expert as an assistant to the judge. However, it incorporates the principles of cooperation and proportionality, which could lead to a radical change in the dynamics of expert evidence.[51]

In Brazil, the Civil Procedure Code (2015) contains a chapter on *Auxiliares da justiça*, which includes the figure of the expert. The judge appoints the expert,[52] but this authority is exercised when the parties fail to reach an agreement on who should conduct the expertise. The parties have the option to suggest technical assistants[53] who are free from any conflicts of interest or suspicion.[54] Additionally, an expert may be disqualified.[55] Experts are appointed by legally-qualified professionals and technical or scientific bodies on the register kept by the court. The judge relies on this register when choosing the expert. The register is drawn up by the courts, which are obliged to hold a public consultation, in addition to contacting universities and other qualified entities. They are also required to perform periodic evaluations of the experts included on the list to assess their professional training, updated knowledge and experience.[56]

The Brazilian Procedural Code (2015) differs from similar Latin American regulatory bodies by incorporating the principle of collaboration. This principle obliges all parties to cooperate with each other to achieve a fair and effective decision within a reasonable timeframe.[57]

[48] Arts 458 and 465.

[49] Art 462.

[50] Art 476.

[51] The draft Bill can be consulted at www.saij.gob.ar/anteproyecto-nuevo-codigo-procesal-civil-comercial-nacion-anteproyecto-nuevo-codigo-procesal-civil-comercial-nacion-nv21914-2019-07-01/123456789- 0abc-419-12ti-lpssedadevon. Arts 1 and 10. See the principles of the draft Bill in E Oteiza, 'Principios procesales' (2020) 1 *Revista de Derecho Procesal, Rubinzal-Culzoni* 27–40.

[52] Art 465.

[53] Art 471. Art 190 establishes that when the conflict is about rights that admit self-composition, it is lawful for the parties to stipulate modifications to the process to adjust it to the specificities of the causes and to agree on the burdens, powers and procedural duties before and during the process. See the regulation of expert evidence in Brazil, PH Santos Lucon, 'Prova pericial no CPC/2015' (2015) 267 *Revista de Processo* 212–223. One of the novelties of the new Brazilian Code of Civil Procedure is the simplified technical evidence in matters of minor complexity (Art 464, s 3°).

[54] Art 466.

[55] Art 467.

[56] Art 156.

[57] Art 6. G Marinoni, SC Arenhart, & D Mitidiero, *Curso de Processo Civil*, 8th edn, (Rio Del. Janeiro, 2023) vol I, 454–485, where they explain the scope of the principles of the Procedural Code and specifically the scope of the duty of cooperation. See also on the same topic C Scarpinella Bueno, *Curso Sistematizado de Direito Processual Civil*, 13th edn (Saraiva Jur, 2023) 98–102.

In Colombia, the General Code of Process (2012), although it gives experts the role of auxiliaries of justice,[58] establishes that their opinions may be provided by the parties when filing a lawsuit.[59] The opinion provided by a party-hired expert must be issued by an authorised professional able to confirm their suitability for the task. They must also declare that they have no impediments preventing them from providing the opinion. If the judge deems it necessary, at the request of the opposing party the expert may be summoned to a hearing to allow for the contradiction of their opinion.[60] The judge possesses the authority to appoint an expert, but the circumstances under which this can occur are not specified, except in cases involving *in forma pauperis*.[61] The Code allows for legal aid to be provided to individuals who cannot afford their legal expenses. This assistance is granted when the costs of the proceedings would jeopardise the party's ability to cover their basic needs.[62] As a result, those who receive this benefit are not required to pay the fees of judicial assistants.[63] Colombia is known for being one of the most unequal countries in Latin America. This inequality is juxtaposed with regulations encouraging the use of expert witnesses, which can affect people's access to justice.[64] Impartiality is safeguarded through various measures, including the expert's oath and the signing of the opinion. By signing, the expert attests that the opinion has been provided independently and with genuine conviction.[65] The parties are also required to refrain from providing opinions rendered by individuals who meet any of the disqualification criteria established for judges.[66] The explanatory memorandum of the Colombian Procedural Code merely says that the party's opinion and the possibility of being able to discuss this with the party's expert in a hearing will improve its reliability.

Including experts with specific scientific and technical training, as outlined by the Colombian Procedural Code, reflects a trend seen in numerous countries

[58] According to Art 48.2 for the appointment of experts, the parties and the judge may resort to specialised institutions, public or private, or to professionals with recognised experience and suitability. This rule characterises experts as auxiliaries of justice.

[59] Arts 82.6 and 227. See DM Ramírez Carvajal, *La prueba en el proceso. Una aventura intelectual* (Librería Jurídica Sánchez, 2017) 161–169.

[60] Art 228.

[61] Art 229.2.

[62] Art 151.

[63] Art 154.

[64] According to the World Bank report for 2021, income inequality in Colombia is the highest among all countries in the Organization for Economic Cooperation and Development (OECD) and the second highest among 18 countries in Latin America and the Caribbean (LAC). The Gini coefficient of household income (a standard measure of inequality) reached 0.53 in 2019, after paying taxes and receiving transfers. For comparison, the Gini coefficient of the most equitable OECD country, the Slovak Republic, was 0.24. The income of the richest 10% of Colombians is eleven times greater than that of the poorest 10%. Again, for comparison, in the Slovak Republic, the richest 10% of the population earn three times more than the poorest 10%. See p. 11 of the report documents1.worldbank.org/curated/en/602591635220506529/pdf/Main-Report.pdf.

[65] Art 226.

[66] Art 235.

across South and Central America.[67] However, this approach can have an impact on impartiality and, in contexts of significant inequality, may severely limit access to justice.

In the nineteenth and twentieth centuries, the party-appointed expert witness was the dominant model in Anglo-American courts. Both the right of 'adversaries' to identify and present evidence favourable to their case, and the establishment of the pre-trial phase where they agreed on how the trial would be developed, were two of the reasons why the party-appointed expert was seen as essential.

In the United States, the expert witness is normally presented by the party. The significant reliance of US courts on the lawyers involved in the case for obtaining evidence, along with the considerable control granted to judges over the proceedings, has greatly influenced the rules governing expert evidence in US courts. This influence is compounded by the institution of the jury, which contributes to the unique configuration of the US judicial process. Courts and legislators have tried to implement measures to filter out excessively biased and inadequately grounded expert evidence. However, in doing so, they have mostly delegated control over expert evidence to lawyers rather than judges. Lawyers do not want to give up their control, and judges, in general terms, are satisfied with the way things are.

The United States has a federal court system, and each of the states has its own state court system. Federal courts are governed by the Federal Rules of Evidence (FRE). Almost all states regulate proceedings that in most cases are directly modelled on federal regulations. According to the FRE, the motion to appoint

[67] Examples of the adoption of the expert's part are: (i) The Civil Procedure Code of Honduras (2007) establishes that the expert evidence will be proposed by the parties, who may choose between contributing to the process the opinion of a private expert who has the corresponding knowledge or requesting that an opinion be issued by an official expert appointed by the court (Art 315.2). Each party has the right to provide the opinion of a private expert when suing or answering the claim (Arts 317 and 318). In any case, the party that renounces or cannot avail itself of a private expert opinion may request an official expert opinion in their claim or response (Art 321). The party that enjoys the right to free legal assistance does not have to provide the expert opinion with the claim or response, but only announce it for the purposes of the court appointment of an expert. The court will proceed to appoint an official expert, provided that it considers the requested expert opinion pertinent and useful (Art 322). (ii) The Civil and Commercial Procedural Code of El Salvador (2008), which provides that the parties presenting the claim will accompany the expert reports (Art 276.7 and 288). Each of the parties has the right to appoint its own expert and to prepare the corresponding opinion privately, accompanied by their respective allegations (Art 377). When the party seeks the appointment of a judicial expert and the urgency of the case requires it, they must indicate as much in the corresponding initial appeal document. This includes an identification of the object of the evidence and the court, if it is considered that this evidence is relevant and useful, leading to the appointment of the expert regardless of which of the parties had requested the judicial expertise (Art 381). (iii) The General Organic Code of the Process of Ecuador (2015) establishes that expert reports are accompanied by the claim (Art 142.7) and requires the party expert to perform their work with objectivity and impartiality (Art 223). In the event of a contradiction between the oral reports of the party experts and the judge places the conclusions of the expert reports into question, he may order a new expert report at the hearing, for which an expert will be drawn from among those accredited by the Council of the Judiciary (Art 226).

an 'expert witness' can be at the request of the parties or the judge.[68] The second alternative is very little used.

The partisan nature of expert evidence in the United States has long been recognised and deplored;[69] it is frequently reported that trials become 'battles of experts', where one biased invocation of expertise counterattacks another. According to Damaška:[70]

> … with expert witnesses, paid by the litigants, this alignment has additional and more palpable reasons to occur. But the danger of a partisan slant in testimony is most manifest when lawyers prepare witnesses, instructing them how to sound more credible, or by employing some other 'coaching' method. Under these circumstances, the spontaneity of testimony can entirely disappear – at least from direct examinations. The interrogation process begins to resemble theater.

Taruffo indicates that the figure of the expert witness emerges as a 'hired gun' ready to serve the party who contracted them.[71] In a controversial article that highlighted the lack of impartiality of the experts, Langbein[72] emphasised that 'at the American trial bar, those of us who serve as expert witnesses are known as "saxophones". This is a revealing term, as slang often is. The idea is that the lawyer plays the tune, handling the expert as he would a musical instrument, on which the lawyer sounds the desired notes.'[73] Langbein's position sparked significant controversy, as he maintained that the German civil process had advantages over its American counterpart[74] which, as Chase points out,[75] can lead to a simplification lacking the analysis of the cultural bases underpinning each society. Beyond the imprecision and error of underscoring the advantages of one system over the other, the issue of bias among expert witnesses in the American system raises valid concerns that merit consideration.

A significant development occurred in the United Kingdom following Lord Woolf's reports, which served as the direct precursor to the Civil Procedural Rules (CPR) of 1998. In the chapter dedicated to expert evidence in his *Access to Justice. Final report*,[76] Woolf was adamant that:

> A large litigation support industry, generating a multi-million pound fee income, has grown up among professions such as accountants, architects and others, and new

[68] FRE, 706.

[69] See the background to the use of the expert witness in the United States and its scope. SR Gross, 'Expert Evidence' [1991] *Wisconsin Law Review* 1113–1232.

[70] RM Damaška, *Evidence Law Adrift* (New Haven, Yale University Press, 1997) 98.

[71] Taruffo (n 10) 44.

[72] JH Langbein, 'The German Advantage in Civil Procedure' (1985) 52 *University of Chicago Law Review* 823–866.

[73] ibid 835.

[74] Responses to Langbein's article: RJ Allen, S Köck K Riechenberg, & TD Rosen, 'The German Advantage in Civil Procedure: A Plea for More Details and Fewer Generalities in Comparative Scholarship' (1988) 82 *Northwestern University Law Review* 705, 1988, answered by Langbein in 'Trashing the German Advantage' (1988) 82(3) *Northwestern University Law Review*763–784.

[75] O Chase, 'Legal Processes and National Culture' (1997) 5 *Cardozo Journal of International and Comparative Law* 1–24.

[76] *Final Report to the Lord Chancellor on the civil justice system in England and Wales*, published for the Lord Chancellor's Department, 1996, see Section III, Chapter 13, Expert Evidence, 137–152.

> professions have developed, such as accident reconstruction and care experts. This goes against all principles of proportionality and access to justice … its most damaging effect is that it has created an ethos of what is acceptable which has in turn filtered down to smaller cases.

His conclusion is clear regarding the potential escalation of costs resulting from the uncontrolled use of expert witnesses hired by one of the parties. Woolf's discussion of the cascade effect is intriguing as he points out that this can significantly affect vulnerable individuals as well as those who may face challenges when seeking expert advice to pursue a legal claim. This is not merely a theoretical concern, as it directly affects the ability of lower-income litigants to present their case effectively.[77] He adds that, 'there is widespread agreement with the criticisms I made in the interim report of the way in which expert evidence is used at present, especially the point that experts sometimes take on the role of partisan advocates instead of neutral fact finders or opinion givers.' This criterion reinforces the risks of overlooking the essential need for the expert's impartiality.

According to the CPR, the expert has a duty to assist the courts in the field of their expertise, which takes precedence over any other obligation with respect to the party offering evidence.[78] 'This duty overrides any obligation to the person from whom he has received instructions or by whom he is paid.'[79] To understand the CPR, it must be remembered that the judge, and not the parties, is the apex of the civil process. It requires moving from a process of laissez-faire which is adversarial, to one oriented towards a case management model.[80] At this point, it should be added that, 'at the end of an expert's report there must be a statement that the expert understands his duty to the court; and has complied with that duty.'[81]

There is an issue regarding terminology, as the CPR replaced the term of 'expert witness' with that of 'expert'. Although Dwyer downplays this change by suggesting that experts are shielded by witness immunity for their statements, which appears to be a vestige of assimilation. However, the removal of added qualifications alongside the incorporation of objective overrides demonstrates a clear shift in their role.[82]

The Protocol for the Instruction of Experts to give Evidence in Civil Claims has been in use since 2005, where the term employed is 'experts' and not 'expert witnesses'. This expressly states that:

> Experts should provide opinions which are independent, regardless of the pressures of litigation. In this context, a useful test of independence is that the expert would express the same opinion if given the same instructions by an opposing party. Experts

[77] N Andrews, *The Modern Civil Process: Judicial and Alternative Forms of Dispute Resolution in England* (Tübingen, Mohr Siebeck, 2008) 130.

[78] CPR 35.3.

[79] See regarding the scope and complexity of overriding duty.

[80] Dwyer (n 18) 283 et seq.

[81] CPR 35.10.

[82] Dwyer (n 18) 186.

should not take it upon themselves to promote the point of view of the party instructing them or engage in the role of advocates.[83]

This consistently reinforces the notion of impartiality required of the expert.

V. Soft Law

Two substantive contributions on possible improvements to be implemented in civil proceedings have been prepared with the support of the International Institute for the Unification of Private Law (UNIDROIT). These are the projects developed with collaboration from the American Law Institute (ALI) on the *Principles of Transnational Civil Procedure* (PTCP),[84] and the European Law Institute (ELI) on *European Model Rules of Civil Procedure* (EMRCP).[85] Due to the rigour with which these projects were discussed and developed, they offer attractive proposals that may be useful for future reform processes undertaken by the states.

In 1997, Geoffrey Hazard Jr. and Michele Taruffo published their first version of the draft transnational rules of civil procedure.[86] After the ALI took the decision to follow through on this initiative, it was joined by UNIDROIT.[87]

The first principle of the PTCP is dedicated to the independence, impartiality and suitability of judges. The reporters' comments suggest that independence is an objective trait, whereas impartiality is subjective, yet both are closely interconnected. This distinction offers clarity on the usage of these terms, which has been extensively discussed concerning judges but not as much regarding experts. The third principle emphasises the importance of procedural equality among parties, which the judge must ensure, along with providing litigants with a fair opportunity to assert and defend their rights. Additionally, the concept of cooperation is underscored in two of its principles.[88]

With respect to experts, the judge is encouraged to appoint an expert.[89] If the parties agree to appoint an expert, the judge, in principle, must proceed with the

[83] Rule 4.3 of the 2005 Protocol.

[84] Adopted in 2004.

[85] Adopted in 2020.

[86] G Hazard Jr, & M Taruffo, 'Transnational Rules of Civil Procedure – Rules and Commentary' (1997) 30 *O'Connell International Law Journal* 493–539. About the background see: American Law Institute/UNIDROIT, *Principles and Rules of Transnational Civil Procedure* (Cambridge, Cambridge University Press, 2005) xxiii–xxiv, xli–xlvii; R Stürner, 'The Principles of Transnational Civil Procedure. An Introduction to Their Basic Conceptions' (2015) 69 *The Rabel Journal of Comparative and International Private Law* 201–254.

[87] During the project, in addition to Geoffrey Hazard J. and Michele Taruffo, Rolf Stürner was appointed co-reporter and Antonio Gidi, associate reporter.

[88] In 7.2, the duty of collaboration is referred to with reference to procedural speed. Section 11.2 proposes that the parties share with the judge the responsibility of promoting a fair, effective and reasonable rapid resolution of the process.

[89] 22.4.

appointment. The parties have the right to present an opinion prepared by an expert that they have chosen. Both the expert appointed by the judge and the one presented by each party are bound by the judge to carry out a complete and objective evaluation of the issue submitted for consideration.

The Rules of Transnational Civil Procedure (RTCP) drafted together with the PTCP did not have the approval of ALI-UNIDROIT. Despite this, they contain some interesting suggestions. One example is the section entitled Impartiality of the Court, which says that: 'a judge or other person having decisional authority must not participate if there are reasonable grounds to doubt such person's impartiality'.[90] The mention of other people with decision-making authority can broadly be interpreted as a guarantee of neutrality. Although the expert does not adjudicate, his contribution when the knowledge is singular, has a determining effect. For that reason, it can be justified that experts are covered by said guarantee. In the comments to this rule, it is specified that 'other persons with decisional authority include a lay member of the court, and an expert appointed by the court'. Then, when regulating expert evidence, it is proposed that:

> … the court appoint a neutral expert or a panel of experts when required by law and may do so when it considers that expert evidence may be helpful. If the parties agree upon an expert, the court should ordinarily appoint that expert. A party has the right to present expert testimony through an expert selected by that party on any relevant issue for which the expert testimony is appropriate. An expert, whether appointed by the court or by a party, owes a duty to the court to present a full and objective assessment of the issue.[91]

For seven years, a group of renowned procedural lawyers worked on the development of the ELI-UNIDROIT European Model Rules of Civil Procedure (EMRCP).[92] This is not the place to provide details about the EMRCP since my intention is to focus mainly on the activity of the experts. However, it is necessary to point out the importance that the EMRCP assigned to the principles of collaboration and proportionality, as well as case management,[93] given that these three basic lines affect the configuration of the role assigned to experts.

The EMRCP accept the duty of cooperation, establishing that the parties, their lawyers and the judge must cooperate in the interests of achieving the fair, efficient

[90] Rule 10.

[91] Rule 22.

[92] The Project Steering Committee was formed with the following as Co-Chairs: Jose Angelo Estrella Faria (Unidroit Secretary-General), Anna Veneziano (Deputy Secretary-General) and Diana Wallis (President of ELI); Members representing the ELI: Remo Caponi and John Sorabji. Members representing Unidroit: Rolf Stürner and Anna Veneziano. For information about the main stages of the Project and the methodology of the European Law Institute, see the International Institute for the Unification of Private Law, *ELI-UNIDROIT Model European Rules of civil Procedure from transnational Principles to European Rules of Civil Procedure* (Oxford, Oxford University Press, 2021) 1–6.

[93] See CHR van Rhee, 'Judicial Case Management and Loyal Cooperation. Towards Harmonized European Rules of Civil Procedure', in R Aarli, & A Sanders (eds), *Courts in Evolving Societies. A Sino-European Dialogue between Judges and Academics* (Brill | Nijhoff, 2021) 168–202.

and rapid resolution of the dispute. The comments issued by ELI/UNIDROIT state that:

> These rules consider the proper conduct of proceedings to require effective co-operation between the court, parties and their lawyers. The emphasis on co-operation, which has been a feature of some European civil procedural codes since the 19th century and others since the turn of 21st century, is an important move away from the traditional divisions between adversarial and inquisitorial conceptions of civil procedure. It is intentionally adopted here, not least as a means to avoid this historical division that has acted as a barrier to procedural harmonization.

This duty dovetails with judge's responsibility to ensure active and effective case management, and therefore the judge must ensure that the parties enjoy equal treatment.[94] This is related to the imposition of due proportionality that requires the judge to take into account the nature, importance and complexity of the matter, as well as the requirement to discharge his own duty of procedural management and, in general, the interest in seeing justice administrated properly.[95]

Regarding the integration of expert knowledge, the EMRCP combine the involvement of the parties' experts with that of the expert appointed by the judge.[96] The EMRCP refer to both the PTCP and the RTCP as sources. As for the expert designated by the parties, the comment recognises that this:

> … may give rise to the risk of expert bias, whether structural or personal. The former arises where an expert genuinely holds a specific opinion on an issue and is instructed by the party on that basis. The latter arises where an expert either develops an animus towards the opponent of the party instructing them, or identifies with the party instructing them, such that in either case they consciously or subconsciously tailor their evidence accordingly. Given this, it is in the party's interest to present party-appointed experts with proper qualifications and skills, and who understand and comply with the duties, not least with their duty of objectivity and impartiality.

Regarding the expert appointed by the judge, the parties reserve the right to object for reasons of bias, when there is a reasonable fear of biased action.

VI. Balance and Neutrality

The principle that equality of the parties and the independence of the judge are essential pillars of the judicial process holds the status of an axiom. The absence of any of these elements hinders the pursuit of a rational and fair resolution of the proceedings. Despite constituting constitutive factors, the two notions are guaranteed with unequal intensity. Incontrovertible on an abstract level, they face

[94] Rules 3–4.
[95] Rule 5.
[96] Rules 119, 120.

multiple difficulties when it comes to their effective realisation. While the substantial import of these notions is acknowledged, given their status as indispensable and essential requirements of the proceedings, the extent to which they are upheld opens up a broad field of analysis.

Achieving the impartiality of the judge towards the parties is not sufficient. To ensure a fair process, it is essential that those involved in a dispute do not encounter any obstacles preventing them from presenting and substantiating the facts and rights that they invoke. The decision on what right to attribute to the facts takes as premises, on the one hand, the neutrality of the decider, understood as impartiality and, on the other, the similarity of forces, considered as the absence of barriers and as the effective opportunity to argue and provide evidence in favour of a certain position.

Regarding the right of access to justice, and its direct relationship with the principle of isonomy, it is necessary to guarantee a balance between the parties with respect to the possibility of incorporating expert knowledge into the proceedings. The path forward should be guided by the realisation of the values embodied in the right of access to justice, which has a distinctly egalitarian foundation. The possibility of having expert advice should not lead to situations of disadvantage and discrimination.

According to the European Court of Human Rights (ECtHR), the principle of equality of arms, with respect to disputes involving opposing private interests, requires each party to be given a reasonable opportunity to present their case, including evidence, in conditions that do not place them at a substantial disadvantage with regard to their opponent.[97] For its part, the Inter-American Court of Human Rights has recognised that in every process, the necessary elements must be present so that the greatest balance between the parties can be achieved to ensure the due defence of their interests and rights.[98]

The assistance of the parties by a lawyer is considered a central element to guarantee access to justice. It is assumed that assistance provided by a legal professional is essential, given the complexity of legal systems. If a person cannot afford to pay, the state provides support systems to ensure they have the necessary legal representation to defend their rights. However, procedural systems often fail to provide assistance in cases where recourse to an expert is essential, particularly those based on the parties' ability to contribute the opinions of their experts.

The essence of judicial activity lies in the fact that it is undertaken by an impartial and neutral third party. When I talk about independence, I am referring to the diverse measures taken by the constituent, the legislator, or social practice

[97] See, eg, ECtHR: *Andrejeva c. Latvia* [GC], well. 55707/00, § 96, 2009; and *Dombo Beheer BV v. the Netherlands*, 1993, § 33.

[98] Inter-American Court of Human Rights. *Opinión Consultiva OC-17/02. Condición jurídica y derechos humanos del niño*. 2002, para 132. Inter-American Court of Human Rights. Caso *Palamara Iribarne vs.* Chile FRC. 2005, para 178. Inter-American Court of Human Rights. *Caso Ruano Torres y otros vs. El Salvador.* FRC. 2015, para 152.

to safeguard those involved in the judicial protection of the rights of subordinations aimed at restricting their freedom to decide in accordance with prevailing regulations and the facts proven during the proceedings. Respect for judicial independence is what serves as the safeguard ensuring the impartiality and neutrality of the court in a specific case. When employing the concepts of independence and impartiality within the context described, a certain level of subordination between them becomes apparent. Andres Ibañez[99] understands that independence is a prior guarantee, a 'condition of possibility of impartiality'. This is an assumption that allows for its realisation, and in that sense, is a condition of possibility. It is necessary but insufficient, as a judge who is free from political influence in performing his duties may not necessarily maintain equidistance in his relationship with the parties involved in the proceedings and the subject matter of the trial. In matters of expert knowledge, both terms are used interchangeably, as is the idea of neutrality, or so with respect to judges.

The purpose of proof, insofar as it can be considered as the search to represent a reality that is external to the proceedings, requires those providing that knowledge to be fair-minded and unaffected by the interests of the parties. Witnesses such as experts are obliged to give the correct view of the facts – or at least that which is correct for them – regardless of the convenience of those confronting them and debating their existence. The procedural means enabling the questioning of a witness or an expert's admission or statement are rooted in the pursuit of fairness, aiming to accurately uncover the full scope of the facts. Both witness and the expert must be independent of the outcome of the proceedings. Both contribute knowledge that is equidistant from the descriptions of what happened as described by those litigating. As Picó i Junoy suggests,[100] regarding whether it is feasible to transfer the essential requirement of impartiality from the judge to the expert, it is important to recognize that impartiality is equally essential for the expert. This is because when the subject matter requires scientific, technical, or specialised knowledge, the judge relies on the expert's assistance. Therefore, the lack of independence of the expert indirectly affects the judge and his independence (or lack of objectivity) when deciding.

The ECtHR has produced decisions to help differentiate the notions of experts' impartiality and independence. It has been understood that Article 6 § 1 of the European Convention on Human Rights, in principle, does not expressly require an expert heard by a 'court' to meet the same requirements of independence and impartiality as the court itself.[101] However, given that their opinions influence the outcome of the process, the neutrality of the experts is important and, with regard

[99] P Andrés Ibañez, *Tercero en discordia. Jurisdicción y juez del Estado Constitucional,* (Madrid, Editorial Trotta, 2015) 216 et seq.

[100] J Picó I Junoy, 'La debida independencia del perito judicial' (2018) 1 *Revista Justicia* 59–84. Although Picó i Junoy speaks of the independence of the expert, the scope with which he uses the term can be understood to encompass impartiality.

[101] Protection *Sara Lind Eggertsdóttir v. Iceland*, 2007, § 47; *Letinčić v. Croatia*, 2016, art 51.

to expert evidence, the Court has relied on the principles of independence and impartiality applicable to a 'court'.[102] In particular, factors such as the procedural position of the expert and his role in the relevant procedure must be taken into account.[103]

VII. Inequality and Bias as Dangers to Consider

Cappelletti[104] justly maintained that the ultimate value, the essence and nature, so to speak, of the judicial function is to have a decision taken by an impartial third person (*tertius super partes*) after a fair opportunity to present and defend your case. These minimum conditions require a correct incorporation of expert knowledge, respecting the fundamental human right of access to justice, and maintaining the essential impartiality of the decision-maker.

Procedural designs must guarantee respect for these values. Over time, it has become clear that it is possible to achieve this by striking the right balance between the expert appointed by the judge and the one proposed by the party. This is done by applying the principles of cooperation and proportionality, while ensuring an adequate relationship between the judge and the parties involved.

The equality of the parties and the impartiality of those involved in clarifying the facts can be effectively harmonised by challenging the notion of rivalry and instead embracing a paradigm of collaboration. This approach aligns better with a rule of law founded on institutions that prioritise dialogue and consensus over antagonism.

[102] See *Çöçelli and others v. Türkiye*, 2022, §§ 58–6.

[103] See *Bönisch v. Austria*, 1985, §§ 31–35.

[104] M Cappelletti, '"Who watches the Watchmen?" A Comparative Study on Judicial Responsibility' (1983) 31(1) *The American Journal of Comparative Law* 1–62. The quote is taken from p 16.

11

Experts on Foreign Law in German Civil Procedure

MICHAEL STÜRNER*

I. Foreign Law in Civil Proceedings

One of the fundamental issues of procedural law concerns the relationship between the court and the parties. The core question is how actively the judge controls the course of the proceedings. German civil procedure is conceived as a liberal model with the two guiding principles of disposition maxim and the principle of production. According to this model, the parties are in control over the proceedings as a whole, and they also determine the subject matter of the proceedings through their factual submissions. Nevertheless, the formal and substantive conduct of the proceedings lies within the responsibility of the court, specifically the presiding judge. From the perspective of common law, this active role of the court is so pronounced in German civil proceedings that the process here has repeatedly been described as 'inquisitorial',[1] though this is hardly convincing at closer scrutiny.[2] However, it can be said that the responsibility for the facts is shared between the court and the parties.

With regard to legal questions, however, the responsibility lies almost entirely with the court: *Da mihi facta, dabo tibi ius*. Nonetheless, the procedural duty of the parties to cooperate covers all aspects of the proceedings; the court can therefore also request the parties or their representatives to state their views on specific legal questions. However, there are no sanctions in this respect. More specifically, there is no risk of losing the case by simply not presenting legal arguments: A party does

* This chapter is partly based on a previous contribution by the author: M Stürner, 'Die Abgrenzung der Aufgaben von Gutachter und Richter', in R Michaels and J P Schmidt (eds), *Das Gutachten zum ausländischen Recht im Prozess des 21. Jahrhunderts* (Tübingen, Mohr Siebeck, 2024), forthcoming.

[1] See J Jacob, *The Fabric of English Civil Justice* (Cambridge, Cambridge University Press, 1987) 7.

[2] In favour for a classification as *adversarial* on the other hand A Zuckerman/A Zuckerman, *Civil Justice in Crisis – Comparative Perspectives of Civil Procedure* (Oxford, Oxford University Press, 1999) 1, 31; J Langbein, 'The German Advantage in Civil Procedure' (1985) 52 *University Chicago Law Review* 823, 841.

not bear any burden of presentation with regard to the legal norms that are favourable to her. If, for example, a party argues in support of the claim only on the basis of fault-based liability and the proof of fault fails, the court must nevertheless grant the claim if, according to the facts presented, a claim based on a strict liability provision is also well-founded: the party does not have to explicitly rely on this norm as well – *iura novit curia*.

The same applies to the private international law norms applicable in Germany: the disposition maxim does not extend to questions of conflict of laws; the conflict of laws regime is not optional.[3] Last but not least, the *effet utile* of the relevant European regulations also speaks against this.

With regard to foreign law, its content is by no means regarded by the ZPO (German Code of Civil Procedure) as a question of fact, but as a question of law. However, the ZPO does not assume that the principle *iura novit curia*, which is thus called upon, also applies without restriction with regard to foreign law. Rather, it provides the court with the broadest possible assistance in determining it via section 293 ZPO. This rule provides as follows:

> The laws applicable in another state, customary laws, and statutes must be proven only insofar as the court is not aware of them. In making inquiries as regards these rules of law, the court is not restricted to the proof produced by the parties in the form of supporting documents; it has the authority to use other sources of reference as well, and to issue the required orders for such use.

In a nutshell, foreign law is law from a German perspective but is treated as a factual question with regard to the process of establishing its contents. Moreover, the parties do not bear a burden of proof with regard to the norms of foreign law that are favourable to them.[4] Rather, the responsibility for determining the foreign law lies entirely with the court.[5] The court is not completely relieved of this responsibility even if the parties agree on the foreign law.[6] This legal dialectic is not always easy to justify, especially to foreign observers. But it is accepted and followed in legal practice, as a 2018 empirical study shows, from which this article has gained many insights.[7]

[3] See M Stürner, 'Einleitung vor Art. 3 EGBGB para 75', in *Erman BGB*, 17th edn (Berlin, Otto Schmidt, 2023).

[4] BGH NJW 1961, 410; BGH NJW 1982, 1215, 1216; BGH NJW-RR 2005, 1071.

[5] BGHZ 36, 348, 353; BGHZ 77, 32, 38; BGH NJW 1981, 1006; BGH NJW 1987, 591; BGH NJW 1988, 647 und 648; BGH NJW 1992, 2096, 3106; BGH FamRZ 1994, 434; BGH NJW 1997, 324; BGH NJW 1998, 1321, 1396; BGH NJW 2003, 2685; BGH NJW-RR 2005, 1071; BGH VersR 2020, 614.

[6] H Schack, *Internationales Zivilverfahrensrecht*, 8th edn (München, CH Beck, 2021) para 765; S Lorenz, 'Einleitung IPR para 81' in *Beck Online Kommentar*, 66th edn (München, C.H Beck, 01.05.2023); BGH NJW 2022, 2547 Rn. 17; see also K Thorn, 'Einleitung IPR para 34' in *Grüneberg BGB*, 82nd edn (München, C.H Beck, 2023), as well as J von Hein, 'Einleitung IPR para 323' in *Münchner Kommentar zum BGB*, 8th edn (München, C.H Beck, 2020), according to which the concurring submissions of the parties should generally be assumed to be correct.

[7] M Stürner and F Krauß, *Ausländisches Recht in deutschen Zivilverfahren. Eine rechtstatsächliche Untersuchung*, (Tübingen, Mohr Siebeck, 2018), summarised in M Stürner (2018) 117 *Zeitschrift für Vergleichende Rechtswissenschaft* 1.

II. Ways to Ascertain Foreign Law

According to section 293 ZPO, the court has a fairly large discretion as to how the content of the foreign law is established.[8] The approach towards foreign law is even more flexible as compared to the power the court has when establishing the facts of the case: The court is not necessarily bound by the strict law of evidence applying to the proof of factual allegations.[9]

A. Court's Own Knowledge

First, the court relies on its own knowledge about the relevant foreign law.[10] The court can use any source of information, eg, manuals,[11] databases,[12] internet sites,[13] etc. A further valuable source of information could be the European Judicial Network in civil and commercial matters.[14] Such sources, however, will only rarely give guidance on every single aspect in question and will only help in fairly straightforward cases. An example might be a case where the only issue at stake is whether or not the applicable law allows a choice of law. In such a case, the mere text of the relevant foreign (conflicts) law might suffice.[15]

Second, the court can (and often will) ask parties to provide information on foreign law.[16] The parties are under a duty to assist the court in fulfilling its task to

[8] *cf.* BGHZ 118, 151 (so-called *Freibeweis* as opposed to the more formal *Strengbeweis*).

[9] Very recently, the Hamburg Guidelines on the Ascertainment and Application of Foreign Law in German proceedings have been published under the auspices of the Max Planck Institute of foreign and comparative law in Hamburg, *cf.* R Michaels and JP Schmidt, 'Die Hamburger Leitlinien zur Ermittlung und Anwendung ausländischen Rechts in deutschen Verfahren – Entstehung, Ziele, Inhalt', in *Neue Juristische Wochenschrift (NJW)* 2024, 24.

[10] See W Lindacher, *Festschrift für Schumann*, (Tübingen, Mohr Siebeck, 2002) 283; T Pfeiffer, *Festschrift für Leipold* (Tübingen, Mohr Siebeck, 2009) 283, 286.

[11] There is good deal of excellent manuals on foreign law in German language, see, eg, S Lorenz, R Michaels and HP Mansel (eds), *IPG – Gutachten zum Internationalen und Ausländischen Privat- und Verfahrensrecht* (collection of experts' reports on foreign law prepared at the request of German courts); Bergmann, M Ferid and D Henrich (eds), *Internationales Ehe- und Kindschaftsrecht* (family law), M Ferid, Firsching, H Dörner and R Hausmann, *Internationales Erbrecht* (law of successions). An excellent source of information can be found in C von Bar, *Ausländisches Privat- und Privatverfahrensrecht in deutscher Sprache. Systematische Nachweise aus Schrifttum, Rechtsprechung und Gutachten.*

[12] The manual edited by C von Bar (previous note) is also available via the juris database.

[13] Sometimes unreliable and not properly organised.

[14] See ec.europa.eu/civiljustice/index_en.htm. That site mainly contains information on procedural issues, and not on substantive law.

[15] See S Jastrow, 'Zur Ermittlung ausländischen Rechts: Was leistet das Londoner Auskunftsübereinkommen in der Praxis?' [2004] *Praxis des Internationalen Privat- und Verfahrensrechts (IPRax)* 404; M Fornasier, 'Auf dem Weg zu einem europäischen Justizraum – Der Beitrag des Europäischen Justiziellen Netzes für Zivil- und Handelssachen' [2010] *Zeitschrift für das Europäische Privatrecht* 477, 493 ff.; P Melin, 'Das Europäische Justizielle Netz für Zivil- und Handelssachen: Ein EU-Instrument zur Verbesserung der justiziellen Zusammenarbeit auf dem Prüfstand' [2010] *Deutsche Richterzeitung* 22, 25.

[16] See W Lindacher, 'Zur Mitwirkung der Parteien bei der Ermittlung ausländischen Rechts' in *Festschrift für Ekkehard Schumann* (Tübingen, Mohr Siebeck, 2001).

ascertain the relevant content of the applicable law.[17] However, given the parties' obvious bias, it will be only in simple cases that the court can really rely on such information. Moreover, parties can adduce private expert evidence, which has to be taken into account by the court. The same caveat applies.[18] The court cannot delegate its duty to gather the necessary information on foreign law entirely to the parties. Under section 293 ZPO, the responsibility to get reliable access to foreign law applicable remains with the court. As already stated, there is no 'burden of proof' as to the content of foreign law.

B. External Sources of Information

If the court is unable to get satisfactory access to the relevant foreign law with onboard means, it will have to make use of external sources. Generally speaking, there are two different possibilities: one is to ask for judicial assistance, the other is to appoint a court expert. The court has a fairly large discretion. However, the exercise of that discretion might be reviewed on appeal.[19]

i. Judicial Assistance

Judicial assistance is provided through the European Convention of 7 June 1968 on Information on Foreign Law (the 'London Convention') which has been set up under the auspices of the Council of Europe.[20] According to Article 3 of the Convention, a judicial authority may make a request for information concerning the law of another Contracting Party. The reply shall be free of cost (Article 15 of the London Convention). However, the practical use of the London Convention seems to be marginal in Germany. In 2007, German courts have used this channel only in 38 cases; in 2008, only in 22 cases.[21]

The reasons seem to be the following:[22] The request for information under the London Convention is time-consuming. There are intermediaries in both the requesting state and the receiving state. The receiving state may pass on the request to another official or even private body to draw up the reply (Article 6 of the London Convention). There is no time-limit for the reply (Article 12 of the London Convention). Furthermore, the reply covers mostly only abstract legal questions (see Article 7 of the London Convention).[23] The court files are

[17] See BGH NJW 1976, 1581, 1583.

[18] See H Krüger, 'Zur Ermittlung ausländischen Rechts in Deutschland: Ein Bericht aus der Praxis' in *Ergin Nomer'e Armağan* (Istanbul, Beta Yayınları, 2002) 357, 374; Schack (n 6) para 244.

[19] See, eg, BGHZ 118, 151.

[20] Ratification in Germany: BGBl. 1974 II, 938, 1975 II, 300. See Jastrow (n 15).

[21] Stürner and Krauß (n 7) 43. More recent data is hard to obtain.

[22] See D Schellack, *Selbstermittlung oder ausländische Auskunft unter dem europäischen Rechtsauskunftsübereinkommen*, (Berlin, Duncker & Humblot 1998).

[23] Pfeiffer (n 10) 283, 288.

not being transferred to the receiving state, thus the requested agency does not normally provide a tailor-made answer for the individual case at hand.[24] The request has to be formulated in the language of the receiving state (Articles 4 and 14 of the London Convention). The necessary translations multiply the risk of error. Finally, the agency or person drawing up the reply cannot be summoned to court to explain the reply (section 4 of the German Act implementing the London Convention into national law). The court cannot clarify open questions in a simple and straightforward way. To sum it up, judicial assistance under the London Convention is not seen as a suitable way to get speedy and precise information on foreign law.[25]

The Federal Court of Justice has ruled that in order for the court to comply with the duty to ascertain and apply the foreign law, it may not be enough to base the decision solely on information that has been obtained under the London Convention.[26] If it turns out that the required information on the foreign law has not been provided by the receiving state, or is insufficient because it consists only of the text of the relevant provisions or a number of court decisions, it would be a procedural error to deliver judgment solely on this basis. For it is precisely the task of the court to apply the foreign law just as a court of that state would do that.[27] In light of this, obtaining legal advice under the London Convention can only be considered in straightforward cases.

ii. Expert Evidence

In complex cases, German courts mostly appoint a court expert (section 402 ZPO).[28] That court expert gets the complete picture of the case as he is normally provided with the entire file of the case. The expert draws up an expert statement about the foreign law aspects of the whole case. Foreign law experts are usually law professors or specialists at large research institutes such as the Max Planck Institute of foreign and comparative law in Hamburg. They need not be based in Germany.[29] However, as the court is not in a position to summon foreign experts to explain their expert statement in an oral hearing[30] normally Germany-based experts are appointed. In that case, the parties can request the court to summon

[24] It seems that in some jurisdictions requested agencies do not give information in cases where contractual rights or obligations are at stake as such rights or obligations stem from the contract, not from the applicable law. See Pfeiffer (n 10) 283, 288.

[25] See Krüger (n 18) 357, 389 (high risk of error).

[26] See BGH *IPRax* 2002, 302 with comments by R Hüßtege, *IPRax* 2002, 292; BGH NJW 2014, 1244; F Krauß, 'Anforderungen an die tatrichterliche Ermittlung ausländischen Rechts in Zivilverfahren' (2014) *Zeitschrift für das Privatrecht der Europäischen Union (GPR)*, 175.

[27] See also BGH NJW 1991, 1418, 1419 on the Venezuelan ship lien; *cf.* also BGH NJW 1976, 1588, 1589; Schack, (n 6) para 705.

[28] See Pfeiffer (n 10) 283, 294 et seq.

[29] See W Hau, 'Gerichtssachverständige in Fällen mit Auslandsbezug' [2003] *Recht der Internationalen Wirtschaft (RIW)* 822.

[30] BGH, *IPRax* 1981, 57, 58, where reference is made to the questioning by way of legal assistance in accordance with s 363 ZPO; *cf.* also Schack (n 6), para 246.

the expert to explain the expert opinion in an oral hearing, section 411 (3) ZPO.[31] The court has to form its own opinion on the merits of the case (section 286 ZPO); it cannot just repeat the expert's opinion. The preparation of such expert opinions may take anything between a few weeks and a year or even more, depending on the nature and complexity of the case.[32]

Obtaining a legal opinion on foreign law is probably not statistically the rule within the framework of section 293 ZPO, but rather is normally only requested if the relevant norms and their interpretation cannot be ascertained with sufficient certainty by other means.

III. Expert Opinions: The Court's Perspective

To sum it up: The court has the main responsibility for ascertaining foreign law. According to section 293 ZPO, it can make use of all possible sources of knowledge.[33] The appointment of an expert is the sole responsibility of the court (section 404 (1) ZPO), even though the parties may of course suggest this type of taking of evidence, and regularly do so by designating the legal questions to be examined by an expert (section 403 ZPO).[34] If the parties agree on an expert, 'the court shall follow this agreement' (section 404 (5) ZPO); in any case, they must be heard before the appointment (section 405 (2) ZPO).

A. Expert Evidence as Ultima Ratio?

According to section 293 ZPO, the ascertainment of foreign law is at the discretion of the court.[35] This applies both to the type of investigation and its intensity.[36] In the case law of the Federal Court of Justice, a kind of dynamic relativity principle has emerged, according to which the investigative effort to be made increases the more 'exotic' the foreign law to be determined is. The same applies to complex factual and legal situations, which also require a more thorough investigation of the foreign law.[37]

However, the ZPO does not state as a general principle that the costs of investigating the foreign law must not be disproportionate to the amount in

[31] BGH, *NJW* 1975, 2142, 2143; BGH, *NJW-RR* 2001, 1431, 1432.

[32] See, eg, G Otto, *Festschrift für Firsching*, (München, CH Beck, 1985) 223, who reports an average duration of one year.

[33] R Hüßtege, 'Internetrecherche contra Sachverständigengutachten – Zur Ermittlung ausländischen Rechts durch deutsche Gerichte' [2021] *IPRax* 261.

[34] In practice, evidence is often provided ('Under Italian law, there is a presumption of contributory negligence in this respect. Proof: expert opinion.').

[35] BGH *NJW-RR* 2007, 574, 575.

[36] BGH *NJW-RR* 2002, 1359; BGHZ 165, 248, 260.

[37] BGHZ 165, 248, 260; BGHZ 118, 151, 163; BGH NJW 2022, 2547 Rn. 17.

dispute.[38] English law is much bolder here, where rule 1.1 (2)(c) and (e) CPR postulate a general procedural principle of proportionality.[39] A similar approach cannot be advocated for German law. The danger seems too great that, for reasons of proportionality, only a minimum effort is made to ascertain the foreign law. However, there are isolated statements to this effect in decisions of some lower courts. For example, the Regional Court of Oldenburg[40] held that the court had to try to gain knowledge of the foreign law required to assess the facts of the case 'in the simplest, quickest and cheapest way'.[41]

The Federal Court of Justice rightly did not accept such limitations of section 293 ZPO:[42] They would either lead to potentially wrong results or would de facto result in a homeward bias. Naturally, however, when exercising its discretion under section 293 ZPO, the principle of procedural economy, the court must take the costs that would be caused by the respective method of investigation into account. Moreover, against the backdrop of the requirement to accelerate proceedings, it must also consider the question of how great the delay in the proceedings caused by obtaining an expert opinion would be.[43] However, the fact that an expert opinion will cost a multiple of the amount in dispute does not prevent the court from appointing the expert all the same.[44]

In fact, the readiness to obtain an expert opinion is lower in the local courts (including family courts) than in higher courts. In many cases, this type of evidence is considered ultima ratio. A few statements from the judiciary may illustrate this:[45]

> Also, I have never asked for an expert opinion from the Max Planck Institute. That would be the last lifeline.

This was justified by the fact that the preparation of an expert opinion would significantly delay the proceedings:[46]

> Well, the whole thing will be delayed by half a year.

[38] But see J Kindl, [1998] *ZZP* 111, 177, 183; S Lorenz, 'Einleitung IPR para 83' in *Beck Online Kommentar*, 66th edn (München, C.H Beck, 01.05.2023).

[39] M Stürner, 'The Search for Principles: Paradigmenwechsel im englischen Zivilprozessrecht?' (2004) 103 *Zeitschrift für Vergleichende Rechtswissenschaft (ZVglRWiss)* 349, 366 ff.

[40] LG Oldenburg *IPRspr.* 1984 Nr. 2, S. 2, 3.

[41] The particularity of this decision, however, lies in the fact that the obiter remarks on the determination of foreign law were directed against the court's order to take evidence, which had obtained an expert opinion because the relevant country report in Bergmann/Ferid [today: Henrich/Dutta/Ebert] was not available in an up-to-date version or only incomplete in the court library. Here, the LG considered the discretionary limit of section 293 ZPO to have been exceeded; the court had to take other paths to obtain the required materials. The instructions to the local court were probably also so clear because the order to take evidence had generally referred to the compatibility of a property law contract 'with German or Yugoslav law' and had thus clearly exceeded the possibilities of s 293 ZPO.

[42] BGH *NJW* 2014, 1244 para 24.

[43] Explicitly in OLG München *IPRspr.* 2010, Nr. 1, p. 1; OLG München *DAR* 2008, 590.

[44] BGH *NJW* 2014, 1244 para 24.

[45] Stürner and Krauß (n 7) 197.

[46] ibid 198.

> The fact that I haven't tried the Max Planck Institute yet is certainly due to the time factor. That's quite clear.
>
> The time/performance ratio. For me, it takes time to find out who the contact person is, then to write to them, then to wait several months, then to get an answer, which may not really answer my question. I do that twice and then I drop it for good.

However, the situation is different in proceedings before the regional courts.[47] This is due to the higher amounts in dispute. In addition, proceedings before the regional courts take longer on average, so that the delay resulting from obtaining an expert opinion is not so significant in relative terms. According to the assessment of the judges working at the Regional Court, the delay caused by a case with a foreign element had little or no influence on the process of ascertaining foreign law work as such:[48]

> The question of how things are done in foreign law often arises, and that's why, if you just can't find a clear result, I tend to simply call in a professional who knows what he's talking about.
>
> Yes, I just say: I can't do it myself and I want to know what it's about .... And of course, on the one hand, that's totally convenient, because we don't somehow commission someone, but someone who, because he plays the role of quasi-judge, does it very well at a very high level.
>
> I think that if the judge ... is simply stuck, no matter how extensive it is or how economically significant it is, and can then no longer defend his decision, then a responsible judge will seek an expert opinion.
>
> It is simply not realistic for us to go to a foreign law school for the sake of a case.

It must be noted that at local courts, except for the Hamburg Max Planck Institute, there was only very little knowledge on who could act as an expert on foreign law.[49] By contrast, there is no empirical evidence that the organisational tool used by the judiciary to allot time to each case could have a direct influence on the amount of time and effort that individual judges spend on ascertaining foreign law, especially at local courts.[50] Only in very isolated cases was the net time allocation of 150 minutes per case seen as a disturbing factor; for the most part, the focus of the judges was solely on the correct decision on the merits.

The fact that an insufficient investigation may amount to a violation of section 293 ZPO and thus a relevant procedural error in possible appeal proceedings also seems to be of little relevance to the judges. An example of this is a decision by the Munich Higher Regional Court, which saw a procedural error in the fact that the lower court assumed that the position of the applicable foreign law on the relevant factual questions could not be ascertained, after a university institute had refused to prepare an expert opinion.[51] However, according to the

[47] ibid 355 ff.
[48] ibid 355.
[49] ibid 264 ff.
[50] ibid 219 ff. The personnel requirement calculation system is called PEBB§Y.
[51] OLG München *NJW* 2017, 338 Rn. 18.

case law of the Federal Court of Justice, a recourse to the lex fori is permissible if 'no certain findings can be made, or findings could only be made possible with disproportionate effort and considerable procedural delay'.[52]

B. The Right Point in Time to Appoint an Expert

Once the court's discretion has been exercised to the point that an expert opinion is necessary, it is important to determine the right time to obtain it: On the one hand, this could be as early as possible so that the determination of the facts may be based on the standards of the foreign law in the first place.

On the other hand, there are also good reasons for obtaining an expert opinion as late as possible, ideally only after the facts of the case have been fully established, so that the expert does not have to formulate alternative decisions. From the expert's point of view, the latter is generally to be advocated. If it is possible for the court to obtain a certain basic understanding of the applicable law with a reasonable effort so that the fact-finding can be advanced in light of this knowledge, then obtaining the expert opinion as late as possible seems generally preferable.

C. The Content of the Order for Evidence

As obtaining the expert opinion is part of the gathering of evidence, the expert is appointed by means of an order for evidence.[53] This court order also states the foreign law issues to be clarified and regularly also a deadline within which the written expert opinion is to be drawn up (section 411 (1) ZPO), which in normal court practice seems to be three months.

Section 293 sentence 2 ZPO provides the legal framework: According to this provision, the court is authorised to use 'other sources of knowledge beyond the evidence provided by the parties and to order what is necessary for the purpose of such use'. From the outset, only such issues which is unknown to the court may be considered necessary, which clearly limits the request to foreign law.

Against this backdrop, the law applicable in Germany can never be the subject of an order for evidence. It happens time and again that courts directly or indirectly ask questions about private international law, about transnational uniform

[52] See BGHZ 69, 387, 393.

[53] At least according to the prevailing opinion, see BGH NJW 1994, 2959; H Prütting, '§ 293 Rn. 29', in *Münchener Kommentar zum Zivilprozessrecht*, 6th edn (München, C.H. Beck, 2020). The opposing view is more open with reference to the wide discretion under section 293 ZPO, see H Linke and W Hau, *Internationales Zivilverfahrensrecht*, 8th edn (München, C.H. Beck, 2021) para 9.14. However, if an order to take evidence has been issued, the evidence is subsequently taken in the form of strict evidence.

law such as the CISG or also about EU regulations and directives. In spite of the international provenance of the relevant norms, basically it is German law that is involved. Their determination is therefore not covered by section 293 sentence 2 ZPO and cannot be the subject of the order for evidence.

However, namely conflict-of-laws rules do not per se fall outside the scope of application of section 293 sentence 2 ZPO, as can be seen, for example, when it comes to overriding mandatory provision: the expert can certainly inform the court on whether a foreign mandatory provision that may have to be taken into account according to Article 9(3) Rome I Regulation exists. The same applies to foreign norms of safety and conduct within the meaning of Article 17 Rome II Regulation. Finally, it may be useful to have an expert clarify the law to be applied in the case of a violation of public policy of the forum,[54] which in any case makes a provisional assessment of the violation itself advisable. And just for the sake of completeness, it should be noted that foreign private international law can, of course, be the subject of expert investigations, for example, in the context of the question of whether a relevant legal issue is the subject of a renvoi.

Furthermore, it the court is limited to ask for clarification of such questions that are relevant for the decision. Against this backdrop, as explained above, it might be problematic to obtain the expert opinion at a very early point in time, when the relevant factual basis still has insufficient details.

Finally, section 293 ZPO does not exempt the court from applying the foreign law to the specific case. Sometimes, when reading the order for evidence, one gets the impression that the court is rather asking the expert: 'Please prepare a judgement for me applying the foreign law!' However, the expert opinion can in no way replace the application of the law by the requesting court. Of course, it is not very helpful for the court if the expert limits himself to referring to provisions of the relevant foreign law, including case law, detached from the case at hand. The concrete framework for the expert opinion is provided by the case to be decided with its specific factual basis. In this respect, it is the purpose of the expert's explanations to present the application of foreign law to the specific facts of the case. However, the room for interpretation that the court needs for its own assessment should always be respected.

It seems that courts are well aware of this rather thin dividing line:[55]

> You send it to Mr. So-and-So and he solves the case for you, in colloquial terms, he solves the case for you with all eventualities, with all intellectual strands, no matter who else will say something, and you get it back after a year and the case comes back in such a way that in essence no one has anything more to say. Because it was evaluated at a really good scientific level for an hourly wage.
>
> Generally speaking, it's not a bad thing to be able to get an expert opinion. At the Max Planck Institute. That's actually not so problematic. Someone sits there who writes

[54] See M Stürner, 'Art. 6 EGBGB Rn. 286 ff.', in *BeckOnline Grosskommentar* (01.05.2023 edn), (München, CH Beck, 2023).

[55] Stürner and Krauß, (n 7) 356.

a legal opinion in German on my problem, I present it to the lawyers and then we move on. I don't think that's a bad way to approach it.

However, this outsourcing of decision-making competence to the expert may certainly be viewed in a critical light, namely from the perspective of the appellate court:[56]

It must be said that sometimes one has the feeling that they ... are not so unhappy when they are told: it is foreign law. Then they will send the file to some smart professor and he will solve the case for them.

But also judges sitting in first instance courts share this point of view:[57]

... And if you have the impression that there are too many uncertainties and it is also a question of certain economic importance, then you would obtain an expert opinion as pointedly as possible, because you are only allowed to borrow the expertise of other people to answer the question selectively, but not to deal with the case, that is our very own business.

D. Whom to Appoint as Expert?

Experts are often appointed from the Max Planck Institute for Foreign and Private International Law in Hamburg or from larger foreign law institutes at German universities such as Cologne, Heidelberg or Munich.[58] The expert appointed must have sufficient knowledge of the pertinent foreign law. According to Federal Court of Justice case law, sufficient knowledge regarding the content and interpretation of foreign law is to be assumed if the expert can already demonstrate relevant experience regarding the foreign law in question.[59]

[56] ibid 357.

[57] ibid 358.

[58] J von Hein, 'The Determination and Application of Foreign Law. A Blind Spot of European Private International Law?', in *Realization of Substantive Law through Legal Proceedings* (Tübingen, Mohr Siebeck, 2017). A list of experts who come into consideration can be found in W Hetger, 'Sachverständige für ausländisches und internationals Privatrecht' [2003] *Deutsche Notar-Zeitschrift* 310 ff. R Schütze, 'Die Anwendung ausländischen Rechts durch deutsche Notare' [1992] *Zeitschrift für das Notariat in Baden-Württemberg* 122, 124 also refers to a previous version with regard to the application of foreign law by German notaries. In addition, he mentions academic institutes and chairs that come into consideration. An updated list has not been published since then. Only an extract from this list was reproduced in *ZEV* 2006, 450 ff. In the course of conducting the expert interviews, a further list of experts in foreign family law was identified. This database can be accessed at sachverstaendige.ftcam.de.

[59] See in this respect BGH, *NJW-RR* 1991, 1211, 1212 with regard to an expert opinion that a scientist of the Max Planck Institute had prepared for the first time in Venezuelan law: '[The court] could not rely on the expert opinion of the Max Planck Institute in clarifying this question. The author himself stated at his hearing that this was the first time he had examined a case from Venezuelan law and that he had no special knowledge of this law and, above all, of the existing legal practice there. Afterwards, he ultimately limited himself to the evaluation of the literature accessible to him and the interpretation of the relevant laws. This was not sufficient for the determination of foreign law.'

However, one may assume sufficient knowledge of the respective law not only if the person appointed can demonstrate experience with regard to the application and interpretation, in particular with regard to the legal practice to be observed in the legal system in question, but also if he had gained such experience with regard to other states of the corresponding legal family.[60] In addition to the necessary language skills, a solid basic knowledge of the structure and the essential terminology of the legal system should be a minimal requirement.[61]

IV. The Expert: The Centrepiece of Proceedings?

This brings us to the addressee of the order for evidence: the expert.

A. Procedural and Factual Position in the Proceedings

The expert assumes a public office and must comply with the appointment. This holds true not only for publicly appointed experts (note that with regard to foreign law, there is no such thing as a public appointment). It suffices that a person 'publicly exercises the science […], the knowledge of which is a prerequisite for the expert opinion […]' (section 407(1) ZPO). With a broad understanding of this, all professors with a comparative law focus would thus be suitable expert witnesses. However, this leaves a back door wide open: Should the task not fall within his or her area of expertise or if the expert opinion cannot be completed within the time limit set by the court, the expert 'shall inform the court without delay' (section 407a(1) ZPO). As a consequence, the expert will be released from preparing the expert opinion (*cf.* section 408(1) sentence 2 ZPO).

In practice, therefore, preliminary enquiries are often conducted in the form of negotiations between the court and the potential expert, in which the basic willingness to prepare the expert opinion is ascertained and the time frames for delivery are established. In some cases, one expert declines after the other, in others, it goes smoothly. The clear 'imbalance of power' between the court and the expert, which the ZPO establishes through the unilaterally conceived process of appointment, the duly enforced deadline for the preparation of the expert opinion and the authority to issue instructions, is understood and practices in a strikingly different way in practice. This may be due to the fact that

[60] Von Hein (n 58).

[61] See A Heldrich, 'Probleme bei der Ermittlung ausländischen Rechts in der gerichtlichen Praxis' in *Festschrift für Nakamura* (Berlin, De Gruyter, 1996).

there are comparatively few potential experts on foreign law or also because the courts respect the position of the mostly professorial experts, as there is no alternative way to ascertain foreign law. This also explains the sometimes rather self-confident way in which the experts deal with the order for evidence. In my impression, the priority is to solve the case correctly and less to simply work through all the questions the court put to the expert.

B. Elaborations on Private International Law?

In the light of this, the expert could be inclined already to correct what he considers to be an incorrect application of private international law. Strictly speaking, this is not up to him, as the expert's assignment – in a reciprocal manner to the court's sphere of competence resulting from *iura novit curia* – does not extend to German law. In this respect, it is advisable as a general rule to accept the reference to foreign law assumed by the court without further questions and to document this accordingly in the expert opinion.

Only in clear-cut cases, for example, if the court has obviously overlooked or misapplied a relevant conflict-of-laws rule, and the expert therefore has doubts as to the content and scope of the order, should he immediately seek clarification from the court in accordance with section 407a(4) sentence 1 ZPO. This is in the interest of procedural economy, the importance of which arises from section 407a(4) sentence 2 ZPO, especially in the reverse case of expert's fees getting out of hand.

Of course, a distinction must be made between this and the case already mentioned where it is precisely foreign private international law that becomes relevant in the context of a renvoi constellation.

C. The Interpretation of the Order for Evidence

Very similar principles apply to the question of the extent to which the evidentiary issues are open to interpretation by the expert. The main interest of the expert is to determine the norms and principles of foreign law relevant for the legal treatment of the case to be decided, as interpreted by the case law there. In this respect, it should regularly be implicit to the expert's mandate to concretise and sharpen evidentiary questions in the light of the findings on foreign law.

More far-reaching changes are regularly only to be made with the utmost care, as this involves the risk of usurping the position of the court. It is preferable, for example, to form alternatives between which the court can choose depending on its conviction. As a matter of principle, the expert should not deal with questions that clearly lie outside the order for evidence without consulting the court.

D. The Expert's Own Legal Opinion

Similarly, the expert should be careful with his or her own legal opinion. As it is their duty to inform the court about the legal situation in another legal system, they should act as neutrally as possible. First and foremost, their task is to set out the interpretation of the relevant norms in the light of the jurisprudence of the higher and supreme court of the relevant legal system. Where guiding case law does not exist, the expert faces what is perhaps the most difficult terrain of expert witness work. This applies in particular to the legal systems of common law, in which precedents have binding force. If the expert considers a certain legal opinion to be preferable, this must be indicated accordingly. In extreme cases of one-sided interpretation of the law, there could even be a threat of rejection by the parties due to lack of neutrality and fear of bias (section 406(1) sentence 1 and section 42(2) ZPO).

Another sensitive issue concerns the application of the foreign law on the facts of the case. On the one hand, as has been shown above, this will often lie in the very interest of the requesting court. On the other hand, the application of the law is one of the tasks of the court, so that the expert can at best make suggestions for a possible result. These must always be made clear in an appropriate manner ('without being in a position or willing to prejudge the assessment of the requesting court, the expert is of the view that …').

E. The Expert's Access to Information

In which way the expert, for his part, obtains access to the necessary information about the foreign law is entirely up to him. For the courts, it is implicitly assumed that the expert is also competent in the legal language and methodology of the legal system in question.

By contrast, the question of the extent to which the expert should have access to other information, such as facts, does not play a decisive role in the present context. The case file, including all annexes, is accessible to them, traditionally by sending the file by mail, but increasingly also in the form of access to an electronic copy of the file. It is not usually necessary for the expert to gain access to objects relevant to the proceedings (such as the vehicle involved in the accident or the property to be vacated) or people (such as in the context of the proceedings for the appointment of a guardian), as is the case in other proceedings.

For all those cases, the legal framework is set out in section 404a(4) ZPO. According to this provision, the court determines, as far as it is necessary, 'to what extent the expert is authorised to clarify the question of evidence, to what extent he may contact the parties and when he must allow them to participate in his investigations'. Conversely, it follows that the expert may not contact the parties without prior judicial permission.

V. The Assessment of Evidence by the Court

With the return of the file to the court and the submission of the expert report, it is up to the court to make use of the findings in the process of assessing the evidence. The parties must be informed of the contents of the expert report and have the right to comment on it (section 411(4) ZPO).

A. The Court Decides, not the Expert

It should be emphasised once again at this point that only the court is authorised to apply the foreign law determined by an expert to the facts in dispute. The court may not uncritically adopt the contents of the expert opinion, rather it must make its own assessment (section 286 ZPO), otherwise this constitutes a procedural error. However, it is also clear that nothing impossible may be demanded of the court here. The risk of the expert dominating the proceedings cannot be altogether ruled out in practice. A court will hardly be able to do more than a plausibility check, as two statements from local courts prove:[62]

> How to check it, well, yes. If it's prepared more or less systematically, then my assumption that it's accurate speaks for itself, then of course you look for the references. Maybe not every one, but the decisive ones, to see if it's true. And if you can confirm it, then so be it. Because I don't have access to the secondary literature.
>
> Well, I'm not going to start asking for the decision of the, I don't know, highest Italian court and have it translated to see if it's all correct. Instead, I will assume that everything that has been presented to me has been done correctly.

B. The Incomplete Expert Opinion or the Expert Opinion that has Become Incomplete

However, sometimes an expert opinion is incomplete. This can have various reasons. It may simply happen that the expert did not answer all of the court's questions due to negligence. On the other hand, it may also happen that the court overlooked relevant aspects or that such aspects only emerged from the expert report itself. Finally, the parties' factual submissions can also change subsequently and raise new legal questions. According to section 411(3) ZPO, the court has various options here, which include a written or – more rarely – oral explanation of the expert opinion or a written supplement.

Section 412 ZPO lists the most serious escalation levels: Should the expert opinion be deemed insufficient, the court may order a new expert opinion by the

[62] Stürner and Krauß (n 7) 202.

same or by other experts; the latter also applies if an expert is successfully rejected after the expert opinion has been provided.

VI. Impossibility to Ascertain Foreign Law

Foreign law may not be ascertainable if no viable sources regarding the applicable law are available, the legal situation is not sufficiently clarified, or an unambiguous result cannot be reached despite having exhausted the accessible sources of knowledge.[63] In such cases, a substitute solution must be found, since a decision on the case cannot be omitted. This follows from the parties right of access to justice and a fair trial.

The Federal Court of Justice hardly conceals its support for direct recourse to the lex fori.[64] This is 'most practicable' and should already be used if 'no certain findings can be made or findings could only be made possible with disproportionate effort and considerable delay in proceedings'.[65]

However, such a solution could create strong incentives for the lower courts not to set the effort of determining the foreign law too high.[66] Such an 'attempt to strive homeward on new paths'[67] would negate the conflict-of-laws rules in the first place. From the perspective of the effectiveness of the conflict-of-laws rules, it is necessary to clarify how much effort the court must expend before it can resort to the lex fori.[68]

VII. Foreign Law on Appeal

The application and interpretation of foreign law have always been considered non-reviewable. Only the process of ascertaining foreign law can be reviewed by the Federal Court of Justice. The reason for this assumption was initially

[63] Lindacher (n 16); J Kindl, *ZZP* 111 (1998), 177, 196; K Sommerlad and J Schrey, 'Die Ermittlung ausländischen Rechts im Zivilprozeß und die Folgen der Nichtermittlung' [1991] *Neue Juristische Wochenschrift*, 1377, 1382.

[64] BGHZ 69, 387, 394; BGH, *NJW* 1982, 1215, 1216.

[65] See BGHZ 69, 387, 393.

[66] Schack (n 6), para 718, describes this case law as a 'dangerous siren song'.

[67] Hence the title of the contribution by A Heldrich, *Festschrift für Ferid* (Frankfurt, Verlag für Standesamtwesen, 1988) 209.

[68] A special problem arises in criminal proceedings: There, the application of the lex fori when foreign law is not available is difficult to reconcile with criminal law concepts of certainty, see A Brutscher, *Zivilrechtsakzessorietät des Strafrechts bei Sachverhalten mit Auslandsbezug* (Tübingen, Mohr Siebeck, 2014) 238 et seq. On the comparison of civil and criminal proceedings with regard to the determination and application of foreign law, S Gössl and D Effer-Uhe, *Einheit der Prozessrechtswissenschaft?* (Stuttgart, Boorberg, 2016) 127.

section 549 ZPO old version.[69] According to this provision, the second appeal could only be based on the violation of federal law or a provision whose scope extends beyond the district of a higher regional court. The violation of foreign law was in any case not covered by that, and consequently also not by section 545 ZPO, old version.

According to the new version of section 545(1) ZPO[70] the second appeal may be based on the fact that the decision violates a legal right. The restrictions existing under the old law are precisely no longer found in the possible grounds for appeal. Since foreign law in Germany is treated as law and not as fact, a review of the application and interpretation of foreign law would be flatly covered by the wording of section 545(1) ZPO.[71] However, due to historical and systematic considerations, the prohibition to review the application and interpretation of foreign law is still assumed by many commentators.[72] In particular, this is also justified by the systematic reference to section 560 ZPO, according to which the decision of the court of appeal on the existence and content of laws, on the violation of which the revision cannot be based pursuant to section 545 ZPO, is decisive for the decision rendered on the second appeal. Since, according to the Reform Act, only foreign law is classified as non-reviewable, the provision would otherwise no longer make sense.[73] Accordingly, foreign law is treated as a fact in the appellate instance, despite its basic classification as law.

[69] The original provision of s 511 ZPO was promulgated as new federal law in 1950, Annex 2 to the Act on the Restoration of Legal Unity in the Field of Court Constitution, Civil Justice, Criminal Procedure and Costs Law of 20 September 1950, BGBl. I, 533.

[70] As amended by the Act on the Reform of Proceedings in Family Matters and in Matters of Non-Contentious Jurisdiction (FGG Reform Act) of 17 December 2008, BGBl. I, 2586, entered into force on 1 September 2009.

[71] In favour of reviewability therefore von Hein (n 58) 35, 52 ff.; Riehm, 'Vom Gesetz, das klüger ist als seine Verfasser- Zur Revisibilität ausländischen Rechts' [2014] *Juristen Zeitung* 73; R Hübner, *Ausländisches Recht vor deutschen Gerichten* (Tübingen, Mohr Siebeck, 2014) 376; M Stürner, 'Effektivität des europäischen Kollisionsrechts und nationales Verfahrensrecht', in *Festschrift für Rolf Stürner* (Tübingen, Mohr Siebeck, 2013); H Gotsche, *Der BGH im Wettbewerb der Zivilrechtsordnungen* (Stuttgart, Nomos, 2009) 154; F Eichel, 'Die Revisibilität ausländischen Rechts nach der Neufassung von § 545 Abs. 1 ZPO' [2009] *IPRax* 389, 393; B Hess and R Hübner, 'Die Revisibilität ausländischen Rechts nach der Neufassung des § ZPO § 545 ZPO' [2009] *Neue Juristische Wochenschrift* 3132, 3135; Gössl and Effer-Uhe (n 68) 127, 136 ff.; G *Mäsch*, 'Die Rolle des BGH im Wettbewerb der Rechtsordnungen oder: Neue Nahrung für den Ruf nach der Revisibilität ausländischen Rechts' (2004) 11 *Europäische Zeitung für Wirtschaftsrecht* 321.

[72] Against reviewability, for example H Roth, 'Die Revisibilität ausländischen Rechts und die Klugheit des Gesetzes' [2014] *Neue Juristische Wochenzeitschrift* 1224, 1226; F Sturm, 'Wegen Verletzung fremden Rechts sind weder Revision noch Rechtsbeschwerde zulässig: Zur Auslegung von §§ 72 Abs. 1 FamFG, 545 Abs. 1 und 576 Abs. 1 ZPO' [2011] *Juristen Zeitung* 74; J Stamm, *Festschrift für Klamaris* (Athens, Sakkoulas, 2016) 769; H Reichold in H Thomas/H Putzo, '§ 545 para 8/9' in *Zivilprozessordnung*, 44th edn (München, C.H. Beck, 2023); W Ball, H Musielak and W Voit, '§ 545 para 7', in *Zivilprozessordnung*, 20th edn (München, C.H. Beck, 2023).

[73] Commentaries often do not define exactly what is meant by non-reviewable law. This usually only emerges from the context and from the synopsis with s 545 ZPO, see, eg, only W Krüger '§ 560 Rn. 3 ff.', in *Münchener Kommentar zum Zivilprozessrecht*, 6th edn (München, C.H. Beck, 2020); H-J Heßler, '§ 560 Rn. 2 ff.', in *Zöller ZPO*, 35th edn (München, C.H. Beck, 2023).

The Federal Court of Justice confirmed that the traditional view should prevail under the new wording of the provision on the possible grounds for second appeal.[74] Thus, only the incorrect or omitted determination of the content of the foreign law is reviewable, as this would constitute a violation of section 293 ZPO.

This position may well be criticised.[75] Since it is precisely with regard to the application of foreign law that there is a higher risk of error, it is surprising that it is not subject to the same scrutiny of correctness as the application of German law.[76] Furthermore, the incorrect application of the law is often due to an insufficient determination of the foreign law, in particular the failure to take foreign legal practice into account.[77] As this can also be asserted by means of a procedural objection in the appellate instance,[78] this in any case indirectly results in a review of the substantive foreign law.[79]

VIII. Outlook and Proposed Reforms

In conclusion, it can be said that in many cases the appointment of an expert will be unavoidable. This practice, which is prevalent in Germany, has certainly proven itself as very helpful. It causes rather moderate costs[80] due to the linking of expert fees to a system of fixed hourly rates and usually provides high-quality and, above all, fact-oriented information on the foreign law to be applied.[81]

Nevertheless, the relevant institutes and chairs have been operating at or above their limits for many years.[82] From a European perspective, it should also

[74] BGH, *NJW* 2014, 1244.

[75] *cf.* with further references the proponents of revisability mentioned in footnote 237.

[76] Linke and Hau (n 53) para 9.20.

[77] *cf.* Fastrich 'Revisibilität der Ermittlung ausländischen Rechts' (1984) 97 *Zeitschrift für Zivilprozess* 423, 424.

[78] *cf.* here only the already mentioned judgment of the Federal Court of Justice, *NJW* 2014, 12. Here it was argued that obtaining information on the London Convention was not sufficient to interpret various foreign terms in the same way as legal practice would do. In effect, the Court of Appeal's interpretation of these legal norms became the subject of the appeal. Such an approach was already criticised by Fastrich (n 77) 423, 424, who noted that the incorrect application of the law was practically always put up for revision via the diversions of the investigation complaint.

[79] There are also other exceptions regarding the reviewability of the foreign law itself, *cf.* the list in Gotsche (n 71) 127 et seq. For example, the BGH can determine the foreign law itself if a foreign provision that is applicable to the facts of the case only came into force after the decision of the court of appeal.

[80] *cf.* Seibl, *ZZP* 128 (2015), 431.

[81] P Neuhaus, *Die Grundbegriffe des Internationalen Privatrechts*, 2nd edn (Tübingen, Mohr Siebeck, 1976) 331, already considered this to be the 'relatively best means [...] to support the judge in determining foreign law'.

[82] This is already stated by G Kegel, *Festschrift für Nipperdey* (München, C.H. Beck, 1965) 453, with reference to a similar complaint by E Rabel, *25 Jahre Kaiser Wilhelm-Gesellschaft zur Förderung der Wissenschaften Vol. 1*, (Berlin, Springer, 1936) 142. See additionally Neuhaus (n 81) 332 ('From the point of view of the purpose of the scientific institutes, the heavy burden of expert opinions is highly questionable'). See also Stürner and Krauß (n 7) 49 ff.

be noted that only very few member states have established research institutes on foreign and comparative law with significant specialisation and extensive law libraries.[83] Especially for those states, better access to foreign law must be guaranteed in order to increase the effectiveness of conflict-of-laws rules.[84]

This leads me to some proposals for reform relating to expert evidence.[85] A first measure, which would be quite simple to implement, relates to improving the information on potential experts. Another proposal is much more demanding; it starts with an enhanced professionalisation of potential experts on foreign law. Finally, a third proposal strives at making conventional expert evidence obsolete and replacing it with a system of mutual legal assistance.

Just for the sake of completeness, it should be noted that artificial intelligence is currently not yet able to determine the necessary information on foreign law with sufficient precision. This may change in the near future, but for the time being, large language models such as ChatGPT are likely to be able to replace expert evidence only in simple cases.

A. Databases on Available Experts on Foreign Law

As far as can be seen, there is no publicly maintained or even accessible list of experts on foreign law. Names of potential experts are time and again published by notaries public. However, the last such publication seems to date from 2003.[86] An exception exists for the area of family law. Here the so-called FTCAM system[87] has been in existence since 1980 and is available online for 15 federal states at www.ftcam.de.[88] The aim of this system is the computerisation of family law. Its aim is the computer-aided preparation of draft decisions on the basis of foreign law.[89]

Part of the FTCAM system is also a database available at sachverstaendige.ftcam.de, in which experts can be searched free of charge according to country, place of work and name. Experts are admitted upon application and payment of a one-off fee of €200.[90] A closer examination of the qualification by the operators

[83] This could also be a reason why the *lex fori* is readily and quickly resorted to in many places, see Kegel (n 82).

[84] On this aspect in particular, see Stürner (n 71).

[85] For further reform proposals *cf.* Stürner and Krauß (n 7) 457 ff.

[86] Hetger (n 58) 310, excerpts also reproduced in *Zeitschrift für Erbrecht und Vermögensnachfolge* (2006) 450; see also Schütze (n 58).

[87] *cf.* D Höbbel, O Seibert and T Möller, 'FTCAM', *Internet Zeitschrift für Rechtsinformatik und Informationsrecht*, Web-Dok. 76/2012, available at www.jurpc.de/jurpc/show?id=20120076.

[88] Baden-Württemberg, Bayern, Brandenburg, Bremen, Hamburg, Hessen, Mecklenburg-Vorpommern, Niedersachsen, Nordrhein-Westfalen, Rheinland-Pfalz, Saarland, Sachsen, Sachsen-Anhalt, Schleswig-Holstein, Thüringen.

[89] See also D Höbbel, O Seibert and T Möller, 'Wie wirkt sich die ROM III-VO auf die Praxis aus?' [2013] *Familie und Recht* 28.

[90] The application form is available here: sachverstaendige.ftcam.de/reg45mnb83c.php.

of the database does not seem to take place. A rough check has shown that only a little more than a dozen experts have registered in this database.

The creation of such a database for general civil law would certainly correspond to a widespread wish of the judiciary.[91] However, the large-scale registration of expert witnesses that is necessary here certainly poses problems. In many cases, there is little incentive to prepare such expert opinions at all. First, this is due to the comparatively modest remuneration under the fee system in Germany. On the other hand, it may also be related to anecdotical evidence that some court administrations are extremely petty with the invoices submitted by the experts. With private expert opinions at the direct request of a party, one may earn considerably more. Nevertheless, it seems to have become established in case law that a classification in the highest hourly rate according to section 9(1), (2) sentence 1 of the Act on the Remuneration of Experts etc. (JVEG) is regularly appropriate.[92]

The large institutes on foreign and comparative law, whether they are research institutes such as the Max Planck Institute in Hamburg or university institutes such as those in Cologne, Heidelberg, Munich or Freiburg, are generally well known among the judiciary,[93] but they are not well enough equipped to deal with the numerous requests in a reasonable amount of time, so that courts sometimes have to make several attempts to obtain the required expert opinion.[94] Law professors at smaller universities, on the other hand, may have expertise in the field, but regularly do not have a sufficiently well-stocked library that would allow them to seriously process requests for expert opinions on more than a handful of legal systems.[95]

Apart from that, there is the time and cost factor. Especially at lower courts, there is a great reluctance to obtain an expert opinion, as the legal dispute would regularly be delayed by six to twelve months.[96] At regional and higher regional courts, the willingness definitely seems to be higher.[97] A change in the fee structure would hardly be explainable to potential experts. It can also be assumed that setting tight deadlines and enforcing them would have a prohibitive effect on them. The 2016 Act Amending the Law on Expert Witnesses[98]

[91] Stürner and Krauß (n 7) 264 ff. and 401.

[92] OLG Dresden *NJW* 2019, 1236.

[93] This applies above all to the Max Planck Institute, see Stürner and Krauß (n 7) 355 ff.

[94] The decision of the OLG Munich *NJW* 2017, 338 para 18 shows that the refusal to accept an expert opinion by the appointed expert does not authorise the decision to be made without further attempts to investigate the foreign law.

[95] Possible solutions below B. and C.

[96] See Stürner and Krauß (n 7) 198.

[97] ibid 355 ff.

[98] Gesetz zur Änderung des Sachverständigenrechts und zur weiteren Änderung des Gesetzes über das Verfahren in Familiensachen und in den Angelegenheiten der freiwilligen Gerichtsbarkeit sowie zur Änderung des Sozialgerichtsgesetzes, der Verwaltungsgerichtsordnung, der Finanzgerichtsordnung und des Gerichtskostengesetzes vom 11.10.2016, BGBl. I, S. 2222. S dazu J Lüblinghoff, 'Das Gesetz zur Änderung des Sachverständigenrechts' (2016) Neue *Juristische Wochenzeitschrift* 3329; M Huber, 'Das Gesetz zur Änderung des Sachverständigenrechts in der Praxis des Zivilprozesses' [2017] *Juristische Schulung* 34.

already went in this direction: With regard to the deadline to be set for the expert to submit the expert report, there is now no longer any discretionary leeway (section 411(1) ZPO).[99] In case of failure to meet the deadline, an administrative fine is now to be imposed (section 411(2) sentence 1 ZPO), which may amount to up to €3,000 (section 411(2) sentence 4 ZPO). The expert's negligence required for this does not already cease to exist through the reference to work overload.[100] Thus, the imposition of an administrative fine can only be waived in exceptional cases, according to the 2016 Act, for example, if the deadline is slightly exceeded or the expert is only slightly at fault.[101]

In my estimation, courts are very cautious in their use of these instruments with regard to expert opinions on foreign law. This is because they are also dependent on the cooperation of the experts. Otherwise, many of them will refuse to provide an expert opinion from the outset with reference to section 408(1) sentence 2 ZPO. The extension of the time limit according to section 224(2) ZPO is certainly also used in appropriate cases.

B. Bundling and Professionalisation of Expert Evidence

A 2011 study by the Swiss Institute of Comparative Law proposes,[102] among other things, the establishment of a European Centre of Expertise at EU level, in which – following the example of the Max Planck Institute in Hamburg or the Swiss Institute of Comparative Law in Lausanne – legal experts from each Member State would be employed to answer questions about their respective jurisdictions. The possibility to ask this Centre of Expertise for guidance on foreign law should be optional and should not replace the existing channels of investigation in each member state. With regard to the costs for legal information provided within this framework, it is proposed that these be borne by the judiciary, at least in the first instance.

For Germany, this proposal of pooling competences would be comparatively easy to implement, as the structures are already in place at the Max Planck Institute. Certainly, an improvement in resources would be necessary. A number of other university institutes could also be upgraded accordingly. Whether a European Centre of Expertise would eventually have a chance of political realisation is another matter. In any case, it can be assumed that German courts would initially tend to turn to the German institutions mentioned above with enquiries about foreign law.

[99] See the statistics in Bundesrats-Drucksache No 438/15, 11.

[100] See, eg, OLG Celle *NJW* 1972, 1524.

[101] Bundesrats-Drucksache No 438/15, 12.

[102] The Application of Foreign Law in Civil Matters in the EU Member States and its Perspectives for the Future, available at op.europa.eu/en/publication-detail/-/publication/c92e8d95-ac55-4c9c-91b6-36a5a7564838/language-en. On its contents Stürner and Krauß (n 7) 58 ff.

C. Substitution of Expert Evidence by Referral Procedure

A completely different direction is taken by the proposal to determine the relevant foreign law within the framework of a formal referral procedure to a court of the state in question. This could be set up in such a way that any court of a Member State before which a question of law relating to the law of another Member State arises would have the possibility to refer this question to a court of that state of equal rank.[103] The referral decision should not have any binding effect on the proceedings pending before the referring court. The question of foreign law is not to be appealable as such, but should be brought to a higher court within the framework of the regular appellate procedure. No costs (other than translation costs) are to be incurred for the reference procedure.

Similar approaches were already implemented by some jurisdictions. In the Australian state of New South Wales, for example, a rule has been in force since the end of 2010[104] that allows a court, on the application of one party and with the consent of all other parties with regard to a legal question on foreign law, to order that proceedings be opened to resolve that legal question before a foreign court.[105] However, since an Australian court cannot order the court of another sovereign state to open interlocutory proceedings to resolve a point of law, international agreements are necessary to enable this type of mutual legal assistance. Corresponding memoranda of understanding exist to date between the Supreme Court of New South Wales and the Supreme Court of Singapore, as well as between the Chief Justice of New South Wales and the Chief Judge of the State of New York.[106]

This type of legal assistance, and even more so the aforementioned referral procedure, could certainly enter new dimensions, especially in comparison to the

[103] Proposal by O Remien in J Basedow, *Aufbruch nach Europa* (Tübingen, Mohr Siebeck, 2001) 617, 631; similarly M Jänterä-Jareborg, *Foreign law in national courts: a comparative perspective* (2003) 204 *Recueil des cours* 181, 322 f. Agreeing with this approach A Flessner, 'Diskriminierung von grenzübergreifenden Rechtsverhältnissen im europäischen Zivilprozess' [2006] *Zeitschrift für Europäisches Privatrecht* 737, 741; J Müller, *Die Behandlung ausländischen Rechts im Zivilverfahren* (Bern, Peter Lang, 2011) 195 ff.; G Rühl and J von Hein, 'Towards a European Code on Private Law' (2015) 79 *Rabels Zeitschrift für ausländisches und internationales Privatrecht* 701, 749. See previously A Schwartze, 'Die Ermittlung und Anwendung des Vertragsrechts anderer EU-Staaten im deutschen Zivilprozeß nach § 293 ZPO – ein besonderer Fall', in *Festschrift für Fenge* (Hamburg, Verlag Dr. Kovač, 1996) 127, 145 with reference to the English Foreign Law Ascertainment Act 1861, repealed in 1973. Neuhaus (n 81) 329, had also mentioned, but rejected, the involvement of an expert 'juge ad hoc'.

[104] New South Wales Uniform Civil Procedure Rules 2005, Part 6, Division 9. The legal basis for this is s 125 New South Wales Supreme Court Act 1970, which became effective on 7 December 2010.

[105] Rule 6.44(1) UCPR 2005 states: 'The Supreme Court may, on the application of one or more of the parties and with the consent of all of the parties, order that proceedings be commenced in a foreign court in order to answer a question as to the principles of foreign law or as to their application.'

[106] See J Spigelman, 'Proof of Foreign Law by Reference to the Foreign Court' (2011) 127 *LQR* 208; PLG Brereton, 'Proof of Foreign Law: Problems and Initiatives' (2011) 85 *Australian Law Journal* 554 and, for a first application, Y Nishitani/Y Nishitani, *Treatment of Foreign Law – Dynamics towards Convergence* (Cham, Springer Verlag, 2017) 3, 52.

London Convention.[107] Nevertheless, it does not appear certain that the quality of legal information would be decisively improved. Even in the case of judicial information, the problem remains that oral questioning of the foreign judge will probably continue to be excluded.[108] It would still need to be clarified whether the parties should have any right to be heard before the foreign court.[109] If this were the case, high costs and considerable delays would be the consequence. If not, the foreign judge would simply act as an expert.[110] The progress compared to the London Convention would then be rather limited. There is also the question of whether a referral procedure would be mandatory or whether – preferably – it would only be at the discretion of the judge as an additional possibility of determining the law alongside the existing ones. Finally, the question of costs is essential: legal assistance is based on reciprocity and is thus borne by the states involved. This is to be welcomed by the parties, as it eliminates the costs for an expert witness.[111] From a fiscal point of view, however, the opposite view may be taken.

At this stage, it seems unlikely that the Member States would be willing to introduce a referral procedure.[112] The EU Commission's joint efforts with the Hague Conference on Private International Law to create a 'global legal instrument' to improve access to foreign law have stalled. The recommendations at the joint meeting of the EU Commission and the Hague Conference in February 2012[113] were that a possible legal instrument should facilitate access to foreign law, but not standardise the legal assessment of foreign law in the respective national procedural law (Recommendation No. 3). Also, such a legal act should only apply in addition to already existing or to be introduced possibilities of ascertaining foreign law and not supersede them (Recommendation No. 4). From the perspective of the states involved, however, the Judgments Project had priority, so that no further impetus has been noted since around 2014.[114] A continuation of the negotiations is currently not in sight.

[107] Emphasising their role model function for possible legal harmonisation, P Lortie and M Groff, 'The 1993 Hague Intercountry Adoption Convention and Subsidiarity: Is the Subsidiarity Principle still 'Fit for Purpose'?' in *Essays in honour of Hans van Loon* (Cambridge, Intersentia, 2013).

[108] *cf.* Stürner and Krauß (n 7) 44.

[109] See, eg, C Trautmann, *Europäisches Kollisionsrecht und ausländisches Recht im nationalen Zivilverfahren* (Tübingen, Mohr Siebeck, 2011) 430.

[110] See generally P Hay, 'The Use and Determination of Foreign Law in Civil Litigation in the United States' (2014) 62 *American Journal of Comparative Law* 213, 223.

[111] See especially Schwartze (n 103).

[112] A competence of the EU to issue a corresponding legal act could follow from Art 81 para 2 lit. f TFEU, according to Müller (n 103) 119 ff., 149 ff., 218 f. See also Trautmann (n 109) 410 ff.

[113] Available at www.hcch.net/upload/foreignlaw_concl_e.pdf. See P Lortie and M Groff in Y Nishitani, *Treatment of Foreign Law* (Cham, Springer Verlag, 2017) 615, 625 f., as well as Stürner and Krauß (n 7) 71.

[114] Doc. Prel. No 14 of April 2014 – Enhancing access to foreign law and case law – Presentation of solutions by the European Union, available at www.hcch.net/de/publications-and-studies/studies/access-to-foreign-law1.

12

Part of the Solution or Part of the Problem? Party-appointed Experts in Serbian Litigation Proceedings

BRANKA BABOVIĆ VUKSANOVIĆ[1]

I. The Background

The Republic of Serbia is a civil law country whose litigation system is based on the Austrian model created by Franz Klein. This model is defined as a 'social model' and was developed as a reaction to the liberal[2] one developed in France. Key features of the 'social model' of litigation are that it is based on the idea that the welfare of society has primacy over the welfare of the individual and that litigation and enforcement proceedings should be affordable for citizens.[3] In 1929, in the Kingdom of Yugoslavia, a law was passed that represented almost literal transplantation of the Austrian 1895 Code of Civil Procedure ('aCPC') written based on Klein's ideas. Even the Austrian Commentary written by Neumann was translated and used in Serbia as if it were a national one. This law acted as a basis for all the subsequent Yugoslav laws on civil procedure.[4]

Austrians found a way to implement the abovementioned ideas through a litigation model, which includes an active judge. Furthermore, the duty of an Austrian judge is to manage the litigation to truthful fact-finding and to apply the law to these facts.[5] This means that after the parties have presented the facts, both parties and the court have to collect evidence.[6]

[1] The author acknowledges financial support from the University of Belgrade, Faculty of Law, within the project Contemporary Problems of Serbian Legal System in 2023.

[2] For the influence of the social model on the French liberal model, see L Cadiet, 'Introduction to the French Civil Justice System and Civil Procedural Law' (2011) 28 *Ritsumeikan Law Review* 366.

[3] RR Verkerk, *Fact-finding in civil litigation, a comparative perspective* (Cambridge, Intersentia, 2010) 257.

[4] B Poznić, V Rakić-Vodinelić, *Građansko procesno pravo* (Beograd, Pravni fakultet Univerziteta Union, 2015) 34–35.

[5] B Nunner-Krautgsser, P Anzenberger, *Evidence in Civil Law- Austria* (Maribor, Institute for Local Self-Government and Public Procurement, 2015) 2.

[6] W Rechberger, D Simmota, *Grundriss des österreichischen Zivilprozessrechts- Erkentnisverfahren* (Wien Manzsche Verlags- und Universitätsbuchhandlung, 2010) 226.

Unlike in Austria, where the inquisitorial principle prevails over adversarial,[7] in Serbia nowadays, it is the other way around.[8] After the 2004 Civil Procedure Act – the first CPA after the process of EU integration started (2004 CPA) – and the 2011 Civil Procedure Act (2011 CPA) were enacted, this feature of Klein's model was abandoned, and now the adversarial principle prevails over inquisitorial. The idea underpinning this change was the efficiency of the proceedings. Nevertheless, many characteristics of Serbian litigation remained the same as in Austria. The underlying structures of legal institutes are mostly transplants from Austria.

For example, in Austria, paragraphs 350 and 351 of the aCPC stipulate that the court expert is to be appointed if specialised knowledge, which the court does not have, is necessary to establish the facts.[9] The proposal of expert evidence by the parties is not necessary in Austria. The court can request the evidence after the parties have pleaded on the facts. Conversely, in Serbia, the notion of the court expert is the same, but the parties furnish facts and propose evidence to the court.

Even though ex-Yugoslav and Serbian litigation proceedings derived from Klein's model, it has changed over time. The main ideas of Klein's model, the active role of the judge, the concentration of the proceedings, and its efficiency, were never implemented in the practice of courts in the post-socialist countries.[10] Serbia has not been an exception, neither in the socialist era nor when the process of European integration started in Serbia.[11] This was one of the reasons why the concept of litigation proceedings was changed in 2004 (the first CPA after the process of EU integration has started) and in 2011 when the current CPA was enacted, introducing the most significant diversions from the Austrian model so far.[12]

The Serbian litigation system has become part of the Mediterranean legal system.[13] The main characteristics of these legal systems have nothing to do

[7] ibid 226.

[8] A Jakšić, *Građansko procesno pravo* (Beograd, Pravni fakultet, 2018) 175–180, Poznić, Rakić-Vodinelić (n 4) 171–173.

[9] This understanding of court expert is analysed below in more detail.

[10] A Uzelac, 'Evidence and the principle of proportionality. How to get rid of expencive and time consuming evidence?', in CH van Rhee ana A Uzelac (eds), *Evidence and Contemporary Civil Procedure. Fundamental Issues in a Comparative Perspective* (Cambridge, Intersentia, 2015) 19.

[11] Poznić, Rakić-Vodinelić (n 4) 35. While Uzelac states that the practice of post-socialist countries was 'drastically different' from Klein's ideas, Rakić-Vodinelić concludes that Klein's ideas 'were never fully implemented'.

[12] ibid. However, the opposition to the novelties is still there: See B. Babović Vuksanović, 'Blast from the past- Consumer Collective Redress in Serbia', in C Poncibo and M Đurović (eds), *Private Law, Rule of Law and European Court of Human Rights: Comparative Perspectives from South- Eastern Europe* (Oxford, Hart Publishing, 2024) 153–174; B Vuksanović, 'Revision (second appeal on the point of law) in Serbian Litigation Proceedings' (2023) 4 *Strani pravni život,* 707–725; B Vuksanović, 'Ročišta na daljinu u parničnom postupku' (2022) 2 *Belgrade Law Review* 533–549.

[13] Defined by A Uzelac, 'Reforming Mediterranean civil procedure: is there a need for shock therapy?', in A Uzelac and CH van Rhee (eds), *Civil justice between Efficiency and Quality, From ius commune to the CEPEJ* (Antwerpen, Ius Commune Series, 2008) 77–99.

with Europe's coastline. Hence, the Mediterranean designation, in its term, is a consolation prize for the legal systems suffering from inefficiency and other dysfunctionalities.[14] Professor Uzelac has explained these dysfunctionalities and defined the main characteristics of these legal systems: judiciary-centred perspective, opposition to the novelties, a high level of formalism, etc. The enactment of the 2011 CPA was final proof that the Serbian litigation system, when diverting from the socialist legal system, has also diverted from Klein's model as well as from the modern Austrian model.

Part of the process of diversion from the Austrian model was the introduction of the party-appointed experts in 2011 as one of the legal institutes that should modernise Serbian civil procedure. The main focus of this chapter is on this novelty. This change in the rules of evidence was a consequence of a strongly boosted adversarial principle in the Serbian litigation system in 2004 and 2011. This chapter will examine the reasons for the introduction of party-appointed experts and the way it is implemented. After more than ten years of application of the 2011 CPA, it is possible to analyse if the application of this institute has helped overcome underlying problems of the Serbian judiciary and to assess the effects of its application in Serbia.

II. The Role of Court Experts in Serbian Litigation Proceedings

In this chapter, we will examine the role of court experts in Serbian litigation proceedings from two perspectives. The first perspective will be the formal – how the Serbian legislation defines court experts, and the second perspective will be the role that court experts have in legal practice.

A. The Core Notion of Court Expert

Continental countries traditionally consider court experts to be judges' assistants, which is the case in Serbia. Serbian understanding of the role of court experts has its roots in Austrian legal tradition.

According to the Explanatory Memorandum to the 1895 Austrian codification, the duty of experts was defined as a duty to support the court in its duty to establish the facts truthfully. Austrian theory has followed with the designation of the expert as not only an 'auxiliary of the court' but also as a 'public law official'.[15]

[14] According to Uzelac, Mediterranean systems are located in different parts of Europe. However, the core of the systems characterized as the Mediterranean is on the shore of the Mediterranean Sea.

[15] Sperl, 1925, 445, according to Verkerk (n 3) 160.

The relationship between the expert, the court, and the parties is not a private one. It is regulated by the acts of parliament and not by contracts.[16] In Austria, the experts perform part of the duties reserved for the judge only because the judge has no expertise in their field. Nevertheless, the court experts' opinion is subject to the free assessment of evidence.[17]

This role of the expert has not fundamentally changed ever since. Both in Austria[18] and in Serbia,[19] the core understanding of court experts is that the court experts are traditionally considered to be primarily proxies for the judge and also means of evidence. Finally, in Serbia, experts can be technical consultants for the parties.[20] Party-appointed experts appeared in Austrian and Serbian litigation systems in different forms.

In Serbia, nowadays, parties can hire a permanent court expert or an expert solely to comment on the report submitted by the court expert or to submit the new report. The court allows those experts to participate in a hearing by asking questions and giving explanations for the party that hired them (Article 271(2) 2011 CPA). Besides, a party-appointed expert can be hired to furnish the report only if that expert is registered as a permanent court expert. In this case, parties can hire an expert, but the pool of experts is limited to the experts certified by the Ministry of Justice. These novelties are the main focus of the analysis contained in the last section of this chapter.

B. The Role of the Judge in Appointing a Court Expert

There are two decisions that should be made when appointing a court expert: choice of the person to be appointed expert and definition of his mission (scope of his work) based on the information about the object of the expertise.

In Austria, the competence of the judges with regard to the expert evidence is broad because the judge is the only one to know for which issues he needs assistance and which he could resolve by himself.[21] Even though the parties should be consulted on the person to be appointed as expert, unlike in Serbia, the court may skip this step due to efficiency.[22]

In Austria, paragraph 353 of the aCPC sets out that experts who are publicly enlisted are, as a rule, obliged to undertake the expertise when appointed. The same applies to the professionals officially authorised to practise their expertise

[16] Verkerk (n 3) 160.
[17] R Holzhammer, *Österreichisches Zivilprozeßrecht Erkentnisverpahren* (Wien, Springer Verlag, 1970) 215.
[18] Rechberger and Simmota (n 6) 462.
[19] Jakšić (n 8) 507.
[20] Jakšić (n 8) 507.
[21] Holzhammer (n 17) 216.
[22] Verkerk (n 3) 162.

publicly.[23] In case the court expert fails to comply with the procedural law, the judge can order the expert to bear the costs caused by its actions and impose monetary sanctions.[24] Permanent court experts have a duty to undertake the expertise when appointed in Serbia as well (Article 265 CPA). This duty is a reflection of the party's right to evidence in the litigation proceedings and the fact that the court does not have specialised knowledge.[25]

Like in Austria, the court can order that the expert bear the costs caused by its actions and impose monetary sanctions (Article 267 CPA). According to paragraph 351(2) of the aCPC, the judge can replace the expert. Similarly, in Serbia, when an expert fails to submit the report timely, the court may, upon request of a party, appoint another expert (Article 272 CPA). The survey conducted by the World Bank Group has established that in practice, sanctions are rarely imposed. The reason for that could be that judges are reluctant to sanction the experts they often appoint.[26] On the other hand, the reason could be that the judges are generally reluctant to impose sanctions in litigation proceedings.

In Serbia, court experts are appointed upon the proposal of a party. Unlike in Austria, Serbian judges, who no longer have as active a role as before, can request expertise only exceptionally. That is the case if fact-finding is necessary to examine the disposals of parties contrary to imperative rules of public policy, and good customs (Article 3.3 CPA). This exception to the rule that parties are the ones to request an expert has been rarely applied. The judge can also request expertise as an ultimate tool when two experts' opinions cannot be aligned (Article 271.4 CPA). If one of the parties has submitted an expert report, the opposing party can object and appoint an expert to reply. Should these experts' reports not be sufficient for a court to establish a fact, it may appoint a third expert and request parties to share the costs of this expertise.[27] Serbian judges are no longer as active in taking evidence as they used to be. The situation is different in Austria (even though the provisions drafted in line with the Kleins model have changed in its home country as well) – the court appoints the court expert, but both the court and the parties can adduce an expert.[28]

In Serbia, the parties present facts, respond to the assertions of the opposing party, and propose evidence to the court. Even though the parties are the ones to

[23] 'Chapter 2: Litigation', in M Heider, M Nueber, et al. (eds), *Dispute Resolution in Austria: An Introduction* (Alphen aan den Rijn, Kluwer Lawnational, 2015) 121.

[24] G Kodek, P Meyer, *Zivilprozessrecht* (Wien, facultas.wuv, 2013) 297.

[25] G Stanković, V Boranijašević, *Građansko procesno pravo* (Beograd, Službeni glasnik, 2023) 453.

[26] The World Bank Group, *Examining the Experts – The Role of Expert Witnesses in Serbia, and How Reform Could Improve Efficiency and Quality of Justice* (Belgrade, The World Group, 2018).

[27] Commercial Appellate Court of the Republic of Serbia, Interpretative Opinion adopted by the Department for Commercial Disputes on 8 November 2018 and 9 November 2018, 'Bulletin of the Commercial Courts 4/2018'.

[28] Nunner-Krautgsser (n 5) 39.

propose the evidence, the court has a final word in choosing a particular court expert (in case parties do not agree on the person to be appointed as court expert). Apart from that, the court has a final word in designating the mission of the court expert. After the 2004 CPA and 2011 CPA introduced the shift in the balance between inquisitorial and adversarial principles in favour of the adversarial, it was unclear in the practice if the court could only decide on the party's proposal of the expert's mission[29] or if it was the court's duty to formulate the mission for the expert. The interpretation that the court has the final word in formulating the mission of the court expert prevailed in practice.[30]

C. Freedom to Choose an Expert?

The focus of this chapter is the selection of the person to be appointed as a court expert. It will examine how the freedom to choose an expert as evidence in litigation proceedings is limited in Serbia and how it is different from Austria, the home country of Serbian litigation.

In Austria, courts keep the experts' registry and update it. However, depending on the circumstances of the case, the judge is competent to appoint an expert who is not enlisted.[31] Unlike in Austria, where the court keeps the registry of court experts, in Serbia, court experts are certified by the MoJ, which is competent to administer and update this registry.

This way of appointing court experts has its roots in SFRY. Nevertheless, in SFRY, when applying the 1976 CPA, courts were allowed to appoint an expert not licensed by the MoJ in case parties agreed on that appointment.[32] This was stipulated by the 1987 Law on Conditions for Conducting Expertise in Courts and Other Proceedings (*Official Gazette of the Socialist Republic of Serbia* 16/87), which provided for the appointment of an individual who is not a licensed court expert in simple cases. The Yugoslav 1976 CPA stipulated in Article 251 that the court appoints the court expert upon consultation with the parties. In the case of urgency, the court can appoint an expert without hearing the parties about the appointment. These provisions were very similar to today's Austrian law.

As a rule, the judges appointed permanent court experts (Article 252 (2) 1976 CPA). However, they were competent to appoint an expert who is not registered

[29] According to legal scholars, the proposal of the parties must contain the object of the expertise, but not the mission of the court expert, G Stanković, V Boranijašević, *Građansko procesno pravo* (Beograd, Službeni glasnik, 2023) 451.

[30] Answer to the questions asked at the 22nd annual commercial court conference held in September 2014, available in the database IngPro.

[31] Kodek, Meyer (n 24) 297.

[32] M Jankovic, H Karamarkovic, Ž Janković and D Petrović, *Komentar Zakona o parničnom postupku* (Beograd Savremena administracija, 1990) 290. B Poznić, *Komentar Zakona o parničnom postupku- prema tekstu zakona iz 1976 sa docnijim izmenama i dopunama* (Beograd, Službeni glasnik, 2009) 653.

as a permanent court expert if he fulfils all conditions to be appointed. In practice, this was rarely the case – for example, if there are no experts registered in an area of expertise.[33]

This practice was not sustained in all countries formed after the breakup of Yugoslavia. In the 1980s, the Supreme Court of Croatia ruled that the judges' choice was not limited to the list made by the ministry since that would affect their freedom to choose the type of evidence.[34] This way of thinking has been preserved in Croatia for a long time.[35] However, it did not take root in Serbia – the government changed the law in the direction of mandatory choice of permanent court experts. There is an exception to this rule: if, for a particular type of expertise, there is no court expert listed in the registry, expertise can be done by a person of appropriate expertise, with a declaration to the court that the findings and opinions were given professionally and to the best of his knowledge, objectively and impartially (Article 264 (2) 2011 CPA). The case law established when the 1976 CPA applied, became the law, and the judges have lost the possibility to interpret the exemption to the rule that the permanent court expert should be appointed. This formalistic approach and self-oriented judiciary are features of the Mediterranean legal system. Comparative law analysis conducted within the European Parliament[36] identifies at least one additional reason to appoint an expert who is not registered as a permanent court expert – in the cases in which highly specialised knowledge is necessary to establish facts, the appointment of a scientific authority would make sense for one case only.

The Law on Court Experts ('LEW') provide for an even distribution of cases between the court experts. Article 18(2) of the Serbian LEW stipulates that the court must appoint an expert whose residence is on the territory within its jurisdiction. Apart from that, the court should evenly distribute work among experts registered in its jurisdiction's territory. While the courts in practice insist on appointing registered permanent court experts, they do not evenly distribute the cases among them according to the available data presented by the World Bank Group in a report based on inspiring empirical research. Moreover, it is noticeable that the judges appoint the same experts repeatedly. The research on this topic (as well as on other problems regarding court experts) was done by the World Bank Group, which identified the reasons behind this practice. The main reason that judges pointed out is that some experts are more diligent and produce opinions of higher quality.[37] However, in the long run, experienced court experts become overburdened, and the less experienced do not get a chance to practise their

[33] Poznić (n 30) 653.

[34] Supreme Court of the Republic of Croatia Rev 1849/80- NZp 19/82-140, cited by S Triva, M Dika, *Građansko parnično procesno pravo* (Zagreb, Narodne novine, 2004) 529.

[35] Triva, Dika (n 32) 529.

[36] European Parliament, *Civil-law expert reports in the EU: national rules and practices – In Depth Analysis of the JURI Committee* (2015) 20.

[37] The World Bank Group (n 25).

expertise in court proceedings.[38] Consequently, the court experts, ie, the registered and often appointed ones, have an even more important role in the Serbian litigation proceedings than experts usually have – they are indeed treated as heroes of the judicial periphery.

D. Assessment of Court Experts' Report

Apart from the perception that the use of court experts is common in Serbian litigation proceedings,[39] there is a perception that judges do not review experts' opinions with enough scrutiny. Furthermore, it is common for courts to appoint experts for routine issues that do not require any specialised knowledge.[40] This means that the experts' opinions issued by the certified court experts largely influence the judgment. The CPA does not attribute enhanced or binding value to the expert's opinion, but the case law does. The main reason for such a practice is that it is difficult for judges to evaluate the expert's opinion because the judge is not knowledgeable in that field.[41]

E. Court Experts' Influence on the Efficiency of the Proceedings

The appointment of a court expert in the litigation proceedings influences the course of the proceedings since the expertise is time-consuming. In comparison to the other types of evidence in litigation proceedings, the expert evidence is lingering.

Typically, the proceedings start with the proposal of a party to appoint an expert, followed by the decision of the court. After the resolution on the appointment is rendered and the scope of the expert's work is defined, the court sets the time for the proposing party to deposit the advance costs of the expertise. After the advance payment is made, the court expert takes the whole hard copy of the case file to conduct the findings and to issue an opinion. The time limit set for the expert to finish the report is most often the legal maximum of 60 days. Once the expert submits the report to the court, the party comments on the report; very often, a hearing is scheduled, and sometimes, an additional expert is appointed. In case the court experts are not disciplined, it affects the efficiency of the litigation proceedings. The 2011 CPA introduced tools to establish the

[38] ibid.

[39] ibid, Jakšić (n 8) 505.

[40] V Pavic, D Hiber, 'Experiences from Post-Socialist Legal Systems', in GJ Horvath, S Wilske (eds), *Guerrilla Tactics in International Arbitration* (Aalphen an den Rijn, Kluwer, 2013)153–154.

[41] Jakšić (n 8) 507.

procedural discipline of the court experts. For example, court experts must submit their opinion within a maximum of 60 days.[42] Nevertheless, there are causes of delay in litigation proceedings that could not be prevented or suppressed successfully. Instructions for experts are sometimes too broadly defined. This usually prolongs the proceedings since additional expertise with more precise instructions is necessary after that.[43] There are also other problems leading to the delay in rendering the judgment. Sometimes, the mission for the court expert is defined wrongfully – it includes legal issues[44] that the court expert is not competent to resolve.

F. Role of the Court Experts in Serbian Litigation Proceedings

To sum up, the role of the judge has changed in Serbian litigation proceedings, but the basic notion of the court expert remains the same as in socialist Yugoslavia. The permanent court experts furnish the reports to the court, which are, in practice, regarded as of high value in the process of assessment of evidence. Those who are repeatedly appointed are overburdened, which influences the efficiency of their work. Due to the lack of reaction by the court, procedural (in)efficiencies of the court experts can affect the course of the proceedings. The work of court experts influences both the length of the proceedings as well as the decision on the merits of the case.

To conclude, the permanent court experts are enormously influential in the Serbian judiciary. One could say that in Serbia, court experts are heroes of the judicial periphery. However, it is not clear if these are real or fake heroes of the judicial periphery in Serbia. It will be analysed whether their expertise, responsibility, and accountability match the exaggerated influence they have in the Serbian judiciary.

III. Quality of Permanent Court Experts

We have examined the role of court experts in the Serbian judiciary, but what we need to do now is assess who the experts are and what skillset they bring to the table. The analyses of the legal framework regulating the certification requirements should be an indicator of the knowledge, skills, and ethics that court experts have in Serbia. Moreover, it will be examined if the legal framework builds the basis for the regular assessment of the competence of court experts and of the improvement of the quality of their work.

[42] Art 269(2) 2011 CPA.
[43] Pavic, Hiber (n 38)153–154.
[44] Statement of Reasons to the 2011 CPA, 12.

A. Entry Criteria

In Serbia, the MoJ administers the registry of permanent court experts.[45] Court experts can be individuals but also companies whose employees are registered court experts, as well as faculties, institutes, and other entities.

The LEW stipulates conditions to be included in the list of permanent court experts. Two of these conditions are clearly defined: one must possess a relevant university degree and have at least five years of professional experience. Apart from these conditions, LCE contains two broad criteria: that a candidate possesses expertise and experience in applying it and, finally, that dignity is needed for a permanent court expert. These conditions are not in line with international standards on requirements for certification of court experts.

The European Expertise & Expert Institute, in its Guide to Good Practices in Civil Judicial Expertise in the European Union,[46] recommends the proof of: (i) the expert's qualifications, (ii) professional curriculum, (iii) knowledge of investigative techniques, (iv) his legal knowledge of the standards governing the exercise of his main activity and the rules relating to the expert's obligations and rights, (v) as well as of the guiding principles of fair trial.[47] Examination of the trial requirements, organisation, or needs of the judiciary is usual in legal systems developed from the same root as the Serbian legal system. For example, in Croatia, court experts need to prove their knowledge of court organisation, organisation of state administration and legal terminology.[48] In Austria, court experts are required to have a basic understanding of provisions on court experts contained in procedural law and methods of writing expert report.[49]

In Serbia, there are no requirements related to the legal standards, requirements of the proceedings, or standardised techniques of writing expert reports. There is no entry test on any judiciary-related or other issues, nor are there any organised training activities after the registration. Paradoxically, the registration of the court experts is permanent and must not be renewed. No mandatory training is required to be licensed as a court expert. The duty to regularly update and improve the knowledge of court experts is stipulated only as an ethical duty prescribed by the Ethical Codex of court experts.[50]

Serbian legislation in this field has abandoned the ex-Yugoslav model of the organisation of training for court experts but never introduced a new system. In the SFRY, the Organisation of Court Experts was competent to inform court experts on modern professional developments and organised training activities.[51]

[45] Both an individual as well as a legal entity could be registered as a permanent court expert.
[46] Rule 3.12 EEEI Guide to Good Practices in Civil Judicial Expertise in the European Union.
[47] The World Bank Group (n 26).
[48] Art 2(1), 4 Croatian Rulebook on Court Experts.
[49] Para 2(2), 1 Austrian Law on court experts.
[50] N Šarkić, M Nikolić, *Veštačenje- građanskopravni aspekti* (Beograd, Glosarijum, 2014) 49.
[51] Art 7 SFRY Law on Conditions for Conducting of Court Expertise.

The 2010 LEW omitted this part – it has no provision about the training or any mandatory activities that should be organised to improve the skills and knowledge of court experts. Those have been excluded together with the provisions on the centralised Organisation of Court Experts. Nowadays, there are several associations of court experts in Serbia. Some of them are formed on the regional criteria,[52] others on the criterion of the area of expertise – primarily medical.[53] However, it is not clear if training activities are being organised regularly or at all. Anyhow, those training activities are voluntary.

The other problem regarding the certification of court experts is related to the areas of expertise defined in the registry. These areas are broad. For example, an expert is licensed in the economy and finance, including calculating interest, evaluating company shares, and the real estate market. Sub-specialisation is the only criterion in the registry to narrow the scope of expertise. The areas of sub-specialisation are not standardised, and for some experts, those are also broad and, for some, relatively narrow. Even though the sub-specialisation could be used as an additional criterion for a party to choose one court expert over the other, in practice, it does not play a crucial role in the appointment of a court expert. If one of the parties proposes the court expert, and the opposing party objects, the objecting party is not legally obliged to elaborate on the reasons since the court is the one to appoint the court expert in case the parties do not agree.

B. Quality Assessment

The entry requirements are only part of the problem. The legal framework regulating the assessment of the work of court experts does not provide adequate tools to control the quality of their work. The court experts are licensed permanently. Even though the international standard is that the court expert licence should be reissued after several years,[54] in Serbia, this is not the case.

Courts are the ones to monitor the work of court experts and to report its remarks and information about the sanctions imposed on the experts to the MoJ. The MoJ is also competent to revoke the court expert's licence. In cases of unprofessional, unethical, or expertise conducted without due diligence, both the court and the parties are authorised to file a motion for revocation of the court expert certification to the MoJ. This function of the MoJ is essential since the registration of the court expert does not expire. Once certified as a permanent court expert, the expert has no further requirements to fulfil. There is neither a mandatory training requirement nor an obligation to re-register. Having in mind that the court

[52] Association of Cout Experts of Vojvodina (northern part of Serbia).
[53] Association of Court Experts in Occupational Health, Association of Court Experts.
[54] Up to five years according to the EGLE European Guide for Legal Expertise EEEI, October 2015.

experts' licences are being revoked very rarely,[55] the only quality filter is the practice of courts to appoint the best experts.

C. Accountability

Unlike public notaries or enforcement agents, court experts are not obliged to have a professional indemnity insurance policy.[56] Therefore, the parties can only sue for compensation of damages.[57] Judges are competent to impose monetary sanctions on the court experts for procedural inefficiency.

Therefore, one could get the impression that becoming part of the group of experts certified to help the court in the process of taking evidence is not difficult. On the contrary, the reality is different. The courts meet annually to discuss the issues related to the work of court experts. They should also initiate the admission procedure for the new court experts in case there is a need for new appointments in practice. Courts inform the MoJ when the court experts in a specific field are lacking. Unlike in Croatia,[58] also an ex-Yugoslav country, or Austria,[59] the homeland of our litigation system, there is no option for an expert to initiate the process of admission to the court expert's profession. This means fewer possibilities for the new experts to be registered as permanent court experts. The involvement of courts in the process of certification of court experts is only initial. The ministry conducts the whole process of certification with no requirements connected to the needs of courts or the process.

All these problems in the work of permanent court experts do not remain unnoticed in Serbia. Laws and policies that regulate this profession are about to be reformed. National Strategy for Judicial Reform for the period 2013–18 – the quality of court experts should be improved through training[60] as well as accountability of court experts through the introduction of transparent control.[61] National Strategy for Judicial Development for the period 2019–24 tackles the inefficiency of court experts. It proposes adequate policies to improve court experts' work accountability, as well as to define the role of court experts more precisely.[62] However, the reform of court experts has not started yet. Moreover, the MoJ has

[55] The World Bank Group (n 25).

[56] Šarkić, Nikolić (n 47) 49.

[57] Jakšić (n 8) 452.

[58] Art 5 of the Croatian Rulebook on Court Experts (*Official Gazette of the Republic of Croatia* No. 38/14, 123/15, 29/16).

[59] Para 4 Austrian Law on court experts.

[60] National Strategy for Judicial Reform for the period 2013-2018, available at www.mpravde.gov.rs/files/Nacionalna%20Strategija%20reforme%20pravosudja%20za%20period%202013.-2018.%20godine.pdf, 36.

[61] ibid 39.

[62] National Strategy for Judicial Reform for the period 2019-2024, available at www.mpravde.gov.rs/sekcija/703/reforma.php, 9 and 27.

not updated the registry for a long period of time, nor did it announce calls for new experts.

IV. Party-appointed Experts in Serbian Litigation Proceedings

A. Reasons Underpinning the Introduction of the Party-appointed Experts in Serbia

The only currently applicable law that has addressed some of the problems analysed above so far is the 2011 CPA. The solution to some of these problems was found in the introduction of the party-appointed experts. The official statement of reasons provided reasoning for the introduction of this provision. The core idea was to change the rules on evidence as a consequence of the change of balance between the adversarial and inquisitorial principles in favour of the former. The problems underpinning this novelty were described in the statement of reasons for the 2011 CPA. According to the legislator, the main problem was that the experts were appointed by the courts exclusively. This problem had two aspects: the courts have established cooperation with some experts they appointed regularly, and the instructions for court experts were sometimes imprecise or even included instructions to provide expertise on the legal issue. Moreover, the uncritical assessment of the expertise furnished by the court-appointed expert has led to the exaggerated value of the expertise in comparison to the other types of evidence.[63] Therefore, introducing the party-appointed experts was intended to enable parties to choose the expert and define a mission for the expertise.

B. The Same Pool of Experts

According to the official Statement of Reasons of the 2011 CPA, the party's choice is limited to the registered permanent court experts. Case law has followed the same understanding: parties are allowed to appoint experts but not to choose an expert not included in the list administered by the MoJ. The Supreme Court case law in criminal matters confirms this position – the expert's report is treated as inadmissible evidence if the registered permanent court expert did not produce it.[64] This way, the opportunity to choose experts was provided to the parties, but the pool of experts remained the same.

[63] Statement of Reasons to the 2011 CPA, 12.
[64] Supreme Court of Cassation, Judgement Kzz 72/2016 as of 22 June 2016.

C. Submitting the Report

The parties can decide if the expertise will be submitted or not. There are no provisions stipulating that the court shall first decide on whether to permit an expert. This is the case in other legal systems, giving major importance to the principle of proportionality[65] in giving evidence, such as England.[66] Similarly, in the US, a country where party-appointed expertise is a rule, Rule 26(a)(2) FRCP requires parties

> at least ninety days before trial (or at times directed by the court) to disclose the identity and report the expected testimony of their testifying required report must include a complete statement of the expert's opinion, as well as the basis and reasons for the opinion, any underlying data and supporting exhibits, the expert's qualifications and publications within the preceding ten years, the expert's compensation, and a listing of other cases in which the expert has testified in the preceding four years.[67]

In Serbia, according to the 2011 CPA, the report is treated as a motion to submit evidence after the party-appointed experts have completed it. If the CPA were applied strictly, the court would be competent to reject the report submitted by the party.[68] Nevertheless, this is not the case due to the party's right to evidence[69] and the report is being read and commented on by the opposing party.[70]

D. The Understanding of Party-appointed Expert

The court expert is no longer only an assistant to the judge but also a consultant for the parties to support their claim. However, the report written by this expert is a court expert's report and not only a document or allegation of the party. The expert appointed by the party must be one of the permanent court experts, after all. This way, the focus of the legal institute is on the court experts.

The party will discuss the potentially inadequate selection of the expert in its objections to the expertise. Of course, party-appointed experts must be independent and impartial, irrespective of the fact that the parties have chosen and hired them. Enrolment in the list of permanent court experts should be the only acceptable guarantee of court experts' accountability (despite the problems described above), save for the situation when there are no experts registered in an area of expertise.

[65] Uzelac (n 10) 22.

[66] S Sime, *A Practical Approach to Civil Procedure* (Oxford, Oxford University Press, 2010) 424.

[67] GR Shreve, P Raven-Hansen, *Understanding Civil Procedure* (Durham, Carolina Academic Press, 2024) 123.

[68] Jakšić (n 8).

[69] ibid.

[70] N Bodiroga, *Parnični postupak* (Beograd, Pravni fakultet, 2022) 349.

When parties appoint an expert, they submit their report to the court. They can do so in the initial stage of the proceedings – to support the claim or the answer to the claim, an expert report is obtained from a party-appointed expert; the court will proceed in the same manner as when an expert is being adduced at the hearing.[71] The choice of an expert who is not registered is, for the court, a reason to reject this evidence.[72]

According to Serbian case law, a report furnished by the party-appointed expert is not documentary evidence since the court is competent to request an oral examination of the expert after the opposing party has objected to the expertise.[73] The understanding of the party-appointed expert in countries with similar traditions is different. Party-appointed expertise will be regarded as a mere allegation of the party in Slovenia,[74] and as documentary evidence like in Austria.[75] Conversely, the Serbian legislator has decided to designate this evidence as expert evidence.

E. Access to Information

Van Rhee wrote that 'party-appointed experts in the continental system should have the duties of a lawyer, and court-appointed experts should have the duties of a judge'.[76] This principle is reflected in the rules on the party-appointed expert's access to the information and evidence in the litigation proceedings. According to Rule 123 ELI/UNIDROIT Model European Rules of Civil Procedure 'Court-appointed experts should be provided with access to all relevant and non-privileged information necessary to prepare their written report.' However, this should not apply to the party-appointed experts.[77] Party-appointed experts have the same type of access to the facts and evidence as parties have.

In Serbia, the CPA does not regulate access to information by the party-appointed experts. There is a difference, though. When the court orders an expert, then it obliges the parties, by a resolution on ordering the expert evidence, that they are to cooperate with and provide to the court expert information regarding the subject matter of expertise.[78] In the event of party-appointed-experts, the parties submit to the court the expertise prepared based on the information provided by the parties themselves. Therefore, from this perspective, a

[71] Art 308 and 315 CPA.

[72] Judgement of the Appellate Court in Belgrade, Gž 2929/2016, 29 January 2016.

[73] Commercial Appellate Court, 2022, Interpretative opinion adopted on the Department for commercial disputes on 22 and 23 November 2022.

[74] A Galič, *Civil Procedure in Sllovenia* (Alphen aan den Rijn, Walters Kluwer, 2020) 169.

[75] Kodek, Meyer (n 24) 297.

[76] CH van Rhee, 'Towards Harmonised European Rules of Civil Procedure: Obligations of the Judge, the Parties and Their Lawyers' (2020) 6 *Access to Just E Eur* 13.

[77] Rule 123 ELI/UNIDROIT Model European Rules of Civil Procedure.

[78] Stanković, Boranijašević (n 25) 452.

party-appointed expert, even though required to be selected from the list of the permanent court experts and examined at the hearing as the court-appointed expert, does not have the role of a court assistant as is traditional for court experts in the Serbian legal system.

F. Remuneration of Court Experts

Both court-appointed and party-appointed experts can reimburse the costs of the expertise and collect their fees. If an expert is court-appointed, then a party will be first required to pay the costs of expertise in advance, and the court will determine the amount of the expert's fee. Subsequently, the losing party will be obliged to reimburse such costs. If the parties have proposed an expert, they themselves have hired, the reimbursement of the costs of this party-appointed expert will be ordered based on the proof of payment. The court may adjust this amount using the criteria of time required by the expert, as assessed by the court, to prepare the report.[79] Since both court-appointed and party-appointed experts are permanent court experts, they calculate their fees based on the same Rulebook.

The Supreme Court of Serbia has also given an explanation for the reimbursement of costs and calculating the fee. According to the highest court in Serbia, court experts are not considered to be commercial entities, and the goal of their activities as court assistants is 'not to acquire commercial gain'.[80] Instead, their activity aims to provide the court with relevant expertise to determine or clarify facts in court proceedings.[81] The 2011 CPA stipulated that a court expert is entitled to reimbursement of travel expenses and expenses for food and lodging, lost profit and cost of expert testimony, as well as to the award for expert testimony given. Reimbursement of the lost profit implies that court experts also have other professional activities outside of the court. However, as already explained, most of them who are appointed in practice are overburdened, and it is hard to imagine that they have enough time to do anything else professionally. The law and the concept of court expert are disconnected from the practice.

Party-appointed experts do not charge for their service based on market prices. This is the case in some countries with a long tradition of party-appointed experts, like England.[82] In Serbia, the basis for the calculation of the court experts fee is a double average net salary in the Republic of Serbia.[83] The fee is calculated based on the estimation of billable hours needed for the expertise. The fee can be increased in cases when it is necessary to work at night, on holidays or under other difficulties.

[79] Commercial Appellate Court, 'Interpretative Opinion adopted by the Commercial Disputes Department on 26. November 2014 and 27. November 2014', *Bulletin of the Commercial Courts* 4/2014.

[80] Supreme Court of Cassation, Resolution R1 362/2021 of 17 June 2021, Resolution R1 338/2021 9 June 2021.

[81] ibid.

[82] S Sime, *A Practical Approach to Civil Procedure* (Oxford, Oxford University Press, 2010) 424.

[83] Art 18 of the Rulebook on Reimbursement of Costs in the Court Proceedings in the Republic of Serbia.

G. Party-appointed Experts in Practice

Party-appointed experts in Serbia, therefore, should allow the parties to assume the role of the judge in selecting an expert and establishing his mission while the experts remain the same. The problems analysed above regarding the court expert's qualification, training etc, remain the same even with regard to party-appointed expertise. This does not imply that court experts are producing evidence which are not of good quality – it means that the legislative framework is not good enough to assure the good quality of court experts.

The appointment of a court expert by the court or by a party usually does not include discussion on the qualifications that the experts need to have in order to be able to do expertise. Namely, it is also not unusual that continental legal systems lack disclosure and that courts rely on the permanent court experts list. In addition, Serbia is not an isolated example of a country where its MoJ administers the permanent court experts list.[84] Nevertheless, the conditions for entry into the registry and the method of administering such a registry do not inspire confidence in courts or parties aiming to rely on it.

In the US, where the expertise system is different from that in European continental law, when the expert's report is delivered, it needs to contain 'the reasons for which the expertise has been sought, including the main qualifications of the expert – his or her experience and the publications in the past ten years, including the list of cases subject to his or her expertise in the past four years'.[85] In Serbia, as is the case in continental law countries, relying on the permanent court experts list is provided for.[86] However, the legislative framework concerning the permanent court experts list is such that it does not encourage the experts' career improvement.

H. Are Party-appointed Experts Part of the Problem or Part of the Solution?

Party-appointed expertise has been offered as a solution to some problems identified in practice. The question is whether party-appointed expertise is part of the problem or part of the solution.

Party-appointed expertise has been offered as a solution to the issue of experts being appointed solely by the judges, unless the parties agree on the personality of the expert. When the parties appoint an expert, then it is possible to affect the expansion of the circle of those most often appointed by courts. Nonetheless,

[84] This is the case in other ex-SFRY countries as well, for instance, Slovenia.

[85] GR Shreve, P Raven-Hansen, *Understanding Civil Procedure* (Durham, Carolina Academic Press, LLC, 2018) 123.

[86] CEPEJ Guidelines on the role of court-appointed experts in judicial proceedings of Council of Europe's Member States, para 50.

that effect cannot be sufficient to resolve the problem of irregular updates of the standing court experts list. Furthermore, the parties cannot deliver expertise by any other expert. They can only hire another expert to give objections to the expert findings and in that case the objections are treated as the parties' claims. To conclude, the parties can expand the pool of frequently appointed experts to those unexperienced certified by the MoJ. The experienced experts cannot be certified before the MoJ decides to publish a call for experts.

Another problem to be resolved by introducing party-appointed expertise is the formulation of the mission of the court expert. It was supposed to prevent the stalling of the proceedings when the task was imprecise. This is a broader problem concerning the backlog of the civil judiciary in Serbia. The mission of the expert can be more precise if defined by the party or their attorney. The assignment of tasks for an expert is part of the solution in simpler cases where the ascertaining of the fact in question requiring expertise ends up with the delivery of an expert opinion by the plaintiff and the defendant each. However, if those expert opinions are insufficient or incapable of being aligned, the process will continue through court-appointed expertise. This way, the proceedings will be prolonged when using party-appointed experts.

The efficiency of the proceedings involving experts may be improved by introducing electronic communication with experts. Serbia's civil proceedings are still without an organised system of electronic communication in courts, so the experts are also communicated with using traditional means of communication. Furthermore, experts are sometimes hired in simple cases, verging on general information and expertise. For some of them, it is realistic to expect that the trends in the growing usage of software and AI will lead to experts being replaced by software extrajudicially as well. Presently, this is the case in the Republic of Serbia about interest calculations. This problem was also identified by the World Bank Group. There is software available to the public used extrajudicially to calculate interests, whereas an expert is appointed to calculate an interest on a debt before the court. It prolongs the proceedings for at least 60 days, which is the time frame for the expert to deliver his or her opinion, also causing additional costs. The judiciary, not only in Serbia, has not yet taken the position regarding the use of such tools, but in time, this will have to be taken into consideration.

The party-appointed expert, even though a practical solution in simple cases, is not a big step forward in more complex litigations. The real problems are in the regulation of a process of certifying a court expert and choosing an expert on trial. The CPA cannot introduce the bigger changes without changes in this field.

V. Conclusion

The profession of court experts has not witnessed major changes in the Republic of Serbia since the country embarked on the path of European integration. The 2010 legislation introduced changes compared to socialist times, but these changes were not enough to establish the new system of court experts. For example, the training models for experts dating from the SFRY were abandoned, but the new models, namely those used in European countries, were not introduced. Furthermore, the criteria for certification of court experts are not the ones from the comparative law since the process does not involve check-ups on any trial-related knowledge. The judiciary is not involved in the procedure of appointing experts, as is the case in other countries. Instead, the entire procedure takes place under the ministry, a body of the executive branch. The courts can initiate the process of opening the call for appointing new experts, though. However, the experts, unlike the models offered in comparative law, cannot initiate registering as permanent court experts.

The legislation on court experts does not always follow the needs of legal practice. Although it can be concluded from the norms on compensation for the expert's work that the experts are expected to have their primary employment, while the expert services to courts are a temporary arrangement, it is questionable if this is feasible in practice. Given that there is no mandatory training or the system of registering permanent court experts, practical experience becomes the primary method for promoting court experts and increasing their competitiveness vis-à-vis their colleagues.

In Continental Europe, it is not unusual to have lists of permanent court experts. Still, in Serbia, in recent decades, we have had an overly formalistic approach in which there is a minimal possibility that the court will appoint an expert who is not on the list of permanent court experts – in cases where there are no available experts for a certain area. This choice of evidence is available to the parties as well. However, parties can hire a consultant to make objections to the findings and opinions made by experts on the opposing party, which is not on the list of permanent court experts. Excessive formalism is another trend in the Serbian judiciary that is reflected in this domain.

Faced with this state of affairs, it is unrealistic to expect that the CPA will resolve the problems related to court experts. This was the only law that was changed in Serbia in an attempt to resolve some of the abovementioned problems with court experts. This attempt was made through the introduction of party-appointed experts. In order to assess the real impact of introducing party-appointed experts in Serbian litigation proceedings, the law regulating the issue of court experts would need to be implemented first. Otherwise, every comment is primarily related to overcoming inadequate solutions contained in the LEW. Until then, all we can conclude is that party experts contribute to more efficient proceedings in simple litigations. In perspective, besides changing the LEW, what is a hope is the digitalisation of litigation and the eventual transfer of the simplest expertise to computer programs.[87]

[87] Policy papers (The World Bank Group (n 25)) include recommendation that the judges are trained on the simple expertise like calculation of interest. However, no discussion on this issue has taken place so far.

13

Party-appointed vs Court-appointed Experts: Considerations in Light of the Macedonian Experience

TATJANA ZOROSKA KAMILOVSKA[1]

I. Introduction

The world today is facing an unprecedented pace of change as a result of the daily advancement in science and technology. It has a great impact in almost every sphere of human life and activity, including the judiciary. The judiciary has not been immune to this invasion in general, including the adjudication of civil cases. More than ever, complicated questions of fact in vast numbers of civil cases increasingly demand scientific and technical knowledge. As judges generally lack expert knowledge and distinctive skills beyond their own field, ie, they have no expertise of their own other than legal one, the courts grow invariably dependent on experts, and thus on the reliability of experts' approaches, used methods, and analyses, but also on their integrity and honesty. This, in turn, seems to pull the experts out of the judicial periphery and puts them right in the centre of carrying out procedural, specifically, evidentiary activities, and adjudication itself. As in many complex cases, expert evidence has often a central, if not decisive, position; it raises again some old questions: how to regulate the use of expert evidence, particularly the manner of adducing expert evidence in civil proceedings? Can it be asserted that party-appointed experts are real problems, and court-appointed experts are the only possible solutions, and vice versa? The debate on this topic, which has been going on intensively for some time in both common law and civil

[1] This chapter repeats a number of points (and reproduces parts of the content) in TZ Kamilovska, 'The New Rules of Expert Evidence in Macedonian Civil Procedure: are they a failed effort at reform?', in CH van Rhee and A Uzelac (eds), *Evidence in Contemporary Civil Procedure, Fundamental Issues in a Comparative Perspective* (Cambridge, Antwerp, Portland, Intersentia, 2015). However, the chapter has been substantially updated to reflect the state of affairs eight years later.

law jurisdictions,[2] results in the adoption of different models of this evidentiary mean, without giving a clear preference to one of them.[3] Between the pure-adversarial and pure-inquisitorial models of expert evidence, new and innovative approaches to this evidence are emerging in many jurisdictions nowadays as more attractive and generally more promising.

During the last decade or so, North Macedonia was not left out of these developments, but it seems that it was more experimenting in extremes than walking the line. The radical turnaround that has been made in 2010 has not achieved the expected results. Although this topic has already been written about and an initial assessment has been given, the present text is a good opportunity to go back to it again and see if, from a different time perspective and with greater practical experience, the rules of expert evidence that were introduced in Macedonian civil procedure in 2010 have withstood the test of time. Let us recall what actually happened in 2010, what the implications were, but also what is the situation today.

II. A Brief Roundup on the Rules on Expert Evidence in Macedonian Civil Procedure

Until 2010, regarding the expert evidence, the Macedonian civil procedure maintained continental legal tradition inherited from the Austrian Code of Civil Procedure. For decades, the duty of the judge to manage the process of fact-finding and evidence-taking actively went along with the court-centred approach to expertise.

Under the Macedonian Civil Procedure Act (MCPA) of 1998[4] the court had the power to take the evidence that was not proposed by the parties if that evidence were important for decision-making. When it comes to expert evidence, the MCPA of 1998 stated that the court shall take expert evidence when professional knowledge, which the court does not have, is necessary in order to determine or clarify any fact. The expertise was performed by experts determined by the court.

[2] See, eg, M Fernández-López, 'Expert Evidence in Civil Law Systems' in V Guillén-Nieto, D Stein (eds), *Language as Evidence* (Cham, Palgrave Macmillan, 2022), PC Chan, UU Rehman, 'Curbing Adversarial Excesses: An Evaluation of the Expert Evidence Regime in Hong Kong After the Civil Justice Reform (with a Focused Study on Personal Injury Litigation)', in CH van Rhee, A Uzelac (eds), *Evidence in Contemporary Civil procedure, Fundamental Issues in a Comparative Perspective* (Cambridge, Antwerp, Portland, Intersentia, 2015), E Arnold, E Soriano, *The Recent Evolution of Expert Evidence in Selected Common Law Jurisdictions around the World*, A commissioned study for the Canadian Institute of Chartered Business Valuators, January 23, 2013, available at www.kpdf.com.

[3] Eg, even the Model European Rules of Civil Procedure maintain a neutral position towards this party-centred or court-centred dilemma and do not contain an explicit answer. See Part VII, Section 3, D. Expert evidence and commentaries thereon in *ELI-UNIDROIT Model European Rules of Civil Procedure, From Transnational Principles to European Rules of Civil Procedure*, (Oxford, Oxford University Press, 2021).

[4] Official Gazette of the Republic of Macedonia, No.33/1998.

The MCPA of 2005[5] introduced a more passive role of the judge concerning fact-finding and evidence-taking, as it became the responsibility of the parties to assert facts and to present means of evidence. In that direction, the expert evidence regime became more adversarial, promoting the principle of party presentation of expert evidence. Nevertheless, this principle was significantly softened by the judicial power to introduce this means of evidence ex officio without any proposal of the parties. Although this was supposed to be an exception in introducing this kind of evidence, it gave the court broad discretion to turn to experts in order to resolve complex or difficult factual questions, whenever professional knowledge was needed.

Furthermore, according to the MCPA of 2005, in both situations – when expert evidence is proposed by a party or ordered by the court on its own motion – the expert was appointed by the court. The MCPA of 2005 adhered to the continental tradition pursuant to which the expert is selected and commissioned by the court (the so-called court-appointed expert). The court itself selected and appointed a neutral expert, who was treated as the judge's aide. Experts were appointed primarily (but not exclusively) from the list of permanent court experts on a certain type of expertise kept by the court. Furthermore, the court itself instructed the expert (in terms of formulating the expert's task) to prepare written findings and an opinion within a set time limit. In order to be truly of assistance to the court, the expert should not only give an opinion, but also support it, showing the court that it was well substantiated. The expertise was taken from one expert as a rule, but in cases of complex expertise the court had the power to appoint two or more experts. In the latter case, the experts could prepare a joint report (findings and an opinion) if they agreed on the issues. Otherwise, separate reports were submitted to the court. The MCPA of 2005 had also foreseen the mechanisms for correcting inaccurate, sloppy, partial or contradictory reports by repeating the expertise with the same or other experts if those deficiencies cannot be remedied by rehearing the experts. Finally, once the expert has reported, the court freely evaluates his findings and opinion. The expert's findings did not bind the court, and the court had a duty to weigh the expert's opinion against other available evidence. Nevertheless, in practice, the courts were not inclined to assess the expert's findings and the opinion critically – they rather took a decision in line with the expert's findings and opinion.

On the other hand, despite the legally accepted concept of the court-appointed expert, in the practice of Macedonian civil procedure, it was not uncommon for the parties to engage their own experts in order to rebut the court-appointed expert. However, being traditionally sceptical about the benefits of party-appointed experts, both theory and practice attributed only limited evidentiary value to expert opinions put forward by the parties. They were treated as private findings and opinions, or as private documents that verify the professional

[5] Official Gazette of the Republic of Macedonia, No.79/2005.

knowledge of their compliers. In the assessment of the evidentiary value of such a document, the circumstance of whether the expertise was ordered by one of the parties and which of the parties paid for the expertise has to be taken into consideration.[6]

With all being said, it is clear that the MCPA of 2005 still reflected a certain divide that exists between the common law approach and the continental approach to expert evidence. The court still played a pivotal role in the involvement of expertise in civil procedure. In particular, the MCPA of 2005 did not recognise the concept of party-appointed experts.

As a matter of fact, even though the MCPA of 2005 nominally strengthened the principle of party presentation of expert evidence, it changed almost nothing in the judicial practice. It remained expert-prone, just as before. Even in the new procedural context, the courts were hardly refusing the parties' proposals for expert evidence. The courts granted the parties' requests to order expertise almost automatically, without assessing whether in the particular dispute expertise was really needed. It may be assumed that it was based on the reasoning that it is easier to order expertise than to explain the rejection of a request for expertise.

In response to this, the amendments to the MCPA of 2010[7] have radically changed the regime of expert evidence, introducing the pure adversarial approach to expert evidence whereby the parties appoint and instruct their respective experts.[8] According to these amendments, the court shall take expertise as evidence if the party in his statement of claim or in his statement of defence has submitted expert findings and an opinion. Under the new rules, the court is no longer empowered to take expert evidence ex officio: it has no discretion to turn to experts in order to resolve difficult factual questions that are beyond the knowledge and experience of a judge. Indeed, the court has the power to determine expertise by written order, but only upon the party's request, and if the party proves that there are facts or circumstances for which he cannot provide expert findings and an opinion. However, this does not mean taking expert evidence ex officio. Moreover, the court has no discretion to determine how many experts should be appointed and who should be appointed as an expert, as long as they are a certified expert.

Regarding the last point, it should be stressed that the new approach to expert evidence was followed by the introduction of 'certified' or 'licensed' experts

[6] See especially M Dika, 'O vještacima i vještačenju u hrvatskom parničnom postupku', in *Zbornik na Pravniot fakultet 'Justinijan Prvi' vo čest na Stefan Georgievski* (Skopje, Praven fakultet 'Justinijan Prvi', 2009) 46.

[7] Official Gazette of the Republic of Macedonia, No.116/2010.

[8] Of course, the party-appointed expert costs are initially borne by the party who appointed the expert. Yet, even though the experts are appointed by the parties, their fees are not agreed by contract and market forces, but the system of a legally prescribed scale of charge exists (Art 29 of the Law on expertise and the bylaw prescribed by Minister of Justice). According to the new Law on expertise of 2023 this bylaw (Tariff) will be prescribed by the Chamber of experts, subject to previous positive opinion from the Minister of Justice.

(by enactment of the new Law on Expertise[9] in the same year), who replaced the previous so-called permanent court experts. It led to a national registration of experts (who met the conditions to provide expertise in certain fields, as prescribed by the law) in a register kept by the Ministry of Justice.

Without going into further procedural details here, this brief roundup will be concluded with the statement that the rules on expert evidence of 2010 were actually a continuation of the reforms started in 2005 in a direction of turning civil procedure towards a more adversarial approach. Nevertheless, it's worth mentioning that the changes in 2010 regarding expert evidence were introduced with almost no debate and with no opportunities for criticism from the Macedonian legal profession. The reactions have come post festum, and they were very doubtful whether party-driven experts are the best solution for Macedonian civil procedure.

III. Observations and Criticism after Five Years of Application of the New Rules

As a part of the procedural community, we provided our observations of the new rules, which, together with the views of the wider public, were sublimated in the paper that was published under the title 'The New Rules of Expert Evidence in Macedonian Civil Procedure: are they a failed effort at reform?' in 2015.[10] What did we observe in that paper?

Starting from what was stated in the explanatory memorandum to the amendments of the MCPA of 2010, that

> The general idea of the new concept of expert evidence is to introduce a procedural tool that will raise the capability of civil litigation to deliver a simple, cost-effective and prompt resolution of disputes, so that the court system will be fair and accessible to all.

through a detailed and in-depth analysis of the new rules, we ended the paper with the following conclusion:

> Up to now, it is obvious that the new approach to expert evidence has no merit either in accelerating the proceedings or in cutting costs. Rather, it seems that the new concept of the party-appointed expert has become an even bigger source of increased complexity because of the excessive and inappropriate use of experts, and thus of excessive expenses and delays.[11]

[9] Official Gazette of the Republic of Macedonia, No.115/2010, being afterwards replaced with the Law on expertise of 2014, and most recently with the new Law on expertise of 2023 (Official Gazette of the Republic of Macedonia, No.154/2023).

[10] Zoroska Kamilovska (n 1).

[11] ibid 237.

IV. The Perception of Party-Appointed Experts Eight Years Later

Eight years later, still within the same procedural framework, we come back to the topic, with old-new considerations on the matter at hand.

Again, we do not deviate from the thesis which was a starting point in the mentioned paper that

> At first glance, the new concept of expert evidence (a party-appointed or a party-driven, added) seems to be very fair in the sense that it provides both parties sufficient and equal legal opportunities to try to convince the court on the merits of their position.[12]

In addition, having in mind that the greatest benefits of this approach to expert evidence are in exposing different expert points of view for evaluation by the judge, who is an ultimate decision-maker (denoting that expert opinions play a subservient role), it seems that nothing is wrong with the new rules. On the contrary, provided things work as intended, Macedonian civil procedure should really take advantage of them. Just as professor Oberhammer speaking about the advantages of party-appointed experts and the lessons that could be learnt in this regard from arbitration practices wrote that

> Party appointed experts have a strong motivation as they compete to convince the tribunal; they have no hidden agenda as it is plain to see that they are there to help the party that has hired them and they normally have much broader access to the fact and much more time for their work than court-appointed or tribunal- appointed experts, if necessary.[13]

But, what does experience suggest?

What can be said with certainty is that in these additional eight years there is, to put it mildly, the status quo in relation to what was concluded above. The judicial practice mainly confirms the drawbacks of the concept of a party-driven expert that were previously detected. The changed position of experts has not lived up to the expected improvement in efficiency and cost cutting, which were the prime reasons for the change. Let's reiterate the key drawbacks once again with enhanced explanations as a result of practical experience over the years.

[12] ibid 234.

[13] P Oberhammer, 'Evidence: Learning from Arbitration' in CH van Rhee and A Uzelac (eds), *Evidence in Contemporary Civil Procedure, Fundamental Issues in a Comparative Perspective* (Cambridge, Antwerp, Portland, Intersentia, 2015) 246. It should be noted that the arbitration practice that Oberhammer is referring to is the one tailored to large-scale business-to-business disputes, and in that vein, the lessons from the arbitration that he points to cannot be fully applied to civil litigation in general, particularly in small claim proceedings as Oberhammer stressed himself.

A. Duty to Provide the Expert Reports at the Very Outset of Proceedings

Under Article 235(1) of MCPA of 2010, the court shall take expertise as evidence if the party in his statement of claim or in his statement of defence has submitted expert findings and an opinion.

It can be interpreted that this provision 'exhorts' the parties to consider whether expert evidence is needed in the first place. In essence, what this means is that the use of experts has come to be recognised as a necessity for the parties in order to put forward the most convincing case and is actually explicitly required by law. That is to say, each party, if he deems it necessary so as to verify his factual assertions, can provide expert findings and an opinion. The plaintiff should provide an expert report before filing a statement of claim with the court and attach the report to the statement of claim. The defendant should submit expert findings and an opinion in a written statement of defence. Furthermore, following the wording of this provision, the submittal of the statement of claim and the statement of defence are actually the last moments in which the parties cannot just propose, but also submit, expert findings and an opinion (ie, written expert reports) to the court. Still, due to legal inconsistency, it was disputed whether the submittal of a statement of claim and statement of defence are the last moments for submitting expert reports. Specifically, the MCPA governs that the parties are obliged to present all facts and evidence on which they base their findings, and to submit the documents and objects that they intend to use as evidence in the proceedings, at the preparatory hearing at the latest (Article 271(2)). It was disputable whether this applies to expert evidence, too. In this regard, the position has already been taken in judicial practice that

> There is no substantial violation of the provisions of the civil procedure from Article 343 paragraph 1 i.c.w. Article 235 paragraph 1 of the CPA, when the party made it probable that there are facts that the preparation of an expert report, proposed and announced in the statement of claim, is in progress, and the expert report was submitted before holding a preparatory hearing/main hearing in accordance with Article 271 paragraph 2 of the CPA.[14]

The criticism that was primarily addressed against this provision in 2015 is still valid. This criticism largely derives from the inconsistency of the rule for submitting the expert report at the very beginning of the proceedings with some other procedural rules. As the MCPA still requires the court to identify the facts that need evidence-taking, and that evidence be taken for disputed facts,[15] it is obvious that this cannot go along with the rules that insist on submitting the expert reports

[14] See Judgment of the Appellate Court in Skopje, TSZ-654/16 of 01.09.2016, confirmed by judgment of the Supreme Court Rev1.301/16 of 24.01.2018.

[15] See Arts 206 and 207 of MCPA of 2005.

at the very beginning of the proceedings. At the very outset of the proceedings, it is almost impossible to identify which facts are disputed and need evidence-taking, more precisely expertise. Furthermore, since the experts preparing the reports are instructed by the parties and not by the court, what often happens is that the expert reports have a different focus than the court has.

The experts instructed by the parties often develop points that are not decisive from the court's point of view. Namely, the main difficulty with this rule arises from the fact that the court is involved in considering the factual basis of the dispute at a relatively late stage. In the majority of cases, if not all, both parties have chosen to obtain an expert report before proceedings were initiated (plaintiff) or within the time limit for a statement of defence (defendant), ie, much earlier than the involvement of the court in the evidence procedure. One should not overlook the fact that the parties (or their lawyers) are not particularly careful in precisely identifying the issues in dispute that would benefit from having an expert report. Hence, the indicated discrepancy is inevitable. Finally, when the expertise is done at this early stage, practically both parties engage an expert to give an opinion on the same subject matter, and hence it is likely that much of the work done by one expert is also done by the other expert. The duplication of work is obvious. That being the case, Macedonian judges and attorneys have many times addressed the problem of unnecessary proof or cumulative evidence on the same subject matter, while at the same time a number of relevant factual questions remain unanswered.[16] This somehow suggests that even within the party-driven expert approach, the parties should not be permitted to adduce expert evidence unless its substance has first been the subject of disclosure during the preparatory phase of the proceedings.

The drawback of the new expert evidence regime discussed here is also noted in the Justice System Reform Strategy for the period 2017–22 with an action plan where it is explicitly stated as follows:

> In the area of procedural laws, the reform that was undertaken with the adoption of the new Civil Procedure Act (CPA) in 2005 and the amendments of 2010 and 2015 contributed significantly to shorten the duration of the procedure and reduce the overloading of the courts by … However, the practical application of some of the new provisions, especially those relating to the cross-examination, the mandatory expert findings and report with the filing of the statement of claim itself, etc, indicates the need for reviewing these provisions by organizing public hearings and inclusive debates to the wider scientific and professional public.[17]

[16] A Dimovska, 'Pregled na rešenijata koi sozdavaat problemi vo primenata na Zakonot za parničnata postapka so osvrt na najnoviot Predlog-zakon za izmeni i dopolnuvanja na Zakonot za parničnata postapka' (2013) 29 *Delovno pravo, Izdanie za teorija i praktika na pravoto*, 128; T Popovski-Buloski, 'Koi problemi se javuvaat pri primenata na ZPP?' (2013) 29 *Delovno pravo, Izdanie za teorija i praktika na pravoto* 140–141.

[17] See Justice System Reform Strategy for the period 2017–22 with an action plan, www.pravda.gov.mk.

B. No Power of the Court to Take Expert Evidence Ex Officio

A second and closely related drawback concerns the abolition of the power of the court to take expert evidence ex officio. As explained above, within the new regime, the court has the power to determine expertise by written order and appoint experts proposed by a party, but only upon the party's request, and only if the party proves that there are facts for which he cannot provide an expert report. Still, this does not mean taking expert evidence ex officio. The court is bound by the initiative of the parties, ie, by their proposals. It comes within the general evidence-taking approach that the court should address only such evidence as may be placed before it by one or more of the parties and should not seek out other evidence that may occur to the court to be relevant.[18]

Nevertheless, the daily court practice shows that since its abolition in 2010, the court's discretion to order expert evidence and appoint its expert is missing in Macedonian civil procedure. The following questions, which are frequently raised by judges, are illustrative of the point:

> Is it not the role of experts to assist the court, in a fair and impartial manner, on matters within their own expertise in which the judges do not themselves have the relevant knowledge? If so, why do we not have the opportunity to take expert evidence ex officio once we have determined the disputed facts? Is it not the role of the judge to decide whether the issue is a matter for expert opinion at all?

The situations when one of the parties failed to present an expert report because of a party's inability to pay for it should also not be overlooked.[19] In these cases, the judges have expert opinion by one party and could resolve the dispute in favour of that party because of the failure of the opposing party to present a countervailing expert report in support of a critical issue. In such situations, the judges make clear their uneasiness in basing their decisions strictly on the expert opinion of one party, regardless of whether they apply the burden of proof rules. Though the judges perceive it as an inadequate presentation of issues, they have no power to order expertise ex officio.

These questions and situations per se indicate that judges more likely prefer independent court-appointed experts, which is somewhat understandable considering that the continental tradition still has a strong influence in the Macedonian civil procedure, since reliance on parties' expert evidence has never been the norm ever before.

Such attitudes of judges are generally common in civil law jurisdictions and even wider, and they are often encountered in the literature.[20] Yet, some solitary

[18] See Art 7 of MCPA.

[19] Of course, it should be noted that in North Macedonia a system of free legal aid has been normatively established (which also includes cost for expertise), but in practice it is still slowly functioning.

[20] Moreover, many researches have shown that judges prefer neutral court-appointed experts, who are generally afforded a greater degree of trustworthiness, while the party-appointed experts are often

but essentially very accurate opinions that reflect the reality of the behaviour of court-appointed experts and the difficulties faced by that concept in general should be mentioned. Here we refer to the excellent observation that Oberhammer made writing for the lessons that could be learnt from arbitration, namely

> However, after being acquainted with arbitration practice I found out that court-appointed or tribunal-appointed experts often have a significant lack of motivation, hidden prejudices and a certain bias for the 'easy way out'; moreover they are hard to examine from the parties' perspective because they always are to some extent on the court's or tribunal's side' as an 'assistant' in the fact- finding process; therefore, a tough examination of such an expert always runs a certain risk of insulting the court or tribunal.[21]

The next question one might ask is whether the court has the power to restrict a submitted expert report in terms it is not reasonably required to resolve the subject matter. It seems that the law does not give a clear answer to this question either. In fact, under Article 238 of MCPA of 2010, the court will not accept the expertise as evidence if the opposing party challenges the expert for bias (on the same grounds as judges), and the court is of the opinion that this challenge is justified. And now the question is whether this is the only situation in which the court will not accept the expertise. At first blush, that much is clear from the wording of Articles 236 and 238 of MCPA. However, it bears noting that notwithstanding the mandatory language used in Article 235(1) of MCPA of 2010 ('the court shall take expertise') another provision of the law empowers the court to disallow or reject the use of expert evidence. Namely, the MCPA still contains the provision that empowers the court to select evidence. It is Article 206(2) that states that the court decides which of the proposed evidence shall be presented for the purpose of determining the decisive facts. In addition, Article 285 states that the presentation of evidence shall be determined by a court decision, indicating the contentious fact on which the evidence should be taken and the means of evidence. The court shall reject the proposed evidence not considered relevant to the merits and shall specify the reason for the rejection. It seems that these provisions empower the court not to allow the written expert reports that have been already submitted to court to be part of evidence-taking procedure. However, in the context of the provisions of the MCPA as a whole, this position could hardly be defended. Even if we take that the existing rules are quite apt to filter out expert evidence which is inappropriate and excessive, it is not so simple from the court's position to manage expert evidence. Since the parties are permitted to present the expert report furnished by the expert who they have selected (as an aspect of a right to be heard), and they did that at the very outset of the proceedings, very often on the same subject matter, the

considered to have low credibility due to the risk of bias. See E Friis and K Åström, 'The Use of Court- and Party-Appointed Experts in Legal Proceedings in Sweden: Judges' Experiences and Attitudes' (2017) 4 *Oslo Law Review* 63.

[21] Oberhammer (n 13) 246.

question is whether the court, even if it invokes its right from Articles 206 and 285 of MCPA, will be able to justify its decision to reject one of the submitted reports.

C. Party-appointed Experts as 'Hired Guns' in Practice

Much has been written about that the dependence on the instructing parties may result in commissioning or adversarial bias. Even though the experts are assumed to be neutral, the adversarial approach may bias experts in favour of the side that engaged them – the tendency, which is known as partisanship or adversarial allegiance,[22] or as advocacy by experts. It was also noted as one of the major problems with the manner of adducing expert evidence by Lord Woolf, who in this regard commented as follows

> Expert witnesses used to be genuinely independent experts. Men of outstanding eminence in their field. Today they are in practice hired guns. There is a new breed of litigation hangers-on, whose main expertise is to craft reports which will conceal anything that might be to the disadvantage of their clients.[23]

The term 'hired guns', or even older one 'paid agents'[24] are used to denote the extent to which the experts are prone to adapt their opinions to the need of the parties who engaged them. This, in turn, creates a great distrust of experts as a means of evidence and devalues their evidentiary value. By the same token, it is well pointed out that 'expert shopping', if taken to the extreme, distorts the intended function of expert evidence and threatens procedural fairness in the fact-finding process.[25]

Little of this appears to have been taken into account in the introduction of party-appointed experts in Macedonian civil procedure in 2010. In fact, it should be recognised that the reform regarding the expert evidence was carried out without a minimal comparative analysis and with a complete disregard of evolving trends that at that time were already on the scene in the common law jurisdictions, where legislators, due to such identified problems, have encouraged the use

[22] Although numerous older titles can be found on this topic, we will point out the following newer ones: JL Mnookin, 'Expert Evidence, Partisanship and Epistemic Competence' (2008) 73 *Brooklyn Law Review* 1009, D Murrie and MT Boccaccini, 'Adversarial Allegiance among Expert Witnesses' (2015) 11 *Annual Review of Law and Social Science* 37.

[23] Lord Woolf MR, *Access to Justice: Interim Report to the Lord Chancellor on the Civil Justice System in England and Wales* (London, Lord Chancellors Department, 1995) 183. These observations resulted in specific solutions in UK Civil Procedure Rules, more precisely Rule 35.3 which expressly states that '1. It is the duty of an expert to help the court on the matters within its expertise. 2. This duty overrides any obligation to the person from whom he has received instructions or by whom he is paid.'

[24] Used by Sir George Jessel, The Master of the Rolls in the English case of Lord *Abringer v Ashton* (1873) 17 LR Eq 358 at 374, who observed that: 'There is a natural bias to do something serviceable for those who employ … and remunerate you.'

[25] Chan, Rehman (n 2) 194.

of court-appointed experts.[26] Namely, the kind of reform that is most popular in these jurisdictions relies upon single expert evidence, often appointed by the court.

Nevertheless, the problem of expert bias was discerned quite early after the introduction of the new rules. As far back as 2013, even from the lawyers' perspective, it was pointed out that the expert report is always one-sided and directly confirms the position of the party presenting it.[27] But if at first this was timidly hinted at, over time it became increasingly clear that although expert opinions should be the reliable tag in the balance of justice, they are the first stumbling block when it comes to the objectivity and impartiality of experts. In the sidelines of judicial practice, there has been a lot of gossip, but also some confirmed cases (which even include corruption) about experts as hired guns or paid agents. Indeed, the practice in North Macedonia has shown that the experts' behaviour fits into the patterns of behaviour of the party-appointed in general, as explained by Moonken:

> … given that experts are called by one party and paid by that party, there is an inevitable danger of bias in favor of that party. The less extreme version of this concern is that as the expert prepares for and becomes enmeshed in the case, he will increasingly, if unconsciously, side with the party that hired him, lose some degree of objectivity, and slant his testimony in that party's favor. The more dramatic version of the same fear is that some unscrupulous experts will literally offer themselves for hire, selling their opinions and their credentials to anyone who meets their price.[28]

It is undisputable that the experts engaged by the parties, instead of being neutral and providing honest opinions, give opinions favourable to the respective party because, at least financially, they depend on the parties, and this, of course, influences their objectivity. Bulks of complaints have been made as to the evidentiary value of the expert reports because they advocate too heavily in the interest of the party presenting them. Therefore, it will not be speculative to say that the maxim 'who pays you, owns you' reflects the situation in this sphere.

On the other hand, it should be clear that the problem of experts' bias is not a result of the lack of a regulatory framework regarding objectivity and independence applicable to party-appointed experts. The duty of objectivity and independence of experts is expressly regulated by law. It is the Law on Expertise which prescribes the following basic principles to which the experts are obliged to adhere when performing the expertise: legality, honesty, impartiality, professionalism, independence, economy, responsibility, conscientiousness, efficiency

[26] See R Verkerk, 'Comparative Aspects of Expert Evidence in Civil Litigation' (2009) 13 *The International Journal of Evidence & Proof* 167. See also Arnold, Soriano (n 2).

[27] Popovski-Buloski (n 16) 141. The lawyers' perspective has been highlighted here, as it seems like they should be the first to manage the clients' expectations in terms that party-appointed experts are not acting for the instructing party, but are to provide an unbiased opinion on the issues in question.

[28] Mnookin (n 22) 588–89.

and equality (Article 3). These duties are also imposed in Article 4 of the same law which states that:

> The expert is obliged to perform the expertise professionally and conscientiously in accordance with the rules of science and the profession and ethical norms and to deliver it to the person ordering the expert opinion in a timely manner in accordance with the deadlines prescribed by law.

Accordingly, on the normative level, experts – even when appointed by a party – should be objective and independent and present an unbiased opinion to the court. Hence, the problem is not the lack of a regulatory framework but the lack of, or more precisely, difficulty in, enforcement. It should not be forgotten that if the experts do not mould their reports to suit the case of the party retaining them, obviously they will not be engaged in the particular case. So, what the experts have to do is expose the matters that support the hypothesis, which most favours the party engaging them, and at the same time take care to be impartial. But it seems to be very difficult to walk the line in practice: 'to be initially recruited as part of the team which investigates and advances a party's contentions and then has to change roles and seek to provide the independent expert evidence which the court is entitled to expect'.[29]

D. Super Expertise as a Tool – Solution or Burden

What do we finally have on a table? The usual scenario: two directly conflicting expert opinions on a topic that is beyond a court's comprehension and a court that should deal with them.

As a matter of fact, within the new system, the experts engaged by both parties always reach diametrically opposite and hardly reconcilable conclusions, so the court is faced with the problem of deciding between the opinions of opposing experts. Of course, it should not be neglected that not only the court, but also the parties and their lawyers have an opportunity to test each party's expert during the examination and cross-examination at the hearing.[30] This can greatly contribute

[29] In order to address the issues, Lord Woolf's observations are used here. See Lord Woolf MR, *Access to Justice:* Interim Report, ch 23, para 5.

[30] Art 244 of MCPA (as amended in 2015, introducing direct examination and cross-examination by the parties) states that:

> (1) The party, his legal representative or attorney, has the right to immediately ask questions to the expert.
> (2) The party, its legal representative or attorney, who proposed the expert, has the right to be the first to ask the expert questions and to request explanations regarding the given expert findings and opinion.
> (3) The opposing party, its legal representative or attorney, then has the right to ask the expert questions and requires explanations regarding the given expert findings and opinion.
> (4) The court may then ask the expert questions and request explanations regarding the given expert finding and opinion.

to shaping the opinion on the evidentiary value of each individual expert report.[31] Nevertheless, at the end of the day, the court is left with the delicate and challenging task of assessing the value of two different expert opinions on the same nucleus of relevant facts.

At first sight, having two different expert opinions at hand should not be disputed, as the experts may have applied a different methodology and approach while valued the facts. The Hon Geoffry L Davies put it in this way

> Many questions involving expertise, including scientific ones, do not admit of an unequivocal answer, let alone one which necessarily favours one side rather than the other. Yet that is what the adversarial system demands; one side or the other must be 'right'. And so experts are engaged by clients on each side only if their opinions are deemed favourable. From that point on there are polarized opinions. That may be, but is not necessarily because of adversarial bias. But the likelihood will be that each will be at one extreme end of the range of opinions on that question, the end most favourable to the client.[32]

Now what is a judge to do with that? The answer would be: to subject the opposing expert reports to evaluation. In that direction, it is well observed that if we consider that the role of a judge includes assessing where the truth lies in situations of conflict, why this role should be any different or any less well achieved where the subject of the conflict is a field of expert knowledge.[33] This has the air of being easy in theory, but not in judicial practice. On the contrary, it seems to be a rather unsatisfactory situation for the court: it is difficult, if not impossible, for the court to bridge the gap between the opposing reports. In theory, it is called 'a problem of lack of epistemic competence' which compounds the problem of partisanship.[34]

In fact, the problem of epistemic competence is always present, regardless of the manner of adducing expert evidence in proceedings, as the expert evidence is necessary precisely because the court lacks the knowledge that the expert provides, which further limits the judge's control over the expert.

This is most noticeable in the evaluation of the evidentiary value of expert reports, even when there is one expert report in the procedure. It is indisputable that the court should subject the expert's report to free evaluation, just as it does with other evidence.[35] The expert's findings and opinion do not bind the court, and the court has a duty to weigh the expert's opinion against other available evidence. Nevertheless, in practice, the courts are not inclined to assess the findings and the

[31] It is a good opportunity for the court to be sure that a party-appointed expert is not just a 'hired gun' as discussed earlier.

[32] GL Davies, 'Court Appointed Expert' (2005) 5 *QUT Law Review* 90.

[33] See the Hon. Justice Garry Downes AM, Expert Evidence: 'The Value of Single or Court-Appointed Experts', Australian Institute of Judicial Administration Expert Evidence Seminar, Melbourne, 11 November 2005, 4, available at www.aat.gov.au.

[34] Mnookin (n 22) 592.

[35] See, eg, Art 8 of MCPA, which governs the principle of free evaluation of evidence by the court.

opinion of the expert critically. On the contrary, the judge always took a decision in line with the expert's findings and opinion: in majority of cases, if not in all, the judgments are mere quotations from expert findings. If the issue of lack of epistemic competence is present when there is one expert opinion in the procedure, one can imagine the problems that the judges encounter when they have to critically evaluate two opposing expert opinions.

In Macedonian civil procedure, the problem of multiple expert opinions tends to be solved by super-expertise, as an exceptional feature of the new concept of expert evidence.[36]

The idea of super-expertise is to provide a higher degree of expertise or critical expertise of two conflicting expert opinions, performed by a team composed of at least the experts in the relevant field.[37] Still, it is noteworthy that the normative framework of super-expertise in MCPA (under the amendments of 2010) does not fully and consistently reflect this idea. Namely, according to the amendments of the MCPA of 2010 (apparently due to an oversight), the court is not expressly empowered to order super-expertise in cases of two conflicting expert opinions submitted by the plaintiff and the defendant, although this should be the typical situation for it. Instead, under the MCPA of 2010, the court is empowered to determine super-expertise only when the judge has ordered expertise in a written order and entrusted the expertise to two or more experts, who afterwards submit vague, incomplete, or contradictory reports, and these drawbacks cannot be eliminated by an alignment and a re-examination of the same experts.[38] Even the alignment of experts is not expressly provided for in the cases of conflicting expert reports submitted by the parties. Yet, in practice, the provisions of Article 246 (1) and (2) are interpreted more widely and used to align the expert findings and opinion or to order super-expertise also in cases where conflicting expert opinions are submitted by the plaintiff and the defendant. Namely in 2018, the four appellate courts in North Macedonia agreed on the issue that has not been expressly resolved in the existing law and formulated the following conclusion:

> In the event when the parties submit different expert opinions, and the experts cannot align, the court can determine super-expertise, even though there is no order from the court, in accordance with Article 246 paragraph 2 of the CPA.[39]

With this being accepted, it is not surprising that super expertise becomes a regular part of almost every civil proceeding. But super-expertise is not just

[36] For the possible strategies and models judges use to deal with conflicting expert evidence see O Perez, 'Judicial Strategies for Reviewing Conflicting Expert Evidence: Biases, Heuristics, and Higher-Order Evidence' (2015) 64 *The American Journal of Comparative Law* 75.

[37] As stated in Art 2.2 of the Law on expertise. Furthermore, in order to provide guarantees for fair and objective expertise, the amendments of 2010 lay down that the court determines super-expertise electronically by using the rule of random selection from the register of experts, in the presence of both parties/their attorneys.

[38] Art 246(1) and (2) of MCPA as amended in 2010.

[39] Appellate Court in Skopje, Bulletin No. 11, Skopje, April 2019, 9.

time-consuming; it is also an expensive evidentiary means. With regard to this, I will recall the words of one of our famous judges that:

> Almost every judge will confirm that even in a small claims procedure there is a necessity to order super-expertise and this leads to the absurd situation where in a dispute of 50,000 denari we have 150,000 denari of costs.[40]

Exploring the available court practice on this issue, we came across some cases where the court did not order super-expertise, as it managed to resolve the difference in opposing expert reports by the judge's inspection. It is stated that

> The first-instance court did not make a substantial violation of the provisions of the civil procedure from Article 343 paragraph.1 i.c.w. Article 246 paragraph 2 of the CPA, by not determining super-expertise, in a situation where a fact can be established or a circumstance to be clarified by immediate observation of the court, i.e. by an on-site inspection, and such a factual situation is also determined by the findings and opinion of an expert submitted by one party, regardless of the fact that a different situation results from the findings and opinion submitted by the other party … According to the second-instance court, the first-instance court acted correctly in not appointing super-expertise, despite the fact that there were two different, or opposite, expert findings and opinions. The first-instance court gave credence to the findings and opinion of an expert who was in accordance with what the court determined during the on-site inspection.[41]

However, this is not possible in all cases because, for the majority of complex technical issues, expert findings and opinions have a key role.[42] Hence, as already said, in most cases, super- expertise is ordered. This leads us to another drawback of the new system: the use of party-appointed experts plus super-expertise is far more expensive than the use of a single court-appointed expert.[43] Obviously, the costs outweigh the benefits of involving party-appointed experts.

V. The Cooperative Future under the New Law?

The mentioned, but also many other problems that the judicial practice is facing (which in part are results of the inconsistency of the law's provisions), clearly indicate that the new approach to expert evidence introduced in 2010 is a failed effort

[40] Dimovska (n 16) 128.

[41] Judgment of the Appellate Court in Bitola Gz- 42/18 of 14.12.2018.

[42] Here, as eg, litigations for compensation for damage caused in a traffic accident will be mentioned, where in the inspection minutes there is often a note that there could be 'hidden damages', which cannot be noticed only by a visual inspection of the vehicle.

[43] In judicial practice, there are some cases where, due to the existence of two opposing expert reports, the court ordered super-expertise, but in the final evaluation, referring to the principle of free evaluation of evidence, the court still based its decision on the expert report submitted by one of the parties. Of course, the court has the right to evaluate the evidence freely, but on the other hand, precisely because of the dilemmas in the evaluation, super-expertise was determined and thus the procedure was significantly delayed and more expensive. See, eg, Case Rev.1 – 171/22 of 01.06.2023.

at reform. It has become an even bigger source of increased complexity because of the excessive and inappropriate use of experts, and thus of excessive expenses and delays.

Being one of the hottest topics of civil procedure regarding fact-finding and evidence-taking, expert evidence was subject to reconsideration during the drafting of the new MCPA. Taking into consideration the perceived problems with the pure-adversarial model of expert evidence, the proposal of the new MCPA (which has already passed the stage of public debate and is pending in Parliament) provides for a mixed model of court-appointed and party-appointed expert evidence as a more promising one. Of course, we should wait to see whether this Act will be adopted by the Parliament and, importantly, what results it will deliver in court practice. In the following section, we will take a closer look at what is new, focussing on the way in which the main shortcomings of the previous concept that were discussed above have been removed.

First of all, the proposal of the new MCPA provides the answer to the questions: why to call an expert and when? It is clearly stated that the court shall take expert evidence when professional knowledge, which the court does not have, is necessary in order to determine or clarify any fact. As a matter of fact, this means a return to the norm that existed in the Macedonian civil procedure before the reform in 2005. Nevertheless, the major novelty lies in a provision that in matters beyond the reach or knowledge of the court, the court may determine expertise without a proposal from a party, if it considers it necessary. The letter means that the proposal of the new MCPA identifies two approaches in relation to adducing expert evidence in proceedings: either on the parties' proposal or by the court ex officio.

Furthermore, the party proposing to produce expert evidence is obliged to designate the subject matter of expertise in its proposal and to nominate/propose a certain person as an expert.[44] The court is obliged to circulate the proposal to the opposing party for the purpose of pleading, and if the opposing party does not object to it, the court shall determine the expertise to be performed by the proposed expert. On the contrary, the court shall determine the expert electronically by applying the rule of random selection from the register of experts, in the presence of either parties or their representatives. The rule for random selection of the expert by electronic means from the register of experts shall also be applied in cases where the court determines an expert ex officio.

On the other hand, the proposal of the new MCPA allows the parties to present expert evidence on any relevant issue for which such evidence is appropriate. Namely, the party may submit to the court a written expert report regarding the facts for which professional knowledge is needed. They may do so through an expert of their choice. The court is obliged to circulate the written expert report

[44] Under the proposal of new MCPA, as before, the expertise shall be performed only by experts registered in the register of experts, for a specific area of expertise.

to the opposing party for the purpose of pleading, and may determine that the production of this evidence shall be carried out by reading the written expert report submitted by the party. Since the party-appointed expert may give rise to the risk of expert bias, it is expressly stated that the court shall not accept the written expert report submitted by the party, if the opposing party challenges the expert for bias and the court finds the challenge justified.

Further novelty refers to the time limits for adducing expert evidence in proceedings. Specifically, the party may propose the production of expert evidence, submit a written expert report, as well as plead to the proposal or report of the opposing party at the preparatory hearing at the latest, or at the first main hearing when the law does not provide for the holding of a preparatory hearing. The same time limits apply to the court when determining expertise ex officio. The crucial novelty is that the court decides a mandate for the appointed expert/experts after listening to the parties' points of view. Namely, when determining expertise (either on the party's proposal or ex officio) at the mentioned hearings, the court shall render a separate decision, which contains: the subject of the dispute, the subject matter of expertise, the deadline for submitting the written expert report to the court (not longer than 45 days, or in complex cases not longer than 60 days), the name of the person or entity entrusted with the expertise, as well as other data from the register of experts.

As a rule, the expertise is performed by one expert, which is consistent with the principle of proportionality. However, the court may determine the expertise to be performed by two or more experts if it considers that the subject matter of expertise is complex. The court should bear in mind any increase in costs arising from multiple appointments.

Without going into many details, it will be noted at this point that the proposal of the new MCPA also contains provisions on the following issues: 1) the reasons for exempting from the duty of expertise; 2) the procedure for challenge for bias of an expert; 3) the duty for reasoning an expert findings and opinion; 4) the sanctions that the court may impose on the expert who does not fulfil his duties; 5) the possibility of the expert being called for an oral hearing and the procedure related to that; 6) the procedure for alignment of experts when the expertise is entrusted to several experts whose opinions essentially disagree, as well as the cases when super-expertise may be determined, as a measure of final resort; and 7) an expert's right to compensation of expenses and reward for performed expertise.

VI. Concluding Remarks

Thirteen years have passed since the concept of an expert appointed by a party was introduced in the Macedonian civil procedure. It is enough to perceive the key problems of this system, as it is established in its pure form. The expectation that the adversarial approach will more likely uncover the truth about a contested event as the result of the efforts of the parties who have a self-interest in presenting evidence, including an expert report and further exposing the weaknesses of an opponent's expert report, than from the efforts of a judge having an official duty to investigate the case by appointing a neutral court expert, is not fulfilled. It became obvious that the modification of the hardcore adversarial system was a necessary path to consider. We use the term modification, because the goal this time was not to go to another extreme: a pure judge-centred alternative. Instead, it aimed to establish a concept that would promote cooperation between the parties, their lawyers, and the court, which is not a novel concept, but rather a part of emerging trends aiming to reduce the costs and delays of litigation. How effective the new solutions will be remains to be seen (of course after they are adopted in Parliament). But this time, they are at least the result of a broad discussion of the professional public.

14

Appointment of Experts in Norwegian Civil Proceedings

MAGNE STRANDBERG

I. Introduction

In an ever more complex society, courts very often need assistance or help from experts. In this context, an expert is a person who has specialised knowledge beyond the level of an ordinary person on a matter that is relevant to a legal dispute. While witnesses contribute to a case through their experience with a singular event, the expert is relevant due to their extraordinary knowledge on that type of event. Typically, the expert is a professional trained in scientific or other methods and familiar with the leading research within his or her field. Most often, their role involves the evaluation or interpretation of existing pieces of evidence. For instance, an expert may be asked, based on the available evidence in a case, whether a harm suffered by the tortfeasor was caused by a specific medic. From a formal and legal point of view, both the expert`s written report and their oral testimony in court may be considered distinct and novel pieces of evidence. However, when analysing the inner relationships of the evidential situation, the report and the testimony are not entirely separate pieces of evidence – it is the expert's opinion on other materials in the case. This corresponds with the very reason to include experts, which is to help parties or judges in assessing evidence that cannot be interpreted or evaluated correctly or adequately without specialised knowledge. Moreover, experts may also be involved in order to advise a party or a judge on the production of evidence. Even in that situation, the expert's testimony or report should not be regarded as a single or new piece of evidence but rather as evidence about potential evidence.

Experts from any kind of scientific discipline could become relevant in civil proceedings. Medical expertise is essential in many personal injury cases, economists with diverse expertise are needed in many competition cases, experts in chemistry are needed in many environmental law disputes, climate experts are needed in modern climate change litigation, experts in music and literature are needed in intellectual property cases, and so on. Within civil procedure law, there is – hopefully – no debate on whether the system shall allow the use of experts. However, the exact role of experts has been a debated topic for decades.[1] The debate has focused on many aspects, such as what an expert is and who may appear as an expert, the interplay between judges and experts, addressing the admissibility of expert opinions, and the evaluation of reports produced by experts.

The debate also concerns the appointment of experts, which is the topic for this chapter. This discussion has been a part of a broader debate concerning the role of parties and judges in civil proceedings. The most important question in this regard concerns the competence to appoint experts. Is it for the parties to appoint experts, the judge, both parties and the judge, or is it a mix of all these? These questions are important, especially because of the limited capacity of the court to correct or overrule the expert's opinion, which can ultimately determine the outcome of a case. In this chapter, I will first and foremost focus on the appointment of experts in Norwegian law. However, I will not dwell on these questions just for the sake of telling stories about the law of a small, frozen country up north. I will dwell on Norwegian law because it may shed light on ongoing comparative tendencies, and because it may provide potential middle-way solutions between more famous and influential procedural traditions or paradigms.

My primary focus will be on the regular state court proceedings. I will not focus on arbitration, complaints boards, or other sorts of ADR-mechanisms, even though such institutions in practice are more important than the regular state courts. This is because regular state proceedings are paradigmatic solutions to procedural problems. Furthermore, the solutions to factual issues are very often copied or used as a role model, also when establishing complaint boards and other institutions. Before dealing with the matter of appointment of expert in regular Norwegian state proceedings, I must emphasise the very simple Norwegian court structure. It consists of three levels: district courts, appeals courts, and the Supreme Court. These are all general courts dealing with all sorts of cases, such as criminal cases, administrative cases, family and inheritance cases, and cases based on regular private law.[2] Most of the civil procedure rules apply to all cases, with the exception of criminal cases.

[1] See from the perspective of theories of evidence, D Faigman, DH Kaye, MJ Saks and J Sanders, *Science in the Law* (Minnesota, West Group, 2002), DH Kaye, *Science in Evidence* (London, LexisNexis, 1997), S Haack, *Evidence Matters. Science, Proof, and Truth in the Law* (Cambridge, Cambridge University Press, 2014), and L Wahlberg and C Dahlman, 'The Role of the Expert Witness', in Dahl man/Stein/Tuzet (eds), *Philosophical Foundations of Evidence Law* (Oxford, Oxford University Press, 2021) 53–66. For some views on use of experts in Europe: F Ferraris, 'Expert Testimony in the Italian Judicial System: Characteristics, Questions and Comparative Views', in van Rhee/Uzelac (eds), *Truth and Efficiency in Civil Litigation. Fundamental Aspects of Fact-finding and Evidence-taking in a Comparative Context* (Cambridge, Intersentia, 2012) 81–95, S Voet, 'Experts', in Rijavec/Kerestes/Ivanc (eds), *Dimensions of Evidence in European Civil Procedure* (Alphen aan den Rijn, Wolters Kluwer 2016) 179–193.

[2] Most of the Norwegian rules on the courts and their competence are found in the court act of 13 August 1915 no 5 (*Domstolloven*) ss 1 and 2.

Experts may be appointed to address both factual and legal issues, see the Norwegian Code of Civil Procedure (Norwegian CCP)[3] section 11-3 which, on certain conditions, makes the rules on evidence applicable for matters of law. I will only deal with the appointment of experts concerning factual matters, which by far is the most frequent use of experts. Specifically, I will deal with party-appointed experts (section III) and court-appointed experts (section IV).

It is important to acknowledge that experts may play additional roles within legal proceedings, which I will not discuss in detail here. First, experts may be appointed as co-judges, a situation in which the court, either on its own motion or on a party's request, decides that two experts may act as co-judges.[4] Such appointments are typically made when the court needs experts to evaluate evidence, in particular when factual and legal issues are complicatedly intertwined. Second, experts can serve as contractors or consultants for the court. Even though such uses of experts are not in any detail regulated in the procedural code, expert contractors have become more and more important during the last decades, especially for pre-commencement securing of evidence.[5] In Norwegian law, similar to English and American law,[6] parties can ask the court for securing massive amounts of information in the control of the opposite party or a third party. In handling such information, the court may appoint an expert to secure or control the evidence, filter relevant evidence from irrelevant evidence, and conduct searches or other analyses of the evidence.[7]

II. Comparative Framework: American versus German Advantage and Modern European Cooperativism

Before delving into the appointment of experts in Norwegian law, I will take a step back and establish a comparative framework, which hopefully will shed light on the following discussions. The topic of appointment of experts serves as a particularly suitable subject for comparative research for two reasons. Firstly, the activity

[3] Code of 17 June 2005 no 90 (*Tvisteloven*). An unofficial English translation under the name of 'The Dispute Act' is found at: lovdata.no/dokument/NLE/lov/2005-06-17-90.

[4] Norwegian CCP, s 9–12 (1)–(3).

[5] Norwegian CCP, ch 28.

[6] M Strandberg, 'Access to Evidence in US, Germany, and Norway', in Woo/van Rhee (eds), *Comparative Civil Procedure* (Cheltenham, Edward Elgar, 2025) (FORTHCOMING).

[7] Unfortunately, most articles concerning securing of evidence are only available in Norwegian, see MA Hjort, 'Sorteringsprosessen i bevissikringssaker og ved beslag inneholdende taushetsbelagt informasjon', *Lov og Rett* (2017) 178–192 and 'Behov for reform av tvistelovens bevissikringsregler', *Lov og Rett* (2017) 131–158. On some similar subjects in Anglo-American law: MR Grossman and GV Cormack, 'Technology-Assisted Review in E-Discovery Can Be More Effective and More Efficient Than Exhaustive Manual Review' (2011) 27 *Richmond Journal of Law and Technology* 1–48, G Christian, 'Predictive Coding: Adopting and Adapting Artificial Intelligence in Civil Litigation' (2019) 97 *The Canadian Bar Review* 486–525.

itself is rather straightforward. Secondly, the need for experts is seen in every fairly modernised jurisdiction, and the subject highlights some general aspects concerning methods of fact-finding, the roles of parties and judges, and a procedural system's attitude towards important factors such as costs, proportionality, and efficiency. An illustrative, and still highly relevant, contribution to this comparative endeavour came from Mirjan Damaska, who set up two macro-ideological schemes for legal processes.[8] These schemes provide a framework for understanding civil litigation in general and for understanding and justifying many elements of civil and criminal proceedings, including the fundamental role of experts and, in particular, the methods for bringing expertise into legal proceedings. A classical and well-known dichotomy of adversarialism and inquisitorialism, including the contrasts between party-autonomy and state-control, is thereby brought to the playing field.

The debate surrounding the pros and cons of adversarialism and inquisitorialism, or, to put it in a more nuanced manner, the contrast between court-activity versus court-passivity, has been notably exemplified in the comparison between German and American traditions of civil procedure law. In a famous article published in 1985,[9] John Langbein compared US civil procedure law to German civil procedure law, ultimately arriving at the rather surprising conclusion that German law had numerous advantages. In general, Langbein championed a more court-oriented mode of proceeding, advocating for judges to take a more active role. Langbein underlined, correctly, that both US law and German law have an adversarial nature – litigation is generally commenced and defined by the parties, with lawyers responsible for presenting evidence on behalf of their clients.[10] While underlining that German law and US law were two different versions of adversarial-styled proceedings, Langbein especially criticised the American practice of 'the battle of the experts', where each party's expert is pitted against the other, often prioritising loyalty to their respective teams over the pursuit of truth and justice.[11] In contrast to such a battle, Langbein argued in favour of a more judge-controlled system, encompassing not only fact-finding in general but also the appointment of experts in particular. Within this system, experts are not regarded as witnesses; instead, they are expected to be neutral and are appointed by the court itself. According to Langbein, the court should have the power to appoint and select experts both on its own motion and when initiated by a party. The parties, on the other hand, should be able to introduce their own expertise if they challenge the court-appointed expert's opinion.

[8] General comparative view on the law of evidence: MR Damaska, *The Faces of Justice and State Authority. A Comparative Approach to the Legal Process* (New Haven, Yale UP, 1986) and MR Damaska, *Evidence Law Adrift* (New Haven, Yale UP. 1997).

[9] JH Langbein, 'The German Advantage in Civil Procedure' (1985) 52 *University of Chicago Law Review* 823–866.

[10] Langbein (n 9) 824.

[11] ibid 824 and 836–841.

Langbein's proposals met critique. Scholars from civil law countries argued that Langbein's analysis was too general, lacked details, and overstated the active role of judges within the German legal system.[12] A remarkable response came from Samuel Gross.[13] He did not challenge Langbein's comparative analysis as such but challenged the assumption of Langbein's normative findings. Gross challenged the starting point of efficiency. Although challenging the goal of efficiency as such, he mainly stressed that the apparent inefficiency of American trials should be considered within the broader context of American pre-trial discovery. Furthermore, he argued that a comprehensive assessment of all relevant factors might reveal American courts to be more effective compared with German courts. In essence, Gross was not convinced that German courts were more accurate than American courts.

We may never reach a definite answer to the general questions concerning the accuracy and effectiveness of adversarialism versus inquisitorialism. However, the American-comparative debate of the late 1980s highlights the critical role played by experts and the pros and cons of party-controlled versus judge-appointed experts. The very existence of fundamental differences between procedural traditions concerning the appointment of experts was to a certain degree confirmed in a comparative European survey from approximately ten years ago. While court-appointed experts hold a dominant position in civil law jurisdictions, the use of party-appointed experts is by far the most important within common law jurisdictions.[14] However, the picture is far from being black-and-white. Across European jurisdictions, there appears to be a common practice of permitting party-appointed witnesses under certain conditions, just as all jurisdictions allow for court-appointed experts, either at the request of a party or initiated by the court on its own motion.[15]

The ELI-UNIDROIT Model European Rules of Civil Procedure (ERCP) continues along the line of combining court-appointed and party-appointed experts:[16] After recognising that most jurisdictions allow both party-appointed experts and court-appointed experts,[17] the two kinds of experts are dealt with in Rule 119 and Rule 120, respectively. To some extent, these rules cohere with the general patterns of evidence law outlined in the ERCP. The model rules provide the court with a general competence to initiate evidence production,

[12] RJ Allen, S Köck, K Riechenberg and TD Rosen, 'The German Advantage in Civil Procedure: A Plea for More Details and Fewer Generalities in Comparative Scholarships' (1988) 82 *Northwestern University Law Review* 705–762. See also the response: JH Langbein, 'Trashing the German Advantage' (1988) 82 *Northwestern University Law Review* 763–784.

[13] S Gross, 'The American Advantage: The Value of Inefficient Litigation' (1987) 85 *Michigan Law Review* 734–757.

[14] Voet (n 1) 179–180.

[15] ibid 181.

[16] M Stürner, 'The ELI/UNIDROIT European Rules of Civil Procedure: Access to Information and Evidence' in Gascón Inchausti/Hess (eds), *The Future of the European Law of Civil Procedure. Coordination or Harmonisation?* (Cambridge, Intersentia, 2020) 205–221.

[17] ERCP Rule 119 Comment 1.

even though evidence-gathering is first and foremost placed in the hands of the parties involved.[18] Nevertheless, the court's role is still more active concerning the production of expert evidence compared with the production of evidence in general. While the court's general competence to initiate evidence gathering is secondary to the party's competence and probably should be used under extraordinary circumstances, the court's role in initiating expert evidence is neither secondary nor exceptional. The project places significant emphasis on the principle of cooperation, which serves as a fundamental cornerstone.[19] This was, among other things, due to a need to by-pass the comparatively troublesome division between adversarialism and inquisitorialism.[20] Notably, this principle of cooperation also plays a central role in shaping the rules governing the appointment of experts.

Norwegian law shares several basic features with the ELI-UNIDROIT Model Rules, both in general and in its approach to the appointment of experts. Within Norwegian law, a combination of party-appointed and court-appointed experts is a key feature. Additionally, the principle of cooperation holds significant importance in both contexts. While not disregarding the present non-existence of a general principle of cooperation in Norwegian civil procedure,[21] the following analyses will demonstrate how such a principle may explain key components concerning the appointment of experts.

III. Party-appointed Experts

Under Norwegian law, a party is free to engage whoever he or she may see fit as an advisor or consultant. That is an integral part of the overarching principle of contract autonomy. Parties often involve private experts. This practice is particularly prevalent in certain categories of cases, encompassing personal injury cases and other tort disputes, but also in cases concerning complex contract matters, property law, and intellectual property rights. In a lot of cases, the expert is engaged well in advance of any formal court proceedings, sometimes long before proceedings commence. During the early phases of a dispute, these experts may play numerous roles, which can encompass advising one of the parties, interpreting existing evidence, suggesting the introduction of new evidence, and offering guidance on the prioritisation of evidentiary elements when a party is unable to present all possible evidence. In some scenarios, several parties may agree on engaging a

[18] ERCP Rules 25 and 94.

[19] ERCP f ex Rules 2, 3, 4, 6, 9 and 10.

[20] ERCP Rule 2 Comment 1.

[21] The principle is relevant for the procedural contracts as well, see A Nylund, M Strandberg and M Tjelmeland, 'Contractualisation of civil litigation in Norway. Flexibility and Cooperation in a Rule-Based Tradition' in Nylund/Cabral (eds), *Contractualisation of Civil Litigation* (Cambridge, Intersentia, 2023) 333–348.

joint expert. Such practice is customary for parties sharing common interests in a dispute, at least if the underlying factual issues are similar. However, parties on opposing sides may also involve a joint expert. That may happen if there is a good playing field between the parties or a mutual desire to reduce costs. Nonetheless, it is customary for claimants and defendants to involve separate experts, regularly culminating in what is known as the 'battle of the experts', which is also a well-known description of civil proceedings in Norway. Plenty of experts are also known for repeatedly accepting assignments from particular types of parties, for instance, insurance companies involved in personal injury cases may maintain a list of preferred experts, while lawyers representing the tortfeasors tend to involve different experts.

Party-appointment of experts is not governed by the Code of Civil Procedure, and frankly speaking, it falls outside the realm of procedural law. What the CCP does address, however, is the role of the party-appointed expert as a source of evidence in litigation; see section 25-6:

(1) A party may call witnesses to give expert testimony.
(2) An expert witness may attend the entire hearing and may be permitted to ask questions to parties, witnesses and experts. The examination shall, in other respects, be conducted in accordance with the provisions relating to the examination of ordinary witnesses.

In accordance with the right to be heard and the parties' right to present evidence supporting their case,[22] a party may call an expert for oral testimony. The opposing party has a right to cross-examine the expert, a practice that in Norway normally is conducted during the main hearing with all parties and judges present.[23] An expert may, as ordinary witnesses, either be physically present in the courtroom or participate online if it proves more suitable.[24] In contrast to regular witnesses, expert witnesses may attend the entire hearing, which illustrates their specialised expertise in assessing the evidence and acting as consultants to the party who engaged their services.[25]

A party may call as many expert witnesses as deemed necessary, yet the court possesses the authority, and indeed the obligation, to reduce the number of witnesses based on the general principle of proportionality.[26] Furthermore, the court may exercise discretion to disallow an expert witness if the court regards the witness as lacking genuine expertise in the relevant matter, sometimes necessitating a distinction between expert witnesses and ordinary witnesses.

Normally, party-appointed experts produce a report or another kind of document explaining their perspectives on the subject matter under consideration.

[22] The Norwegian CCP, s 21-3 (1).
[23] ibid ss 9-14, 9-15 (6) and 21-9.
[24] ibid s 21-10.
[25] ibid s 25-6 (2), *cf.* s 24-6.
[26] ibid s 21-8, *cf.* s 1-1.

The admissibility of such documents as evidence is addressed in section 21-12, second paragraph, of the Norwegian CCP:

> (2) Written statements made for the purpose of the case by other persons may be presented as evidence if the parties agree or they have the opportunity to examine the person who has made the statement. The evidence shall not be presented until it is confirmed that the person who made it will attend. If it is impossible to examine the person who made the statement, it may be presented as evidence unless it would be contrary to the legislative intent pursuant to Section 1-1.

Apparently, reports from party-appointed experts are allowed as evidence only when the opposing party consents or if the expert is available for cross-examination. However, if the opposite party disagrees and the expert is neither presented as a witness nor intended to stand as witness, the report may be admitted if it was not produced 'for the purpose of the case'. This criterion reflects a criterion found in section 197 of the 1915 Code, which was interpreted rather flexibly by the courts, and which should persist under the Code of 2005.[27] In line with this tradition, a report is deemed to have been produced 'for the purpose of the case' only if its primary intent was to deploy it in the particular proceeding where the report is offered as evidence.[28] If the report is produced well in advance of the trial, the court may reasonably conclude that its primary purpose was to enhance a party's position during pre-trial negotiations for settlement. In such circumstances, the expert's role was, arguably, more one of a consultant or advisor for the settlement, engaged in the collection or production of evidence for a forthcoming trial. Under these circumstances, the report may be admissible, even though the expert is not called as witness.

IV. Court-appointed Experts

A. Introduction

Experts may be appointed by the court, either as an alternative to or in conjunction with party-appointed experts. Both the district courts, the courts of appeals, and the Supreme Court are vested with this prerogative. In general, decisions on production and admission of evidence shall be taken during the preparatory stage and prior to the main hearing.[29] The appointment of experts may be initiated by

[27] NOU 2001: 32 *Rett på sak* 954–955.

[28] *cf.* the Supreme Court decisions in *Norsk Retstidende* (Rt.) 1972, 831, Rt. 1997, 93, Rt. 2002, 637 and Rt. 2007, 920.

[29] The Norwegian CCP s 9-4 (2) f. On the main hearing model of Norwegian civil proceedings: A Nylund, 'Preparatory Proceedings in Norway: Efficiency by Flexibility and Case Management', in Ervo/Nylund (eds), *Current Trends in Preparatory Proceedings. A Comparative Study of Nordic and Former Communist Countries* (Cham, Springer, 2016) 57–79.

the court on its own motion or on request of the involved parties, see section 25-2, first paragraph, of the Norwegian CCP:

> The court may appoint an expert when requested by a party or at its own initiative pursuant to Section 21-3 second paragraph when such an appointment is necessary to establish a sound factual basis for the ruling in the case.

According to the wording of this section, an expert shall be appointed whenever considered necessary to establish a sound factual basis. The court is entrusted with the responsibility of determining whether an appointment of an expert is necessary for establishing a solid factual foundation, and this determination must be based on an assessment of the additional value an expert could contribute to the case, beyond the evidence already presented. An expert shall be appointed only if the costs will be proportionate to the case, a criterion that is applied by the court on its own motion.[30] In practice, however, the parties' opinion is of great importance and can heavily influence this assessment. The parties are entitled to express their views on the necessity of appointing an expert, a right that stems from both the general principle of party-driven evidence production and the fact that the parties are financially responsible for the appointed experts. The massive influence exercised by the parties and the style of decision or procedure in such matters reflect important aspects of the principle of cooperation.

First, as a main rule, the court shall appoint an expert only when initiated by one or both of the parties. However, there are a few exceptions to this rule. The court shall appoint experts on its own motion if the case is non-dispositive, which pertains to situations where the parties do not have full competence to reach a settlement, and the court bears the responsibility of establishing a sound evidential basis.[31] Additionally, the court may appoint experts on its own motion in other cases, provided this action is not met with active protest from both parties.[32] As a part of the general rules on substantive guidance ('*materielle Prozessleitung*' in German),[33] the court may suggest the introduction of new evidence and encourage the parties to form an opinion on whether the court should appoint an expert. Second, if the parties jointly request the appointment of an expert, the court typically accedes to their request.[34] When both parties are willing to take the associated costs and time of appointing an expert and consider such an appointment substantial to the case, the judge usually honours the parties' preferences. The court may refuse to appoint an expert only if the appointment is deemed devoid of evidential value or highly disproportionate relative to the value of the claims at hand. Third, in instances where one party requests the appointment of an expert

[30] The Norwegian CCP, s 21-8 and NOU 2001: 32, 974.

[31] The Norwegian CCP, s 11-4, *cf.* s 21-3 (2).

[32] ibid s 21-3 (2).

[33] ibid s 11-5 (4) and (5), *cf.* ERCP Rule 92 (2).

[34] T Schei et al., *Tvisteloven kommentarutgave*, 2nd edn (Oslo, Universitetsforlaget, 2013) 933 and JEA Skoghøy, *Tvisteløsning*, 4th edn (Oslo, Universitetsforlaget, 2022) 827.

while the opposite party protests, the court considers whether the expert 'is necessary to establish a sound factual basis'. In this situation, the court must take into account arguments presented by both parties but is obligated to independently make a determination based on the criteria set up in the code.

One of the key objectives of the Norwegian Civil Procedure Code of 2005 is to ensure that economic and other disbalances between the parties do not influence the outcome of the case.[35] As a consequence of that purpose, the court may appoint an expert in order to balance the powers between the parties, as stipulated in section 25-2 of the Norwegian CCP:

> If the case can have consequences beyond the specific ruling for a party and, for that reason, the party wishes to call expert witnesses, the court may appoint experts if this is necessary to ensure balance between the parties in the presentation of evidence.

A situation where this clause becomes applicable is in a personal injury case involving a single claimant and a pharmaceutical company, where the injury allegedly is caused by a drug manufactured by the company.[36] In such a case, the court's judgment may have massive importance for the company, as a ruling in favour of the claimant could impact the drug's sales and potentially the company's stock market value. Typically, the company has access to in-house experts whom they may present as expert witnesses. While such expert witnesses are normally admissible, their involvement may significantly tilt the evidentiary balance. Pursuant to section 25-2, second paragraph, the court is empowered to appoint one or several experts in order to rectify any such evidentiary imbalance. Furthermore, a special cost provision allows the court to order those expenses incurred be covered by the party who has an interest in a general effect of the case.[37]

B. The Number of Experts Appointed

Traditionally, the main rule of Norwegian civil procedure was that two experts should be appointed unless the parties agreed otherwise. However, a reform of 1994 shifted the main rule,[38] and the outcome of that reform was upheld in CCP section 25-3, second paragraph:

> One expert shall be appointed. More than one expert may be appointed if this is justified by the nature of the expert issues, the importance of the case or other circumstances, and provided that it shall not result in undue expense or delay.

The alteration of the main rule represents a significant modification rather than a radical shift. Although this rule is first and foremost justified by reasons of

[35] The Norwegian CCP, s 1-1 (2).
[36] The example was brought forward by the law commission, see NOU 2001: 32, 974.
[37] Act on court fees (*rettsgebyrloven*) of 17 dec 1982 no 86 section 2 second paragraph fourth sentence.
[38] Ot.prp. no 45 (1993–1994) *Om lov om enkelte endringer i rettergangslovgivningen*.

cost-reduction, it also reflects an advantage of court-appointed experts compared to party-appointed experts. Specifically, a court-appointed expert is neutral and independent from both the parties involved and the court itself. A court-appointed expert aligns more closely with the purpose of objectivity, a quality essential both in the realms of science and law. In principle, a single expert should be capable of presenting both negative and positive aspects of the case impartially.

A need for more than one court-appointed expert may, of course, still be imperative. For instance, in a case encompassing multiple expert issues that cannot be adequately addressed by a single specialist, the need for multiple experts may arise. A personal injury case arising from product liability may require one kind of expertise concerning whether the product suffered a malfunction and another distinct expertise to evaluate whether the claimant suffered the alleged injury, whether the injury was a result of the product, and how the injury will develop in the future. In accordance with section 25-3 (1) of the Norwegian CCP, several experts shall be appointed in such a situation. This interpretation aligns with the correct understanding of appointing a single expert: the main rule is interpreted so that one expert shall be designated for each distinct expert issue at hand.[39]

Pursuant to CCP section 25-3 (1) second sentence, the court exercises wide discretion when appointing multiple experts to address an issue. First, two or more experts may be appointed when this is justified by 'the nature of the expert issues'. For instance, in cases involving multi-disciplinary matters where various fields of expertise are necessary to cover the relevant scientific perspectives, the court may appoint multiple experts. This may also apply when the subject matter within a single field of expertise is fiercely debated, and particularly when distinct schools of expertise within that field could yield differing conclusions. One such field of expertise can be found in whiplash cases, where one school of medicine is inclined to regard whiplash as a special causal mechanism, while another rejects this assertion.[40] Second, the court may appoint several experts when necessary due to the importance of the case. This includes situations where the case itself holds substantial importance for one or both parties, as well as cases that may have broader implications for a party or parties beyond the immediate matter. Third, the Supreme Court has emphasised that the relationship between an expert and one of the parties is a separate argument for appointing multiple experts.[41]

Since the question of appointing one or several experts involves assessments of proportionality, a balance of evidential soundness against costs and potential delays and the values at stake, the decision rests with the judge. However, the parties have a right to be heard before the court makes its decision,[42] and their viewpoints are to be taken into serious consideration.

[39] Schei et al. (n 34) 935.

[40] Underlined by the Norwegian Supreme Court in Rt. 1998, 1565.

[41] Rt. 2011, 812.

[42] Norwegian CCP, s 9-6.

C. The Choice of Expert and the Expert Instructions

The selection of an individual to serve as an expert is a frequently contested matter between the parties. Obviously, the court is tasked with the responsibility of making this determination, and it is guided by the provisions outlined in section 25-3 (2) of the Norwegian CCP:

> Persons appointed as experts shall have the necessary skills and experience. If a panel of experts has been established, experts shall be appointed from the panel unless it is desirable to appoint someone else. An expert who is nominated by both parties and who is willing to serve, shall be appointed unless special reasons dictate otherwise.
>
> A person who due to conflict of interest could not have sit as judge in the case, shall not be appointed as an expert. It is not an impediment to appointment that a person has served as an expert in a lower instance.

First, the suggested expert must be a real expert on the particular subject. Norwegian law provides for the establishing of expert panels, which compile lists of individuals recognised as genuine experts in various fields. However, such lists of experts are not yet widely developed, particularly for the majority of expertise categories relevant to traditional civil proceedings.[43] Consequently, the evaluation of a suggested expert's competence must be conducted on a case-by-case basis. In most cases, there is no doubt as to whether a person is an expert, but uncertainty may very well arise regarding whether that particular person possesses expertise on the specific issue at hand.

The selection of experts is based on the principle of cooperation. The parties have a general right to be heard on all procedural matters, including the designation of experts. When both parties reach consensus regarding the choice of expert, that person is appointed unless 'special reasons' dictate otherwise.[44] In practice, the court typically upholds the parties' joint selection and actively encourages them to find common ground in this regard. Now, what exactly are these 'special reasons'? They may arise if the expert in question has, or previously has had, a conflict of interest, for instance a prior affiliation with one of the parties or if one of the parties has suggested that particular expert in numerous other cases. If the parties diverge in their preferences for an expert, the court must make the final determination after considering both parties' arguments. The court has the authority to explore several options such as appointing two experts, seeking a third expert, or may appoint the expert suggested by one of the parties.

The significance of cooperation between the parties, as well as the court, becomes even clearer and more important when it comes to expert instruction, as outlined in section 25-4 of the Norwegian CCP:

> The court shall determine the issues to be examined by the expert and shall give the necessary instructions. The court may order the parties to prepare draft terms of reference for the experts.

[43] See ch 15 in this volume.
[44] Similarly, ERCP Rule 120 (3).

Pursuant to CCP section 25-4, it is for the court to determine both the issue which the expert shall address and the instructions governing the expert's fulfilment of his mission. In practice, however, the court will make efforts to find an agreement between the parties and itself. To this end, the court may order the parties to prepare drafts for the instructions or the expert's mandate, underscoring the significant influence the wield over the content of these directives. These drafts are not binding, of course, but the court will normally accept the draft, at least as a starting point for its decision. In most cases, there are compelling reasons to embrace the consensus reached by the parties. After all, it is the parties who have the most knowledge of the case, especially concerning the factual details essential for formulating adequate instructions for the expert.

In instances where the parties do not reach a consensus on a joint draft, the court may still ask each party to prepare individual drafts. While the court ultimately retains the authority to make the final decision, each party's suggestions and inputs must be taken into consideration. The instructions are important in facilitating precise communication between the court, the parties, and the expert. They serve as the conduit for obtaining the expert's opinion on crucial factual matters.

D. Challenging Appointments of Expert

As elucidated within this chapter, the parties shall be afforded an opportunity to express their views before the court decides on the appointment of one or several experts. Furthermore, the court is obliged to duly consider the opinions presented by the parties during this process. A party may still disagree with the court's decision and has plenty of opportunities to challenge it. Initially, a party may challenge the decision to the court that rendered it. Since there is no formal res judicata effect to decisions concerning the appointment of experts, these decisions may be revised, rephrased, or supplemented by further decisions. Consequently, these decisions are not strictly binding in the sense that the court retains the latitude to appoint additional experts even after an initial appointment has been made.[45]

Second, a party may challenge the decision by an interlocutory appeal. A decision rendered by the district court can be challenged to the court of appeals, and subsequently, a second appeal may be brought before the Supreme Court.[46] The Supreme Court's competence is limited to considering whether the district court's decision aligns with 'the general legal interpretation of a written legal rule', see the Norwegian CCP section 30-6 letter c. In situations where the court of appeals has decided to appoint one or several experts, the decision may be appealed to the

[45] The Norwegian CCP, s 25-3 (1) third sentence.
[46] ibid ss 29-2 (1) and 30-3 (1).

Supreme Court. In this scenario, the Supreme Court's competence is limited by the Norwegian CCP section 29-3, second paragraph:

> An interlocutory procedural order which, pursuant to statute, shall be made on an assessment of what is appropriate and necessary for the proper conduct of the case may, as far as the discretionary assessment is concerned, only be appealed on the grounds that the ruling is unsound or clearly unreasonable.

This limitation also extends to the court of appeals when handling appeals on decisions made by the district court. When such decisions are brought before the court of appeals or the Supreme Court, it will also check whether the decision has been made on adequate reasoning. A court's order regarding the production or admission of evidence must be substantiated in writing. On numerous occasions, the Supreme Court has overturned lower courts' decisions that declined to appoint experts or appointed fewer experts than requested by a party, if the decision lacked sufficient reasoning.[47]

Third, a party who disagrees with a court decision regarding the appointment of an expert may use it as a procedural ground for appeal against a subsequent judgment.[48] In such a situation, the appellate court has the competence to assess whether the decision was in line with procedural law. However, a judgment shall only be reversed if the procedural error may have affected the final outcome of the case.[49]

V. Some Concluding Remarks

In general, the system of appointment of experts found in Norwegian civil procedure law functions fairly well. While party-appointed experts serve as a means for the parties to be heard and to challenge other involved experts, court-appointed experts serve as a means for objectivity and neutrality. As far as I am aware of, the combination of these two categories of experts has been under severe criticism in Norway. However, certain aspects of the involvement of experts are regularly put under debate. In a small country, the problem of frequently used experts is pressing both for party-appointed and court-appointed experts. Especially during the last decade, a quite dramatic rise in the legal costs involved in civil litigation has been very high on the agenda. The system of appointment of experts, especially the opening-up for both party-appointed and court-appointed experts, may significantly impact the costs. A major problem with the combination of such experts is that civil litigation tends to involve many experts and perhaps a higher number of experts than what is rational or reasonable.

[47] Rt. 2010, 18, Rt. 2014, 1334, Rt. 2015, 9.
[48] The Norwegian CCP, ss 29-3 (1) and 30-3 (1).
[49] ibid ss 29-21 (1) and 30-3 (1).

15

Expert Evidence in Custody Disputes and Child Protection Cases. Much Debate and Limited Research

CAMILLA BERNT[1]

I. Introduction

Expert evidence, especially from psychologists, plays an important role in child protection cases and in court disputes between parents on parental responsibility, custody, and contact (custody disputes) in Norway. The experts provide the courts and other decision-making bodies with expert knowledge that most judges and other jurists do not have, and they conduct investigations to provide scientifically based evidence on issues such as the quality of care provided for children in their parents' homes and the individualised care requirements of each child. Their assessments and conclusions are often given considerable weight in judgements and decisions rendered by various bodies in these cases, partly because of the experts' expertise and thorough investigations, and partly because appointed experts hold a significantly more neutral position vis-à-vis the parents than most other witnesses.

The use of experts and expert evidence in custody and child protection cases is frequently debated in Norway. This is not surprising, considering the importance of such evidence and the considerable cost an expert investigation entails for the client – usually the state or local municipality. One issue is the quality of the investigations, and another is the weight the expert evidence is given, and how the courts and other decision-making bodies otherwise relate to the investigations

[1] This chapter and the author are connected to the research project 'The Use of Expert Reports as Evidence in Child Protection Decision-Making' financed by the Norwegian Research Council #334711. Further information about the project is given on the webpage The use of Expert Reports as Evidence in Child Protection Decision-Making – Psykologisk institutt (PSI) (uio.no). I would hereby like to thank Professor Magne Strandberg for valuable feedback on different aspects of this text, and research assistant Øystein Nordmo at The University of Bergen, Faculty of Law for his invaluable assistance with language, sources and footnotes.

in their decisions. A related issue is the relationship between the experts' investigations and the adversarial and immediate presentation and examination of evidence that takes place in court hearings and hearings at the child welfare tribunals.[2] In custody disputes, child protection cases and other types of cases, it has been discussed whether experts conclude more clearly than they should, considering the limitations of their expertise and the scope and thoroughness of their investigations.[3]

In child protection cases, objections have also been raised regarding the involvement of child protection services in the selection and engagement of experts. This practice raises questions about the independence, neutrality, and impartiality of these experts.

An additional issue regarding the use of expert evidence has occurred after several judgments against Norway in the European Court of Human Rights in cases related to child protection.[4] In some of the judgments it has been stated that while the Norwegian proceedings in child protection cases are thorough, some aspects of the decisions have not been based on sufficient evidence. The criticism highlights the need for expert evidence regarding complex issues. Furthermore, in a few instances, the court has stated that there should have been a *more updated* expert assessment.[5]

[2] See, eg, G Nordhelle, 'Kritisk blikk på sakkyndigrollen i barnefordelingssaker' (2010) 8 *Tidsskrift for Norsk psykologforening, Temanummer: Mekling* 744–747; G Nordhelle, 'Praktiseringen av sakkyndighetsarbeid i barnefordelingssaker – til barnas beste?' (2011) 3 *Tidsskrift for familierett, arverett og barnevernrettslige spørsmål (FAB)* 176–196; IR Lundeberg, 'Sannhetsvitnet' (2009) 4/5 *Tidsskrift for rettsvitenskap* 611–646; T Haugli and G Nordhelle, 'Sikker i sin sak? Om barn, sakkyndighet og rettssikkerhet' (2014) 2 *Lov og Rett* 89–108; K Sandberg, *Tilbakeføring av barn etter omsorgsovertakelse* (Oslo, Gyldendal Akademisk, 2003), S Asmervik, 'Hva er det med (noen) sakkyndige?' (2016) 4 *FAB* 262–272 and C Bernt, 'Sakkyndige i barnelovssaker for domstolene: roller og rettssikkerhet' (2014) 3/4 *FAB*.

[3] K Koch, 'Når mor og far møtes i retten – barnefordeling og samvær', *NOVA-rapport* 13/2000, and Ot.prp. nr. 29 (2002–2003) 44, Nordhelle (2010) (n 2) 744, Haugli and Nordhelle (2014) (n 2) 99–100 and RA Greve, T Jørgensen, O Christiansen, V Samsonsen and HC Braarud, 'Independent experts in care order proceedings: A scoping review' (2023) 26(6) *European Journal of Social Work*. From other fields: A Schiøtz, 'Den (retts)medisinske sakkyndighet. Rasjonalitetsformer og rolleoppfatninger i medisin og juss' (2006) 1 *Tidsskrift for Strafferett* (Schiøtz 2006) 20–38, 22–23 and IR Lundeberg, 'Sannhetsvitnet' (2009) 4/5 *Tidsskrift for rettsvitenskap* 611–646.

[4] *Strand Lobben and others. v Norway* App no 37283/13 (ECtHR 30 November 2017); *Jansen v Norway*, no 2822/16 (ECtHR, 6 September 2018); *K.O. and V.M. v Norway* App no 64808/16 (ECtHR 19 November 2019); *A.S. v Norway*, no 60371/15 (ECrHR 17 December 2019); *Hernehult v Norway* App no 14652/16 (ECtHR 10 March 2020); *Pedersen and others v Norway*, no 39710/15 (ECtHR 10 March 2020); *M.L. v Norway* App no 64639/16 (12 December 2020); *K.E. and A.K. v Norway* App no 57678/18 (1 July 2021); *R.O. v Norway* App no 49452/18 (ECtHR 1 July 2021); *F.Z. v Norway* App no 64789/17 (ECtHR 1 July 2021); *E.H. v Norway* App no 39717/19 (25 November 2021); *M.F. v Norway* App no 5947/19 (ECtHR 25 November 2021); *Abdi Ibrahim v Norway* App no 15379/16 (ECtHR, 10 December 2021); *E.M. and others v Norway* (ECtHR 20 January 2022); *A.L. and others v Norway* App no 45889/18 (ECtHR 20 January 2022); *D.R and others v Norway* App no 63307/17 and 38105/19 (ECtHR 12 September 2023); *K.F. and others v Norway* App no 39769/17, 9167/18, 48372/18, 38097/19, 45985/19, 58880/19 (ECtHR 12 September 2023); *S.S. and J.H. v Norway* App no 15784/19 (ECtHR 12 September 2023); *D.R. and others v Norway* App no 63307/17 and 38105/19 (ECtHR 12 September 2023).

[5] See, eg, *Strand Lobben and others. v Norway* (2017) (n 4).

In this chapter, I will start by discussing the purpose of expert evidence and how it should affect the mandates assigned to experts, as well as the role they should assume (II). Subsequently, I will provide an overview of some important issues that have been debated, and/or that have been uncovered by research in Norway (III). This will highlight areas where there is a particularly pressing need for further research. This article exclusively focuses on Norwegian research conducted within the context of Norway. The reason for this delimitation of the scope of the chapter, is that there are substantial differences between the legal systems and societies, making the use of findings from other countries about this issue impossible to assess without far more extensive analysis than what is possible within the format of this chapter. Nevertheless, it is hoped that this overview can provide a basis for comparative discussions with academics from other jurisdictions concerning the use of experts, particularly in custody and child protection cases, and to some extent, also in other types of cases. In the final section of this chapter (IV) I will give a brief presentation of the research project *The Use of Expert Reports as Evidence in Child-Protection Decision Making*, where several matters regarding the use of expert evidence in child protection cases will be investigated.

II. What should be Investigated by Experts and how? The Intended Role of Expert Evidence

To effectively assess the criticism and debate regarding different aspects of the use of experts in custody and child protection cases in Norway, it is vital to have a clear understanding of the purpose of expert evidence. The Dispute Act chapter 25 has general rules for expert evidence in general, both for court-appointed experts and expert witnesses summoned by any of the involved parties, including the child protection service, parents, or children. These rules apply to custody cases and child protection cases alike.[6] The rules also apply for the proceedings at the child welfare tribunals, which are court-like independent administrative tribunals that decide on whether coercive measures in child protection cases should be imposed.[7] Their decrees can be brought to courts for a full review.

The rules in the Dispute Act, chapter 25 are concise and provide relatively limited guidance regarding the questions of what expert evidence is and what its purposes are. In section 25-1, it is merely stated that 'Expert evidence is an expert assessment of factual issues in the case', and in section 25-2 it is stated that the court may appoint an expert 'when such an appointment is necessary to establish a sound factual basis for the ruling in the case'. Furthermore, on the matter of party appointed experts, section 25-6(1) states that a party 'may call witnesses to give expert testimony'.

[6] *cf.* The Children Act, s 59, subsection three.
[7] *cf.* The Child Welfare Act, ss 14–18, subsection one, litra d.

The child protection services engage experts at different stages of a child protection case, either during the investigative stage or as a part of the preparation for a hearing before the child welfare tribunal regarding coercive measures, such as a care order. In the Child Welfare Act section 12-7 subsection one, it is stated that the child protection services 'may engage experts to prepare an expert report on the case' but provides no guidelines regarding the specific issues for which the appointment of an expert is warranted. The question of whether an expert should be engaged, and with what mandate, therefore becomes a question of proper case management; *cf.* section 17 of the Public Administration Act.[8]

However, it is stated in the Child Welfare Act, section 12-7 subsection two that the ministry 'may issue regulations on requirements for experts' mandates, reports and self-declarations'. Such regulations are currently being drafted within the ministry. It must be noted that the statute giving regulatory authority to the ministry is placed in a provision regarding the *child protection service's* use of experts, and therefore does not include the appointment of experts by the child welfare tribunal or the courts.

The Children Act section 61 subsection one number three appears to offer additional guidance regarding the appointment of experts in custody cases:

> When necessary, the court should appoint an expert to express an opinion on one or more of the questions raised by the case. Where allegations have been made concerning violence, abuse, drug or alcohol abuse or mental disorder and sufficient information concerning the case has not otherwise been provided, the court may appoint an expert.

The first sentence offers no further guidelines than the Dispute Act. However, the second sentence, introduced through an amendment to the act in 2013,[9] serves to clarify that an expert should be appointed in cases where it is necessary. The preparatory works exemplify this with cases in which one parent raises allegations of violence or abuse against the other parent or another member of the household. It also applies to cases involving allegations of substance abuse or mental disorders, such as personality disorders, which can affect the parent's ability to provide for their children. If other evidence does not shed sufficient light on these matters, an expert should be appointed.[10] The amendment of the statute did not result in any real change of the law, and it is emphasised in the preparatory works that it is still a matter of judicial discretion to decide whether to appoint an expert.[11] The Norwegian Supreme Court has stated that whether an expert should be appointed in custody cases depends on whether it is considered necessary for a proper handling of the case, ensuring the safeguarding of the best interest of the child.[12]

[8] Act relating to procedure in cases concerning the public administration (Public Administration Act) (forvaltningsloven) 10 February 1967.

[9] Act on amendments to the Children's Act (the child perspective in custody disputes) 21 June 2013 nr 62, entered into force 1 January 2014.

[10] Prop. 85 L (2012–2013) 88.

[11] Prop. 85 L (2012–2013) 88.

[12] Rt. 2005 p 466 U, para 21.

In section 61 b of the Children Act, there is a similar provision as in The Child Welfare Act section 12-7: 'The Ministry can issue regulations on the design of the mandate of the experts and their reports.' This statutory provision is situated within chapter 7 of the Children Act, a section that encompasses special procedural rules for the court proceedings in these particular cases.[13] No regulation on appointment of experts by courts in custody disputes is issued thus far.

The Norwegian Courts' Administration has however provided national guidelines for the courts' handling of both custody cases and child protection cases, encompassing recommendations regarding the use of experts in both contexts. The documents include various templates, including standard mandates.[14] Considering the principle of judicial independence,[15] these guidelines are not legally binding upon the courts. Nevertheless, they serve as a useful tool and are likely to affect judicial practice.

In summary, the statutory regulation regarding the use of experts primarily comprises two key elements, which are most clearly expressed in the Dispute Act. First, expert evidence is defined as 'an expert assessment', *cf.* section 25-1, distinguishing it from other forms of evidence. The expert is appointed or engaged by virtue of his or her expertise rather than their prior knowledge of the specific case, which is the situation for other witnesses, *cf.* section 24-1. On the contrary, appointed experts must fulfil requirements for judicial impartiality, as stipulated in section 25-3 of the Dispute Act.

Second, it is stated in section 25-1 that the expert assessment must concern 'factual issues in the case'. This emphasises that the expert's role in the case is giving evidence and thus limits the expert's role vis-à-vis the court and the child welfare tribunal. Statutory interpretation and application of the law is not within the purview of the expert's mission, *cf.* the Dispute Act section 11-3.

The expert's role is thus to contribute a special type of evidence, namely their professional assessment of psychological issues within the case, subsequently becoming an integral part of the evidence in the case. It is for the court or tribunal to assess the evidence, including deciding what weight the expert evidence should be given in view of all evidence presented, *cf.* the Dispute Act section 21-2.

It is first and foremost the responsibility and task of the parties to collect and present evidence; *cf.* the Dispute Act section 11-2 (2) and section 21-3 (1). However, in custody and child protection cases, the court – and child welfare tribunal – 'has

[13] In custody disputes in Norway there is no administrative decision-making process where the use of experts out-of-court is an option. Deciding matters of custody and contact is considered a matter of private law which is to be handled by the parents by means of amicable settlement.

[14] National guide for handling child welfare cases, updated 14 February 2023, Nasjonal veileder for behandling av barnevernssaker – oppdatert 10.02.23 (domstol.no) (reading date 10 august 2023) and National guide for handling parental disputes, version 3.0, 11 May 2023 Nasjonal veileder foreldretvister versjon 3.0 (domstol.no) (reading date10 August 2023).

[15] *cf.* The Norwegian Constitution of 17 May 1814, s 95, *cf.* The European Convention of Human Rights, Art 6.

a duty to ensure that the presentation of evidence provides a sound factual basis for the ruling', cf. sections 21-3 (2) and 11-4.[16]

Considering that the expert's mandate is to provide 'an expert assessment', *cf.* the Dispute Act, section 25-1, it is undoubtedly not the expert's responsibility to conduct interviews with potential witnesses or collect and assess additional evidence, except what is required to be able to perform his or her expert assessment. As will be discussed in III.A and III.B, it is, however, common for expert reports to contain a fairly comprehensive account of documentary evidence and statements from witnesses – so-called *comparatives*. This practice may raise some procedural law issues, particularly regarding the parties right to refute the arguments and evidence, *cf.* the Dispute Act, section 1-1 and the European Convention on Human Rights (ECHR) Art 6, and the procedural principle that 'the evidence shall be presented directly to the adjudicating court', *cf.* the Dispute Act, section 21-9.

The fact that an expert should not *interpret the law or apply it to the facts of the case* may seem obvious, but in practice the boundary between matters for legal assessment and matters for psychological investigation and assessment can become unclear. This typically occurs when the expert's mandate necessitates them to express a stance on matters that also encompass legal requirements or principles, such as whether there is serious neglect of care[17] or evaluating the best living arrangement for a six-year-old, such as whether residing with his father is in the child's best interest. Undoubtedly, such issues will in many instances give rise to questions necessitating a psychological assessment. However, if both the courts or tribunals and the experts themselves are not sufficiently aware of the distinction between legal issues on the one hand and subjects appropriate for psychological assessment on the other, it may lead to a situation where experts are assigned the responsibility of opining on matters that fall within the jurisdiction of the courts or tribunals. As will be further discussed in III.B, psychology as a science is characterised by a diversity of theories, and psychological assessments involve a substantial element of discretion. Enquiries regarding what constitutes suitable childcare also involve value-based decisions, which are typically reserved for the legislator. It is therefore interesting and important that the national guidelines for managing child protection cases emphasise the distinction between legal matters and subjects requiring psychological assessment in their standard mandate templates,[18] see, for instance, the standard mandate for cases concerning the return of children to their biological parents' care, *cf.* the Child Welfare Act, section 5-7:[19]

> The mandate should not ask what is in the child's best interest, whether there is an overriding likelihood that the parents may provide proper care, or whether the child has

[16] For the child welfare tribunal, the Child Welfare Act, s 14-5, subsection two states that the tribunal 'shall ensure that the presentation of evidence provides a sound basis for decision-making'.

[17] *cf.* the Child Welfare Act, s 5-1 subsection one, litra a.

[18] National guide for handling child welfare cases, 37, 39 and 41.

[19] National guide for handling child welfare cases, 39.

formed such attachment to its foster parents that it may lead to serious problems for the child if it is returned to its parents' home. These are legal matters which the court must consider.

It is important for decision makers and experts alike to be conscious of what expert evidence is and its purposes. This awareness should guide the formulation of mandates as well as the conduct of expert investigations and report preparations. Furthermore, this should also affect how courts and other decision makers assess and give weight to expert evidence. The findings from academic and public debate and Norwegian research on the use of experts in custody and child protection cases, indicate significant practical variations. These findings underscore the need for increased awareness. In the next section of this chapter (III) an overview of current issues regarding the use of experts in Norway will be given. It will be organised thematically and structurally, with a division into three stages: the initial selection of experts and the assessment topics (III.A), questions regarding how these assessments are and should be conducted (III.B), and last how courts and child welfare tribunals use and should use expert evidence (III.C).

III. Issues and Criticism in Debate and Research

A. *Input*: Who should be Appointed and with what Mandate?

Statutory provisions do not prescribe who may be appointed as an expert in *custody cases*. The preparatory works of the procedural rules in the Children Act state that the legislation should refrain from stipulating specific requirements for professional competence prerequisites. It argues that the lack of such requirements contributes to better access to experts.[20] This is a common argument when the question of regulating matters of professional competence is discussed. The rationale behind this argument is that Norway has a fairly low population (approximately 5.5 million people[21]) spread across rather large geographical distances, with many small municipalities and relatively small court districts.

Furthermore, it is stated in the preparatory works that there are 'no formal requirements – it is the relevant person's real competence regarding the issues to be assessed that is decisive'. Subsequently, it is stated that, in most cases, psychologist or child psychiatrist are utilisised.[22]

[20] Ot.prp. nr. 29 (2002–2003) (n 3) 43.

[21] Store norske leksikon (Norwegian encyclopedia), 'befolkning' (eng. 'population') at snl.no/befolkning (last accessed 20 September 2023).

[22] Ot.prp. nr. 29 (2002–2003) (n 3) 89.

Until recently, the legislation on child protection cases had no provisions on the qualification of experts. However, tn the new Child Welfare Act, section 15-6, a qualification requirement was introduced, requiring a relevant master's degree for experts employed by the child protection service. Nevertheless, an exception exists for experts who have at least four years of experience and relevant further education of at least 30 ECTs, *cf.* subsection two, b. The purpose of this new requirement was to ensure that experts have, as a minimum, education at the same level as the child protection services' own employees, where the new Act section 15-6 introduced such a qualification requirement. The preparatory works emphasise that it is the responsibility of the municipality to assess what qualifications are required for the expert to be suitable to assess the case in question. At the same time, it is underlined that the qualification requirement does not apply to experts appointed by the child welfare tribunals or the courts, where the head of the tribunal or the judge has the competence to assess what qualifications are required.[23]

The relative lack of specificity in the qualification requirements can mainly be explained by two factors: First and foremost, as previously mentioned, setting too specific requirements may prove challenging in terms of securing experts in all cases where it is needed. The second factor appears to be rooted in a more principled concern: one must avoid conflict with the principle of the parties' right 'to present such evidence as they wish', *cf.* the Dispute Act, section 21-3, subsection one, or with the court's 'duty to ensure that the presentation of evidence provides a sound factual basis for the ruling' in child law and custody cases, *cf.* section 21-3, subsection two, 11-4. The latter factor is expressed in the two aforementioned statements in the preparatory works of the Children Act and the Child Protection Act, affirming that the assessment of the necessity for expert evidence falls under the discretion of the courts.

In Norway, experts are engaged and appointed on a case-by-case basis. These experts are often self-employed practitioners, and their role as experts may constitute a substantial portion of their income. This arrangement may lead to a dependency relationship with the client. In child protection cases, it has consequently been argued that it could be potentially problematic that the child protection services engage experts extensively. The child protection services function as parties in these proceedings and conduct their own investigations and assessments. This raises the question of whether the child protection services may favour experts whose previous conclusions align with their own. Regardless, the fact that an expert is employed by the child protection services may give rise to concerns about the expert's impartiality among private parties involved in the case.

Following the ECtHR judgments against Norway in child protection cases, there were media reports in which lawyers and experts conveyed their

[23] Prop. 133 L (2020-2021) New Child Protection Act and amendment. in the Child Protection Act, 502.

observations. They shared that some child protection services blacklisted certain experts who had either assisted parents in ECtHR cases, gone against the child protection services' assessments in other cases where they have been appointed, or had publicly expressed criticism of aspects of the child protection services' operations through the media.[24]

A possible course of action could involve transferring the responsibility of expert selection for each individual case from the child protection services to the child welfare tribunals. However, this may cause considerable delays, potentially conflicting with the best interest of the child. Expert assessments are typically relatively time consuming, and when the child protection services have serious concerns regarding the quality of care within a child's home, leading to a belief that the child should be removed from the home and placed in care, the process needs to be both swift and efficient. A delay may result in the need to remove the child from the home by means of an emergency decision, ie, before the hearing at the child welfare tribunal.[25] Such situations are typically highly dramatic for both parents and children. Furthermore, the child protection services often engage experts at an early stage of a case, using them as part of their investigations and assessments to determine whether any measures – voluntary or coercive – are required. In these cases, it might not be a particularly suitable system to assign the responsibility of appointing experts to the child welfare tribunal. Nevertheless, the question about whether an independent public body should be tasked with assigning experts remains relevant, possibly even when child welfare tribunals and courts need to appoint an expert. However, the format of this article does not allow for a comprehensive exploration of this topic.

An equally important question, aside from *who* should be appointed as an expert, is *what the experts should investigate.* As previously demonstrated, there is little legislation on this matter. There is relatively limited research on the use of experts in custody and child protection cases, but Melinder, Koch and Bernt have conducted a study on 201 mandates given by the child protection services to experts. The study revealed a significant degree of variation among the mandates. When formulating a mandate, the initial consideration should revolve around the nature of the case, including the measures under consideration – with due regard to the associated legal requirements. However, the study revealed that legal provisions in the Child Protection Act are rarely referred to within the mandates.[26]

[24] See, eg, AM Odland, 'Advokat: Sakkyndige blir svartelistet av barnevernet' in *Fri Fagbevegelse* (9 February 2023) at frifagbevegelse.no/fontene/advokat-sakkyndige-blir-svartelistet-av-barnevernet-6.158.936453.497630aa77 (last accessed 4 September 2023), AM Odland, 'Barnevernet nektet å bruke fire psykologer på grunn av deres uttalelser i mediene' i *Fontene* (10 February 2023) at fontene.no/nyheter/barnevernet-nektet-a-bruke-fire-psykologer-pa-grunn-av-deres-uttalelser-i-mediene-6.47.935662.f6f9496325 (last accessed 4 September 2023).

[25] *cf.* the Child Protection Act, ch 4.

[26] A Melinder, K Koch and C Bernt, 'Som du spør, får du svar: En gjennomgang av mandater til sakkyndige i barnevernssaker' in [2021] *Tidsskrift for familierett, arverett og barnevernrettslige spørsmål (FAB)* 52-76, 67.

This can potentially result to investigations and findings that extend beyond the issues requiring examination, and ultimately may also conflict with the principle of minimal intervention and, ultimately, the principle of proportionality, as outlined in Article 8 no 2 of the ECHR.[27] This risk primarily arises when the mandates otherwise lack specificity. The study found that the mandates were often worded quite openly and generally, without clearly specifying which psychological aspects seemed particularly relevant in the specific case.[28] On the other hand, most mandates avoided the opposite pitfall: they refrained from instructing experts to take a position on the legal issues of the case, such as whether the criteria for a care order were met.[29]

However, in some instances, the mandates lacked certain questions that one would expect to be included, particularly considering the purpose of the investigations. For example, half of the mandates failed to solicit an assessment of the parents' caregiving abilities, seen in relation to the child's needs.[30]

Another type of issue arises when experts are tasked with assessing matters beyond the scope of their professional expertise, for instance, when experts are asked to provide prognoses regarding factors such as the stability in the child's home environment and network, which carry significance for their future upbringing, and the assessment of whether the child can be returned with their parents. Psychologists typically lack the expertise required for making such prognoses, and, in most cases, the child protection services possess a lot of relevant information from their reports from contact sessions, health services, schools, and other arenas, which provide a basis for the child protection services to assess these issues themselves.[31] Furthermore, courts and child welfare tribunals should arrive at their conclusions regarding these matters based on the comprehensive evidence presented during proceedings with oral hearings.[32] In the study, requests for such prognoses occurred in approximately one third of the mandates.[33]

When a matter does not require psychological expertise, it is not an appropriate allocation of resources to enlist an expert for the investigation. Another instance indicative of unnecessary utilisation of experts, as identified in the study, is that in 75 per cent of the mandates, experts were tasked with assessing and recommending

[27] ibid 59 and 71 with further references. The principle of least intervention is considered a fundamental principle of child protection law, which is expressed in, among other things, the Child Protection Act, s 2-2 (child welfare's investigations) and s 5-1 (decision on taking over care). More generally, the European Convention on Human Rights, Art 8 on the right to private and family life also establishes such a principle, through the requirement in Art 2 of proportionality, but it probably takes a lot to establish that an investigation has violated Art 8. See, eg, *K.T. v. Norway* 2008, s 63, and an analysis of the decision in KH Søvig, 'Barneverntjenestens rett til å sette i verk undersøkelsessak og foreldrenes rett til å angripe avgjørelsen – K.T. mot Norge, klagenr. 26664/03 (EMD-2003-26664), dom av 25. september 2008'(2008) 4 *FAB* 276–282, 277–288.

[28] Melinder, Koch and Bernt (2021) (n 26) 68.

[29] ibid 67 (only in 15.4 % of the total cases).

[30] Melinder, Koch and Bernt (2021) (n 26) 68 and 72–73.

[31] ibid 74.

[32] ibid 74.

[33] ibid 69.

measures. These are matters that the child protection services should assess. The child protection services possess knowledge about available measures and are proficient in devising appropriate measures for each individual family.[34]

To include questions in the mandate that fall outside the realm of a psychological expert's expertise also raises principled concerns. When including such matters in the expert report, these assessments acquire an air of professional authority. Consequently, there is a risk that these assessments may be given more weight than they should when child welfare services, tribunals, or courts make their decisions.

Of course, there may arise occasions when the expert is required to evaluate the psychological implications of information provided by different institutions. This is emphasised in Melinder, Koch and Bernt, who illustrate this with an example of a question that a client could pose to the expert: Assuming that it is true that the child exhibits a specific behaviour pattern in certain situations, for example at school or following parental contact sessions, what psychological insights can be gleaned from this? In response, the expert can offer their professional opinion on the matter, leaving it to the decision-makers to assess the actual information about the child's behaviour purely in terms of evidence.[35]

A more general issue appears when experts conclude without acknowledging doubts and uncertainties in their assessments, creating an impression of greater certainty than actually exists. In the study conducted by Melinder, Koch and Bernt, there were no mandates that required experts to express and discuss doubts and uncertainties.[36] However, this sample was from mandates given by the child protection services, and the current situation is probably different in the courts, as the standard mandates outlined in the national guidelines now clearly state that experts must clarify where uncertainty surrounds their conclusions. Furthermore, in the standard mandates for child protection cases, experts are instructed to discuss alternative hypotheses when applicable.[37]

In a recent study conducted by Melinder, Jahren and Bernt, the authors analysed data registered by the Child Experts' Commission (CEC) in 1,855 child protection cases.[38] CEC is a body responsible for evaluating all expert reports submitted in child welfare and custody cases. For an expert report to be used as the basis for a decision by the child protection services, the child welfare tribunals, or the courts in a child protection or custody case, expert reports must be submitted to the commission, cf. the Child Welfare Act, sections 12-7 and 12-8, 14-18 subsection two, and section 61 c of the Children Act.[39]

[34] ibid 69 and 73–74.

[35] ibid 74.

[36] ibid 71.

[37] National guidelines for handling child protection cases, Apps 8 to 10 and National guidelines for handling parental disputes, App 8.

[38] A Melinder, MES Jahren and C Bernt, 'Hvordan arbeider sakkyndige psykologer med barnevernssaker? En gjennomgang av 1855 saker fra årene 2018–2020' (2023) 3 *Tidsskrift for familierett, arverett og barnevernrettslige spørsmål (FAB)* 175–195.

[39] For custody disputes, the BSK assessment was introduced as late as 2022. The amendment entered into force on 15 August 2022, according to res. 3 June 2022 no. 959.

The CEC registers key information about each individual case and the expert investigations conducted within them, forming the basis for the aforementioned study. A factor that was analysed is the correlation between the legal aspects of a case and the psychological issues that the expert was asked to investigate and assess. There was a particularly interesting finding regarding the matter of contact. The question of contact arises in nearly all child protection cases regarding coercive measures and, in some instances, may constitute a case of its own. In the ECtHR judgments against Norway, the issue of contact was a recurring theme. Key criticisms centred on the fact that very restrictive and limited visitation had been granted without sufficient justification and that sufficient assessments had not been made of how to improve the parents' abilities to interact with their children in a safe and positive way during contact, as well as how to prevent negative reactions in the children.[40]

Based on the frequency and complexity of matters of contact in child protection cases, one would naturally expect that the legal issue of contact would be a prevalent inclusion in most of the expert mandates, as an indication of which topics in the case prompted an expert assessment. Therefore, it was a rather surprising finding that contact was only the third most frequent legal theme indicated in the mandates. Furthermore, the study uncovered a mild negative correlation between the legal theme of 'quality of care' and both the legal theme 'contact' and the psychological assessment issue concerning the parents' ability to provide good and safe contact sessions.[41] Considering the criticism from ECtHR regarding decisions and assessment related to contact, it is a reasonable argument that assessment themes concerning contact should occur far more often in the mandates.

There is a need for further research to explore the scope of assessments delegated to experts within their mandates and to scrutinise the significance of these mandates on expert investigations. These issues are part of the research project, which will be presented in section four.

B. How should the Investigations be Conducted?

The next question of importance for the quality of expert evidence is how experts implement their investigations and what their conclusions are based on. This

[40] *Strand Lobben and others. v Norway* App no 37283/13 (ECtHR 30 November 2017); *Jansen v Norway* App no 2822/16 (ECtHR, 6 September 2018); *K.O. and V.M. v Norway* App no 64808/16 (ECtHR 19 November 2019); *Hernehult v Norway* App no 14652/16 (ECtHR 10 March 2020); *M.L. v Norway* App no 64639/16 (12 December 2020); *K.E. and A.K. v Norway* App no 57678/18 (1 July 2021); *R.O. v Norway* App no 49452/18 (ECtHR 1 July 2021); *F.Z. v Norway* App no 64789/17 (ECtHR 1 July 2021); *E.H. v Norway* App no 39717/19 (25 November 2021); *M.F. v Norway* App no 5947/19 (ECtHR 25 November 2021); *Abdi Ibrahim v Norway* App no 15379/16 (ECtHR, 10 December 2021); *A.L. and others v Norway* App no 45889/18 (ECtHR 20 January 2022); *D.R and others v Norway* App no 63307/17 and 38105/19 (ECtHR 12 September 2023); *K.F. and others v Norway* App no 39769/17, 9167/18, 48372/18, 38097/19, 45985/19, 58880/19 (ECtHR 12 September 2023); *S.S. and J.H. v Norway* App no 15784/19 (ECtHR 12 September 2023).

[41] Melinder, Jahren and Bernt (2023) (n 38)184–185.

includes what kind of methodology they use, the theoretical foundation their assessments are based on, and how they portray the basis for their conclusions within the reports.

The aforementioned study conducted by Melinder, Jahren and Bernt investigated to what extent experts used structured assessment tools and/or semi-structured interview protocols in their assessments. The use of such tools not only enhances the verifiability of findings but also mitigates the risk of bias. They prove particularly relevant in certain assessment domains, such as evaluating substance abuse, specific aspects of mental health, and when interacting with children.[42] The study found a relatively low occurrence of such tools, accounting for only nine per cent of the cases. The authors express concerns regarding this low frequency, particularly because it could jeopardise the adherence to recommended practices during conversations with children. Additionally, the authors highlight that the use of structured instruments in cases involving drug related issues did not exhibit a statistically significant connection, even though well-established and frequently used tools for assessing substance abuse are available.[43]

An issue that has been raised both in public and professional debate is that some expert reports seem to be characterised by none or little discussion of alternative hypotheses to explain behaviour and problems in parents and children, and that this can lead to incorrect conclusions.[44] Addressing this concern may involve more frequent utilisation of the tools as mentioned above, but it also underscores the importance of establishing guidelines for the composition of expert reports.

Psychology is a field encompassing a multitude of theories, and a notable concern has been that psychologists do not sufficiently show the theoretical basis for their assessments in the reports and do not indicate that other theories exist.[45] This issue is illustrated in an article from 2021 authored by Melinder, van der Hagen and Sandberg. In this article, they explain the strong influence of psychology on the understanding of the best interest of the child in Norway, emphasising the predominant influence of attachment theory in assessments. Within the Norwegian context, it might seem as if attachment theory is the only valid theory, while the internationally perspective portrays a more nuanced landscape.[46] Similar issues pertaining to the lack of transparency regarding theoretical foundations have also been identified in Norwegian research across other domains involving the utilisation of experts.[47]

[42] ibid 179–181 with further references.

[43] ibid 189.

[44] See, eg, Haugli and Nordhelle (2014) (n 2) 89–108 and 100–104 with further references.

[45] See, eg, Haugli and Nordhelle (2014) (n 2) 99–100 and Bernt (2014) (n 2) 207–209.

[46] A Melinder, MA van der Hagen and K Sandberg, 'In the Best Interest of the Child: the Norwegian Approach to Child Protection' (2021) 4 *International Journal on Child Maltreatment: Research, Policy and Practice* 209–230.

[47] Lundeberg (2009) (n 2) 611–646 (on experts in compensation cases due to inadequate education in schools in cases of special needs education) and A Schøitz, 'Den rettsmedisinske sakkyndighet.

An issue that has been raised, somewhat related to the above, is that experts may experience external pressure leading them to deliver definite conclusions that surpass the boundaries of their professional expertise.[48] It is worth noting that, as of now, no research has been conducted to explore this particular aspect concerning experts in custody or child protection cases in Norway.

As mentioned in the introduction, the extent to which experts should talk to *comparatives* as part of their investigations and how child welfare tribunals and courts should relate to this part of the expert reports has been a matter of ongoing debate.[49] A comparative is a person, for instance, the child's teacher, a school nurse, or a relative, who can provide the expert with information relevant to the questions posed in the mandate. On one hand, experts may find it necessary or beneficial to interview individuals who play significant roles in the lives of the children or parents as part of their investigations of the psychological issues in the case. On the other hand, involving comparatives in expert assessments and reports introduces the possibility of experts acquiring potentially crucial witness evidence. This could potentially infringe the parties' right to have access, and the opportunity, to refute the evidence presented, *cf.* the Dispute Act. section 1-1, if the comparatives are not brought as witnesses in the oral hearing. Furthermore, there is an increased risk of misinterpretation if certain pieces of information only reach the tribunal and the court indirectly, via the expert.[50] Another potential problem is that the contact between the expert and the comparatives may influence the latter, making them less unbiased and therefore negatively affect the evidentiary value of their statements.[51] Additionally, there arises a question concerning effective use of time and resources: To what extent should an expert's valuable – and often expensive – time be allocated to engaging with comparatives who should ultimately appear as witnesses?

Research on the use of comparatives in custody and child protection cases in Norway remains scarce. However, the study conducted by Melinder, Jahren and Bernt revealed significant variation in the inclusion of comparatives. There was a positive correlation between the number of comparatives involved, the number of psychological themes explored and the number of children under consideration. An interesting discovery, however, was that while the most frequent scenario entailed the absence of comparatives, the second most frequent entailed the inclusion of more than nine comparatives.[52]

Rasjonalitetsformer og rolleoppfatninger i medisin og juss' (2006) 1 *Tidsskrift for Strafferett* 20–38 (part of the NFR project 'Den rettsmedisinske sakkyndighet. Møte mellom to profesjoner belyst gjennom rettsmedisinens historie').

[48] Haugli and Nordhelle (2014) (n 2) 99–100 and Greve et al. (2023) (n 3). For similar discussions in related fields, see Schøitz (2006) (n 47)22–23 and Lundeberg (2009) (n 2) 644–645.

[49] Haugli and Nordhelle (2014) (n 2) 99 and Bernt (2014) (n 2) 206–207.

[50] Haugli and Nordhelle (2014) (n 2) 99.

[51] Melinder, Jahren and Bernt (2023) (n 38) 180.

[52] ibid 187.

C. *Output*: The Use of Expert Evidence in Child Welfare Tribunals and Courts

The third and final question is how child welfare tribunals and courts engage with expert evidence, an area that has seen relatively limited research. Kirsten Sandberg was a pioneer within the field of legal science ago when, as part of her jurisprudential doctoral thesis on the return of children placed in care to their parents' home, she conducted a qualitative study into the treatment of expert reports within judicial decisions. Her study encompassed an examination of both the reports and the judgments and raised critical concerns about her findings. In her opinion, the reasoning in the judgments regarding the choice to emphasise or disregard assessments in expert reports lacked sufficient professional or scientific justification.[53]

A more recent study was conducted by Audun Løvlie, who examined the use of evidence in child protection cases involving domestic violence. His study uncovered, among other things, significant variation in how decision makers use and give weight to expert evidence. While some decision-makers concurred with the assessments without articulating explicit justification, others engaged in more independent and partly critical deliberations, based on theory or additional pieces of evidence.[54]

In 2015, Augusti, Bernt and Melinder participated in an evaluation of the CEC, a study commissioned by the Ministry of Children and Families.[55] Some important findings in the evaluation were made. First, it was observed that the assessments from CEC were consistent from case to case.[56] Additionally, judges and tribunal heads themselves expressed that the CEC assessments were useful in identifying reports of low quality that should be disregarded.[57] However, the decision-makers were more reserved in their responses regarding questions on whether the BSK assessments were important when deciding the evidentiary weight of the expert reports.[58] Subsequently, a qualitative analysis of 45 judgments and tribunal decrees in cases where the CEC had expressed criticism of the reports was conducted. It found that the reports were not presented as an independent argument in the justification in the decisions on points were the reports were criticised by CEC.[59]

[53] Sandberg (2003) (n 2).

[54] A Løvlie, 'Evidence in Norwegian child protection interventions – Analysing cases of familial violence' ([2022] *Child & Family Social Work* 236–247.

[55] Agenda Kaupang, *Evaluering av Barnesakkyndig kommisjon og vurdering av utvidet ansvarsområde*. Ministry of Children, Equality and Social Inclusion (2015). From Agenda Kaupang participated Gitte Haugnæss (project leader), Dag Stokland and Odd Helgesen.

[56] Agenda Kaupang (2015) (n 55) 84 and E-M Augusti, C Bernt and A Melinder, 'Kvalitetssikring av sakkyndighetsarbeid – en gjennomgang av vurderingsprosesser i Barnesakkyndig kommisjon, fylkesnemnder og domstoler' (2017) 4 *Tidsskrift for familierett, arverett og barnevernrettslige spørsmål* (FAB) 265–289, 278–282 and 289.

[57] Agenda Kaupang (2015) (n 55) 34 and Augusti, Bernt and Melinder (2017) (n 56) 287.

[58] Agenda Kaupang (2015) (n 55) 34 and Augusti, Bernt and Melinder (2017) (n 56) 287.

[59] Agenda Kaupang (2015) (n 55) 34 and Augusti, Bernt and Melinder (2017) (n 56) 284–286.

It must be noted that these findings do not provide sufficient grounds to determine whether the decision-making bodies chose not to emphasise the criticised points in the reports *because of* the CEC remarks or whether they did so based on their own assessment and other evidence in the case. Nevertheless, the study's observation that no cases were identified where the court or tribunal deviated from CEC's assessments suggests that the CEC assessments likely carried some degree of significance.

IV. Research Project: 'The Use of Expert Reports as Evidence in Child Protection Decision-making'

As shown, existing research on the role of expert evidence in courts and tribunals in child protection cases, and even more so in custody cases, is relatively fragmented. There is a need for more up-to-date, thorough, and comprehensive research across various dimensions of this topic. Both public and academic debate, coupled with the findings from existing research, uncovers the pressing need for a better knowledge foundation to ensure that the utilisation of experts contributes effectively to improving the quality of proceedings and decision-making in child protection and custody cases. This alignment with the fundamental procedural and material rights of children and parents is paramount.

In the last section of this chapter, I will introduce an ongoing research project focused on the use of experts in child protection cases. This project aims to investigate various aspects presented in this article, delving deeper into the subject matter.

In September 2022, the Norwegian Research Council allocated 12 million Norwegian kroner, which is approximately €1 million, to an interdisciplinary four-year research project on the use of experts in child protection cases. This project officially commenced on the 1 July 2023, under the leadership of Professor Annika Melinder from the psychology department at the University of Oslo. The primary project team comprises the author of this article and Professor Kirsten Sandberg from the University of Oslo, Faculty of Law. The project also includes two Ph.D. candidates, one with a legal background and the other a psychologist. Additionally, senior researchers from Sweden, the USA, England, and Germany are collaborating on this initiative as partners. The project has a broadly composed reference group where all stakeholders are represented.

The project is dedicated to an extensive examination of expert evidence in child protection cases, encompassing all stages, from the formulation of mandates to the application of expert evidence in judgments. The first research question (work package 1) is what experts are asked to investigate and what they should be asked to investigate. To address this, a comparative analysis will be conducted, evaluating regulatory frameworks for experts' usage in Norway, Sweden, England,

and Germany, and perhaps a few other countries. Furthermore, the project group develops standard mandates in close cooperation with an expert group of judges that will be used by the courts. Subsequently, a study will be devised, comparing cases where these mandates have been used to cases where no standard mandates have been used.

The second work package of the project focuses on the experts' interactions with children. The project will develop and validate an *application* tailored for these interactions. This application will encompass an interview guide and further guidance for the experts based on the type of case, a secure recording feature for conversations, and a mechanism enabling experts to give feedback within the app. In addition to analysing the feedback received from experts who have used the app, a comparison will be made of the feedback from CEC on the reports written by experts who have used the app, compared to cases where the app was not used. As mentioned in III.B, Melinder, Jahren and Bernt revealed limited use of structured methods in child protection cases. This may give cause for concern regarding the quality assurance of conversations with children, particularly in light of the absence of legislation mandating experts to possess special competence in conducting such conversations.

The third work package of this research project focuses on the utilisation of expert evidence by the courts. This section aims to address critical research enquiries such as how the courts refer to the mandate and describe the expert investigations in their verdicts, along with the findings that receive emphasis and the extent to which they are emphasised. An issue that will be analysed is the significance of the psychological assessments for the courts' perception of the child's best interest. Another issue is what affects how much weight a report is given when rendering a decision, encompassing a number of questions: What significance does the court place on the mandate, the theoretical foundation indicated in the report for the assessment, and the expert's choice of methods? How independently does the court assess the investigations, the findings, and the assessments in the reports? What other forms of evidence are available in the case, and how does the court weight alternative evidence given compared to the expert report? Additionally, the study investigates the interplay between the use of comparatives and the testimony of witnesses within the case. Norwegian and Swedish court decisions will be analysed and compared to gain a comprehensive understanding of these aspects.

As the mentioned research questions indicate, several scientific methods will be used in this research project. In addition to studies of the legal framework in different countries, a qualitative study of 100 judgments and corresponding expert reports based on traditional individual mandates will be compared with 100 judgments and corresponding expert reports based on standardised mandates. Quantitative analyses involving 100 court decisions from both Norway and Sweden, respectively, will also be conducted, with an additional in-debt qualitative analysis of 25 to 35 decisions from each country. A scoping review by Greve et al.

concludes that there is a need for research on the decision-making bodies' use of expert evidence, and particularly the lack of quantitative research is emphasised.[60]

Although the project is extensive, it is evident that there will remain unexplored territory within this field even after the project is concluded. The need for further research is particularly pressing in custody cases, where there is even less research on the use of experts than in child protection cases. In many custody cases, expert reports assume great importance as evidentiary material, given the frequently limited availability of alternative evidence regarding the child's situation and needs, compared to child protection cases.

[60] Greve et al. (2023) (n 3).

16

The Heroes of Judicial Periphery

Court Experts and Shadow Actors: A View from South Africa

DANIE VAN LOGGERENBERG[1]

I. Introduction

In the conference outline it is stated that the principal focus of the conference will be on experts and the way they are appointed, managed and remunerated across Europe and the world. The goal is to focus on cooperation and interplay between judges and experts and to reflect on the manner in which experts affect the quality and speed of civil justice having regard, amongst other things, to changes in the appointment of experts, if any.

In addition, the conference aims at assessing the role of the 'judicial periphery' – the actors in the shadow who nevertheless often determine the pace, outcome and flavour of the judicial process.

The goal of the conference necessitates a distinction between:

(a) the procedural aspect, namely the appointment, management and remuneration of experts;
(b) the evidential aspect relating to expert evidence,[2] namely the cooperation and interplay between judges and experts and how the latter's evidence affect the quality and speed of civil justice;
(c) different shadow actors and their role in the judicial process.

These aspects will be addressed *seriatim* from a South African perspective of civil litigation in the High Court,[3] keeping in mind that in South Africa party autonomy, embedded in an adversarial system of civil procedure, prevails.

[1] Prepared by Danie van Loggerenberg for the XVII PPJ Course and Conference, IUC Dubrovnik.

[2] In South Africa 'expert evidence' is also referred to as 'opinion evidence'. In this chapter the term 'expert evidence' will be used.

[3] In terms of s 166 of the Constitution of the Republic of South Africa, 1996 ('the Constitution'), the courts are:

(a) the Constitutional Court;

II. Experts: The Procedural Aspect

Section 34 of the Bill of Rights in South Africa's Constitution guarantees the right of everyone to have any dispute that can be resolved by the application of law in a fair public hearing before a court. A public trial that allows each party to put its case fully and freely in a setting that is open to the public and the media before an independent judge, ensures the constitutionally entrenched right of fairness of the proceedings.[4]

Section 171 of the Constitution provides that all courts function in terms of national legislation, and their rules and procedures must be provided for in terms of national legislation. The national legislation envisaged in section 171 of the Constitution comprises the Superior Courts Act 10 of 2013 and the Rules Board for Courts of Law Act 107 of 1995, both of which provide for the framing of rules of court. In the High Court these rules are embedded in the Uniform Rules of Court.

The appointment and management of experts are regulated by the Uniform Rules of Court. In addition to the Uniform Rules of Court, Practice Directives issued by the heads of the various divisions of the High Court regulate experts and their functions.

A. Rule 36(9) and (9A) of the Uniform Rules of Court

Rule 36(9) and (9A) of the Uniform Rules of Court provides as follows:

> (9) No person shall, save with the leave of the court or the consent of all parties to the suit, be entitled to call as a witness any person to give evidence as an expert upon any matter upon which the evidence of expert witnesses may be received unless —
>
> (a) where the plaintiff intends to call an expert, the plaintiff shall not more than 30 days[5] after the close of pleadings,[6] or where the defendant intends to call the

(b) the Supreme Court of Appeal;
(c) the High Court of South Africa, and any high court of appeal that may be established by an Act of Parliament to hear appeals from any court of a similar status to the High Court of South Africa;
(d) the Magistrates' Courts; and
(e) any other court established or recognised in terms of an Act of Parliament, including any court of a status similar to either the High Court of South Africa or the Magistrates' Courts.

[4] *De Lange v Smuts NO* 1998 (3) SA 785 (CC) at [131].

[5] Prior to the substitution of this paragraph with effect from 1 July 2019, the subrule imposed the same time limits on both parties, namely 15 days before the hearing for a notice of intention to call a witness to give evidence as an expert. By now imposing different time limits and providing for the calculation of the time periods with reference to the close of pleadings, the subrule in its amended form is of a more efficient and practical nature, amongst other things, by allowing a defendant, on receipt of a plaintiff's notice of intention to call an expert witness, to consider its position and, if necessary, to find an expert to give evidence at the hearing.

[6] Pleadings normally consist of, at least, a summons and particulars of the plaintiff's claim, a plea by the defendant and a replication to the plea by the plaintiff. Once these 'pleadings' have been delivered, pleadings are closed.

expert, the defendant shall not more than 60 days after the close of pleadings, have delivered notice of intention to call such expert; and

(b) in the case of the plaintiff not more than 90 days[7] after the close of pleadings and in the case of the defendant not more than 120 days after the close of pleadings, such plaintiff or defendant shall have delivered a summary of the expert's opinion and the reasons therefor:

Provided that the notice and summary shall in any event be delivered before a first case management conference held in terms of rules 37A(6) and (7) or as directed by a case management judge.[8]

(9A) The parties shall —

(a) endeavour, as far as possible, to appoint a single joint expert on any one or more or all issues in the case; and

(b) file a joint minute of experts relating to the same area of expertise within 20 days of the date of the last filing of such expert reports.

i. Rule 36(9)(a)

The main purpose of rule 36(9)*(a)* is to require the party intending to call a witness to give expert evidence to give the other party such information about its evidence as will remove the element of surprise from the trial. Furthermore, proper compliance with the rule may enable experts to exchange views before giving evidence and thus to reach agreement on at least some of the issues, thereby saving costs and the time of the court.[9] On the other hand, the rule makes inroads upon a fundamental right of a party, viz to call a witness, and places the party at the disadvantage

[7] Prior to the substitution of this subrule with effect from 1 July 2019, the subrule imposed the same time limit on both parties, namely 10 days before the trial for a summary of the expert's opinions and reasons therefor. That gave rise to questions such as if a party delivered its summary on the 11th day before trial, was the other party entitled to lead evidence in rebuttal of the summary without complying with the subrule, for in such circumstances it was impossible to file a summary of rebutting evidence in time to comply with the rule? It had been held that the subrule (prior to its amendment) '*was not intended to cover evidence strictly in answer to an opposing party's summary*' (by the full court in a judgment which is not reported but is referred to in a note by Brathwaite in (1976) 6 *Newsletter of the Institute of Patent Agents* at 4). In other words, such evidence could be led as of right and was not hit by the subrule. On the other hand, it could be argued that such evidence was hit by the subrule and was evidence which might be allowed without a summary by the leave of the court. In either event there appeared to be a *lacuna* in the subrule. This has been addressed by the subrule in its amended form: first, by introducing different time periods within which the plaintiff and the defendant must deliver their expert summaries; and, secondly, by providing that the time periods are to be calculated from the date of close of pleadings.

[8] Under rule 37A a judicial case management system applies in trial actions in the High Court. The judicial case management procedure is overseen by a judicial case management judge who, eventually, must certify the case as trial-ready.

[9] *Klue v Provincial Administration, Cape* 1966 (2) SA 561 (E); *Coopers (SA) (Pty) Ltd v Deutsche Gesellschaft für Schädlingsbekämpfung mbH* 1976 (3) SA 352 (A) at 371F; *Doyle v Sentraboer (Co-operative) Ltd* 1993 (3) SA 176 (SE) at 181A-C; *Hall v Multilateral Motor Vehicle Accidents Fund* 1998 (4) SA 195 (C) at 200A.

of having to intimate in advance what its expert is going to say. Accordingly, the rule should be strictly construed.[10]

Rule 36(9)*(a)* contains its own sanction in that the party who fails to comply with the provisions thereof is precluded from calling an expert witness. This does not mean, however, that it is the only remedy available to the other party: in appropriate circumstances such a party would be entitled to a postponement of the trial by reason of its opponent's non-compliance with the provisions of the subrule.[11]

Rule 36(9)*(a)* applies to expert witnesses who are asked to express an opinion on a particular subject. There are, therefore, two requirements for the rule to operate: first, the evidence must be in the nature of an opinion; and, secondly, it must be given by a person who is an expert.[12] These aspects will be addressed s v 'Experts: the evidential aspect' below.

The meanings of the words 'summary' and 'opinion', and of the phrase 'reasons therefor' in rule 36(9)*(a)* were considered by the Appellate Division in *Coopers (SA) (Pty) Ltd v Deutsche Gesellschaft für Schädlingsbekämpfung mbH*.[13] In regard to 'summary' and 'opinion' the court adopted as appropriate the meanings given by the *Concise Oxford Dictionary*: 'summary' as a noun means a 'brief account, abridgement, epitome'; 'opinion' means a judgment or belief based on grounds short of 'proof' or a 'formal statement by expert when consulted on what he holds to be the fact'. In regard to the phrase 'his reasons therefor', the court held that it means, or at least includes, the facts or data on which the opinion is based. However, the 'summary' also governs 'his reasons therefor'; hence the testimony that the expert witness intends to give need not be fully set out in the summary. The summary must at least state the sum and substance of the facts and data which lead to the reasoned conclusion (ie the opinion). In this regard Wessels JA stated:[14]

> As I see it, an expert's opinion represents his recent conclusion based on certain facts on [sic] data, which are either common cause, or established by his own evidence or that of some other competent witness.

If the process of reasoning is not a matter of ordinary logic, but involves, for example, the application of scientific principles, it will ordinarily also be necessary to set out the reasoning process in summarized form.[15] In deciding whether there

[10] *Boland Construction Co (Pty) Ltd v Levin* 1977 (2) SA 506 (C) at 508H; *Doyle v Sentraboer (Co-operative) Ltd, supra*, at 180G-J.

[11] *Smit v Shongwe* 1982 (4) SA 699 (T).

[12] *Uni-Erections v Continental Engineering Co Ltd* 1981 (1) SA 240 (W) at 250A; *M J Snyman v Alert-O-Drive (Pty) Ltd* 1981 BP 213.

[13] Above at 371B.

[14] At 371F. See also *Schneider Electric SA (Pty) Ltd v Jim Fung Industrial Limited* (unreported, GJ case no A5058/2015 dated 8 December 2016) at para [69]; *AM v MEC for Health, Western Cape* 2021 (3) SA 337 (SCA) at paras [18]–[21]; and see *JA obo DA v MEC for Health, Eastern Cape* 2022 (3) SA 475 (ECB) (a decision of the full court) at paras [11]–[13].

[15] *Coopers (SA) (Pty) Ltd v Deutsche Gesellschaft für Schädlingsbekämpfung mbH*, above, at 371–2. In *Boland Construction Co (Pty) Ltd v Lewin* 1977 (2) SA 506 (C) Vos J suggested (at 508) that 'the concept "summary" may not have received sufficient weight in *Cooper's* case'. He expressed the opinion that the rule should be restrictively construed and that 'a summary should be no more than a summary'.

has been due compliance with the subrule, it is relevant to have regard to the main purpose thereof, viz to remove the element of surprise. When summarizing the facts or data on which the expert witness premises his opinions, the draftsman should ensure that no information is omitted, where omission thereof might lead to the other side being taken by surprise.[16]

ii. Rule 36(9A)

Proper compliance with rule 36(9A) will enable experts to exchange views and to reach agreement on the issues, or at least some of them, which require expert evidence, thereby facilitating the appointment of a single joint expert, on the one hand, and the preparation of a joint minute, on the other hand, thus saving costs and the time of the court.[17]

B. Costs

An expert attending court and giving evidence (or not) is entitled to an allowance for lost income per day attending court. In addition, and if the court so orders, the expert's 'qualifying expenses' could be allowed. These are the expenses necessarily incurred by a witness who has to qualify himself to give evidence upon some matter, usually technical; they mean the expenses incurred by him in making experiments, investigations or research.[18]

'Qualifying expenses', it seems, covers all acts performed by the expert which relate to the opinion he would express in court. This may include the observation of persons and places, or the investigation of or experiments on the *corpus delicti*. It does, however, not include pre-trial examinations or investigations which go to direct proof of the *factum probandum*.[19] The pre-trial activity of the expert may relate to both qualifying and non-qualifying preparatory acts; indeed it may be difficult to unravel the one from the other. But the basis of the distinction is clear:

[16] *Coopers (SA) (Pty) Ltd v Deutsche Gesellschaft für Schädlingsbekämpfung mbH*, above, at 371E.

[17] Practice Directives issued by a head of a division of the High Court in regard to joint minutes should be adhered to. Non-compliance therewith could be met with a refusal by the court to hear the case (see, eg, *Ntombela v Road Accident Fund* 2018 (4) SA 486 (GJ) at 496A-497E and 498B-C). In *Bee v Road Accident Fund* 2018 (4) SA 366 (SCA) the majority of the Supreme Court of Appeal held (at 386A-388A) that effective case management required experts to stick to the facts agreed in their joint minute. If an expert wished to depart from it, it had to give due warning to the other experts. If an expert testified inconsistently with the contents of a joint minute, it would amount to trial by ambush, which is impermissible.

[18] The scope of qualifying expenses is considered, with full reference to earlier authority, in *Köhne v Union & National Insurance Co Ltd* 1968 (2) SA 499 (N). See also *Champion v Morkel* 1971 (2) SA 121 (R) at 128; *City Deep Ltd v Johannesburg City Council* 1973 (2) SA 109 (W); *Julies v Cape Town Municipality* 1976 (3) SA 138 (C); *Owen v Owen* 1979 (2) SA 568 (C); *Administrator, Cape v Buffalo Park Township (Pty) Ltd* 1980 (2) SA 430 (SE); *Randall v Baisley* 1992 (3) SA 448 (E) at 453D–454C.

[19] This means all the facts which must be proved in order to disclose the plaintiff's cause of action against the defendant, in contradistinction to the facts which prove those facts (ie the *facta probantia*).

qualifying acts bear upon the expert's opinion, all other acts fall outside the scope of the concept.[20]

The court must be requested to make a special order allowing such expenses to be taxed as between party and party, failing which the party calling such witness will have to bear these costs himself.[21] If the expert witness is not called the question whether the qualifying expenses (and the witnesses' allowances) should be claimable on taxation depends on whether they were reasonably necessary when they were incurred, in other words, whether it was reasonable for the legal representatives of the successful party to incur the expenses when they did so.[22] If the answer to this question is in the affirmative, the expenses should be allowed.[23] If the case is settled and the agreement states that one party is to pay the other party's taxed costs, these do not include the qualifying expenses of a witness whom the court has not heard.[24] It is, of course, always open to a party who negotiates a settlement to stipulate for the payment of the qualifying expenses of expert witnesses.[25]

In *Ndlovu v Road Accident Fund*[26] the High Court, after having expressed its disappointment in the quality of some of the experts' reports that were presented to it, remarked[27] that 'a time may come when a court will consider that an expert's lack of care, skill and diligence will have adverse costs consequences upon the successful litigant, or will direct that the expert is limited in what may be recovered from the instructing party (particularly where there is a contingency-fee arrangement and this may constitute an additional disbursement reducing the ultimate award received)'.

[20] *Randall v Baisley* 1992 (3) SA 448 (E) at 454A–C. See also *Van Deventer v Commercial Union Insurance Co Ltd* 1997 (4) SA 890 (T), where it was held (at 891I–892H) that where experts consult with counsel in order to be informed of the issues and matters on which they would be required to testify and to limit those issues to a minimum, their fees for the consultation fall within the ambit of the qualifying process and are allowable as qualifying fees.

[21] *City Deep Ltd v Johannesburg City Council* 1973 (2) SA 109 (W); *Community Development Board v Katija Suliman Lockhat Trust* 1973 (4) SA 225 (N) at 228–9; *Van Wyk v Protea Assurance Co Ltd* 1974 (3) SA 499 (SWA); *Ferreira v Ferreira* 1977 (4) SA 618 (O) at 620; *Luvuno v Southern Insurance Co Ltd* 1980 (2) SA 931 (D) at 934; *South African Forestry Co Ltd v New York Timbers Ltd* 2001 (4) SA 884 (T) at 888D–G; *Transnet Ltd t/a Metrorail v Witter* 2008 (6) SA 549 (SCA) at 558G; *AD v MEC for Health and Social Development, Western Cape* 2017 (5) SA 134 (WCC) at 159B–H. The request that qualifying fees be allowed need not necessarily be made before judgment: it may be made immediately upon judgment being given or 'very soon' thereafter (*Lynmar Investments (Pty) Ltd v South African Railways and Harbours* 1975 (4) SA 445 (D)).

[22] *Stauffer Chemical Co and Another v Safsan Marketing and Distribution Co (Pty) Ltd* 1987 (2) SA 331 (A) at 354I–355H; *Transnet Ltd t/a Metrorail v Witter* 2008 (6) SA 549 (SCA) at 560A–D.

[23] *Transnet Ltd t/a Metrorail v Witter* 2008 (6) SA 549 (SCA) at 560A–D.

[24] *Breetzke v Union Government* 1911 EDL 394; *Roos v Morkel and Somerset West Municipality* 1915 CPD 201; *De Villiers v Stadsraad van Pretoria* 1967 (4) SA 533 (T); *Van Wyk v Protea Assurance Co Ltd* 1974 (3) SA 499 (SWA); *Theron, Van der Poel, Brink, Roos v Simonsig Landgoed* 1994 (4) SA 204 (A) at 208D–G.

[25] As was done in, eg, *Köhne v Union & National Insurance Co Ltd* 1968 (2) SA 499 (N) at 500. An agreement relating to a claim for bodily injuries to pay an amount as damages plus taxed costs plus such medico-legal fees as are allowed by the taxing officer, includes the qualifying fees of medical experts (*Muller v AA Mutual Insurance Ass Ltd* 1973 (2) SA 787 (T)).

[26] 2014 (1) SA 415 (GSJ).

[27] At 440I–441A.

III. Experts: The Evidential Aspect

As pointed out above, expert evidence must be given by a person who is an expert in the form of an opinion.

A. General

In *AM v MEC for Health, Western Cape*[28] the Supreme Court of Appeal said the following about the role of an expert and expert evidence:[29]

> Something needs to be said about the role of expert witnesses and the expert evidence in this case. The functions of an expert witness are threefold. First, where they have themselves observed relevant facts that evidence will be evidence of fact and admissible as such. Second, they provide the court with abstract or general knowledge concerning their discipline that is necessary to enable the court to understand the issues arising in the litigation. This includes evidence of the current state of knowledge and generally accepted practice in the field in question. Although such evidence can only be given by an expert qualified in the relevant field, it remains, at the end of the day, essentially evidence of fact on which the court will have to make factual findings. It is necessary to enable the court to assess the validity of opinions that they express. Third, they give evidence concerning their own inferences and opinions on the issues in the case and the grounds for drawing those inferences and expressing those conclusions.

In *Schneider NO v AA*[30] the role of an expert was explained as follows:[31]

> In this connection it is necessary to deal with the role of an expert. In Zeffertt, Paizes & Skeen *The South African Law of Evidence* at 330, the learned authors, citing the English judgment of *National Justice Compania Naviera SA v Prudential Assurance Co Ltd (The 'Ikarian Reefer')* [1993] 2 Lloyd's Rep 68 at 81, set out the duties of an expert witness thus:
>
> 1. Expert evidence presented to the court should be, and should be seen to be, the independent product of the expert uninfluenced as to form or content by the exigencies of litigation.
> 2. An expert witness should provide independent assistance to the court by way of objective, unbiased opinion in relation to matters within his expertise. … An expert witness should never assume the role of an advocate.
> 3. An expert witness should state the facts or assumptions upon which his opinion is based. He should not omit to consider material facts which could detract from his concluded opinion.
> 4. An expert witness should make it clear when a particular question or issue falls outside his expertise.

[28] 2021 (3) SA 337 (SCA).
[29] At para [17].
[30] 2010 (5) SA 203 (WCC).
[31] At 211E-214B.

5. If an expert opinion is not properly researched because he considers that insufficient data is available, then this must be stated with an indication that the opinion is no more than a provisional one. In cases where an expert witness who has prepared a report could not assert that the report contained the truth, the whole truth and nothing but the truth without some qualification, that qualification should be stated in the report.

In short, an expert comes to court to give the court the benefit of his or her expertise. Agreed, an expert is called by a particular party, presumably because the conclusion of the expert, using his or her expertise, is in favour of the line of argument of the particular party. But that does not absolve the expert from providing the court with as objective and unbiased an opinion, based on his or her expertise, as possible. An expert is not a hired gun who dispenses his or her expertise for the purposes of a particular case. An expert does not assume the role of an advocate, nor gives evidence which goes beyond the logic which is dictated by the scientific knowledge which that expert claims to possess.

B. Expert

It is the function of the High Court to decide whether the witness has sufficient qualifications for him to qualify as an expert. In other words, the court must be satisfied that the witness possesses proper skill, training or experience to assist it in the role of an expert.[32] The expert's skill or knowledge need not necessarily be acquired in the course of his profession. It all depends on the topic. Thus, lack of formal training may indicate inadequate theoretical training but, in the circumstances of a particular case, this may be offset by practical experience.[33] There is no general rule that the expert's knowledge upon the subject-matter of his evidence must derive from personal experience rather than from reading. Opinions on scientific matters usually involve reliance upon data provided by others.[34]

C. Opinion

Expert evidence does not mean any evidence given by an expert but only admissible opinion evidence by such a witness.[35]

Before any weight can be given to an expert's opinion, the facts upon which the opinion is based must be found to exist. As long as there is some admissible evidence on which the expert's testimony is based it cannot be ignored; but it follows that the more an expert relies on facts not in evidence, the weight given to

[32] *Commissioner for the South African Revenue Services v Stepney Investments Pty Ltd* [2016] 1 All SA 1 (SCA) at para [16].
[33] DT Zeffertt and AP Paizes, *The South African Law of Evidence*, 3rd Edition (Durban 2017) at 338.
[34] Ibid.
[35] *M J Snyman v Alert-O-Drive (Pty) Ltd* 1981 BP 213.

his opinion will diminish. An opinion based on facts not in evidence has no value for the court.[36]

Expert evidence is only as sound as the factual evidence on which it is based. The less fixed (or more variable) the assumption and the fewer hard facts available to the expert, the greater the scope for alternative conclusions.[37]

In *AM v MEC for Health, Western Cape*[38] the rules relating to expert witnesses were disregarded in various respects, to the dissatisfaction of the Supreme Court of Appeal, which held *(per* Wallis JA):

> [22] In my view these requirements were disregarded in this case. The experts instructed on behalf of the Ms were in certain respects not instructed on the basis of facts that could be, or were, proved at the trial in regard to the mechanics of J's injury. There was no endeavour to clarify the facts known to Dr Horn, or the facts about her diagnosis and treatment of J. She was criticised in relation to matters that were known to be irrelevant, such as her failure to perform an otoscopy. Her notes and other documents were subjected to forensic scrutiny and criticism of a type one encounters with the most pedantic lawyers. Conclusions contrary to her diagnosis were expressed on the basis that her notes were not as complete as Dr Goosen and Dr Edeling thought desirable. The medical literature was used selectively to bolster arguments and not for the purpose of informing the court of the current approach to the clinical assessment of head injuries in children and the range of accepted medical views. Instead, it was directed at justifying exceptions to the established consensus. Initial theories, advanced to justify claims that a skull X-ray or CT scan should have been performed, were shown under cross-examination to be untenable and abandoned.
>
> [23] In the result, the eventual argument that Dr Horn negligently diagnosed J with a minor injury proceeded on a basis that was not pleaded; was not reflected in the expert's summaries; was not debated at the pre-trial meetings between the experts; was referred to in passing during counsel's opening address; and first emerged, fully formed, in Dr Edeling's evidence on the fourth day of the trial. All the other arguments directed at suggesting that Dr Horn was negligent in arriving at her diagnosis have been abandoned. This is an unsatisfactory state of affairs and resulted in a lengthy trial, much of which was devoted to ploughing through the minutiae of academic articles.
>
> [24] A proper use of the provisions of rules 37 and 37A of the Uniform Rules would have avoided many of these problems and enabled the trial to proceed and finish in the estimated 3-4 days instead of taking 10 days spread over three months. The 10 pre-trial meeting minutes, or progress certificates in relation to such meetings, show that the 'meetings' were conducted telephonically or by way of correspondence, without any engagement on the nature of the disputes between the parties or any real endeavour to clarify and limit the issues. The impression is overwhelming that these were seen as

[36] *AM v MEC for Health, Western Cape* 2021 (3) SA 337 (SCA) at paras [20]–[21].

[37] *Harrington NO v Transnet Ltd t/a Metrorail* 2010 (2) SA 479 (SCA) at 494B-C. Thus, where there are eyewitnesses or direct evidence of an occurrence, that may render the reconstruction of experts less relevant or even irrelevant in determining the cause of the occurrence (*Representatives of Lloyds v Classic Sailing Adventures (Pty) Ltd* 2010 (5) SA 90 (SCA) at 107F-G).

[38] 2021 (3) SA 337 (SCA); and see the majority decision in *HAL obo MML v MEC for Health, Free State* 2022 (3) SA 571 (SCA) at paragraphs (206)-(215).

nothing more than a necessary formality in order to secure a trial date. What should have happened in an endeavour to narrow the issues was that witness statements should have been delivered from both Mr M and Dr Horn. Broadly speaking that is what rule *37A(IO)(e)* contemplates. It is what is customary in many jurisdictions.

[25] Turning to the experts, the instructions given to them on the facts should have been disclosed. Where necessary, clarification should have been sought to enable proper instructions to be given. Instead, opinions were expressed on the basis of conjecture and, in one instance, on a misreading of Dr Horn's notes. An agreed bundle of academic articles should have been prepared together with an executive summary of their contents. That would have largely obviated the need to trawl through them, reading sections into the record disguised as questions. The issues at the trial should have been clearly defined in terms of rule *37A(ll)(c)*. Instead of refusing the particulars for trial requested in relation to the expert summaries of Drs Goosen and Edeling they should have been furnished.

[26] Following that course, as is required in many jurisdictions, especially when dealing with expert witnesses, would have brought greater clarity to the proceedings. While rule 36(9) was innovative when introduced in 1963, times have moved on and the preparation of expert summaries by lawyers, who often have only a tenuous grasp of the real issues in a case, frequently gives rise to problems of this type. It would be desirable for the Rules Board to reconsider the rule. A useful change would be to require the experts to prepare and deliver their reports in their own words and to include both a statement recognising that the report is furnished for the assistance of the court and a statement of truth. Having said that, I turn to consider the three issues described earlier.

D. Rule 36(9)*(b)*

Pursuant to the judgment of the Supreme Court of Appeal in the *AM* case, rule 36(9)*(b)* of the Uniform Rules of Court was introduced during May 2023. The rule reads as follows:

> *(b)* The summary of the expert's opinion and reasons therefor referred to in subparagraph *(a)*(ii) shall be compiled by the expert himself or herself and shall contain a statement by the expert confirming that the report is –
>
> (i) in such expert's own words;
> (i) for the assistance of the court; and
> (iii) a statement of the truth.

Rule 36(9)*(b)* makes it compulsory that the expert's opinion and reasons therefor be compiled by the expert, and not the plaintiff's or defendant's legal representative. The purpose of rule 36(9)*(b)* is to ensure that the expert evidence presented to the court is, and should be seen to be, the independent product of the expert uninfluenced as to form or content by the exigencies of litigation.[39]

[39] Cf *Schneider NO v AA* 2010 (5) SA 203 (WCC) at 211E-214B.

An expert's opinion must be accompanied by reasons in order for the court to understand the opinion and the conclusions contained therein. An expert's bald statement of his opinion is not of any real assistance to the court. Proper evaluation of the opinion by the court can only be undertaken if the process of reasoning which led to the conclusion, including the premises from which reasoning proceeds, is disclosed by the expert.[40]

Courts must guard against adopting the scientific level of proof, namely the ascertainment of scientific certainty, frequently applied by experts in assessing whether a particular thesis had been proved or disproved. Courts must assess where the balance of probabilities lies on a review of the evidence as a whole.[41]

The following are a few topics on which expert evidence is commonly given:[42]

(a) evaluations by psychologists, psychiatrics, social workers, accountants, etc; handwriting;
(b) fingerprints and palm prints;
(c) footprints;
(d) tool marks and ballistics;
(e) foreign law and indigenous law;
(f) intoxication.

IV. Shadow Actors

There are numerous actors who play an important role in the judicial process, including registrars of each division of the High Court (who issues court process such as summonses, files court papers and pleadings; compiles court rolls, etc); taxing masters (who tax bills of costs pursuant to cost orders made by the High Court); judges' secretaries/registrars (who administers judges' court rolls, bench books, etc), stenographers, transcribers, typists and even ushers (who oversee order and the decorum of the court).

In this contribution one novel actor will be highlighted, namely intermediaries.

On 5 August 2022 sections 37A (evidence through intermediaries), 37B (oath and competency of intermediaries) and 37C (evidence through audiovisual link) of the Superior Courts Act 10 of 2013 – which regulates, amongst other things, the structure, constitution and jurisdiction of the High Court – came into operation.[43]

[40] *Coopers (SA) (Pty) Ltd v Deutsche Gesellschaft für Schädlingsbekämpfung mbH*, above, at 371F–G.

[41] *Michael v Linksfield Park Clinic (Pty) Ltd* 2001 (3) SA 1181 (SCA) at para [40]; *MEC for Health and Social Development, Gauteng v MM obo OM* (unreported, SCA case no 697/2020 dated 30 September 2021) at para [6] footnote 3.

[42] DT Zeffertt and AP Paizes, *The South African Law of Evidence*, above, at 345–354.

[43] Proclamation Notice R75 of 2022 dated 4 August 2022.

A. Section 37A of the Superior Courts Act: Evidence Through Intermediaries

This section provides as follows:

> 37A Evidence through intermediaries in proceedings other than criminal proceedings
>
> (1) A Superior Court may, on application by any party to proceedings, other than criminal proceedings before the court, or of its own accord and subject to subsection (4), appoint a competent person as an intermediary in order to enable a witness —
>
> (*a*) under the biological or mental age of 18 years;
> (*b*) who suffers from a physical, psychological, mental or emotional condition; or
> (*c*) who is an older person as defined in section 1 of the Older Persons Act, 2006 (Act No. 13 of 2006),
>
> to give his or her evidence through that intermediary, if it appears to that court that the proceedings would expose such a witness to undue psychological, mental or emotional stress, trauma or suffering if he or she testifies at such proceedings.
>
> (2) (*a*) No examination, cross-examination or re-examination of any witness in respect of whom a court has appointed an intermediary, except examination by the court, may take place in any manner other than through that intermediary.
> (*b*) The intermediary may, unless the court directs otherwise, convey the general purport of any question to the relevant witness.
>
> (3) If a court appoints an intermediary in terms of subsection (1), the court may direct that the relevant witness gives his or her evidence at any place —
>
> (*a*) which is informally arranged to set that witness at ease;
> (*b*) which is so situated that any person whose presence may upset that witness, is outside the sight and hearing of that witness; and
> (*c*) which enables the court and any person whose presence is necessary at the relevant proceedings to see and hear, either directly or through the medium of any electronic or other devices, that intermediary, as well as that witness, during his or her testimony.
>
> (4) (*a*) The Minister may, by notice in the *Gazette*, determine the persons or the category or class of persons who are competent to be appointed as intermediaries.
> (*b*) An intermediary appearing at proceedings in terms of this section who is not in the full-time employment of the State must be paid such travelling and subsistence and other allowances in respect of the services rendered by him or her as is prescribed by the rules made —
>
> (i) by the Rules Board for Courts of Law under the Rules Board for Courts of Law Act, 1985, in respect of the High Court; or
> (ii) in terms of section 29 of this Act, in respect of the Constitutional Court.
>
> (5) (*a*) A court must provide reasons for refusing any application for the appointment of an intermediary, immediately upon refusal, which reasons must be entered into the record of the proceedings.

(*b*) A court may, on application by a party affected by the refusal contemplated in paragraph (*a*), and if it is satisfied that there is a material change in respect of any fact or circumstance that influenced that refusal, review its decision.

(6) An intermediary referred to in subsection (1) may be summoned to appear in court on a specified date and at a specified place and time to act as an intermediary.

(7) If, at the commencement of or at any stage before the completion of the proceedings concerned, an intermediary appointed by the court is for any reason absent, becomes unable to act as an intermediary, in the opinion of the court, or dies, the court may, in the interests of justice and after due consideration of the arguments put forward by the parties —

(*a*) postpone the proceedings in order to obtain the intermediary's presence;
(*b*) summons the intermediary to appear before the court to advance reasons for being absent;
(*c*) direct that the appointment of the intermediary be revoked and appoint another intermediary; or
(*d*) direct that the appointment of the intermediary be revoked and that the proceedings continue in the absence of an intermediary.

(8) The court must immediately give reasons for any direction or order referred to in subsection (7)(*c*) or (*d*), which reasons must be entered into the record of the proceedings.

On 26 August 2022 the Minister (ie the Cabinet member responsible for the administration of justice in South Africa) made the following determination in terms of section 37A(4)(*a*):

'DETERMINATION OF PERSONS OR CATEGORY OR CLASS OF PERSONS WHO ARE COMPETENT TO BE APPOINTED AS INTERMEDIARIES: SUPERIOR COURTS ACT, 2013, MAGISTRATES' COURTS ACT, 1944

I, Ronald Ozzy Lamola, Minister of Justice and Correctional Services, hereby determine under the powers vested in me by section 37A(4)(a) of the Superior Courts Act, 2013 (Act No. 10 of 2013) and section 51A(4)(a) of the Magistrates' Courts Act, 1944 (Act No. 32 of 1944), that:

1. The following categories or classes of persons to be competent to be appointed as intermediaries:

(*a*) Medical practitioners who are registered in terms of section 17 of the Health Professions Act, 1974 (Act No. 56 of 1974), against whose names the speciality of paediatrics or psychiatry is registered.
(*b*) General practitioners and family physicians who are registered in terms of section 17 of the Health Professions Act, 1974 (Act No. 56 of 1974), and have at least three years of experience in working as qualified medical practitioners.
(*c*) Occupational therapists, speech therapists, audiologists, physiotherapists and art therapists who are registered in terms of section 17 of the Health Professions Act, 1974 (Act No. 56 of 1974), and have at least three years of experience in working as qualified therapists or audiologists.

(d) Clinical, counselling or educational psychologists who are registered in terms of section 17 of the Health Professions Act, 1974 (Act No. 56 of 1974), and have at least two years of experience in working as qualified psychologists.

(e) Professional nurses who are registered in terms of section 31 of the Nursing Act, 2005 (Act No. 33 of 2005), who have worked for at least three years in a psychiatric or a paediatric ward in a hospital as qualified nurses, including former or retired professional nurses whose names have not been removed from the register in terms of section 44(1) of the Nursing Act, 2005.

(f) Family counsellors who are appointed under section 3(1) of the Mediation in Certain Divorce Matters Act, 1987 (Act No. 24 of 1987), and who fall under any of the categories or classes of persons referred to in this section.

(g) Social workers and retired social workers who are registered in terms of section 17 of the Social Service Professions Act, 1978 (Act No. 110 of 1978), and have at least two years of experience in working as qualified social workers.

(h) Educators as defined in section (1) of the South African Schools Act, 1996 (Act No. 84 of 1996), who —

(i) have obtained a minimum post Matriculation teacher's education qualification of three years at a recognised tertiary educational institution;
(ii) have at least three years of experience in working as qualified teachers; and
(iii) are registered in terms of section 21 of the South African Council for Educators Act, 2000 (Act No. 31 of 2000),

including former or retired educators, who comply with subparagraphs (i) and (ii), and whose names have not been removed from the register in terms of section 23(1) of the South African Council for Educators Act, 2000.

(i) Early childhood development practitioners, who —

(i) have obtained an education qualification referred to in paragraph *(h)*, or a post Matriculation education qualification in early childhood development, accredited by the South African Qualifications Authority;
(ii) have at least 10 years of experience in working as early childhood development practitioners; and
(iii) are employed by an early childhood development centre which is duly registered with the relevant government department.

(j) Child and youth care workers who —

(i) have obtained a minimum post-matriculation education qualification of three years at a recognised tertiary educational institution in child and youth care;
(ii) have at least three years of experience in working as child and youth care workers; and
(iii) are registered in terms of section 18A of the Social Service Professions Act, 1978 (Act No. 110 of 1978).

(k) Community trauma counsellors who —

(i) are employed by a Non-Governmental Organisation;
(ii) have received training in trauma counselling; and
(iii) have at least 10 years of experience in working as trauma counsellors.

2. A person who falls under any of the categories or classes of persons referred to in section 1, and whose name appears in the register contemplated by section 42 of the Criminal Law (Sexual Offences and Related Matters) Amendment Act, 2007 (Act No. 32 of 2007), is not competent to be appointed as an intermediary.

RO LAMOLA, MP

MINISTER OF JUSTICE AND CORRECTIONAL SERVICES

B. Section 37B of the Superior Courts Act: Oath and Competency of Intermediaries

Section 37B provides as follows:

37B Oath and competency of intermediaries

(1) Subject to subsection (3), any person who is competent to be appointed as an intermediary in terms of section 37A(4) of this Act must, before commencing with his or her functions in terms of section 37A, take an oath or make an affirmation subscribed by him or her, in the form set out below, before the judicial officer presiding over the proceedings:

'I, ... do hereby swear/truly affirm that, whenever I may be called upon to perform the functions of an intermediary, I shall truly and correctly, to the best of my knowledge and ability —

(a) perform my functions as an intermediary; and

(b) convey properly and accurately all questions put to witnesses and, where necessary, convey the general purport of any question to the witness, unless directed otherwise by the court'.

(2) *(a)* Subject to subsection (3), before a person is appointed to perform the functions of an intermediary in a Superior Court, the judicial officer presiding over the proceedings must enquire into the competence of the person to be appointed as an intermediary.

(b) The enquiry contemplated in paragraph *(a)* must include, but is not limited to, the person's —

(i) fitness as a person to be an intermediary;

(ii) experience, which has a bearing on the role and functions of an intermediary;

(iii) qualifications;

(iv) knowledge, which has a bearing on the role and functions of an intermediary;

(v) language and communication proficiency; and

(vi) ability to interact with a witness under the biological or mental age of 18 years or a witness who suffers from a physical, psychological, mental or emotional condition, or a witness who is an older person as defined in section 1 of the Older Persons Act, 2006.

(3) *(a)* The head of a court may, at his or her discretion and after holding an enquiry contemplated in subsection (2), issue a certificate in the form prescribed by

the Minister by notice in the *Gazette*, to a person whom he or she has found to be competent to appear as an intermediary in a Superior Court.

(b) Before the head of a court issues a certificate referred to in paragraph *(a)*, he or she must cause the person who has been found competent to be appointed as an intermediary, to take the oath or make the affirmation referred to in subsection (1) and must endorse the certificate with a statement of the fact that it was taken or made before him or her and of the date on which it was so taken or made and append his or her signature thereto.

(c) A certificate contemplated in paragraph *(a)* may be accepted as proof —

(i) of the competency of a person to be appointed as an intermediary; and

(ii) of the fact that the person has taken the oath or made the affirmation contemplated in subsection (1), for purposes of this section, in any subsequent proceedings in terms of this Act, before a Superior Court and it is not necessary for the presiding judicial officer presiding over the proceedings in question to administer the oath or affirmation or to hold an enquiry into the competence of the person to be appointed as an intermediary.

(d) Paragraph *(c)* must not be construed as prohibiting a judicial officer who presides over proceedings in a Superior Court from holding an enquiry, at any stage of proceedings, regarding the competence of a person to act as an intermediary.

C. Section 37C of the Superior Courts Act: Evidence Through Audiovisual Link

Section 37C provides as follows:

37C Evidence through remote audiovisual link in proceedings other than criminal proceedings

(1) A Superior Court may, on application by any party to proceedings before that court or of its own accord, order that a witness, irrespective of whether the witness is in or outside the Republic, if the witness consents thereto, give evidence by means of audiovisual link.

(2) A court may make an order contemplated in subsection (1) only if —

(a) it appears to the court that to do so would —

(i) *(aa)* prevent unreasonable delay;

(bb) save costs;

(cc) be convenient; or

(dd) prevent the likelihood that any person might be prejudiced or harmed if he or she testifies or is present at such proceedings; and

(ii) otherwise be in the interests of justice;

(b) facilities therefor are readily available or obtainable at the court; and
(c) the audiovisual facilities that are used by the witness or at the court enable —
(i) persons at the courtroom to see, hear and interact with the witness giving evidence; and
(ii) the witness who gives evidence to see, hear and interact with the persons at the courtroom.

(3) The court may make the giving of evidence in terms of subsection (1) subject to such conditions as it may deem necessary in the interests of justice.
(4) The court must provide reasons for —
(a) allowing or refusing an application by any of the parties; or
(b) its order and any objection raised by the parties against the order, as contemplated in subsection (1).

(5) For purposes of this Act, a witness who gives evidence by means of audiovisual link, is regarded as a witness who was subpoenaed to give evidence in the court in question.
(6) For purposes of this section 'audiovisual link' means facilities that enable both audio and visual communications between a witness and persons at a courtroom in real-time as they take place.

The provisions of section 37C are not limited to intermediaries only. They relate to evidence through remote audiovisual link in civil proceedings by any kind of witness, including experts and intermediaries. A discussion of proceedings by means of audiovisual link falls outside the scope of this contribution.

V. Conclusion

Expert witnesses play an important role in South African civil litigation. Their opinion depends on the relevant facts of the case under consideration. Their role is limited to one of assisting the court in making its own findings. They should, therefore, not usurp the functions of the court in determining the issues in dispute in the case.

As far as intermediaries are concerned, time will tell what effect their role will have on the pace and outcome of civil cases where they are employed. As yet, no decided cases in that regard exist.

PART III

Other Actors

17

Beyond Wooden Desks: The Impact of Artificial Intelligence on Reshaping the Role of Court Staff

GINA GIOIA AND SEYEDEH SAJEDEH SALEHI

I. Introduction

Artificial intelligence (AI) is a broad and multifaceted concept that lacks a singular definition.[1] The origin of AI can be traced back to the 1950s, and it encompasses various areas within computer science, including machine learning (ML), computer vision, natural language processing (NLP), speech recognition, and expert systems.[2] In social sciences discussions, AI frequently emerges as a topic of debate concerning ethics, regulations, human rights, and the future of humanity. The Organisation for Economic Co-operation and Development (OECD) defines AI as a machine-based system capable of making predictions, recommendations, or decisions that impact real or virtual environments, within a given set of human-defined objectives.[3] The OECD acknowledges that AI systems can operate with varying degrees of autonomy. However, different entities may offer distinct definitions of AI. The absence of a clear and universally accepted definition of AI has resulted in varied interpretations within legal frameworks and policy contexts.

[1] See, eg, D Kirsh, 'Foundations of AI: The Big Issues' (1991) 47 *Artificial Intelligence* 3 doi.org/10.1016/0004-3702(91)90048-O (accessed 23 December 2023); D Monett and C Lewis, 'Getting Clarity by Defining Artificial Intelligence' (2017) *Conference on Philosophy and Theory of AI www.philpapers.org/rec/LEWGCB*; RJ Brachman, '(AA)AI More than the Sum of Its Parts' (2006) 27 *AI Magazine* 19; P Wang, 'On defining artificial intelligence' (2019) 10 *Journal of Artificial General Intelligence* 1 www.sciendo.com/downloadpdf/journals/jagi/10/2/article-p1.pdf (accessed 23 December 2023).

[2] BW Wah et al., 'Report on workshop on high performance computing and communications for grand challenge applications: computer vision, speech and natural language processing, and artificial intelligence' (1993) 5 *IEEE Transactions on Knowledge and Data Engineering* 138.

[3] J McCarthy et al., 'A Proposal for the Dartmouth Summer Research Project on Artificial Intelligence' (31 August 1955) www-formal.stanford.edu/jmc/history/dartmouth/dartmouth.html (accessed 25 December 2023).

Thus, any legal conversations referring to AI should be understood and analysed within the specific context in which this term is employed.[4]

In the ongoing debate on the potential of AI as a valuable tool for enhancing the functioning of justice systems, specifically in civil proceedings, AI is portrayed as a completely novel technology that states have utilised for judicial administration. The aim of this study is to explore the latest technological advancements in civil proceedings, with a particular focus on the integration of AI as an assistive analytical tool. This research seeks to understand the impact of AI implementation on the roles and responsibilities of court staff in civil proceedings.

This chapter begins by exploring the role of AI in civil proceedings, highlighting its evolution from emerging as a predictive justice tool to becoming a decision-making support system. It then delves into the advantages of using AI-driven technologies in civil proceedings, emphasising their capacity to assist court staff in automating document processing, including e-filings, NLP, and legal research, to reduce the staff workload and optimise the efficient administration of civil justice. Additionally, AI can assist court staff in analysing evidence to identify relevant information.

This chapter also addresses various challenges associated with integrating AI into civil proceedings. These challenges include ensuring transparency in the data processing methods employed by court staff when using AI to conduct tasks. Additionally, a key concern is to ensure that the implementation of AI by court staff adheres to the standards of fair trial as stipulated in Article 6 of the European Convention on Human Rights (ECHR) within civil proceedings.

This chapter argues that, to tackle these challenges effectively, it is essential to primarily acknowledge them and develop transparent and accountable AI systems based on clear ethical and legal principles.

II. The Role of AI in Civil Proceedings

AI has become a transformative force across different areas of law. In civil proceedings, AI was initially used as a predictive tool to assist judges and legal professionals in assessing the possible case outcomes.[5] However, recent advancements have led to AI-powered technologies being integrated as decision-makers within civil justice systems. Nevertheless, in recent years, attention has been given to utilising

[4] F Bell et al., 'AI Decision-Making and the Courts: A Guide for Judges, Tribunal Members and Court Administrators' [2022] *Australasian Institute of Judicial Administration* 7 www.ssrn.com/abstract=4162985 (accessed 26 December 2023).

[5] See F Galli and G Sartor, 'AI approaches to predictive justice: a critical assessment' (2023) 5 *Journal of Humanities and Rights Global Network* www.humanitiesandrights.com/journal/index.php/har/article/view/118 (accessed 22 December 2023); Manvee, 'Predictive Justice with Artificial Intelligence: Enhancing Efficiency and Accuracy of Judiciary' (2023) 3 *Legal Spectrum J* 1 www.heinonline.org/HOL/P?h=hein.journals/lglspuj3&i=91 (accessed 25 December 2023).

AI as an assistive analytical tool by court staff in civil proceedings. Thus, this section explores the nature and evolution of AI, from its role as a predictive tool to a decision-making instrument in civil proceedings. Additionally, it delves into the application of AI in courtrooms by staff as an assistive analytical tool in conducting various analytical and research tasks.

A. From a Predictive Justice Tool to a Decision-Maker Instrument

i. AI in Predictive Justice

AI can aid judges by predicting the outcome of court decisions. It is, however, important to note that human judges ultimately decide cases. Generally, AI-driven systems are integrated into civil proceedings with the aim of enhancing efficiency, consistency, and accuracy in judicial decision-making.[6] These systems employ ML algorithms and extensive data to analyse legal precedents, statutes, and other relevant information, thereby assisting in predicting case outcomes. These predictive tools have proven useful in legal research, case management, and early case assessment.

According to the December 2018 Ethical Charter by the European Commission for the Efficiency of Justice (CEPEJ), AI has the potential to predict outcomes by identifying possible correlations between input and output data in cases where large volumes of decisions are processed.[7] The input data, for example, includes legal criteria, case facts, and legal arguments. On the contrary, the output data consists of official judgments. AI systems can generate models that, when used with new input data, predict decisions based on pertinent correlations. The AI models can essentially predict what an average judge might decide given the evidence.[8]

The CEPEJ Charter defines predictive justice as 'the analysis of a large number of judicial decisions using artificial intelligence technology in order to predict the outcome of certain types of litigation.'[9] As highlighted by Ulenaers (2020), the predictive software evaluates the probability of success of the case in a court decision.[10]

[6] N Kinchin, 'Technology, displaced?: The risks and potential of artificial intelligence for fair, effective, and efficient refugee status determination' (2021) 3 *Law in Context* 45 www.search.informit.org/doi/abs/10.3316/informit.553020919379694 (accessed 25 December 2023).

[7] European Commission for the Efficiency of Justice (CEPEJ), 'European Ethical Charter on the Use of Artificial Intelligence in Judicial Systems and Their Environment' (December 2018) www.rm.coe.int/ethical-charter-en-for-publication-4-december-2018/16808f699c (accessed 20 December 2023).

[8] E Ash, '*Judge, Jury, and Execute File: The Brave New World of Legal Automation*' 7 June 2018 www.smf.co.uk/publications/judge-jury-and-execute-file-paper/ (accessed 25 December 2023).

[9] CEPEJ 2018.

[10] J Ulenaers, 'The Impact of Artificial Intelligence on the Right to a Fair Trial: Towards a Robot Judge?' (2020) 11 *Asian Journal of Law and Economics* 5, 7 doi.org/10.1515/ajle-2020-0008 (accessed 25 December 2023).

In the United States, attorneys and law firms in the private sector have used predictive justice tools to advise their clients on compliance strategies.[11] American scientists have developed a predictive justice model utilising ML – based on AdaBoosted Decision Trees (ADTs) – to predict the voting patterns of individual judges and to forecast whether the Supreme Court of the United States (SCOTUS) will uphold or overturn a lower court decision. This model has demonstrated a significant degree of accuracy,[12] predicting SCOTUS voting outcomes with an accuracy rate of more than 75 per cent.[13] In the EU context, a pioneering systematic study focused on predicting judgments of the European Court of Human Rights (ECtHR) in 2016. This study achieved an average prediction accuracy of 79 per cent.[14] This AI model targeted detecting violations of specific articles in the ECHR, namely Article 3 (prohibition of torture and inhuman or degrading treatment or punishment), Article 6 (right to a fair trial), and Article 8 (right to privacy and family life, including housing and correspondence).[15] The dataset used in this study comprised 584 cases related to these articles, treating each case as a 'bag of words' to determine the significance of specific terms within individual cases.[16] The structured format of ECtHR judgments made them particularly suitable for text analysis.[17] It is important to note that this ML model did not rely on legal reasoning to assess ECHR violations. Instead, it primarily assessed the factual background presented in the 'circumstances' section of ECHR judgments, achieving a higher accuracy rate. Building on this research, in a subsequent study in 2020, the researchers aimed to increase predictive capabilities by implementing NLP tools to analyse language within ECtHR judgments and predict ECHR violations. In this

[11] DM Katz, 'Quantitative Legal Prediction or How I Learned to Stop Worrying and Start Preparing for the Data-Driven Future of the Legal Services Industry' (2013) 62 *Emory Law Journal* 909 www.heinonline.org/HOL/P?h=hein.journals/emlj62&i=923 (accessed 25 December 2023).

[12] This ADTs technique was used by Kaufman et al. based on implementing two datasets – case-level covariates and statements of judges during oral arguments – of the SCOTUS from 2005 to 2015. AR Kaufman et al., 'Improving Supreme Court Forecasting Using Boosted Decision Trees' (2019) 27 *Political Analysis* 381, 383 doi.org/10.1017/pan.2018.59 (accessed 23 December 2023); see also M Medvedeva et al., 'Rethinking the Field of Automatic Prediction of Court Decisions' (2023) 31 *Artificial Intelligence and Law* 195 doi.org/10.1007/s10506-021-09306-3 (accessed 25 December 2023); R Sharma et al., 'Using Modern Neural Networks to Predict the Decisions of Supreme Court of the United States with State-of-the-Art Accuracy' (2015) 9490 *Lecture Notes in Computer Science* 475 doi.org/10.1007/978-3-319-26535-3_54 (accessed 25 December 2023); K Lockard et al., 'Using NLP to Model U.S. Supreme Court Cases' (2023) 7 *SMU Data Science Review* www.scholar.smu.edu/datasciencereview/vol7/iss1/4 (accessed 23 December 2023).

[13] Ulenaers (n 10) 6; see also DM Katz et al., 'A General Approach for Predicting the Behavior of the Supreme Court of the United States' (2017) *4 PIoS One*: e0174698 doi.org/10.1371/journal.pone.0174698 (accessed 25 December 2023).

[14] N Aletras et al., 'Predicting Judicial Decisions of the European Court of Human Rights: A Natural Language Processing Perspective' (2016) 2 *PeerJ Computer Science* 2: e93 www.peerj.com/articles/cs-93.pdf (accessed 25 December 2023); see also Ulenaers (n 10) 6.

[15] Ulenaers, ibid 7.

[16] T McCullan, 'A.I. Judges: The Future of Justice Hangs in the Balance' (2019) *Medium Magazine* 02–2019 (February) www.medium.com/s/reasonable-doubt/a-i-judges-the-future-of-justice-hangs-in-the-balance-6dea1540daaa (accessed 25 December 2023).

[17] Aletras et al. (n 14).

study, an average accuracy of 75 per cent was achieved in predicting violations in nine ECHR articles.[18] Although the accuracy for Articles 3, 6, and 8 was slightly lower in the 2020 model compared to the 2016 analysis (75 per cent compared to 79 per cent), it claimed greater representatives due to the considerably larger data-set comprising 1,942 cases.[19]

These examples illustrate that AI-driven predictive justice models, utilising ML and NLP techniques, can predict case outcomes with relatively high degrees of accuracy. Over the past decade, scholars have argued that AI, when used as a predictive justice tool, has a great potential in being used for categorising and prioritising cases and also informing judges of evolving legal trends in case law.[20] Through the identification of patterns in past cases, AI can use precedents to predict case outcomes, contributing towards fostering consistency and coherence in case law.[21]

ii. AI as a Decision-Making Support Tool

It is predicted that between 2030 and 2040, AI will take on many judicial responsibilities, leading to fully automated decision-making processes within courtrooms.[22] This shift may be perceived as humans relinquishing control and accepting non-human-made decisions.[23]

AI systems have the potential to inform, enhance, or entirely replace the discretionary judgment of judges.[24] The degree of human oversight varies based on the purpose and safeguards integrated in the adopted AI system, ranging from partial human involvement to complete autonomy of the system.[25] While the use of predictive techniques to foresee litigation outcomes can be extended to automate decision-making processes, it raises concerns about preserving due process and upholding the rule of law. This is because the primary role of courts is to uphold the integrity of the rule of law in society.[26]

It is crucial to point out that the utilisation of AI in justice systems is not limited to judicial decision-making; but it has also been employed in non-judicial and administrative decision-making processes. There are several prominent examples

[18] Medvedeva et al. (n 12); see also CEPEJ 2018, 37.
[19] Medvedeva et al., ibid; see also Ulenaers (n 10) 6.
[20] Medvedeva et al., ibid.
[21] Aletras et al. (n 14); see also Ulenaers (n 10).
[22] HJ Van den Herik, 'In 2030 Zullen Computers Rechtspreken' *Redactie Mr.* www.www.mr-online.nl/in-2030-zullen-computers-rechtspreken (accessed 25 December 2023); see also Ulenaers (n 10) 12.
[23] Ulenaers (n 10) 7.
[24] Bell et al. (n 4).
[25] On human oversight in AI, see generally L Enqvist, 'Human oversight' in the EU artificial intelligence act: what, when and by whom?' (2023) 15 *Law, Innovation and Technology* 508 doi.org/10.1080/17579961.2023.2245683 (accessed 25 December2023). On the various degrees of autonomy in AI systems see also Bell et al (n 4).
[26] Ulenaers (n 10).

of successful implementation of AI systems, either by judges or court clerks, for supporting decision-making in non-judicial and administrative context.

In Mexico, in the first application of AI in law, the EXPERTIUS system was developed to provide guidance to 'novice' judges and court clerks in determining pension eligibility and the amount of pension for qualifying individuals.[27] This system guides the user through three distinct steps: a tutorial module to help the user to comprehend the process, an inferential module that allows the user to submit evidence for the case and assign weights to each supporting document, and a financial module for enabling the user to calculate the pension amount based on specified socio-economic factors related to the user.[28]

Similarly, the Bail Assistant program in Australia assists decision-makers in navigating the complexities of the Bail Act 2013 in New South Wales.[29] This program employs ML-based systems, trained on previous bail decision data, to predict future bail outcomes and references to relevant precedents. It is important to note that while this program functions as an ML system, its role remains strictly supportive as an assistant, without any autonomous decision-making capabilities.[30]

The implementation of AI in civil proceedings offers numerous advantages. AI can effectively process and analyse an extensive amount of legal information in a considerably shorter time compared to humans, enabling faster resolution of cases. It identifies patterns and predicts case outcomes based on historical data, which promotes consistency and mitigates human biases. Furthermore, AI's analytical capabilities may uncover correlations and insights that human judges might overlook, improving decision quality. Despite this, integrating AI as a predictive justice tool, whether as an assistive or fully automated decision-maker, raises various challenges and ethical considerations.[31]

A primary concern is the lack of transparency and interpretability of AI algorithms.[32] Unlike human judges, AI systems often operate as 'black boxes',

[27] E Cáceres, 'EXPERTIUS: A Mexican Judicial Decision-Support System in the Field of Family Law' in EBE Francesconi, G Sartor and D Tiscornia (eds), *Legal knowledge and information systems* (Amsterdam, IOS Press, 2008) 78; see also D Carneiro et al., 'Online Dispute Resolution: An Artificial Intelligence Perspective' (2014) 41 *Artificial Intelligence Review* 211, 227–228 doi.org/10.1007/s10462-011-9305-z (accessed 25 December 2023).

[28] Cáceres, ibid.

[29] See especially 'Judicial Information Research System (JIRS)', Judicial Commission of New South Wales, www.judcom.nsw.gov.au/judicial-information-research-system-jirs/ (accessed 25 December 2023); see also Hon TF Bathurst AC, 'Sir Maurice Byers Lecture 2021: Modern and Future Judging', 3 November 2021, [48] www.supremecourt.nsw.gov.au/documents/Publications/Speeches/2021-Speeches/Bathurst_20211103.pdf (accessed 23 December 2023).

[30] Bathurst AC, ibid.

[31] See especially B Carsten Stahl, 'Ethical Issues of AI', in Bernd Carsten Stahl (ed), *Artificial Intelligence for a Better Future: An Ecosystem Perspective on the Ethics of AI and Emerging Digital Technologies* (Cham, Springer International Publishing, 2021) www.doi.org/10.1007/978-3-030-69978-9_4 (accessed 25 December 2023); see also M Dymitruk, 'Ethical artificial intelligence in judiciary' *22nd International Legal Informatics Symposium IRIS 2019 Salzburg, Austria* doi.org/10.5817/MUJLT2019-1-2 (accessed 25 December 2023).

[32] See generally S Gulyamov et al., 'Adapting Legal Systems to the Development of Artificial Intelligence: Solving the Global Problem of AI in Judicial Processes' (2023) 1 *International Journal*

making their decisions difficult to comprehend and challenge. The term 'black box' is commonly used in AI to refer to models that are complex and opaque, meaning their internal operations are not easily understandable or explainable by humans.[33] The main challenge with black box models is the highly complex and nonlinear relationships between the input data and the output predictions.[34] In spite of huge efforts to develop techniques for interpreting and explaining the AI's decisions, the inherent complexity and opacity of certain architectures and algorithms can still make them difficult to fully interpret.[35]

This opacity undermines the principle of explainability, which is crucial for ensuring fair trials.[36] Additionally, the algorithmic bias that may stem from biased training data or flawed algorithms poses a significant risk to the fairness of AI-driven decisions. Questions regarding accountability arise when AI systems make erroneous or unjust decisions, complicating the attribution of liability to an algorithm.

B. AI and Analytical Capacity in Assisting Court Staff

AI as an analytical tool has significant potential to considerably assist civil court staff in their daily tasks. AI technologies can effectively process and analyse large volumes of legal information, saving time and resources for court personnel. One area where AI can be particularly beneficial is in the e-filing of legal documents and their subsequent review and analysis. AI-driven algorithms can enhance effective legal research by swiftly scanning and extracting relevant information from various legal texts, such as contracts, case law, and statutes. This automated process significantly speeds up the time-consuming task of reviewing and categorising legal documents, allowing court staff to prioritise higher-level tasks.[37]

of Cyber Law 1 doi.org/10.59022/ijcl.49 (accessed 25 December 2023); see also G Gioia, 'AI and judicial Independence: At Times an Opaque Relationship', in *Independencia Judicial En El Tercer Milenio. Call for Papers Del XVII Congreso Mundial de Derecho Procesal / Coordinadores, Mónica Bustamante Rúa, Luis Alfaro Valverde, Lima* (Palestra Editores, IAPL, Facultad de Derecho PUCP, 2023); TJ Buocz, 'Artificial Intelligence in Court Legitimacy Problems of AI Assistance in the Judiciary' (2018) 2 *Retskraft–Copenhagen Journal of Legal Studies* 41 www.retskraft.dk/s/Artificial-Intelligence-in-Court.pdf (accessed 25 December 2023).

[33] V Hassija et al., 'Interpreting Black-Box Models: A Review on Explainable Artificial Intelligence' (2023) *Cognitive Computation*, 2 doi.org/10.1007/s12559-023-10179-8 (accessed 28 December 2023).

[34] WJ von Eschenbach, 'Transparency and the Black Box Problem: Why We Do Not Trust AI' (2021) 34 *Philosophy and Technology* 1607, 1608 www.philpapers.org/rec/VONTAT-6 (accessed 25 December 2023).

[35] ibid.

[36] Gulyamov et al. (n 32) 4.

[37] Ulenaers (n 10) 14; see also J Komoda, 'Designing AI For Courts' (2023) 3 *Richmond Journal of Law and Technology* 145 www.jolt.richmond.edu/files/2023/05/Komoda-Final.pdf (accessed 25 December 2023).

Furthermore, AI can assist in identifying relevant precedents and case law, hence aiding court staff to make well-informed decisions based on previous judgments. By utilising AI's analytical capabilities, civil court staff can streamline their workflow, boost efficiency, and contribute to a more effective and expedited legal system.[38]

Furthermore, AI's analytical capacity can support court staff in handling and analysing extensive amounts of data associated with civil cases. In civil litigation, to construct robust reasonings, a large volume of data, including financial records, medical records, and other forms of evidence, must be reviewed and analysed.[39] AI algorithms can efficiently process and categorise this data, enabling court staff to access relevant information promptly. By employing NLP techniques, AI can extract substantial facts and details from unstructured data sources, such as witness statements or expert reports, providing court staff with significant insights.[40] By developing AI's analytical capabilities, court staff can effectively handle and utilise vast amounts of data, leading to improved decision-making, thorough case preparation, and ultimately, a more efficient and equitable civil justice system. The section below delves into some of these supportive capabilities of AI in aiding court staff in more details.

III. AI Implementation in Civil Proceedings for Court Staff

A. E-Filing of Documents

The adoption of electronic filing (e-filing) systems in court proceedings has become a widespread practice in modern court systems. The aim is to reduce or even eliminate the need for physical documents in processing a case. Although most e-filing systems are expert or rule-based, there is potential for AI to enhance this technology.[41]

In the EU, one notable example is Estonia's e-File (e-toimik)[42] system that was introduced in 2005. This system offers a comprehensive digital platform for

[38] See especially D Engstrom and DE Ho, 'Algorithmic accountability in the administrative state' (2020) 3 *Yale Journal on Regulation* 800 www.heinonline.org/HOL/P?h=hein.journals/yjor37&i=812 (accessed 25 December 2023); see also KK Ng et al., 'A systematic literature review on intelligent automation: Aligning concepts from theory, practice, and future perspectives' (2021) 47 *Advanced Engineering Informatics* 101246 doi.org/10.1016/j.aei.2021.101246 (accessed 25 December 2023).

[39] See A Moreno and T Redondo, 'Text analytics: the convergence of big data and artificial intelligence' (2016) 3 *International Journal of Interactive Multimedia and Artificial Intelligence* 57 www.dialnet.unirioja.es/servlet/articulo?codigo=5573981 (accessed 25 December 2023).

[40] RY Li et al., 'Fast AI classification for analyzing construction accidents claims' (2020) *Artificial Intelligence and Complex Systems Conference 2020 Proceedings* 1 doi.org/10.1145/3407703.3407705 (accessed 25 December 2023).

[41] See especially Bell et al (n 4).

[42] 'E-File' www.rik.ee/en/international/e-file (accessed 20 December 2023).

efficient, accessible, and high-quality court services. The e-File system enables claimants and defendants to submit and respond to civil cases electronically, facilitating fully digital interactions with thc courts. Moreover, this platform ensures secure digital sharing of data and documents through digital signatures or encryption.[43]

In another example, the UK Crown Court reported considerable paper savings after transitioning to e-filing, with over 100 million sheets saved by April 2019. Using electronic format simplifies storage and retrieval of documents. It also enables parties, lawyers, and court staff to swiftly search for specific terms or phrases within large volumes of files.[44]

It is crucial to point out that e-filing can also help the staff to reduce errors in filed documents and accelerate the pace of court processes. In this specific context, the UK Crown Court observed a decrease in filing errors in divorce cases from 40 per cent to less than one percent with e-filing. Similarly, in the UK online civil money claims, e-filing helped to reduce the case resolution time from 15 days – in the paper-based format – to just 10 minutes with the digital system.[45]

In the United States, the Case Management/Electronic Case Files (CM/ECF) was introduced in the federal judicial system with the aim of facilitating the filing and organisation of court documents. This initiative resulted in the electronic filing of over 25 million documents in Florida alone in 2020.[46] This e-filing system also facilitates the creation of comprehensive databases to receive submissions from litigants and assists in the issuance of judgments and orders by the courts.[47]

Overall, e-filing systems play a substantial role in improving the court's efficiency in the administration of civil proceedings by simplifying document submission and their assessment. It also enables the staff to promptly dispatch a sealed version of the document to the relevant parties, including judges and any other judicial actors involved in the proceedings. As a result, the exchange of information and communications within the judicial process occurs in a more efficient and expedited manner. Automated workflows in e-filing systems reduce human

[43] A Numa, 'Artificial Intelligence and the New Reality of e-Justice' (e-Estonia.com, 27 April 2020) www.e-estonia.com/artificial-intelligence-as-the-new-reality-of-e-justice (accessed 28 December 2023); see also M Giacalone and SS Salehi, 'Small claims and the pursuit of (digital) justice: a tiered online dispute resolution perspective' (2022) 1 *Revista Ítalo-española De Derecho Procesal* 181, 207–208 doi.org/10.37417/rivitsproc/859 (accessed 25 December 2023).

[44] HM Courts & Tribunals Service, Ministry of Justice and Lucy Frazer QC MP, 'Digital Court System Saves Enough Paper to Cover Central Park Twice', GOV.UK (18 April 2019) www.gov.uk/government/news/digital-court-system-saves-enough-paper-to-cover-central-park-twice (accessed 26 December 2023); see also Bell et al. (n 4) 34.

[45] Digital Court System Saves Enough Paper to Cover Central Park Twice | Ministry of Justice', WIRED GOV (18 April 2019) www.gov.uk/government/news/digital-court-system-saves-enough-paper-to-cover-central-park-twice (accessed 24 December 2023); see also Bell et al. (n 4).

[46] 2019-2020 Annual Report, Florida Courts E-Filing Authority www.documents.myflcourtaccess.com/uploads/2021/08/AnnualReport_2019-2020.pdf (accessed 27 December 2023).

[47] C Coglianese and LM Ben Dor, 'AI in Adjudication and Administration' (2021) 86 *Brook Law Rev* 791, 800 www.scholarship.law.upenn.edu/faculty_scholarship/2118/ (accessed 28 December 2023).

errors that are common in manual handling of documents, saving time and elevating the accuracy of court proceedings. However, it is crucial to maintain adequate human oversight and monitoring to minimise systematic errors in the process and ensure efficiency in the system.[48]

B. Natural Language Processing Function

Scholars generally refer to NLP as a technology that often utilises machine learning techniques to effectively identify, process, and analyse languages.[49] The NLP's primary objective is to facilitate the convenient conversion of various language forms, such as transforming audio into textual content.[50] Moreover, NLP can generate summaries and evaluate text with greater accuracy.[51]

Statistical methods assess the likelihood of certain words appearing together, aiding the system in interpreting and generating coherent textual representations. The integration of machine learning in NLP systems ensures a more context-aware interpretation of textual contexts, facilitating the conversion of languages into different forms and enhancing comprehension of human communication complexities, particularly in legal contexts. NLP, in its essence, seeks to bridge the gap between human communication and computational analysis. This is particularly important when dealing with the multifaceted aspects of communication, where context plays a critical role in interpreting and decoding meanings.[52]

One of the NLP's most significant practical applications is observed in transforming audio into text. In this capacity, the system not only recognises individual words but also comprehends their contextual relationships and overall meaning. Statistical methods are employed to assess the likelihood of certain words appearing together, aiding the system in interpreting, and generating coherent textual representations.[53] A more context-aware interpretation of textual contexts is ensured by the incorporation of ML into NLP systems. Such a synergy between NLP and ML facilitates the conversion of languages into different forms and enhances understanding of the inherent complexities of human communication, especially in legal contexts.[54]

[48] Gulyamov et al. (n 32) 4.
[49] Bell et al. (n 4) 28.
[50] Aletras et al. (n 14).
[51] K Merchant and Y Pande, 'NLP Based Latent Semantic Analysis for Legal Text Summarization' (2018) *International Conference on Advancing in Computing, Communications and Informatics* 1803 doi.org/10.1109/ICACCI.2018.8554831 (accessed 25 December 2023).
[52] J Frankenreiter and J Nyarko, 'Natural Language Processing in Legal Tech' in David Freeman Engstrom (ed), *Legal Tech and the Future of Civil Justice* (Cambridge, Cambridge University Press, 2023) Available at doi.org/10.1017/9781009255301.005 (accessed 25 December 2023).
[53] DM Legg and F Bell, *Artificial Intelligence and the Legal Profession* (London, Bloomsbury Publishing, 2020) 28.
[54] See especially Frankenreiter and Nyarko (n 52).

One of the prominent examples of using NLP in justice administration can be observed in certain Chinese courts. These courts have integrated real-time speech (voice) recognition technology into their civil proceedings to produce court transcripts and automatically generate indictment judgments.[55] Chinese tech-companies, such as iFLYTEK, are employed in certain types of trials to instantly translate audio into both Mandarin and English text.[56] Shanghai Courts also benefit from AI assistants that transcribe cases, retrieve files, and present digital evidence.[57]

The implementation of NLP models by court staff in civil proceedings enhances the speed and accuracy of court hearing records by eliminating the need for using keyboard typing or handwriting the documents. Most significantly, speech-to-text technology notably saves time compared to traditional methods of document creation. Consequently, court staff can efficiently manage their caseload while ensuring the accuracy of hearing reports and reducing the risk of disputes over their content.[58]

This should be noted, however, that one of the most considerable limitations of using NLP in civil proceedings is the lack of accountability for software errors. Addressing this significant challenge is crucial to balancing the potential advantages and disadvantages associated with NLP applications in court proceedings.[59]

C. AI for Legal Research in the Courtroom

AI can assist court staff in efficiently locating specific information within an extensive collection of digital documents. The advantages of employing NLP over conventional keyword searches are exemplified by the widespread use of Google.[60] A certain number of legal research service providers emphasise that using AI-powered techniques in their research has significantly increased their efficiency.

For instance, legal research industry leaders, such as LexisNexis and WestLaw, have incorporated NLP methods into their databases with the aim of dealing with

[55] CX Zou, 'Achievements and Prospects of Artificial Intelligence Judicature in China' (2022) 11 *Chinese Studies* 197, 213 doi.org/10.4236/chnstd.2022.114016 (accessed 25 December 2023).

[56] See generally X Liu et al., 'A Survey on Intelligent Writing Technology' (2022) *Proceedings of 2022 10th China Conference on Command and Control* (Springer Nature 2022); see also Bell et al. (n 4).

[57] Bell et al. (n 4) 37.

[58] See generally FF Bajandas and GK Ray, 'Implementation and Use of Electronic Case Management Systems in Federal Agency Adjudication' (2018) *Administrative Conference Recommendation* 3.

[59] See especially F Contini, 'Artificial Intelligence and the Transformation of Humans, Law and Technology Interactions in Judicial Proceedings' (2020) 2 *Law, Technologies and Humans* 4 doi.org/10.5204/lthj.v2i1.1478 (accessed 25 December 2023).

[60] 'Seeking Legal Help Online: Understanding the 'Missing Majority' Report', Justice Connect (November 2020) www.justiceconnect.org.au/about/digital-innovation/missing-majority-report/ (accessed 25 December 2023); see also Bell et al. (n 4) 40.

massive amounts of legal texts available on their platforms.[61] These AI-powered systems perform analysis on natural language texts ranging from text summarisation to predicting judgments.[62]

In another example, the Australasian Legal Information Institute (AustLII) in Australia deploys expert systems within its database for legal research with the aim to facilitate the conversion of statutes into a machine-readable format.[63] Consequently, AustLII's system enables users to determine the application of statutes in specific scenarios through a structured series of questions. This method accelerates the identification of pertinent reasons for the applicability or inapplicability of a particular provision in providing statutory references. This method is expected to surpass the effectiveness of thoroughly reading all the statutes. Moreover, users can effortlessly find documents relevant to the one they are currently viewing.[64]

In the context of deploying AI for legal research, generative AI (Gen-AI) models have been used by lay citizens and some lawyers to scan through large volumes of data to acquire the relevant rules and legal information about the case.[65] Gen-AI models refer to a broad term encompassing machine learning solutions that utilise extensive legal datasets to generate responses or outputs in response to user prompts, typically presented as input commands.[66] These models have created new opportunities for applications, such as text production and human-like chatbots. However, users must exercise caution when using Gen-AI models for legal research due to significant concerns regarding the reliability and accuracy of the generated output.[67]

In summary, implementation of AI, including NLP systems, for legal research in courts offers advantages for staff. It is, however, important to note the limitations of these systems. AI often struggles to grasp the subtleties of legal language and context, leading to the retrieval of irrelevant or misleading information.[68]

[61] D Hall, 'Google, Westlaw, LexisNexis and Open Access: How the Demand for Free Legal Research Will Change the Legal Profession' (2012) 26 *Syracuse Science and Technology Law Reporter* 53, 75; see also 'Nexis+ AI | Company Research Platform' www.lexisnexis.com/en-us/professional/decision-intelligence/nexis-plus-ai.page (accessed 25 October 2024); 'Westlaw – Legal Research Platforms' www.legal.thomsonreuters.com/en/westlaw (accessed 25 October 2024).

[62] K Sarvajna and F Geldon, 'Semantic NLP Technologies in Information Retrieval Systems for Legal Research' (2021) 2 *Advances in Machine Learning and Artificial Intelligence* 28.

[63] See Australasian Legal Information Institute www.austlii.edu.au/ (accessed 30 December 2023).

[64] Bell et al. (n 4) 40.

[65] One of the most prominent examples of Gen-AI models is ChatGPT(-4) by OpenAI. See for more information 'OpenAI' www.openai.com (accessed 25 October 2024). A Perlman, 'The implications of ChatGPT for legal services and society' Available at *SSRN* 4294197 (2022): 4 papers.ssrn.com/sol3/papers.cfm?abstract_id=4294197 (accessed 25 December 2023).

[66] SH Skaug, 'Generative AI: Here to stay, but for good?' (2023) 75 *Technology in Society* 102372 doi.org/10.1016/j.techsoc.2023.102372 (accessed 25 December 2023).

[67] A Bandi et al., 'The Power of Generative AI: A Review of Requirements, Models, Input–Output Formats, Evaluation Metrics, and Challenges' (2023) 15 *Future Internet* 8260 doi.org/10.3390/fi15080260/ (accessed 25 December 2023).

[68] See especially LK Branting, 'Artificial Intelligence and the Law from a Research Perspective' (2018) 3 *Scitech Lawyer Chicago ABA* 32.

Moreover, biases present in training data, often derived from legal judgments and previous case law, may unintentionally support biased results and unfair outcomes, exacerbating inequalities within the legal system.[69] Accountability is also challenging, as understanding the reasoning behind AI recommendations can be complicated, raising concerns about relying on AI-generated information in legal proceedings. Ongoing debates over legal and ethical considerations, such as responsibility for errors or omissions, as well as issues like privacy and data protection, add to this complexity.[70] Therefore, while AI is a valuable tool, careful consideration of its limitations, coupled with human oversight and critical analysis, is essential in the legal profession.[71]

D. AI for Evidence Analysis

In terms of presenting evidence, AI can assist court staff to retrieve the relevant evidence from massive volume of electronic documents. This AI-powered capability can be specifically useful in big cases, like collective redress or antitrust litigations, where judges may deal with large quantities of documents that must be analysed for evidence. In addition, it can provide the judge with recommendations regarding testimonial evidence. More specifically, AI can assist judges in formulating precise and highly relevant questions for witnesses, ensuring the questions are closely linked to the aspects of the case. At the same time, if necessary, the AI can help the judge check the questions to the witness coming from the lawyers. Evaluating evidence and determining witness credibility are assigned to the judge. Nevertheless, employing algorithmic analysis can assist the judge in evaluating the relevance of each testimony and strengthening the credibility of witnesses, resulting in establishing relevant facts in the case.[72] While human judges primarily concentrate on legal reasoning and decision justifications – areas often beyond AI capabilities – the AI assistant can support the judge by conducting a preliminary evidence analysis and increase the objectivity.[73]

The feasibility of this process relies on the capability of AI systems to aggregate large quantities of data. Fundamentally, these systems receive comprehensive datasets, analyse them, and utilise the significant flow of information to identify

[69] B Neupane and P Sibal, *Artificial intelligence needs assessment survey in Africa* (UNESCO Publishing, 2021).

[70] See specifically K Crawford and J Schultz, 'AI systems as state actors' (2019) 7 *Columbia Law Review* 1941 www.columbialawreview.org/wp-content/uploads/2019/11/Crawford-Schultz-AI_systems_as_state_actors.pdf (accessed 25 December 2023).

[71] CR Taylor, 'Artificial intelligence, customized communications, privacy, and the General Data Protection Regulation (GDPR)' (2019) 5 *International Journal of Advertising* 649 doi.org/10.1080/02650487.2019.1618032 (accessed 25 December 2023).

[72] In criminal proceedings the facial recognition is already used to understand the reliability of the witness's answers.

[73] Ulenaers (n 10) 11.

patterns from the available data.[74] As a result, they surpass traditional human approaches to analysis. The processing of this data is carried out through an algorithm, which sifts through extensive data to select pertinent information. It is essential to clarify that the term 'algorithm' encompasses encoded procedures that transform input data into desired output through specific calculations.[75] While collecting extensive datasets enhances output accuracy, it is crucial that the data maintain a quality baseline to generate valuable predictions.[76] It should be highlighted that these comprehensive datasets can include transcriptions, audio recordings, and video recordings of hearings at any trial phase level. It is, however, essential that the testimonies identified as relevant and decisive during the trial align with the standards set by the ECtHR.[77]

IV. Challenges in Integrating AI into Civil Proceedings

A. Transparency of Data Processing Methods

The lack of transparency in AI systems, specifically when utilised in court proceedings by the staff, can diminish citizens' confidence in the justice system and pose a threat to AI sustainability. This opacity may also provoke concerns about the integrity of the rule of law. Therefore, it is crucial to address the issue of transparency.[78]

Transparency is a multidisciplinary concept with different meanings across various disciplines. In the context of AI, transparency is often perceived as explainable, interpretable, responsible, or comprehensible AI.[79] It refers to the capability of AI systems to make decisions that can be understood and interpreted by humans, who should also have the ability to inspect and the right to appeal those decisions. Transparency in AI should entail both physical and cognitive elements.[80]

[74] S Lim, 'Judicial decision-making and explainable artificial intelligence – a reckoning from first principles?' (2021) 33 *Singapore Academy of Law – Special Issue on Law and Technology* 280 www.law.nus.edu.sg/trail/wp-content/uploads/sites/9/2022/03/9777_09.-Shaun-Lim-Judicial-Decision-Making-and-Explainable-AI.pdf (accessed 25 December 2023).

[75] T Gillespie, 'The relevance of algorithms', in T Gillespie et al. (eds), *Media technologies: essays on communication, materiality, and society* (Cambridge, MIT Press, 2014) 167.

[76] P Nutter, 'Machine learning evidence: admissibility and weight' (2019) 3 *Journal of Constitutional Law* 919 www.scholarship.law.upenn.edu/jcl/vol21/iss3/8/ (accessed 25 December 2023).

[77] C Abegão Alves, 'AI Assistance in the Courtroom and Immediacy' in H Morão and R Tavares da Silva (eds), *Fairness in Criminal Appeal: A Critical and Interdisciplinary Analysis of the ECtHR Case-Law* (Cham, Springer International Publishing, 2023) 177–178 doi.org/10.1007/978-3-031-13001-4_9 (accessed 25 December 2023).

[78] M Zalnieriute et al., 'From rule of law to statute drafting: Legal issues for algorithms in government decision-making', in W Barfield (ed), *The Cambridge Handbook of the Law of Algorithms* (Cambridge, Cambridge University Press, 2021) 251.

[79] S Larsson and F Heintz, 'Transparency in artificial intelligence' (2020) 2 *Internet Policy Rev* 4 www.policyreview.info/concepts/transparency-artificial-intelligence (accessed 25 December 2023); see also Ulenaers (n 10) 26.

[80] V Papadouli, 'Transparency in Artificial Intelligence: A Legal Perspective' (2022) 4 *J of Ethics and Legal Tech* 25, 29 www.jelt.padovauniversitypress.it/system/files/papers/JELT-2022-1-03.pdf (accessed

In the context of civil court proceedings, the physical element refers to the system's capacity to reveal its internal process and its training data sources to staff, who are the users of the system.[81] The cognitive element encompasses the comprehensible explanations provided by AI systems for their decisions and the involvement of humans in the decision-making process. Additionally, there is transparency in policy, which refers to the values and objectives that AI systems should adhere to.[82] To ensure transparent data processing in civil proceedings, court staff need to be well-informed about the methods employed for data processing and the associated risks. The main objective is to define the information that should be disclosed to fulfil transparency obligations towards relevant stakeholders. Providing transparent information aims to ensure that the system and the associated risks can be understood by stakeholders.

According to the principles for accountable algorithms by Fairness, Accountability, and Transparency in Machin Learning (FAT-ML),[83] when AI is employed in civil proceedings and algorithmic decision-making is involved, it is imperative to ensure that these decisions can be explained in non-technical terms to end-users and involved stakeholders.[84] This explanation should include how the system functions, how it uses the data, and the specific decisions it makes. It is crucial to point out that explainability is closely linked with transparency, as it aims to clarify the system's functioning and its decisions to make it more comprehendible on the one hand and accountable on the other.[85]

According to the High-Level Expert Group on Artificial Intelligence (HLEG AI), the European Commission recognises that there are technical limitations to achieving explainability. It has also been emphasised that in certain cases, it may be even impossible to provide an explanation for specific system decisions. The degree of explicability required depends on the context, the seriousness of the decision, and the stakeholders involved.[86] Transparency also requires disclosure of strategies and practices for using data, adhering to the FAT-ML principles definition of accuracy by identifying and articulating sources of error and uncertainty throughout the algorithm and its data sources. The method of presenting this information may vary depending on whether transparency is provided to experts or lay individuals.[87]

25 December 2023); see generally ML Anderson, 'Embodied cognition: A field guide' (2003) 1 *Artificial intelligence* 91 www.core.ac.uk/download/pdf/82652784.pdf (accessed 25 December 2023).

[81] H Felzmann et al., 'Towards Transparency by Design for Artificial Intelligence' (2020) 26 *Journal of Science and Engineering Ethics* 3333, 3347–3348 doi.org/10.1007/s11948-020-00276-4 (accessed 25 December 2023).

[82] Papadouli (n 80).

[83] 'Home: FAT ML' www.fatml.org/ (accessed 14 February 2024).

[84] Felzmann et al. (n 81).

[85] ibid.

[86] High-Level Expert Group on Artificial Intelligence, 'Ethics guidelines for trustworthy AI' (April 2019) 18 www.ec.europa.eu/newsroom/dae/document.cfm?doc_id=60419 (accessed 25 December 2023).

[87] CS Sunstein, 'Output transparency vs. input transparency', in DE Pozen and M Schudson (eds), *Troubling transparency: The history and future of freedom of information* (New York, Cambridge University Press, 2018).

In summary, transparency should also cover cases where human judgement or oversight is involved. It is crucial to clearly disclose and explain the impact of human decision-making, including potential biases introduced during tasks such as selecting and creating training data. Additionally, it is imperative that transparency requirements cover how and where human intervention occurs. The users should also be informed about the risks associated with data processing and how such risks are managed.[88]

B. Adherence to Fair Trial Standards

Safeguarding human rights principles poses a significant challenge for AI.[89] Ensuring a fair trial is essential for protecting citizens' fundamental rights, preserving their freedoms, and maintaining democracy and upholding the rule of law in the European legal framework, at both regional and national level. This imperative is explicitly outlined in Article 6 of the ECHR. This article is dedicated to securing the procedural rights of all parties engaged in judicial proceedings, with the overarching objective of facilitating issuance of precise and equitable judgments.[90] The ECtHR plays a critical role in interpreting and upholding this right, as the Court has identified numerous stances of violations of the right to a fair trial in the lodged cases before it.[91] It should be, however, noted that defining and ensuring a fair trial is a complex task, given that the concept of fairness has evolved considerably over time.[92] According to the CEPEJ, the notion of a fair trial encompasses the entire legal process, and judges have a moral obligation to uphold fairness at every stage of proceedings. The right to a fair trial encompasses key elements, such as the right to access a court, the right to an independent and impartial tribunal, and additional safeguards articulated in Article 6 of the ECHR.[93]

The CEPEJ Ethical Charter emphasises the importance of ensuring that AI tools used in dispute resolution or judicial decision-making firmly and fully adhere to the right to a fair trial.[94]

Moreover, paragraphs 38 and 40 of the Proposal for the EU AI Act make it explicitly clear that when AI systems are not adequately transparent and explainable, their implementation could undermine key fundamental rights, including the right to a fair trial. Therefore, it is substantial to classify them as high-risk when

[88] Felzmann et al. (n 81).

[89] Ulenaers (n 10).

[90] For a deeper study on the issue of fairness in civil proceedings, see specially Dymitruk (n 31) 33–36.

[91] Ulenaers (n 10) 20.

[92] For a deeper understanding on the concept of 'fairness' in the light of 'the rule of law' see T Bingham, *The Rule of Law* (Reprint edition, London, Penguin, 2011).

[93] CEPEJ 2018, 15.

[94] AD Reiling, 'Courts and Artificial Intelligence' (2020) 11 *IJCA* 1, 2 www.ssrn.com/abstract=3736411 (accessed 25 December 2023); see also Ulenaers (n 10) 19.

they are deployed in the administration of justice, considering their potential impact on the rule of law and the right to a fair trial. This classification is particularly crucial for maintaining public trust, ensuring accountability, and providing effective redress for individuals.[95] Thus, any deployed AI system must operate in line with the individual rights outlined in the ECHR.[96]

Central to the right to a fair trial for citizens is access to a court.[97] Barriers to this access, such as costly proceedings and delays, can undermine the fair and efficient functioning of the judicial system. Implementation of AI in the legal process has the potential to enhance efficiency, reduce costs, and improve access to justice by making it more accessible, especially for individuals with limited resources. Despite the acknowledged biases and transparency issues in AI systems, their use in courtrooms can enhance access to civil justice.[98]

The effective functioning of a judicial system is subject to the principles of independence and impartiality.[99] Judicial independence requires immunity from external influences, whether from other authorities or the involved parties. While AI systems are inherently resistant to external pressures, human judges may encounter subtle inducements to excessively rely on AI tools. It is imperative for judges to maintain their independence and not blindly defer to AI outcomes, as their primary task is to uphold the rule of law.[100] With regard to impartiality, AI-powered systems can be trained to identify and address biases in certain contexts. By using behavioural nudges and legal education, these systems can assist judges in recognising and mitigating their biases,[101] fostering a fairer legal system by reducing the impact of external factors on decision-making.[102]

In brief, significant challenges arise in ensuring that AI adheres to the fundamental rights, particularly the right to a fair trial. However, integrating AI into the legal system can improve access to justice for citizens and reduce court backlogs. It is therefore imperative to strike a delicate balance between the advantages of AI-powered systems and safeguarding human rights in the judicial process.[103]

[95] Proposal for a Regulation of The European Parliament and of the Council Laying Down Harmonised Rules on Artificial Intelligence (Artificial Intelligence Act) and Amending Certain Union Legislative Acts, COM/2021/206 final.

[96] CEPEJ 2018, 15.

[97] Ulenaers (n 10) 21–22.

[98] F Pasquale, 'A Rule of Persons, Not Machines: The Limits of Legal Automation' (2019) 87 *George Washington Law Review* 1, 54 www.gwlr.org/wp-content/uploads/2019/01/87-Geo.-Wash.-L.-Rev.-1.pdf (accessed 25 December 2023); see also RM Re and A Solow-Niederman, 'Developing Artificially Intelligent Justice' (2019) 22 *Stanford Technology Law Review* 242.

[99] See especially Ulenaers (n 10) 22–23.

[100] See generally Gioia (n 32).

[101] DL Chen, 'Machine learning and the rule of law' (2019) 16 *Revista Forumul Judecatorilor* 3 www.users.nber.org/~dlchen/papers/Machine_Learning_and_Rule_of_Law_LawAsData.pdf (accessed 25 December 2023).

[102] Ulenaers (n 10) 24; see also D Varona and JL Suárez, 'Discrimination, Bias, Fairness, and Trustworthy AI' (2022) 12 *Applied Sciences* 12:5826 doi.org/10.3390/app12125826 (accessed 25 December 2023).

[103] Ulenaers, ibid.

V. Concluding Remarks: Acknowledging the Challenges and Developing Ethical and Legal Guidelines

This chapter delved into the intricate landscape of AI within civil proceedings and the administration of civil justice. It focused on understanding technological advancements and the transformative effects of AI as an assistive analytical tool on the role of court staff in civil proceedings.

The discussions highlighted that incorporating AI as an assistive analytical tool could offer significant advantages to court staff in facilitating their tasks during various stages of civil proceedings. For instance, AI-powered tools can be significantly effective in e-filing of documents, the application of NLP for tasks like simultaneous translation and transcription of complex legal speech, aid in legal research, and analysing evidence. On this account, AI has the potential to reduce the workload of court staff and enhance the efficiency of civil justice administration.

It was specifically underscored that despite the advantages of incorporating AI-powered systems into civil proceedings, there are associated challenges and risks that require attention. Key concerns include ensuring transparency in data processing methods and adherence to fair trial standards.

This chapter emphasised the need for a balanced approach that acknowledges and tackles these challenges to ensure a proper and ethical implementation of AI in courts. Accordingly, this study suggests establishing ethical and legal guidelines for the use of AI by court staff in civil court proceedings to mitigate associated risks. These guidelines should include transparency measures such as requiring AI systems to provide explanations for their decisions, enhancing accountability, and ensuring a fairer process. Moreover, human oversight, where court staff remain in control of the process and review AI-driven recommendations, is essential. This monitoring can ensure the preservation of human judgement and safeguard against overreliance on technology. Furthermore, AI systems must be subject to continuous monitoring, auditing, and evaluation to identify and rectify any biases or errors that may arise.

Beyond all ethical and legal considerations, a significant question is whether court staff and the public will accept the use of a particular AI system in their daily tasks. This is particularly important to assess as the adoption of generative AI models is on the rise within the legal sphere.

It is also essential to understand the degree of public acceptance. Will litigants feel they are treated fairly knowing that the legal system they are interacting with deploys AI in serving justice? Thus, the development of ethical and legal guidelines for the integration of AI-powered systems in civil proceedings to be used by court staff is crucial for adherence to the core values of the public.

18

Supporting Actors in International Child Abduction Cases before Brazilian Federal Courts

MAURÍCIO MAGALHÃES LAMHA

I. Introduction

Brazilian courts have many complex and varied cases to decide every day. The numbers related to the judiciary branch in the country are absurdly high.[1] Furthermore, the diversity and complexity of the cases are also significant, on account, mainly, of: the social-economic context of a wealthy, but extremely unequal society; an enormous territory and heterogeneous Federation; and a peculiar hybrid-mixed legal system that encompasses a ('broad and wide') federal Constitution, many different codes, and judicial review (administrative and constitutional).

In this scenario, to achieve efficiency and quality, the courts must be supported by many 'auxiliaries', that have an essential role in numerous cases. The non-exhaustive list of Article 149 of the Brazilian Civil Procedure Code (CPC/15) includes, inter alia, clerks, '*oficiais de justiça*', mediators, conciliators, and court appointed experts.

Frequently, the hard and essential work of those supporting actors is even more significant due to the importance of the cases dealt with by the courts. Among cases involving fundamental rights, social benefits, family matters, environment and public policies, child protection, more specifically, child protection from the 'harmful effects of their [international] wrongful removal or retention' is a special field in which the role of the aforementioned auxiliaries is crucial.

[1] The last (September 2023) annual national report (Justice in numbers – *Justiça em números*) shows that 'the Brazilian Judiciary ended the year 2022 with 81.4 million cases in progress, awaiting a definitive solution'. The number of cases closed in 2022–30.3 million – and the number of new cases – 31.5 million – are also massive. The report can be accessed through the National Council of Justice (*Conselho Nacional de Justiça (CNJ)*) website at cnj.jus.br. English (Justice in numbers) and Spanish (*Justicia en Cifras*) versions are also available for the 2022 report.

International child abduction can be considered one of the most complex and difficult types of cases conducted and decided by the judiciary. The affirmative considers not only the fact that the correlated proceedings involve an incessant protection of fundamental substantial and procedural rights and the direct or indirect participation of international organs or institutions, but also all the possible repercussions and impacts of this kind of proceeding in the life of a child.

Not coincidentally, one of the 'core conventions' of the Hague Conference on Private International Law (HCCH) is the 'Convention of 25 October 1980 on the Civil Aspects of International Child Abduction (HCCH 1980 Child Abduction Convention)'.

In this chapter, the special role of the supporting actors of the Brazilian Judiciary will be highlighted in the complex and sensitive context of child abduction cases. The work is concentrated in three specific auxiliaries – the *Oficial de Justiça*; the Mediator; and the Court-appointed Psychologist Expert – on account of their possible 'impact' in the case, even though it must be recognised that international child abduction cases demand a sum of efforts of all the actors that, directly or not, participate in the related proceeding.

After a brief background regarding international child abduction cases, the related international conventions that prevent wrongful removals and retentions or protect the children from its possible effects will be presented. In sequence, the correlated cases will be detailed in its peculiarities and the 'Brazilian-context and reality' will be considered. Finally, the essential role of the auxiliaries of the Court will be explained to contextualise their concrete importance in practice.

II. International Child Abduction Cases – Minimum Background

A. International Child Abduction in a Nutshell

For the strict and specific purposes of this work, 'International Child Abduction' can be summarised as a wrongful removal or retention of a child (a person under 16 years old[2]), by, in the majority of cases, one of his/her parents (taking-parent in contrast to the left-behind-parent), from his/her habitual residence across international boundaries.

Apart from possible criminal consequences, which will depend not only on facts but also on national legislation, the civil aspects of the aforementioned

[2] Even if the 1989 United Nations Convention on the Rights of the Child and many national legislations define the age of 18 years old as the childhood limit, 16 years old is the age usually established in International Conventions and bilateral agreements related to international child abduction. See especially Art 4 of the Hague Convention of 25 October 1980 on the Civil Aspects of International Child Abduction.

'wrongful act' attract in Brazil and in more than 100 other countries, the application of a special International Convention. The Hague Convention of 25 October 1980 on the Civil Aspects of International Child Abduction.

In addition, other important non-Hague conventions (eg, the OAS 1989 Inter-American Convention on the International Return of Children) and bilateral agreements were formulated around the world. Due to its global importance and the fact that Brazilian cases are almost entirely brought in in terms of the Hague Convention, the focus will be on this fundamental international instrument.

B. The Hague Convention of 25 October 1980 on the Civil Aspects of International Child Abduction

The Hague Conference on Private International Law – Conférence de La Haye de droit international privé[3] (HCCH) is an 'intergovernmental organisation' composed of more than 90 members (91 including the European Union) whose 'ultimate goal is to work for a world in which, despite the differences between legal systems, persons – individuals as well as companies – can enjoy a high degree of legal security'.[4] Through many instruments, including 41 conventions and some soft law instruments,[5] the work of the Conference is concentrated in three main areas: International Family and Child Protection Law; Transnational Litigation and Apostille; International Commercial, Digital, and Financial Law.

[3] Historical facts and many other important, interesting and useful information about the Hague Conference and its instruments (including guides, statistics, reports and papers) can be found directly on its website (hcch.net). Regarding the history of the HCCH, in '(…) the end of the 19th century (…) a group of prominent international lawyers, most notable among them Pasquale Mancini and T.M.C. Asser, paved the way for States to establish a uniform system, based on cooperation and mutual respect, for resolving issues related to the cross-border application of laws and recognition of judgments. In 1893, at the behest of T.M.C. Asser, the Dutch Government convened an international conference on the regulation of a number of issues relating to civil procedure and jurisdiction. Attended by delegates from 13 States, this 'Hague Conference' has since then become known as the First Session of the Hague Conference. The first 'Hague Convention', the Convention on Civil Procedure, was adopted shortly after, in 1894, and signed on 14 November 1896'. (…) The first six Sessions of the Hague Conference were held between 1893 and 1928. These were international conferences organised on an ad hoc basis with the participation of a limited number of States, varying from 13 to 22. (…) With the outbreak of the two world wars international cooperation broke down, and progress in the unification of private international law came to a standstill. While the fifth and sixth Hague Conferences were held in the interwar period (in 1925 and 1928 respectively), these did not lead to the adoption of any new Conventions. The end of the Second World War marked the start of a new era for the Hague Conference. After a long hiatus, its seventh Session was held in 1951, resulting in the adoption of a Statute which, upon its entry into force on 15 July 1955, would establish the Hague Conference as a permanent intergovernmental organisation, governed by its Members and supported by a secretariat, the Permanent Bureau'.

[4] According to Art 1 of its Statute (entered into force on 15 July 1955), The purpose of the Hague Conference is to work for the progressive unification of the rules of private international law.

[5] Among the 41 Hague Conventions, the first one was signed in 1896 (*Relative a la procedure civile* – civil procedure) and the most recent in 2019 (Recognition and Enforcement of Foreign Judgments in Civil or Commercial Matters (HCCH 2019 Judgments Convention). The first soft law instrument was approved in 2015 (Principles on Choice of Law in International Commercial Contracts.)

Among the considered 'core conventions' is the Hague Convention of 25 October 1980 on the Civil Aspects of International Child Abduction (1980 Child Abduction Convention), 'which seeks to protect children internationally from the harmful effects of their wrongful removal or retention and to establish procedures to ensure their prompt return to the State of their habitual residence, as well as to secure protection for rights of access' (Preamble).

The scope of the convention is expressly limited by Articles 1 to 5, and its objects are (Article 1) 'a) to secure the prompt return of children wrongfully removed to or retained in any Contracting State [the return mechanism]; and b) to ensure that rights of custody and of access[6] under the law of one Contracting State are effectively respected in the other Contracting States'. Therefore, if the case is considered under the terms of the 1980 Child Abduction Convention[7] and no exceptions[8] are applicable, the prompt return of the child to his/her state of habitual residence (return mechanism) shall be determined by the court. Nonetheless, a basic and crucial point for the proper understanding and application of the 1980 Child Abduction Convention is the fact that 'A return order is not a decision on the merits of custody (Article 19). It is simply an order that the child be returned to the jurisdiction that is most appropriate to determine custody and access'.[9]

The hard task of finding a child abroad and starting the 'return mechanism' requires the contribution of many actors, both at the administrative and judicial levels. Central authorities must be indicated (Article 6) by each contracting party and they are responsible to receive, analyse, prepare, assist, and send applications. Their duties include (Article 7) full cooperation with each other and, in particular,

> (a) discover the whereabouts of a child who has been wrongfully removed or retained; (c) secure the voluntary return of the child or to bring about an amicable resolution of the issues; (f) to initiate or facilitate the institution of judicial or administrative proceedings with a view to obtaining the return of the child and, in a proper case, to make arrangements for organising or securing the effective exercise of rights of access; (g) where the circumstances so require, to provide or facilitate the provision of legal aid and advice, including the participation of legal counsel and advisers.

[6] Rights of custody and Rights of Access are defined 'for the purposes' of the Convention in Art 5 as follows: 'a) 'rights of custody' shall include rights relating to the care of the person of the child and, in particular, the right to determine the child's place of residence; b) 'rights of access' shall include the right to take a child for a limited period of time to a place other than the child's habitual residence'.

[7] According to Article 3, 'The removal or the retention of a child is to be considered wrongful where – a) it is in breach of rights of custody attributed to a person, an institution or any other body, either jointly or alone, under the law of the State in which the child was habitually resident immediately before the removal or retention; and b) at the time of removal or retention those rights were actually exercised, either jointly or alone, or would have been so exercised but for the removal or retention.'

[8] Exceptions are in Arts 12, 13(1)(a), 13(1)(b), 13(2) and 20, but 'must be applied only so far as they go and no further. This implies above all that they are to be interpreted in a restrictive fashion if the Convention is not to become a dead letter'. Explanatory Report by Elisa Pérez-Vera, para 34.

[9] Outline of the Convention. Principal features of the Convention. The return mechanism. Available at hcch.net. Child Abduction Section.

If the judicial proceeding is properly initiated, the work of the judge responsible for the case will be usually supported by many auxiliaries, like clerks, *oficiais de justiça*, mediators, experts, and interpreters. Their fundamental role will be addressed in detail in this chapter.

C. Post Convention Activities

The 1980 Child Abduction Convention has 103 contracting parties, and its growing importance led to many 'post-convention' activities, services, and assistance, and important related resources and instruments (reports and guides)[10] that help the central authorities and the courts in the interpretation and application of its dispositions.

The Preparatory Work, published in the *Actes et documents de la Quatorzième session (1980), tome III*, Child Abduction[11] and the Explanatory Report by Elisa Pérez-Vera (*Rapport explicatif de Mlle. Elisa Pérez-Vera*) are not only essential documents that constitute the grounds and foundations of the convention but 'can be used as a supplementary means of interpretation of the Convention [based on] the Vienna Convention of 23 May 1969 on the Law of Treaties, Arts 31–32'.[12]

The Preparatory Work 'contains the minutes of the discussions of the Fourteenth Session of The Hague Conference on private international law concerning the Convention on the Civil Aspects of International Child Abduction'. The '*avis au lecteur*' summarises the content as follows:

> In this volume you will find, first of all, a number of preliminary documents: a Questionnaire on international child abduction by one parent and a Report on the same subject drawn up by Mr Adair Dyer, the Replies of the Governments, the Conclusions of the discussions held by the Special Commission of March 1979, the preliminary draft Convention prepared by the Special Commission of November 1979 and the Explanatory Report of Miss Elisa Pérez-Vera, as well as, among others, the Comments of the Governments on this Preliminary Draft. Following are the minutes and working documents of the First Commission, which dealt with this subject at the Fourteenth Session. Finally, the volume contains the minutes of the final session which approved the draft Convention, the text of the Convention which was adopted and the Explanatory Report of Miss Elisa Pérez-Vera.

The Explanatory Report of Miss Elisa Peréz Vera is 'not limited to supplementing the Special Commission's Report but rather constitutes an autonomous commentary on the Convention'. The report is divided into two major parts. The First Part explains the general characteristics of the Convention and details its object (definition, objectives, importance, exceptions), nature, instruments for

[10] The 'Child Abduction Section' concentrates all the mentioned resources (hcch.net).
[11] Available online in French and English (hcch.net).
[12] HCCH Guide to Good Practice Part VI – Art 13(1)(b), fn 10.

application (central authorities and model form), structure, and terminology. The second part brings commentaries on the specific articles of the Convention (Articles 1 to 36) and final clauses (Articles 37 to 47).

The 'Guides to Good Practice' (Parts I to VI) also form an important post-convention tool and deal with: Part I: Central Authority Practice; Part II: Implementing Measures; Part III: Preventive Measures; Part IV: Enforcement; Part V: Mediation; Part VI: [Exception of] Article 13(1)(b). A Guide regarding 'Transfrontier Contact Concerning Children' and a Practitioners' Tool: Cross-Border Recognition and Enforcement of Agreements Reached in the Course of Family Matters Involving Children can be mentioned as well. The guides are truly helpful in administrative and judicial practice, not only clarifying certain aspects of the Convention but also indicating possible solutions to hard and complex situations, especially, for the purposes of this work, the enforcement of return orders.

The International Child Abduction Database (INCADAT) and International Child Abduction Statistics (INCASTAT) must also be mentioned as fundamental resources in the practical application of a worldwide convention.

The INCADAT is an easy and quick post-convention service offered by the HCCH for case law searches. It concentrates hundreds of judgments from many national courts (from 1st instance to Supreme Courts), which can be fully accessed, and provides summaries in English. Spanish and French summaries are also available for some decisions.

The INCASTAT depends on the statistical information provided by the contracting states. It provides data regarding not only the number of cases related to each country but also who is usually the 'taking person', the outcomes, and the timing of the cases.

The so-called 'The Judges' newsletter (*La Lettre des juges*) on International Child Protection' is a major knowledge source that combines qualified theory[13] and real practice. The articles are also very important for the development of international judicial cooperation[14] and pure 'gold'[15] for those who seek the record of historical facts related to the development of the application of the Convention in the last 25 years.

The joint work of the International Hague Network of Judges (IHNJ), formed by *Liaison Judges* (*Enlace*)[16] in close cooperation with the Hague Conference and

[13] A vast bibliography is also provided in the Child Abduction Section (hcch.net).

[14] N Sauvage, 'Ten years of The Judges' Newsletter'. *The Judge's Newsletter on International Child Protection*. Volume XV (2009).

[15] Sir M Thorpe, 'Judicial Activism – the IHNJ & the Judge's Newsletter: a 20 year evolution'. *The Judge's Newsletter on International Child Protection*. Volume XXIII (2018/2019).

[16] In Brazil, the current coordination of the network is done by the President of the Federal Regional Court of the 2nd Region (TRF-2), Federal Judge (*Desembargador Federal*) Guilherme Calmon Nogueira da Gama, an expert in the 1980 Child Abduction Convention. The group is formed by Federal judges (*Desembargadores Federais*) Daniele Maranhão (TRF-1), Theophilo Antônio Miguel Filho (TRF-2), Inês Virgínia Prado Soares (TRF-3), Fernando Quadros (TRF-4), Rogério de Menezes Fialho Moreira (TRF-5) and Pedro Felipe de Oliveira Santos (TRF-6). Prof. Calmon and Prof. Carmen Tiburcio, a renowned private lawyer and brilliant scholar in private international law, are the authors of the

the Special Commission (SC) on the operation of the 1980 Convention is essential for the good work and improvement of the Convention.

The last Special Commission meeting occurred in October 2023 and was attended by 471 delegates, in person and online. Many conclusions and recommendations (C&R) were adopted. The SC also 'endorsed the importance of measures to prevent international child abduction and noted the activities in this field of national and international organisations including, but not limited to, Reunite, The International Child Abduction Centre in the Netherlands (Centre IKO), ZAnK, Missing Children in Europe, and the International Social Service (ISS)'.

III. Child Abduction Cases in Brazilian Civil Justice – Theory and Practice

A. The Theory

i. Brazilian National Child Protective Legal System – An overview

Brazil has a very solid and well-established legal system to protect children's rights and best interests in accordance[17] with international standards and instruments, especially the United Nations Convention on the Rights of the Child, adopted in 1989 (entry into force on 2 September 1990).

The Brazilian Federal Constitution of 1988 (CF/88), among other fundamental social-rights (Article 6), confers special protection to the childhood and stresses, in Article 227, that 'It is the duty of the family, the society, and the State to ensure children, adolescents, and young people, with absolute priority, the right to life, health, nourishment, education, leisure, professional training, culture, dignity, respect, freedom, and family and community life, as well as to guard them from all forms of negligence, discrimination, exploitation, violence, cruelty and oppression'.

In the legislative level, fully compatible with the Federal Constitution and already in line with the aforementioned UN Convention of 1989/1990, the most important[18] work is the Federal Law 8.069/90, the so-called Statute of the Child

indispensable book: *Sequestro Internacional de Crianças. Comentários à Convenção Da Haia de 1980* (São Paulo, Atlas, 2014). Both are also professors at the state University of Rio de Janeiro.

[17] Historically, like many other Latin American countries, Brazil initially based its legislation on the theory of children in 'irregular situations', first in a punitive and later in a protective scope. In the second half of the 20th century, the international movement around the theory of 'full protection', derived from the 1959 Declaration of the Rights of the Child and strongly and widely spread after the United Nations Convention on the Rights of the Child, led to a change in national legislation. For a historical, comparative and evolutive perspective in Latin America, see: EG Méndez, *Child Rights in Latin America. From irregular situation to full protection* (UNICEF International Development Child Centre, 1998).

[18] Importance is related to a sum of factors, but here the 'comprehensiveness' of the 'Statute', the quality of the text and the fact that the existence of the law is well known by the society is preponderant.

and Adolescent (*Estatuto da Criança e do Adolescente – ECA – pt*). In its 267 articles, civil, administrative, and criminal law are encompassed, and some special correlated procedural norms are also established.

It is important to say that, despite Article 24, XV of the Federal Constitution indicates that the Federal Union and the federated states *have the power to legislate concurrently on protection of childhood and youth*, Article 22 leaves not much space for the federated states. As a result, the 'ECA' is not only mandatory at all levels but occupies a central position.

Besides many public organs that are responsible for the direct protection of child's best interests, the '*Ministério Público*' (Public Prosecutor Office – Articles 127/130 CF/88) and the '*Defensoria Pública*' (Public Defender Office – Articles 134/135 CF/88), both in the Federal and state levels have a special role.

A public prosecutor responsible for civil matters must act as a '*custos legis*'[19] in all the cases that involve children's interests (Article 178, II CPC/15). That surely includes at the Federal level all the child abduction cases. The importance of the public prosecutor is not only related to the final judgment, but also to all the necessary stages of the proceeding, including the hearings, mediation sessions, and enforcement.

Public defenders are responsible for the judicial guidance, the promotion of human rights, and the full and free of charge defence, at all levels, both judicially and extra judicially, of individual and collective rights of the needy (Article 134 CF/88). They also have a significant protective role in general regarding children, even if more specific aspects of this activity are still under debate. In international child abduction cases, usually, the public defender will act if one of the parents cannot afford a private attorney. It is important to notice that, except (for a part of what is considered) small claims, civil litigation in Brazil is under the mandatory representation rule (Article 103 CPC/15).

ii. International Child Abduction Cases and Brazilian System – Still in Theory

Cases related to children are naturally complex and sensitive. If the case involves, in addition, directly or not, family conflicts, the scenario becomes even harder. One can imagine, then, an international dispute between parents over the return of a child (allegedly) wrongfully removed or retained from his/her habitual residence by one of them.[20]

Another important legislative act is the Federal Law 12.318/10, related to substantive and procedural aspects in prevention and combat of 'parental alienation'.

[19] A possible, but non-literal, translation would be 'guardian of the Law'.

[20] It is important to notice that this is the most usual hypothesis in Brazil, the reason why will be considered the rule for the chapter's purpose. For other possibilities, see Art 3, 4 and 8 of the 1980 Hague Convention on the Civil Aspects of International Child Abduction (hereafter 1980 Child Abduction Convention).

Based on the 1980 Child Abduction Convention, 'cases' are usually[21] preceded administratively by the 'left behind parent' applying *for assistance in securing the return of the child* (Article 8) to the so called national 'Central Authority'[22] of the child's habitual residence. The administrative proceeding initiated must follow some formalities (Article 8), measures (Articles 7 and 10) and good practices,[23] and may involve an attempt to reach the 'taking parent' and establish some kind of conciliation or mediation.

Nonetheless, if the dispute remains, the Central Authority (requesting) of the child's habitual residence shall contact the Central Authority (requested) of the country to which the child was allegedly wrongfully removed or retained by the taking parent. A new proceeding is initiated by the requested Central Authority and some efforts might be made to resolve the dispute amicably.

In Brazil, the current national Central Authority is denominated 'Federal Administrative Central Authority (*Autoridade Central Administrativa Federal – ACAF*[24])', part of the Department of Assets Recovery and International Legal Cooperation (DRCI) that integrates the Ministry of Justice and Public Security. If the case is not resolved by consensus, the *ACAF* must 'send' it to the organ that advises and represents the Federal Union, the Attorney General Office (*Advocacia Geral da União – AGU*).

As the Federal Union is the 'contracting party' of the 1980 Child Abduction Convention, it will[25] assume the position of claimant/plaintiff in the judicial process initiated by the *AGU*. The left behind parent is not necessarily a party but can voluntarily join in assistance. The taken parent, not the child, will be the defendant.

Since the constitutional disposition of Article 109, III[26] determines that the Federal judges have the competence to institute legal proceeding and trial of cases based on a treaty or a contract between the Union and a foreign state or

[21] For other possibilities see Art 8 1980 Hague Convention.

[22] The designation of a Central Authority is an express command of the Hague Convention, which in Art 6 establishes that: 'A Contracting State shall designate a Central Authority to discharge the duties which are imposed by the Convention upon such authorities. The full list of Central Authorities (per party) can be consulted in https://www.hcch.net/en/states/authorities'.

[23] See the 'Guide to good practice under the Hague Convention of 25 October 1980 on the Civil Aspects of International Child Abduction Part I – Central Authority Practice. Available in the website of the Hague Convention in English, French, Spanish and Russian versions.

[24] For the role of ACAF and other relevant information: gov.br/mj/pt-br/assuntos/sua-protecao/cooperacao-internacional/acaf.

[25] There is also the possibility that the left behind parent decide to 'directly apply' to the judicial authority, according to Art 29 of the 1980 Convention. But even in that situation, the Federal Union shall be notified through the *AGU* to act as a part or assistant.

[26] The Constitution of the Federative Republic of Brazil (CF/88) is the supreme rule of the legal system. It shall be observed by Federal and state courts. Some English versions are available online, but the Supreme Court version seems to be a better translation. It can be found at portal.stf.jus.br/internacional. A 'case law compilation' and 'bulletin' are also available through the same portal under 'institutional publications'. In addition, some explanations about 'judicial review' in Brazil are interesting for its 'uniqueness'.

international organisation, the case must be submitted to the Federal Justice. At this point, it is important to say that Brazilian Federal courts, except for the specific matter of international child abduction and a few others also related to international conventions,[27] are not 'used' to dealing with cases that somehow involve 'family' or 'child' disputes. Federal courts are mainly[28] related to public law, particularly what would be considered 'administrative', 'social' and 'tax' cases by many European countries.

It is also important to remember[29] that Federal courts deal only with the request for the prompt return of a child (or access) and the possible exceptions listed in the 1980 Convention. The merits related to custody will be dealt with by the competent court of the habitual residence of the child if he/she returns, or if the child remains in Brazil, by the competent state court, due to national civil procedural rules.

Beyond all the necessary procedural steps, which will follow the common dispositions of the Civil Procedure Code,[30] the *Ministério Público* shall be notified to act as the *custus legis*, and if the defendant does not indicate a private attorney, a public defender will be designated.

That is not difficult to imagine why this type of case is one of the hardest dealt by the courts. It involves not only substantive and procedural rights of the parents and international cooperation, but, principally, the protection of the child and its best interest.[31] As a consequence, the correlated proceeding must ensure efficiency and quality at such a high level that full attention of all those who participate is required.

In practice, general and specific challenges and difficulties are related not only to the legal structure and how the courts interpret and apply the international convention but also to the reality of each country, which will have an impact on the service of process, fact-finding and enforcement. As a consequence, the outcome

[27] The UN (New York) 'Convention on the Recovery Abroad of Maintenance', from 1956 is an example.

[28] Even if Art 109 of the CF/88 'naturally' restrict the possibilities, private law is not excluded from Federal courts, especially, but not only, because cases that involve public Federal companies are also 'attracted' to Federal 'jurisdiction'. For instance, the main Brazilian bank is a public Federal company called *Caixa Econômica Federal*, which, despite many activities related to governmental programs, has more than 100 million private account holders. It is also one of the biggest litigators of the country.

[29] According to the Elisa Pérez-Vera Report (n 8), para 19: 'the Convention rests implicitly upon the principle that any debate on the merits of the question, i.e. of custody rights, should take place before the competent authorities in the State where the child had its habitual residence prior to its removal'.

[30] Many countries have special proceedings for international child abduction cases, but Brazil is not yet one of them. A Federal Procedural Draft Law is still being discussed in the National Congress. Nevertheless, the Resolution nº 449/2022 from the National Council of Justice (*Conselho Nacional de Justiça – CNJ*) is an important instrument regarding the clarification of some procedural aspects.

[31] Best interest is not easy to define, but the words of Baroness Hale of Richmond (President of the Supreme Court of the United Kingdom from 2017 to 2020) are a safe path: 'The child's best interests are not necessarily the same as the child's welfare. Welfare is a paternalistic – or maternalistic – assessment of what will be better for the child. But a best interest's evaluation might go further and ask how the child's rights can best be accommodated and advanced'. 'Child Abduction from the Child's Point of View – London Workshop (22–23 March 2018) *The Judge's Newsletter*. Volume XXII, 40.

and timing of the proceeding will depend on several factors. That is why it is important to explain in detail the social and legal context of the country to which the child was wrongfully removed or retained.

B. The Practice – Brazilian Context

i. General Challenges

Even if, in theory, the legal system is very protective and well structured, the reality of Brazilian infancy is quite far from perfect. On the contrary, many children are permanently in danger or at risk in the country, especially, but not only, regarding domestic abuse/violence and poor-quality public education and health care.

International child abduction cases, as in any case, are not immune to the reality and social-economic context of the country to which the children are wrongfully removed. Unfortunately, the 'international' element of some cases is not sufficient to move them apart from this hard reality. That is why it is important to put those international cases in the national context.

Brazil is one of the biggest economies in the world[32] and has a huge territory. But is also, as most Latin America and Caribbean countries are, a land where inequality found fertile ground and took deep roots. Social deficits are everywhere, and violence is a daily reality, especially but not only in the big cities.

When a child is wrongfully removed or retained, the first challenge is to find him/her. In a country that seems a whole continent in size and where many places are not easily accessible, it is not difficult to 'hide from authorities'. Some regions are hard to access because of natural challenges and a lack of structure. In the big cities, violence clearly restricts in practice many fundamental rights protected in theory. There are some places where, tragically, even trained militaries would think twice before getting in.

Even if the child is found and service of the process is reached, many other challenges may appear.

The first and more obvious is the risk that the taking-parent removes (again) the child to another place, city, or even country. To prevent that, the general measure is a restrict order from leaving the country, or the city, without a previous and formal request, which is communicated to the administrative authorities, including the Federal Police (*Polícia Federal*) responsible 'to perform the functions of maritime, airport and border police' (Article 144, III CF/88). Passports may also be confiscated. It is a strong measure, but it is, certainly not infallible mainly because Brazilian borders are immense.

[32] According to the International Monetary Fund, Brazil is currently the 9th biggest economy of the World. www.imf.org.

The potential risks are real, because some parents may prefer to put themselves (and the child) in a dangerous or precarious situation, rather than 'face the court'.

Apart from this hard social reality, many other challenges can be mentioned. Some are related to the fact that some foreigners have the wrong idea that Brazil is a safe refuge for those who are hiding from justice. It is important to notice that international child abduction cases may involve foreigners on both sides of the dispute (taking parent and left behind parent). So, when a foreigner 'chooses' Brazil to 'hide' many times, he/she is fully convinced that the child would never return to his/her habitual residence abroad. Even if that is not true, one associated consequence is the real challenge to 'bring people to court' (or even to use Zoom) to try at least a mediation session. All the steps are important and shall be carefully prepared, including the explanation of the consequences of a wrongful removal or retention.

Another important element that makes international child abduction cases even harder is the fact that only a few private attorneys are used to this very specific type of judicial dispute. The strong majority deal with it like a 'normal' family case, which makes things much harder. Experience shows that even big law firms can act in a non-specialised manner.

ii. Specific Challenges

a. Fact Finding, Evidence and Exceptions for the Return Order

The 1980 Child Convention's general rule is the return of the child wrongfully removed or retained to the country of his/her habitual residence. Nonetheless, the same international instrument establishes exceptions for this return. These exceptions are expressly listed in Articles 12, 13 (1) (a), 13 (1) (b), 13 (2) and 20 of the Convention, and 'for the most part, these exceptions are only concrete illustrations of the overly vague principle whereby the interests of the child are stated to be the guiding criterion in this area'.[33]

The exceptions were well summarised by the 'Outline of the Convention' as follows:

> The Convention provides for certain exceptions in which the authority seised with the return application has discretion not to order the return of the child. Where it is demonstrated that the child is now settled in the new environment, the authority has the discretion to not make the return order (Art. 12). If the person or institution having care of the person of the child was not actually exercising the custody rights at the time of removal or retention, or had consented or subsequently acquiesced to the removal or retention, the authority is not bound to order the return of the child (Art 13(1)(a)). Where there is a grave risk that the return would expose the child to physical or psychological harm or otherwise place the child in an intolerable situation, the authority is

[33] Elisa Pérez-Vera Report (n 8) para 25.

similarly not bound to order the return of the child (Art. 13(1)(b)). The authority may also refuse to order the return of the child if it finds that the child objects to being returned and has attained an age and degree of maturity at which it is appropriate to take account of the child's views (Art. 13(2)). Return may also be refused if it would not be permitted by the fundamental principles of the requested State relating to the protection of human rights and fundamental freedoms (Art. 20).

Apart from many possible debates regarding all the exceptions, the exception of Article 13 (1)(b) must be analysed in more detail due to its relation to the direct work of the psychologist expert, one of the central supporting actors focused on in this chapter.

'Grave risk' and 'intolerable situation' are both legal expressions that are not easily applicable, especially considering the 'highly fact-specific' context of the cases related to international child abduction. Therefore, they must be not only carefully interpreted but usually demand a practical analysis that depends on the production of vast documental and expert evidence, especially an evaluation of a psychologist expert.

Recognising the complexity and importance of this matter, a special Guide to Good Practice (Part VI) was edited by the HCCH to 'promote, at the global level, the proper and consistent application of the grave risk exception in accordance with the terms and purpose of the 1980 Convention, taking into account interpretative aids such as the Convention's Explanatory Report, as well as past Conclusions and Recommendations of the Special Commission, and existing Guides to Good Practice on the 1980 Convention'. The Guide is a truly useful tool in practice, separating the exposition in 5 Parts: Article 13(1)(b) as part of the framework of the 1980 Convention; Article 13(1)(b) in practice, with examples of assertions that could be raised; Good practices for Courts; Good Practice for Central Authorities; and Useful Resources.

Apart from other 'assertions that could be raised', in many cases the central argument is the fact that the child or the mother (usually the taking parent) was subjected to domestic violence or abuse. And an important point at the centre of the debate is the fact that when the Convention was discussed and adopted the usual situation was the removal or retention of the child by the father, who had no substantial reasons to move the child away from the mother and tried to use national legal systems, disconnected from each other, to protect his own interests. But things changed a lot during the last 40 years and now the usual situation is the mother as the taking parent,[34] many times just trying to escape from domestic violence or protect the child from abuse.

How to deal with this change is a major concern, and the case law of many countries is prodigious in examples of how the courts are analysing, interpreting and applying the exception of grave risk related to domestic violence. Still on a

[34] N Lowe, and V Stephens, V 'Global trends in the operation of the 1980 Hague abduction convention: the 2015 statistics' (2018) 52(2) *Family Law Quarterly*.

national level, some countries, like Switzerland[35] and Japan,[36] decided to establish a clear connection in their national legislation between domestic violence and the grave risk exception.

At the international level, the Guide, not only mentions many cases dealt by national courts related to domestic violence, but also includes 'Domestic violence against the child and/or the taking parent' in the list of the 'Examples of assertions that can be raised under Article 13(1)(b)'. Nonetheless, the conclusion is that:

> The specific focus of the grave risk analysis in these instances is the effect of domestic violence on the child upon his or her return to the State of habitual residence of the child, and whether such effect meets the high threshold of the grave risk exception, in light of such considerations as the nature, frequency and intensity of the violence, as well as the circumstances in which it is likely to be exhibited. Evidence of the existence of a situation of domestic violence, in and of itself, is therefore not sufficient to establish the existence of a grave risk to the child.

In addition, the Guide stresses the possibility of protective measures at national level as follows:

> In cases where the taking parent has established circumstances involving domestic violence that would amount to a grave risk to the child, courts should consider the availability, adequacy and effectiveness of measures protecting the child from the grave risk. Where legal protection and police and social services are available in the State of habitual residence of the child to assist victims of domestic violence, for example, courts have ordered the return of the child. In some instances, however, courts may deem such legal protection and services to be insufficient to protect the child from the grave risk, for example where the left-behind parent has repeatedly violated protection orders, which may put the child at grave risk of physical or psychological harm, or given the extent of psychological vulnerability of the child.

The debate is not closed, and in the last (October 2023) meeting of the Special Commission (SC) on the practical operation of the 1980 Child Abduction Convention, among other conclusions and recommendations (C&R), not only was the Guide 'welcomed', but also 'in the light of the discussions on the issue of domestic violence and the operation of Article 13 (1) (b) the SC supported the proposal of the Secretary General to hold a forum that would allow [further] discussions, (…) ideally to take place in the course of 2024'.

b. Enforcement – The Return Order-mechanism in Practice

The prevention of international child abduction and the protection from its possible harmful effects are sensitive fields. Besides all the natural implications

[35] MH Weiner, 'Intolerable situations and counsel for children: following Switzerland's example in Hague abduction cases' (2008) 58(2) *American University Law Review*.

[36] S Yamaguchi, and T Lindhorst, 'Domestic violence and the implementation of the Hague convention on the civil aspects of international child abduction: Japan and U.S policy' (2016) 17(4) *Journal of International Women's Studies*.

of a wrongful removal of a child from his/her habitual residence and from one of his/her parents, the further existence of a judicial dispute makes the scenario even harder. In addition, the cases are extremely complex. They involve a laborious and challenging fact-finding and decision-making process that demands cautious and planned steps and a juridical analysis that touches fundamental substantive and procedural rights.

Substantive rights are centred in a child's protection, as a consequence of the paramount importance of the 'best interest of the child'. Procedural rights depend on the pillar of international access to justice, which, in turn, relies on the necessary cooperation between administrative and judicial actors of the countries involved. This double connection combined with the very specific field of the topic makes it necessary to broaden the knowledge and practical experience of all the actors involved in order to achieve procedural fairness and a final decision according to the 1980 Hague Child Abduction Convention. Otherwise, the object and limits of the cases will not be fully understood, which may lead not only to inefficiency and injustice but also to personal frustration related to erroneous expectations.

If not sufficient, considering that a fair proceeding was fully observed, the facts were sufficiently elucidated, and the law-convention properly applied, the cases do not end in a mere declaration nor (most of the time) in a voluntary return. Enforcement[37] is necessary, and it is possible to imagine how hard it is to take measures that involve the separation of a child from his/her own mother (or father).[38] Even if, in 'cold' theory, this separation is just temporary or does not occur because the taken parent can accompany the child in the return to the country from where he/she was taken, the reality is much more dramatic, especially due to economic, bureaucratic, or legal reasons/difficulties.

The execution phase must be very well prepared, and the judge shall be in constant coordination with all other actors that somehow will participate in this practical and pivotal stage. The auxiliaries will form a real 'teamwork' and previous conferences may take place. Hearings are also possible, as are mediation sessions.

After all the measures are taken, two '*oficiais de justiça*' (preferably one man and one woman) will be the judge's '*longa manus*' at site, and at least a psychologist and a social worker will join forces in the task. Even if it is not usual, a mediator can also assist them. The presence of the left behind parent during the act will depend on many circumstances, but, if possible and appropriate, may be an important factor. Other supporting actors can be designated, according to the particularities of the case.

The 'team' will be responsible for the direct execution of the 'return order' and must be prepared for all kinds of reactions, not only from the taking parent and the child but also from other people. Neighbours and relatives may try to impede

[37] In general, the execution of the judicial decisions must be processed by the same court that decided the case (Art 516, II CPC/15).

[38] Brazilian cases usually follow the pattern of the mother being the taking parent and the father the left behind one.

or obstruct the return. This is not unusual, and if it is the case, the teamwork will need protection by the police. Nonetheless, the police officers are not allowed to directly execute the order of return (a non-criminal order), but only to stop or prevent possible aggressions against the auxiliaries or to remove possible obstacles.

An important arrangement is to decide where the child will be taken, especially if the left behind parent could not be present at the moment of the execution of the order. Experience shows that the court building is not the best place, mainly because the court's 'environment' is not always[39] appropriate. Usually, a special room in the Consulate or Embassy of the child's country of residence is preferable. It also facilitates and expedites the emission of the necessary documents for the return. There the child will meet the left behind parent, and he/she will become responsible for the further arrangements for the return. The nomination of a 'third person' (a relative or even the left behind parent's attorney) to be responsible in the name of the left behind parent is exceptional and must be well grounded and carefully evaluated.

As a general rule, the judicial proceeding[40] will end with the concrete return of the child to the country that was considered his/her habitual residence (or even a third country indicated by the left behind parent) and until this event, the court and its auxiliaries must be ready to assist and act.

IV. The Supporting Actors – Heroes that Deserve Recognition

A. The 'Oficial de Justiça'

The so-called *oficial de justiça* is a court public servant that can be compared to the bailiff and the '*huissier de justice*'. He/she exercises fundamental activities in civil and criminal litigation, and is responsible, among other tasks, for the service of process[41] and to 'execute the orders of the judge to whom he or she is subordinate'.[42]

In the special context of child abduction cases, the *oficial de justiça* has a double challenge. First, he/she has to find the taking parent (defendant) for serving. That is not something easy, especially in a country that has the size of a continent and (still) many places where access is hard or even 'impossible'.

[39] Some courts may dispose of special 'rooms' for children. Recently, the Federal Regional Court of Rio de Janeiro (TRF2) installed a special room for mediation, which could be an appropriate place to 'receive' children after the return order execution as well.

[40] Administrative assistance from the Central Authorities may continue, which will depend on many factors.

[41] In Brazilian litigation the service of process cannot be done by the parties or their attorneys. It is a public responsibility of the court through the *oficial de justiça* to deliver a summons to the defendant.

[42] Among other activities. See the list of Art 154 CPC/15.

Despite that hard task, the most challenging one is to execute the return order. In close coordination with the judge and assistance of other auxiliaries, the *oficial de justiça* is the main character on site during the execution. He/she is the judge's *longa manus* and his/her work will be decisive for the proper application of the convention.

Actually, for better results, two *oficiais de justiça* are required, and it is preferable that one man and one woman are appointed. They will both be responsible for all the necessary measures to ensure the enforcement of the decision in favour of the left behind parent. Certainly, if the steps provided by the return order are not clear or even incomplete, the head clerk of the court and the judge must be immediately contacted by electronic means or personally. Many factual challenges and difficulties may appear, and this close coordination is pivotal for the success of the activity.

Their work will be done only when the child is in a safe place designated by the judge, preferably immediately with the left behind parent. Then, this parent will be the major responsible for the return, with the possible assistance of the court and Central Authorities.

It shall be clear at this point that the activity requires experience and commitment. One hindering factor is that family and child cases are not usual in Federal courts. Even if the *oficiais de justiça* are accustomed to many different and risky tasks (and there is no doubt about that), this one is obviously special. That is why orientations by the court must be clear and objective, and previous personal contact between the judge and the *oficiais de justiça* responsible for the task is strongly recommended. During the execution of the return order, the judge must be available full time to solve practical and legal doubts. This close, flexible and agile acting may be essential for the success of the whole 'operation'.

Training and specialisation are also 'essential for its smooth operation in the child's best interests'. That is precisely why the Guide to Good Practice under the Hague Convention of 25 October 1980 on the Civil Aspects of International Child Abduction – Part IV- Enforcement, highlights 6 basic commands related to this field:

9.1 The professionals responsible for enforcing a return order should receive appropriate training.

9.2 The professionals responsible for enforcing a return order should be aware of the role of other relevant professionals in their jurisdiction (for example, social workers, psychologists, interpreters) who could assist in the enforcement and its preparation. Interdisciplinary training which brings together representatives of these different professions is recommended.

9.3 All professionals involved in Hague return proceedings and the enforcement of return orders should be made aware of the objects of the Convention.

9.4 All professionals involved in Hague return proceedings and the enforcement of return orders should be made aware of the possible pressure of the media and / or parent initiatives and support groups in such cases, and should be prepared to deal with this pressure.

9.5 Problems can occur when judges, lawyers and other professionals are unfamiliar with the Hague return process. There is merit in a properly trained and educated specialist group of judges and lawyers undertaking this work so as to reduce delays and add integrity to the process.

9.6 It is recommended that practice guidelines, manuals, checklists and / or other documents should be developed which can be of assistance to the different professionals involved in the enforcement of Hague return orders.

Even if complete training and specialisation is not done, the court is responsible for clarifying any doubt and to provide complete and detailed orientation related to the return order. Thus, some of the highlighted points, like 9.2, 9.3, 9.5 and 9.6, are easily attended if the *oficial de justiça* and the judge of the case act in close and permanent contact.

B. The Mediator

Mediation (and Conciliation) is already a daily-practice with no turning back in Brazilian courts.[43]

In the path of the Alternative Dispute Resolution (ADR) scholar boom of the last decades and pressured by the absurdly high caseload and backlog of Brazilian justice, the 'new' 2015 Civil Procedure Code (CPC/15) established that, with a few exceptions, a conciliation/mediation session/conference must be scheduled by the court at the very beginning of the proceedings.

The judiciary had to adapt fast, not just training staff but providing structure. Even if it can be recognised that the legislative imposition just propelled a movement that was, in court's practice, already in course, the 'black letter' was essential to accelerate a process that was slow, not coordinated and not widespread, especially because orality[44] is not a traditional feature of Brazilian Civil Procedure. Surprisingly, the pandemic year of 2020 did not stop the work in progress. In the long run, adaptation was easier because conciliation and mediation turned to the online version, strongly supported[45] by lawyers and judges. At this point, it must be stressed one more time that Brazil is a 'continental' country and distances can be a real obstacle to 'access the court's' buildings.

[43] Litigants (and lawyers) still prefer to settle in court, even if out-Court ADR is growing as well.

[44] Many reasons can be appointed for that, but the number, diversity and complexity of cases dealt daily by the 'civil' courts (better described as non-criminal because, except for some specialised courts, usually public and private matters are decided by the same state or Federal courts/judges) is a central point. An important exception is the Labor courts, which follow a special material/procedural law much based on hearings.

[45] Long distances avoidance (in the big cities, for example, from a neighborhood to another it can take several hours during rush time – the same can occur in small cities due to infrastructural problems) and reduction of costs may explain this strong 'support'. Surely, the Federal courts were already well prepared and used to virtual cases and systems when the pandemic started.

None the less, the real change was just possible because the general culture is also changing. After a long period of 'distrust', parties, attorneys, and judges are becoming much more open and confident about consensual resolution. One of the main factors that can lead to even more promising results is the quality of the training and the real work of the conciliators and mediators. The 'human factor'.

In the field of international child abduction, the work of the mediator is essential not only to speed up the resolution of the case and achieve a real better result, but also to prevent or mitigate the possible harm that a judicial dispute can cause in the life of a child.

During the mediation process or even before the 'formal' mediation starts, it could be necessary that an initial approximation of the parents occur. Some relations may be so damaged that parents would refuse to be in the presence or even talk to each other in a mediation session. This work should be done by a psychologist designated by court, with the assistance of an interpreter if necessary. Some other facts can also make the mediation impracticable. For instance, 'Views differ widely as to whether family disputes involving domestic violence are suitable for mediation'.[46]

If all the barriers are overcome and the mediation initiated, one or more sessions will take place, in person, online or in a hybrid form. The way the mediator will conduct the sessions will vary and depend on his/her methods of work. That is exactly why specialisation and training are crucial.

The 'voice of the child'[47] in child abduction cases and more specifically in the mediation process is not an easy topic, and the way the child will 'be heard' depends not only on the Hague Convention, but also on national legislation, general context, and many aspects of the individual case. The 'age and maturity' of the child are the minimum requirements and the participation of the child can be direct or not. To prevent possible harm, the court shall provide proper structure, including a special room, and designate a high-level specialised mediator or a psychologist. Appropriate staff training is mandatory in any case.

The 'involvement of third persons' in the mediation, like a grandparent, for example, is not usual, but it 'can sometimes be helpful to include within the mediation process a person who has close links with one or both of the parties and whose co-operation is needed to implement the agreed solution successfully'.[48]

If the mediation is successful 'the mediator has to assist the parties with working out the details of their agreement. The mediator will in many cases be the one who drafts the actual 'agreement' or 'memorandum of understanding' in accordance with the parties' wishes.[49]

[46] Guide to Good Practice Child Abduction Convention: Part V – Mediation page 73 (263).

[47] A special focus to the topic was addressed in volume XXII of the Judge's Newsletter. It is mandatory reading for a comparative view.

[48] Guide to Good Practice – Mediation page 72 (253).

[49] ibid 80 (283).

The following points are highlighted by the Guide:[50]

> an agreement on the return or non-return of the child and in the latter case an agreement on where the child is to establish his / her new residence; with whom the child will live; the question of parental responsibilities and their exercise. Furthermore, the agreement is likely to address certain financial issues such as travel expenses, but also, in some cases, issues of child and spousal support.

Most importantly, 'the mediated agreement needs to be realistic and as detailed as possible regarding all the obligations and rights to which it refers'.[51] That is the so-called 'reality check'.

In addition, 'Caution is necessary with regard to conditions that go beyond the sphere of influence of the parties. For example, an agreement should not task one of the parties with the withdrawal of criminal proceedings, if, in the relevant legal system concerned, criminal proceedings, once initiated, can only be dismissed by the prosecutor or the court.'[52]

Besides all the mentioned usual mediation processes, 'prevention' can take place not only through a consensual resolution of the case at any time before the final decision but also, at a later stage, through a facilitation or coordination of the execution/enforcement. Both are important, but as the execution is a 'critical' stage of the proceeding, the role of the mediator acquires a special position.

In coordination with the other actors,[53] especially the judge, the mediator must find a way to facilitate a 'voluntarily' return of the child to the country of habitual residence from which he/she was taken. If it is not possible, the mediator may support the court to mitigate the possible harms related to the enforcement measures. It is important to notice that even tiny details matter (much more than usual) in this potentially traumatic moment. That is why all the efforts cannot be underestimated or neglected.

This 'teamwork' is not easy. It must be very well planned and discussed and depends on the experience and expertise of all the participants. The human factor again. A wrong move can cause serious damages and even turn unfeasible a voluntary or less traumatic solution. That is why the profile of the mediator is a central point. It is definitely not a job that anyone can do. It demands a lot of hard and soft skills and abilities.

Additionally, tailor-made training is required. First because 'child abduction mediative solution' naturally needs specialised training, preferably an interdisciplinary one that goes far beyond legal theory and even 'abstract practical' techniques. 'Field work' is essential. In addition, as stated, the work demands a very specific profile and many abilities.

[50] ibid 80 (284).
[51] ibid 80 (287).
[52] ibid 80 (288).
[53] Here it is possible to mention a real 'team', a working interdisciplinary group necessary to find solutions and mitigate harms.

But a specific challenge is that mediation, and consequently mediators, is not usual in Brazilian Federal courts. Actually, despite international child abduction cases, there must be very little space for mediators. That is due to the fact that 'federal disputes' are mainly public and involve rights that are more suitable to conciliation methods. 'Child' or 'family' cases are not the daily work of Federal courts. That is why 'child abduction cases', dealt by Federal courts due to their grounds in an international treaty/convention (Article 109, III CRFB), becomes even more 'special' in the federal court routine. The specialisation of some courts (judges and staff) helps (actually is essential), but the formation of a good mediator is a step forward, mainly because it is not restricted to legal knowledge and practice.

Last but not least, despite the intrinsic complexity of a mediation, interaction may occur not only between the mediator, parents, and even the child,[54] but also with other essential actors that also play important roles in the child abduction related proceeding, like a public attorney, responsible for the representation of the Federal Union, and a public prosecutor, acting as '*custos legis*'.

C. The Court-appointed Psychologist Expert

Many different experts are required in Brazilian courts. From specialists in the various fields of medicine to engineers and accountants, the possibilities are numerous. Child abduction cases may require other experts, but psychologists seem to be essential.

During the proceeding, a court appointed[55] psychologist expert may act as an auxiliar of the court during the fact-finding process, especially when some substantial 'exceptions' related to previous violence or abuse[56] are presented by the

[54] As already mentioned, the participation of the child in the 'mediation process' will always depend on many factors, including the age and maturity of the child, the court's infrastructure and previous experience of the mediator. In fact, the presence of the child in a mediation conference, online or in-court, must be very well evaluated and, if considered beneficial by the court, shall be structured to a maximum prevent of eventual harms. It is important to notice that all disputes that involve, directly or not, family relations also involve strong emotions and are driven not only by the future but mainly by the past.

[55] Traditionally, the courts have the duty and power to appoint experts (court appointed experts as the rule). But it is important to say that the 2016 CPC innovated in Art 471 and now it is permitted that the parties 'by mutual agreement, choose the expert'. Nonetheless, the practice shows that this kind of 'agreement' is not usual nor easy in international child abduction cases.

[56] According to the Glossary of the 1980 Child Abduction Convention Guide to Good Practice Part VI Art 13(1)(b), 'The term 'domestic violence' or 'family violence' may, depending on the definition used in the relevant jurisdiction, encompass a range of abusive behaviors within the family, including, for example, types of physical, emotional, psychological, sexual and financial abuse. It may be directed towards the child ('child abuse') and/or towards the partner (sometimes referred to as 'spousal abuse' or 'intimate partner violence') and/or other family members. The term "Child abuse', depending on the definition used in the relevant jurisdiction, refers to types of physical, emotional or psychological neglect, maltreatment or sexual molestation of a child, typically resulting from actions or a failure to

taking parent as part of his/her defence. In addition, he/she can also participate in the mediation sessions, helping the mediator to achieve a better understanding between the parents or even the child. Last but not least, the psychologist has a central role during enforcement.

Related to fact-finding, at this point, it is necessary to stress that the 1980 Hague Convention expressly lists some exceptional causes that will prevent the return of the child to his/her habitual residence. Article 13b, for example, states that 'the judicial or administrative authority of the requested State is not bound to order the return of the child if the person, institution or other body which opposes its return establishes that there is a grave risk that his or her return would expose the child to physical or psychological harm or otherwise place the child in an intolerable situation'. The importance of this exception is shown by the fact that the Hague Conference produced a Guide to Good Practice (Part VI) exclusively to deal with this 'crucial provision'. In this scenario, if the taking parent argues that the left behind parent acted in a violent or anyhow abusive manner, this defence can lead to the need to appoint a psychologist expert to analyse the evidence and produce a detailed written report or even present oral clarifications during a conference or a hearing.

In another field, during mediation sessions,[57] the role of the psychologist may also be essential, complementing with his/her skills and knowledge the work of the mediator. Even if the mediator has many abilities, sometimes the 'gulf' between the parents prevents a possible approximation or even the dialogue. This joint work between mediators and psychologists not only opens new possibilities, but also prevents possible harms, especially if the child participates in the mediation process.

Finally, if the return order is imposed, the work of the psychologist will become part of the enforcement 'teamwork', as already described in this chapter[58]

V. Conclusion

Brazilian courts have innumerous and diverse cases and many complex hard cases. Above them, we have child abduction cases. The practical and real influence of the auxiliaries of the courts in the development of the proceeding, fact-finding, decision-making process, and enforcement in this special kind of case is extremely significant. Their role is definitely not peripherical but central.

act by a parent or other person'. The Guide is available online in English, French, Spanish, Portuguese, Italian, Dutch, Croatian and other languages (www.hcch.net – publications).

[57] The 2nd Federal Court (TRF2) recently implemented a joint work between the mediator and a psychologist expert in a special hearing room with all the resources to protect the children and achieve better results.

[58] See topic III.B.ii.b.

That is why the work of these 'heroes' shall not be in the shadow. Not only does every effort and detail count to protect a child from all the potential harms that a court dispute and a final judgment can cause, but without the coordinated work of many actors it would be impossible to solve it.

The work of the *oficial de justiça* at the beginning of the proceeding and as the pivotal actor during the enforcement related to the return order; the role of the mediator and the potential benefits of a rapid and consensual solution; and the expertise of the court-appointed psychologist expert during fact finding and also as part of the 'enforcement teamwork' must be recognised. Their impact in the case is essential, and practice shows that coordination between the judge and those supporting actors of the courts is a key element.

I hope that this chapter has demonstrated not only the real and practical importance, but also my gratitude and admiration for the serious, dedicated and qualified work of all the clerks, *oficiais de justiça*, mediators and experts that joined forces with public and private actors to protect children and proportionate the best possible legal solutions.

A final but not less important remark is that the 'human factor' and 'teamwork' is still essential in courts, which has some value in an environment where artificial intelligence seem to be inevitable[59] in short-run.

[59] AI is essential to deal with the caseload (and backlog) of Brazilian courts, especially considering the numbers related to the Brazilian courts (see n 1). In addition, its potential is extraordinary if the input is qualified and the output is properly checked and refined by the clerks and the judge. But in some cases, especially the ones object of this work, machines cannot (at least in a near future) replace a skilled and dedicated mediator, an experienced and qualified clerk or *oficial de justiça*, or a high psychologist expert. Hopefully, they will not replace the judges as well.

19

Can the King be Wrong? The Brazilian Public Prosecutors as 'Heroes of the Periphery': Prosecutors who Sue the State and Large Corporations in Collective Redress Cases

HERMES ZANETI JR[1]

I. Introduction

This chapter explores the multifaceted role of the *Ministère Public* in the Brazilian civil procedure, specifically its functions in non-criminal proceedings, emphasising its promotional function as investigator and the principal initiator of collective redress actions, an intervening party (*custos juris*), and a defender of the primary public interest linked to access to justice and human and fundamental rights.

The growing relevance of the Brazilian *Ministère Public* coincides with the movement to expand access to justice following the end of military dictatorship in the country and the process of redemocratisation that led to the Federal Constitution of 1988, marking the longest democratic period in the nation's political history.

The *Ministère Public* has become a permanent and essential institution autonomous and independent from the traditional three branches of the state, no longer tasked with the protection of state interests but the people's primarily public rights and interests in their broadest expression, the diffuse and collective rights with the '*ação civil pública*' (public civil action), the initiator of actions for constitutional control, the protection of the democratic regime, and inalienable individual and social rights.

The Brazilian public prosecutors work as lawyers of public interest litigation (PIL). The public interest referred to is precisely that which the new democratic

[1] The author thanks colleagues Alan Uzelac, Antonio Cabral, Camilo Zufellato, Edilson Vitorelli and Manuel Pinheiro Freitas.

constitutions have recognised in the protection of human and fundamental rights, linked to comprehensive protective legislation of the environment, consumers, health, education, housing, traditional communities, and the most vulnerable groups in society.

Demonstrating this trajectory in doctrine, practice, and procedural legislation involves considering how the concept of public interest distinguishes itself and unfolds against the various configurations that the institution has had throughout its history, highlighting the crucial role of the *Ministère Public* in the contemporary legal and social framework of Brazil.

II. To Supervise or Support the King?

The French model of *Ministère Public*, which has spread worldwide, was amplified and modified in the Brazilian constitutional tradition.[2] The traditional function of protecting the incapacitated, orphans, and widows, overseeing foundations, representing the treasury, and supervising judges in the proper application of law in individual cases, *custos legis* intervention,[3] has expanded within the Brazilian *Ministério Público* to include investigations through civil inquiries, collective settlements (ADR),[4] and the filing of actions for the protection of diffuse, collective, and individual homogeneous rights of social groups. This includes, but is not limited to, defending the environment, consumers, education, housing and urban environment, health, persons with disabilities, the elderly, indigenous peoples, and the homogeneous individual rights of persons affected by significant injuries to these rights, as occurs in major environmental disasters and in defending historically marginalised groups in matters such as combating racism and all forms of discrimination.

A. Primary Public Interest and the Role of the *Ministère Public* in Defending Social and Inalienable Individual Rights: Identifying a Model

The *Ministère Public* is not a universal institution and does not exist everywhere. Setting aside the fact that the *Ministère Public* is reserved solely for criminal prosecution in a series of legal traditions, including the current European Public

[2] For the contemporary French *Ministère Public* in civil cases, including the public interest cases E Jeuland, 'The Concept of 'Party'' in A Stadler, E Jeuland and V Smith (eds), *Collective and Mass Litigation in Europe. Model Rules for Effective Dispute Resolution* (Cheltenham, Edward Elgar, 2020) 15.

[3] Art 83, Napoleon Code of Civil Procedure, 1806. The origins are not precise, commonly attributed to Philippe III, after 1300, creating the '*procureurs du roi*' J-M Carbasse (ed), *Histoire du parquet*, 1st edn (Paris, PUF, 2000) 10.

[4] Many cases are resolved through collective agreements, either in court or out of court, as demonstrated in the data from section III.C.

Prosecutor's Office (EPPO), the original function of the non-criminal *Ministère Public* to provide legal opinions supporting the correct application of the law is in decline.[5] Alongside traditional functions, a completely new role has emerged related to defending access to justice for 'meta-individual', fundamental and human rights and addressing emerging social problems in mass societies.[6] Only recently, starting from the 1970s and 1980s, has the potential activity of *Ministère Public* members in defending diffuse, collective, and homogeneous individual interests been identified, as well as their role in ensuring the effective respect of fundamental and human rights by public and private powers.

The starting point and conclusion of the investigation proposed by the IX International Congress of Comparative Law, which had Mauro Cappelletti (1927–2004) as the general rapporteur and was held in 1974 in Tehran, was precisely to recognise *the need for institutions dedicated to the function of protecting the public interest connected to the protection of new rights of groups of people in mass societies.*[7] The conclusion of the global movement for access to justice that emerged from that investigation was the need for broad legitimacy, encompassing both public and private bodies.[8]

At that historic Congress, the investigation focused on whether the *Ministère Public* could play an important role in this broader civil procedural environment, even in combination with other emerging institutions, as well as with direct organisation by civil society in the defence of public interests. The common interest that has driven the topic in comparative law for more than five decades is the need for institutions and methods to protect public interests in civil litigation (public interest litigation, PIL).

B. Institutions and Names: *Ministère Public, Attorney General, Ombudsman* and *Public Prosecutors* (Principle of Actionability) as an Independent Pro-Accountability Agency (IPA)

There was no doubt at the time, and there is still no doubt today, about the need for mechanisms to defend these collective and social rights and interests, the new primary public interest that emerged with mass societies.

[5] Among others, JN Fenoll, *Derecho Procesal I. Introducción* (Madrid, Marcial Pons, 2014) 210; A Ledesma and others, *El Rol Del Ministerio Público En Casos No Penales En América Latina* (Ceja 2018) 20 biblioteca.cejamericas.org/handle/2015/5623?show=full.

[6] Ledesma and others (n 5).

[7] M Cappelletti and JA Jolowicz (eds), *Public Interest Parties and the Active Role of the Judge in Civil Litigation* (Milan, A Giuffrè/Oceana, 1975) 7–8 and 23–24.

[8] M Cappelletti and B Garth, 'The Protection of Diffuse, Fragmented and Collective Interests in Civil Litigation', in WJ Habscheid (ed), *Effectiveness of Judicial Protection and Constitutional Order. The General Reports for the VIIth International Congress on Procedural Law. Würzburg 1983* (Regensburg, Gieseking-Verlag 1983).

Institutional innovation is a characteristic of new constitutionalism. Most constitutional reforms aimed to ensure that fundamental rights had practical effects rather than being merely rhetorical, expanding the mechanisms for protecting and guaranteeing these rights. Many introduced direct judicial protection of rights, such as the Colombian '*Acción de Tutela*', or strengthened existing mechanisms, as in the Brazilian case. Additionally, several nations reinforced or established constitutional justice.[9] Most of the new constitutions also instituted Ombudsman figures, responsible for the promotion and protection of human rights.[10] The function of Ombudsman, originating in Scandinavia and present in various countries, was adapted in Spain and in several Latin countries as *Defensor del Pueblo*. It is a preventive and mediating function, even if it is possible to file suits to fulfill their obligations, crucial for ensuring access to justice. In Brazil, the Ministério Público plays a similar role, as stated in Article 129, II, of the 1988 Federal Constitution.[11]

Considering these needs, translating the functions of the new *Ministère Public* into English can be challenging, as noted by Jolowicz, who preferred the term 'Public Ministry' over 'Public Prosecutor' due to its non-criminal functions. In Brazil, the terminology 'Ministério Público' and 'Promotor de Justiça' indicates an active and independent role in protecting the public interest reflecting functions of oversight and essentiality to justice. The nomenclature of the institution varies internationally, sometimes describing improper relationships of internal or external dependence with the executive or judicial branches, which represent stronger or weaker limitations to functional independence.[12]

In developing countries and post-military dictatorships, such as those in Latin America, autonomous public institutions emerged to hold governments and private entities of the market accountable for their normative commitments. These include IPAs (Independent Pro-Accountability Agencies).[13] These

[9] R Uprimny, 'The Recent Transformation of Constitutional Law' (2011) 89 *Texas Law Review* 1587, 1593–1594; C Cyrillo, ÉH Fuentes-Contreras and S Legale, 'The Inter-American Rule of Law in South American Constitutionalism' (2021) 42 *Seqüência Estudos Jurídicos e Políticos* 1.

[10] H Fix-Zamudio, 'Posibilidad Del Ombudsman En El Derecho Latinoamericano' in JUC Tinoco and J Carpizo (eds), *La vinculación entre los derechos humanos y los derechos universitarios: obra en homenaje al Dr. Jorge Carpizo Mac Gregor* (Mexico, Primera edición, Universidad Nacional Autónoma de México, Defensoría de los Derechos Universitarios, 2013); J Madrazzo, *El Ombudsman Criollo* (Mexico, Academia Mexicana de Derechos Humanos, 1996). The 'Defensor del Pueblo de la Nación Argentina' is provided for in the Argentine National Constitution, Arts 86 and 43, under Law No. 24.284, and has an Organization, Functioning, and Structure Regulation, yet since 2009 remains unappointed in 2024. See defensoria.org.ar/noticias/defensores-solicitan-designacion-del-defensor-del-pueblo-de-nacion/, accessed on 5 May 2024.

[11] 'Art. 129 (…) II – to safeguard respect by the *public authorities* and by the *services of public relevance for the rights guaranteed in this Constitution*, taking the *measures required* to guarantee such rights', CF/1988.

[12] N Picardi, *Manuale Del Processo Civile* 3rd edn (Milan, Giuffrè, 2013) 169–170.

[13] JM Ackerman, 'Rethinking the International Anti-Corruption Agenda: Civil Society, Human Rights and Democracy' (2014) 29 *American University International Law Review* 293, 311.

institutions collaborate in the construction of public policies, if necessary, by invoking the Judiciary. In this latter case, the Ministério Público, acting as the requesting magistrature, becomes the active face of the justice system precisely to preserve the Judiciary, which must remain inert. Luigi Ferrajoli, in his garantiste model (GM), referred to this characteristic as the 'principle of actionability': 'This further principle was introduced into the Brazilian Constitution, whose Article 129 greatly expanded the powers of the Ministério Público (…) the ability to initiate actions for the protection of fundamental rights and, in particular, social rights, as well as public interests and constitutional goods violated by public authorities.'[14]

Even in the classic studies of civil procedure, it is possible to recall the same insistent idea. In his study on the American procedural model, Mirjan Damaska introduced a coordinated state bureaucracy model aimed at implementing public policies, characterised by state and citizen participation. Damaska exemplifies this paradigm in American public interest litigation, highlighting civil actions on behalf of large groups against institutions like schools and hospitals.[15] The remaining doubt is whether the Ministério Público can be appointed as the guardian of these public interest rights in civil procedures.

Which are the conditions to give rise to such an institution? Neil MacCormick argues that law should be analysed through the practices and institutions that support it.[16] The construction of a new institution requires specialisation, autonomy, and independence from central power. Constitutional provisions, statutes and budgets are also paramount.[17]

In Brazil, the Ministério Público is recognised for its role in civil litigation involving public interests, as observed by Lesley K McAllister. The institution is fundamental in protecting collective and social rights, acting as an independent and autonomous guardian essential to the justice system.[18]

The evolution of the Brazilian Ministério Público demonstrates its transition from a connection with central power to an independent and autonomous operation, essential to the justice system and the state's judicial function, defending the primary public interest. Analysing this evolution is fundamental to understanding the political and institutional circumstances of this trajectory.

[14] L Ferrajoli, *A Democracia Através Dos Direitos. O Constitucionalismo Garantista Como Modelo Teórico e Como Projeto Político* (RT/Thomson Reuters, 2015) 246–247.

[15] MR Damaška, *The Faces of Justice and State Authority: A Comparative Approach to the Legal Process* (New Haven, Yale University Press, 1986) 237.

[16] N MacCormick, *Institutions of Law: An Essay in Legal Theory* (Oxford, Oxford University Press, 2008) ch 10.

[17] See III.A.

[18] LK McAllister (ed), *Making Law Matter: Environmental Protection and Legal Institutions in Brazil* (Redwood, Stanford Law Books an imprint of Stanford Univ Press, 2008) 7.

C. Origins of the Ministério Público in Brazil Until the 1988 Constitutional Framework: A True Game Changer?

> Various models have come to the attention. In one model, in which diffuse interests are considered public, the Public Prosecutor is given the right to act for their protection. This is made possible by Art. 129, III of the Brazilian Constitution. In Europe, however, this solution has proven not to be very efficient.[19]
>
> Art. 129 (…) III – to institute *civil investigation and public civil suit* to protect public and social property, the environment and *other diffuse and collective interests* (…) IX – to exercise other functions which may be conferred upon it, if they are compatible with its purpose, with *judicial representation and judicial consultation for public entities being forbidden*.[20]

The Ministério Público in Brazil has historically been linked to both the Executive Power and the Judiciary, from which its initial versions emerged in the national territory. For instance, in 1609, it was part of the *Tribunal da Relação do Brasil*, created in Salvador, Bahia, by the decree of 7 March. In 1891, it was included as a member of the Supreme Federal Court and, locally, as part of the newly established local courts of justice with the advent of the Republic. During the military dictatorship, the Brazilian Ministério Público was included under the Executive Power (Constitutional Amendment nº 1/1969).

In constitutional democratic states, however, its current nature is that of an independent and autonomous institution, defending social and individual rights characterised as public interest. Even where the Judiciary constitutes a single career, with distinctions between requesting magistrates and judging magistrates, the trend is to strengthen this autonomy and independence, despite criticisms of institutional control that limit these characteristics. Although the Ministério Público is detached from the ownership of rights claimed in court and the interests of the state, it is not impartial; it is a public party that must pursue the interests related to its office, which are the general interests of the community. In Brazilian law, these interests include the observance of the legal order, the defence of the democratic regime, and the protection of social and individual rights. It is a 'justice body' that not only participates in the exercise of the Judiciary power but also serves as an access point to justice.[21]

The Ministério Público already had the expertise to protect society in criminal law and criminal proceedings. This approach to criminal law is evident in how cases are registered in court; in criminal actions, the Ministério Público appears protecting 'The people' or 'society' against the defendant, which is the primary

[19] M Cappelletti, *Dimensioni della giustizia nelle società contemporanee: studi di diritto giudiziario comparato* (Bologna, Il Mulino, 1994) 109.

[20] Brazilian Federal Constitution of 1988 (CF).

[21] Picardi (n 12) 169–170.

public interest in the application of criminal law and the protection of society.[22] What structural adaptations enabled the protection of collective rights?

Additionally, due to its criminal jurisdiction and traditional civil curatorship functions, the Ministério Público was well-integrated, spread across all judicial units with the physical structures and personnel necessary for immediate operation. This was an important detail in a continental-sized country.[23]

It is crucial to observe the historical shift from the king's interests, through the state's interests, to the contemporary understanding of constitutional interests, which encompass fundamental and human rights, as the embodiment of public interest and the Rule of Law.[24] A three-act Brazilian opera: (1) Overture to all interests regarding vulnerable parties and public goods in the Brazilian Code of Civil Procedure of 1973. (2) Considering diffuse, collective, and individual homogeneous rights included in the idea of vulnerable groups and public interest rights, enacting statutes and a new constitution after the democratisation of the country that protect these rights and give standing and joint party status to public prosecutors as ombudsmen, while simultaneously forbidding the protection of state interests. (3) A new Brazilian Code of Civil Procedure that expands the idea of *custos legis* to *custos juris*, including precedents and agreements (ADR and procedural agreements) as pillars of the new civil procedure, and establishes that the sole presence of a state party is not a cause for intervention as a joint party by non-criminal prosecutors.[25]

First act. In the 1970s, Brazil was under a non-democratic regime. The Minister of Justice was Alfredo Buzaid, a proceduralist and tenured professor at Brazil's largest university, the University of São Paulo (USP). He authored a draft and used the opportunity to initiate the enactment of the 1973 Civil Procedure Code. During discussions on implementing the Code, a public prosecutor from Rio Grande do Sul, Sérgio da Costa Franco, supported by the institution, argued that the Ministério Público should defend the Public Treasury, including Federal interests where there was no Federal prosecutor, at the 1971 First Congress of the São Paulo State Ministério Público. This thesis prevailed and was inserted via a legislative amendment by Amaral de Sousa, a Federal deputy from Rio Grande do Sul and future appointed governor of the state, becoming, with some adaptations, part of the final text. Thus, the 1973 Civil Procedure Code regulated the intervention of the Ministério Público in *all cases involving public interest by the nature of the dispute or the quality of the parties*, granting

[22] E Vitorelli, 'El Proceso Colectivo Brasileño y El Rol Del Ministério Público: Pasado, Presente y Futuro' in GFP Posada and R Cavani (eds), *Los Procesos Coletivos en Debate* (Palestra, 2024) 76.

[23] H Zaneti Jr., *O Ministério Público e o Processo Civil Contemporâneo*, 2nd edn (Salvador, Juspodivm 2021).

[24] H Zaneti Jr., 'Precedente. Tra Rule of Law e Stato Costituzionale nel Diritto Processuale Brasiliano' in A Briguglio and others (eds), Scritti in Onore di Nicola Picardi, vol III (Pacini, 2016) 2647.

[25] Art 178, CPC/2015.

broader functions of public interest protection, including defending the Public Treasury's interests.[26]

Second act. On the other hand, in the 1970s, many Brazilian proceduralists were researching issues related to access to justice and the Florence Project, significantly influenced by Mauro Cappelletti in national law. Many studies on the subject emerged, primarily those by Barbosa Moreira, Ada Pellegrini Grinover, Kazuo Watanabe, and Waldemar Mariz de Oliveira Jr.[27] In this cultural context, major legislative innovations occurred in the 1980s.

For the first time, public civil action for environmental protection, with standing granted to the Ministério Público, was mentioned in Law No. 6.938 of 31 August 1981; the first national organic law of the Brazilian Ministério Público, Complementary Statute No. 40 of December 14, 1981, was approved, mentioning public civil action as an institutional function.

Broad public civil action ('*ação civil pública*') was created in 1985, Law No. 7.347 of July 24 (LACP), with a broad protection of many collective rights. The Federal Constitution was promulgated on 5 October 1988 (CF/1988), equating the Ministério Público to the Judiciary and separating it from other powers, explicitly prohibiting representation and consultancy for the state and public entities.[28] The Ministério Público became a permanent institution, externally autonomous, internally independent, defending the democratic regime, legal order, and inalienable social and individual rights.[29] This configuration of the Ministério Público was reinforced in 1993 by the National Organic Law of the Ministério Público (LONMP) and the Complementary Statute of the Ministério Público of the Union, both initiated by the President of the Republic. The first serves as a framework norm to minimally discipline what each federative unit should consider when establishing specific organisation, attributions, and statutes for each respective Ministério Público. The second regulates the organisation, attributions, and statutes of the Ministério Público of the Union.[30]

Third act. The 2015 Civil Procedure Code is a new code founded on the pillars of the general duty of cooperation, encouragement of alternative dispute resolution methods, and a culture of binding precedents. It recognised the Public Prosecutor's Office's agenda-setting power to identify the public interest,[31] a duty to promote binding precedents and ensure the uniformity and stability of jurisprudence, and the role of gateway to justice, resolving legal issues outside the Judiciary

[26] Art 82, III, CPC/1973, S da Costa Franco, 'Sobre a Conveniência Da Ampliação Das Atribuições Processuais Do Ministério Público Como 'Custos Legis'' Anais do I Congresso do Ministério Público de São Paulo-1971 [1971] *Justitia* 203.

[27] For complete referencies F Didier Jr and H Zaneti Jr., *Curso de Direito Processual Civil. Processo Coletivo*, vol 4. 15th edn (Salvador, Juspodivm, 2021) ch 1.

[28] Art 129, IX, CF/1988, text above.

[29] 'Art 127. The Prosecution Office is a *permanent institution, essential to the jurisdictional function of the State*, and it is its duty to defend the *legal order, the democratic regime and the inalienable social and individual interests*', CF/1988.

[30] See III.A.

[31] Art 279, CPC/2015.

or mediating the parties in court. It prioritised its constitutional functions. The intervention of the Public Prosecutor's Office was reduced in family and succession cases, jurisdictional conflicts, and other matters of individual disposable rights. The Public Prosecutor's Office ceased to be a guardian of the law to become a guardian of the legal order, which means that it protects not only the application of strict law but also the constitutional order, international human rights norms, valid contracts between parties, including procedural agreements, and primarily the application, formation, and overruling of binding judicial precedents.

Next, we will analyse the broad role of the Ministério Público in the Brazilian Constitution and legislation, highlighting the characteristics of its structure that allowed the establishment of a control body with independence and specialisation for broad protection of access to justice and fundamental and human rights.

III. Conditions of Functionality: Constitutional and Legal Provisions, Specialised in Collective Redress, and the Portrait of the *Ministère Public*

The existence of an independent institution for the control and implementation of fundamental and human rights, with the special task of ensuring that other public bodies and the market effectively respect the rights and duties set forth in the Constitution, requires a well-defined structure, budget, and normative support. In addition to institutional design, it is also necessary to verify whether the substantive and procedural legislation supports effective action and to review performance data to determine if, beyond normative provisions and legal doctrine, there is a real correspondence to the assigned tasks.[32]

Some of these elements are demonstrated as follows: There is much to be done, but the existing structure, the maturity of collective redress in Brazil, and the data are particularly illustrative of what has already been achieved.

A. Structure, Selection, Compensation, and Constitutional and Legal Functions of the Brazilian *Ministère Public*

Brazil suffers from a structural paradox, being influenced by both the American justice system and the French codified model.[33] This paradox is common in many

[32] For the importance of this broad analysis in comparative civil procedure see A Uzelac, 'Estudos Comparados de Processo Civil (Comparative Studies of Civil Procedure)' (2023) 345 *Revista de Processo* 391.

[33] A Gidi and H Zaneti Jr, 'The Cost of Access to Justice Revisited – The 'Age of Austerity' in Brazilian Civil Procedure Five Years Later. Winds of Change?' *University of Miami School of Law Institutional Repository* (Miami, 2021) 82 repository.law.miami.edu/umialr/vol52/iss2/4 accessed 20 May 2021.

Latin American countries.[34] With democratic maturity, its institutions are becoming more independent and autonomous, creating a self-aware mixed culture.[35] The Brazilian Ministério Público, starting from the 1988 Federal Constitution, was designed in a radically new way, with a clear separation between the Executive, Legislative, Judicial branches, without overlap or direct influence among them.

The 1988 Constitution ensures the independence and autonomy of the Ministério Público, guaranteeing functional, administrative, and budgetary autonomy. The minimum guarantees include life tenure, irremovability, and irreducibility of salaries, while prohibitions encompass receiving fees, practicing law, participating in commercial enterprises, and holding other public functions except teaching.[36]

The remuneration of the Ministério Público is attractive, and its members are chosen through public competitive exams, ensuring stability and merit. As observed by scholars, the Ministério Público attracts the best graduates from the best law schools in Brazil, making the career desirable due to its stability and the opportunity to defend significant rights.[37] The institutional principles of the Ministério Público are unity, indivisibility, and functional independence.

The structure of the Ministério Público reflects the geopolitical peculiarities of Brazil. The Brazilian Ministério Público comprises the Ministério Público of the Union (Federal, Labor, Military, and the Federal District and Territories) and the 26 Ministério Públicos of the states. The Procurador-Geral da República (Attorney General of the Union) is appointed by the President of the Republic, after approval by the Federal Senate, for a two-year term with the possibility of reappointment. In the states, the Procurador-Geral de Justiça (Attorney General of the states) is appointed by the Governor after an election among peers, who select a list of three members. This subtle but important difference allows for greater control by class members in the nomination of the state AG.[38]

The Conselho Nacional do Ministério Público (CNMP) in Brazil oversees the administration, financial management, and disciplinary control of the Ministério Público, ensuring its autonomy and accountability.[39] Together, these features compose the system of checks and balances.

[34] RO Berizonce and E Oteiza, *Civil Procedure in Argentina* (Alphen Aan Den Rijn, Kluwer Law International, 2021); E Oteiza, 'Civil Procedure Reforms in Latin America: The Role of the Judge and the Parties in Seeking a Fair Solution' in J Walker and OG Chase (eds), *Common law, civil law and the future of categories: proceedings of a conference of the International Association of Procedural Law held in Toronto, June 3-5, 2009* (London, LexisNexis, 2010) 233–234.

[35] AP Grinover and K Watanabe, 'Brazil and Its European Influences' in J Walker and OG Chase (eds), *Common law, civil law and the future of categories: proceedings of a conference of the International Association of Procedural Law held in Toronto, June 3-5, 2009* (London, LexisNexis, 2010); H Zaneti Jr., *A Constitucionalização Do Processo: Do Problema Ao Precedente. Da Teoria Do Processo Ao Código de Processo Civil de 2015* (Sao Paulo, RT/Thomson Reuters 2021).

[36] Art 127 and 128, CF/1988.

[37] McAllister (n 18).

[38] C Cyrillo, *O Ministério Público Federal Numa Visão Do Garantismo Sul-Americano* (FAPERJ, 2024).

[39] Art 130-A, CF/1988.

The 1988 Constitution highlights the functions of the Ministério Público in the civil area, such as ensuring respect for constitutional rights, promoting civil inquiries and public civil actions, controlling the constitutionality of laws, defending indigenous rights, and requesting information for its administrative procedures. The express prohibition on judicial representation and consultancy for public entities reinforces the separation between the state and the Ministério Público.

Equality with the judiciary and the prohibition of ad hoc prosecutors are achievements of the 1988 Constitution, ensuring the independent and effective performance of the Ministério Público in defending the legal order and fundamental rights.

As can be observed, the original French system of *Ministère Public*, from which descends the Ministério Público, does not adequately address new challenges, leading to a crisis in that model and its related systems. While the American model, with its strategic planning and rigorous efficiency control, might seem compatible, it is unsatisfactory for our needs. It fails to align with impartial justice and creates inequalities and selective law application. We cannot imagine judges and prosecutors elected by the people, as this would lead to campaign financing crises and high corruption levels, some of the problems that are in the *realpolitik* of Latin American countries.[40]

The Brazilian Ministério Público is already a rich and interesting patchwork influenced by the Scandinavian ombudsman and the American public prosecutor. The crisis of the Ministério Público lies between the law firm and judicial models. In the absence of definitive answers and the complexity of the institution, pure models do not exist. To survive and remain legitimate, it must strengthen its unity through internal democracy and value strategic planning, setting goals, and achieving concrete results that align with society's values.[41]

B. Protecting Homogeneous, Diffuse, and Collective Rights in Brazil: The Role of Public Prosecutors

> The adoption of procedural reforms by leading countries such as Brazil can increase the likelihood that the reform will be adopted elsewhere.[42]

Brazil has over four decades of experience with class actions. The current Brazilian system of collective redress has instigated and responded to the nearly 300,000 class actions filed and pending in the judicial system.[43] The necessary coherence

[40] F Calderón and M Castells, *A Nova América Latina* (Rio de Janeiro, Zahar, 2021) 259.
[41] E Garcia, *Ministério público: organização, atribuições e regime jurídico*, 6th edn (Sao Paulo, Editora Saraiva, 2021) 195; Zaneti Jr. (n 23) 192–196.
[42] T Main, 'Country Studies from Beyond the Divide: An Introduction' in OG Chase, and J Walker (eds), *Common Law Civil Law and the Future of Categories* (London, LexisNexis, 2009) 273/274.
[43] See III.C.

of the law was secured by the doctrine and the courts considering the various rules as part of a procedural 'microsystem' for collective redress. This means that, when referring to the Consumer Defence Code (CDC) and the Public Civil Action Law (LACP), the rules generally apply to the entire collective process, irrespective of the area or subject matter, regardless of the name of the judicial action or the legitimate party. This system ensures both effective judicial protection for individual group members and the public interests involved, and adherence to due process of law, as mandated in a constitutional democracy. This topic will consider particularly the collective rights regulation by law, standing, res judicata, and the allocation of damages, costs, and funding.

The Brazilian doctrine on collective redress underwent significant evolution between 1977 and 1981, creating a body of laws, practices, and doctrine that is very solid. The influence of the US class actions, and 1970 Italian scholarship is evident;[44] however, the Brazilian experience and the cultural public values attributed to the '*ação civil pública*' resulted in a distinct and quite unique development. One cannot compare Brazil to the North American problems of the 'Big Bad Wolf'.[45] Brazil does not have punitive damages by jury trial, entrepreneurial lawyering, or contingency fees.[46] Brazil has successful cases in collective redress; it is not a doctrinal 'puzzle' or lost in 'shades of gray'. However, this undermines the defendants' aspirations, as it signifies a robust legal framework that ensures accountability and fairness.[47]

In the Consumers Protection Code (CDC), new categories of rights were created by statutory law to protect collective interests in a broad sense. Article 81 of the CDC establishes three categories of collective *lato sensu* rights: (1) 'diffuse rights' (trans-individual rights of an indivisible nature in which the parties involved are indeterminate persons connected by circumstances of fact – for example, living in the same area); (2) strictly collective rights (trans-individual rights of an indivisible nature, in which the involved party is a group, category, or class of people connected among each other or with the *ex adversa* party through a legal relationship); and (3) 'homogeneous individual rights' (individual rights of a common origin). The most complex category is the latter, as this entails the joinder of individual rights originating *ex post facto* from the same material facts. Taken together, these three categories should allow every kind of right of a group of people to be protected by the courts, not only consumer rights. Brazil protects group rights in a broad, trans-sectoral (trans-substantive) way and is open to new emerging rights in the legislation and the international treaties and conventions to

[44] AP Grinover, 'The Defense of Transindividual Interests: Brazil and Ibero-America' (2014) 1 *BRICS Law Journal* 44, 46.

[45] R Marcus, 'The Big Bad Wolf: American Class Actions' in CH (Remco) Van Rhee and V Harsàgi (eds), *Multi-party redress mechanisms in Europe: Squeaking Mice?* (Cambridge, Intersentia, 2014).

[46] H Zaneti Jr., 'Collective Redress in Brazil: Success or Disappointment?', in S Voet and A Uzelac (eds), *Class Actions in Europe. Holy Grail or a Wrong Trail?* (Cham, Springer, 2021) 347.

[47] L Mullenix, 'For the Defense: 28 Shades of European Class Actions' in A Uzelac and S Voet (eds), *Class Actions in Europe. Holy Grail or a Wrong Trail?* (Cham, Springer, 2021).

which it is bound, admitting all types of procedural remedies, admitting all types of procedural remedies.[48]

Based on the Constitution, statute law, Brazilian procedural tradition, and precedent of the higher courts, such actions can result in payment of amounts owed as collective compensation or to the members of the group; injunction orders to take, desist, or refrain from any given action in order to protect the group rights (eg, the installation of technical equipment to reduce emissions, the closure of a factory, or the shelving of plans of expansion); to recover degraded areas and return the natural environment to the *status quo ante*; structural injunctions in prisons, hospitals, or schools, to change practices in such institutions under the supervision of the public prosecutor or the courts.

The Brazilian model of collective redress challenges the idea that only opt-out class actions can adequately protect societal interests. It advocates for a hybrid approach that combines mandatory class actions (non-opt-out), opt-out, and opt-in mechanisms, including aggregated litigation, which is considered a type of opt-in collective redress.[49] Furthermore, it promotes the use of collective agreements both before and during the legal process.

One of the most critical and effective aspects of the Brazilian Ministério Público is the 'inquérito civil' (Civil Investigation). This administrative procedure allows public prosecutors to investigate and gather evidence on violations of diffuse or collective rights, serving as a preliminary step for negotiating out-of-court settlements or filing Public Civil Actions. Established by the 1985 Public Civil Action Act[50] and reinforced by the 1988 Constitution,[51] the Civil Investigation empowers prosecutors to summon complainants, witnesses, experts, and defendants. They can commission scientific and technical surveys by specialists such as auditors, engineers, and biologists, and request information from both public and private entities. Non-compliance with information requests necessary for filing a Public Civil Action is criminalised, with penalties including imprisonment from 1 to 3 years and fines up to US$5,000.[52]

Moreover, the plaintiffs of the proceedings are not themselves members of the group but rather various private and public entities. The Office of the Public Prosecutor is not the only public body that plays a role in class actions in Brazil: the federal government, member states of the federation, municipalities, and numerous other public institutions and bodies have standing to bring class actions. So too do several private organisations and associations (eg, NGO's). In all cases brought by bodies other than the Office of the Public Prosecutor, however, the public prosecutor will intervene to protect the public interest (*custos juris*). Failure to include the Office of the Public Prosecutor in the proceedings will result in

[48] Art 83, CDC.
[49] Art 985, CPC/2015.
[50] Arts 8 to 10, LACP.
[51] Art 129, III, CF/1988.
[52] Art 10, LACP.

the annulment of the procedure if the public prosecutor considers that this has harmed the public interest. This very liberal approach to legal standing in class actions with many potential co-plaintiffs is a distinctive feature of the Brazilian model for collective redress.

Another significant feature is that, due to the Brazilian extension of the *res judicata secundum eventum litis*, there is no risk to the party autonomy of individual claimants that governs in civil law procedure countries, because every individual can still bring his or her own individual claim. This principle, rooted in Article 103 of the CDC, posits that a class action judgment yields *erga omnes* and *ultra partes* effects, without compromising the interests or individual rights of the constituents of the collective, group, category, or class. Succinctly, a successful class action benefits all absent class members. Conversely, an unsuccessful class action, while preventing any subsequent class action on the same claim(s), does not inhibit the holders of individual rights from pursuing their rights in individual actions. Consequently, there is no *lis pendens* between an individual action and a class action.

This approach to *res judicata* in class action litigation has consistently been a subject of controversy, particularly because the US version of opt-out class actions is characterised by *pro et contra* binding effect, even against the holders of individual rights. However, recent advancements in Brazilian law have significantly mitigated the practical effect of this difference between Brazilian and US law. New rules on claim preclusion, ie, novel methods to prevent the reiteration of the same issue/claim in individual or class action cases, include: (1) test cases (aggregate litigation, applicable in both individual and collective cases); (2) binding precedents (applicable to both individual and collective cases); (3) stay of individual claims related to the class action ('As a result of collective action concerning the macro litigation that generates multitudinous litigations, individual actions are suspended, awaiting the judgment of collective action.')[53]

For these reasons, it is necessary to strike the right balance between the various forms of collective redress available, especially between the use of class actions and aggregate litigation. Due to the importance that the Brazilian system attaches to the public interest, a guideline to strike this balance is the view that the existence of a class action ought to lead to the suspension, even ex officio, of individual cases.

The statute for collective redress ensures that awarded damages can be directed to, for instance, a fund. As an example, the Diffuse Rights Fund was established by law to receive damages awarded in successful class actions based on diffuse rights and strictly collective rights,[54] as well as a kind of *cy-près* fund for cases where insufficiently harmed people claim their awards after a money judgment in a class action to protect individual homogeneous rights.[55]

[53] Superior Court of Justice (STJ), REsp 1110549/RS, Justice Sidnei Beneti 28 October 2009; REsp 1353801/RS, Justice Mauro Campbell Marques, 14 August 2013.

[54] Art 13, LACP.

[55] Art 100, CDC.

There are no costs or attorneys' fees for the plaintiffs. The loser pays rule applies only for the defendant, or in case of frivolous or bad-faith litigation.[56] The state covers the costs if the plaintiffs lose the case.

Regarding the effectiveness of the Brazilian system, it should be noted that Brazil adheres to the Multi-Door Court House movement, with the new Civil Procedure Code providing for a general duty to encourage alternative dispute resolution (ADR). As far as collective redress is concerned, Brazilian law has encouraged collective settlements since 1985. As a result, many cases are resolved through conduct adjustment agreements ('*compromisso de ajustamento de conduta*' *e* 'TAC').[57] Furthermore, the Brazilian system of collective redress has allowed for the agreements, even after the filing of an action and in the enforcing phase.

The key institution in the indispensable coordination of the various mechanisms of collective redress is the Office of the Public Prosecutor. The significance of the public prosecutor's role in collective redress is particularly evident in Brazil, where even if class actions are initiated by other parties, the public prosecutor is obligated to intervene in the proceedings and act as *custos juris*.[58] During the period from 2014 to 2017, over 80 per cent of class actions, including 57,514 collective settlements, were filed by public prosecutors.[59] The collective redress system that yielded these results was lauded by Mauro Cappelletti in 1994, who underscored the role of the Brazilian public prosecutor, stating, 'Clearly, independence and specialisation are two absolutely necessary conditions for the success.'[60]

Public bodies with financial and political independence can provide in combination with ONGs and private attorneys for far better supervision of these actions and their outcomes than the models with foster only private attorneys, like US class actions.[61] From a Brazilian perspective, the important role played by independent public bodies – whether public prosecutors, ombudsmen, or other independent bodies – to protect public interests.

C. A 'Portrait' of the Brazilian Public Prosecution Service: Data

We will analyse the recent data on the number of public prosecutors in Brazil, the monthly salaries paid for their function, the budget of the institutions for fulfilling

[56] Art 18, LACP and 87, CDC.

[57] Art 5, § 5, LACP and Res. Nº 179, CNMP.

[58] See II.C.

[59] E Vitorelli and H Zaneti Jr., 'O Futuro Do Processo Coletivo: Considerações Sobre o Relatório Analítico Propositivo Do Conselho Nacional de Justiça (The Future of Collective Redress: Considerations about the Analytic Survey by the National Justice Council)' (2019) 295 *Revista de Processo* 195.

[60] Cappelletti (n 19) 110.

[61] DR Hensler et al., *Class Actions Dilemmas. Pursuing Public Goals for Private Gain* (Santa Monica, Rand, 2000) 71–72.

their legal and constitutional mission, and the results of their performance in collective actions. These data exemplify what has been discussed so far.

Some data can be extracted from the Business Intelligence (BI) Portal 'MP: A Portrait', maintained by the National Council of the Ministério Publico (CNMP).[62] As of April 2023, there were 13,185 member positions filled in the Public Prosecutor's Offices of the States and the Federal Public Prosecutor's Office, and 37,564 Public Prosecutor's staff positions filled.

The careers in the Public Prosecution Service and the Judiciary represent the pinnacle of public service in Brazil. The starting salaries for a Federal Prosecutor (MPF) and a State Prosecutor (MPE) are attractive, typically around R$33,000.00 monthly at the beginning of their careers. These can rise to amounts equivalent to the salary of a Supreme Court Justice, which is the salary cap for public servants, approximately R$44,000.00 monthly.[63]

The budget data for 2024 highlights the scale of public investment in Brazilian Public Prosecutors' offices. The Fiscal Responsibility Law (Complementary Statute No. 101/2000) sets expenditure limits for personnel costs, including those of the Public Prosecutor's Office. At the Federal level, the Public Prosecutor's Office of the Union (MPU) is capped at 0.6 per cent of the Union's net current revenue. In the states, the State Public Prosecutor's Office (MPE) is limited to 2 per cent of the state's net current revenue. These measures aim to ensure fiscal responsibility, transparency in public resource management, and the prevention of financial imbalances. For example, the budget for the Federal Public Prosecuto's Office is R$5,080,398,289.00.[64] Among the states, the Public Prosecutor's Office of São Paulo has the largest budget, amounting to R$3,172,656,901.00.[65] In the State of Minas Gerais, it is R$3,014,841,492.00,[66] and in the State of Espírito Santo, it is R$502,774,441.00.[67]

The same report, 'MP: A Portrait', presents the results from 2023 regarding the investigations initiated as civil investigations, settlements, litigations filed, and cases archived in the State Public Prosecution Services:[68]

[62] See www.cnmp.mp.br/portal/relatoriosbi/mp-um-retrato-2021, accessed on 4 May 2024.

[63] Approximately €6,270 and €8,360, respectively. Updated data on the salaries of all staff and members of the Public Prosecution Service can be found on the public transparency portals of each institution, for example in the case of the Federal Public Ministry (www.transparencia.mpf.mp.br/conteudo/contracheque/remuneracao-servidores-ativos) and in the case of the State Public Ministry of Espírito Santo (transparencia.mpes.mp.br/informacoes/Contracheque/Remuneracao_de_Todos_os_Membros_Ativos.asp).

[64] Approximately €965,275,675, see www.transparencia.mpf.mp.br/.

[65] Approximately €602,604,811, see www.mpsp.mp.br/portal-da-transparencia.

[66] Approximately €572,819,883, see transparencia.mpmg.mp.br/arquivos_por_nome_links/execucao_orcamentaria_e_financeira/receitas_proprias.

[67] Approximately €95,527,044, see transparencia.mpes.mp.br/informacoes/Execucao_Orcamentaria_e_Financeira/Receitas_Proprias.asp.

[68] A note from the BI itself indicates the possibility of registering more than one subject per procedure. The list of subjects represented are those included in the annexes of CNMP Resolution No. 195/2019, which is not exhaustive and therefore should not be totaled. As we have noted in another study, the data comes from the collection by unified taxonomies between the Judiciary and the Public Ministry, which may show disparities in collection and classification.

State Public Prosecution Service: Measures Adopted
47,572 inquiries initiated
3,342 settlements
3,540 litigations filed
8,171 cases archived

The distribution of predominant subjects demonstrates the scope and priorities of activities across the country. Focusing on the data from state public prosecution services alone, there were 19,811 civil inquiries registered concerning environmental matters, 14,062 on administrative control of corruption, 4,929 on urban law issues, 4,422 on consumer rights, 2,608 on the rights of children and adolescents, 2,511 on health, 1,658 on the right to education, 908 concerning the protection of elderly persons, and 528 regarding persons with disabilities. All these proceedings are presumably regarding group rights, not individual issues.

Another important source of data about collective redress is presented by the National Register of Collective Actions (CACOL), linked to the National Council of Justice (CNJ) and the National Council of the Ministério Público (CNMP). According to this register, there are currently 290,721 pending cases (two hundred ninety thousand seven hundred and twenty-one) in Brazil, considering collective redress proceedings. Public civil actions ('*ações civis públicas*') constitute the largest volume, representing 72.9 per cent of the pending cases.

Recall, many actions in state and federal common courts are filed by the Public Prosecutors, and whenever not a plaintiff, the Public Prosecutor's office acts as *custos juris*, thus serving as an author or joint party in all cases. It is also possible to filter the research by the defendant, and it is not surprising to find that, except in cases of confidentiality, the major defendants are precisely public entities, including, among others, the Federal Union and the States of Pará, Minas Gerais, Paraná, Ceará, Paraíba, and Tocantins.[69] This fact is not surprising considering that official statistics on major litigants in Brazil place public law entities and public institutions alongside major litigants such as financial institutions and telephone companies.[70] In a country with nearly 83 million cases,[71] this information is highly significant.

The CACOL research tool also provides data from the Public Prosecutor's office over a longer time frame, encompassing the results of public civil inquiries initiated (1.23 million) and agreements concluded (209,045).[72]

[69] See paineisanalytics.cnj.jus.br/single/?appid=1d54bc4d-81c7-45ae-b110-7794758c17b2&sheet=87f1a661-cf86-4bda-afe4-61dfc6778cd4&lang=pt-BR&opt=ctxmenu,currsel, (accessed on 4 May 2024). The same caveats about data accuracy and collection apply here.

[70] See grandes-litigantes.stg.cloud.cnj.jus.br/, (accessed on 4 May 2024).

[71] For the number of cases currently in process in Brazil, see grandes-litigantes.stg.cloud.cnj.jus.br/, (accessed on 4 May 2024).

[72] See paineisanalytics.cnj.jus.br/single/?appid=1d54bc4d-81c7-45ae-b110-7794758c17b2&sheet=1fef0785-a20b-4b4d-919b-8d529099eed7&lang=pt-BR&opt=ctxmenu,currsel, accessed on 4 May 2024. The same caveats about the accuracy of the data and the collection are applicable here.

Comparison with European figures highlights the vast differences between the choice for an open model of filing and prosecution of public interest in court, with multiple standings from both public and private bodies, and the emphasis on an independent public institution, autonomously budgeted and specialised, versus more closed options of government lists approved by executive bodies or entities linked to the legislature.[73] The challenges are largely distinct; not all outcomes have been positive, and there is still much to be done. Yet the numbers are very significant.

IV. Conclusion

> Currently, Brazil is living a very serious crisis both ethical and economic, in the political sphere, and the population puts all its hope in the judiciary branch. Brazilian judges have a career, which begins by passing a public admission exam where there is no political bias. In recent years, they have shown that they are independent and entirely fulfil the needs and expectations of Brazilian society.[74]

The Ministério Público is often seen as a highly influential entity within the Brazilian government, characterised by its structured organisation and specialisation. It attracts some of the nation's most talented and ambitious legal minds from top law schools. These individuals, highly accomplished and prepared, navigate Brazil's rigorous university entrance exams and public employment examinations. Enshrined in the Constitution and governed by statutory provisions, the Ministério Público operates with a high degree of autonomy. Although its members are paid by the government, their role involves holding the government accountable, often through litigation, to ensure adherence to the Rule of Law. This environment, which fosters respectability among the public and colleagues alike, creates a unique space dedicated to the protection of human and fundamental rights. As pointed out, imagining a division of the US Department of Justice suing the President and the head of the EPA for failing to enforce environmental laws – an almost unthinkable scenario in the US – highlights the significant power and influence wielded by the Ministério Público.[75]

In conclusion, the Brazilian Ministério Público exemplifies a crucial innovation in the legal framework, particularly within young Latin American democracies. These democracies illustrate the necessity of intertwining political representation legitimacy with constitutional legitimacy, ensuring that political decisions are constrained by human and fundamental rights. Such social guarantee structures

[73] CJS Hodges and S Voet, *Delivering Collective Redress: New Technologies* (Oxford, Hart Publishing, 2018) 284–285; Zaneti Jr., (n 46) 349.

[74] TA Alvim, and CS Bueno, 'Civil Justice in Brazil' (2016) 3(6) *BRICS Law Journal* 38–39.

[75] C Crawford, 'Defending Public Prosecutors and Defining Brazil's Environmental 'Public Interest': A Review of Lesley McAllister's Making Law Matter: Environmental Protection and Legal Institutions in Brazil (2009)' (2008) 40 *George Washington International Law Review* 619, 621; McAllister (n 18).

require the support of judicial institutions, especially when other branches fail to comply. To prevent an overly active judiciary, a control institution with the authority to engage the judiciary in cases of legal non-compliance is essential.

This is the model that the Brazilian Ministério Público adopted in 1988, merging the roles of Attorney General, Public Prosecutor, and Ombudsman with the traditional functions of public interest protection found in the French model. It has been granted powers of investigation, litigation, and collective rights agreements, thereby becoming a gateway to justice itself.

The presence of an autonomous institution dedicated to the oversight and enforcement of fundamental and human rights, specifically tasked with ensuring that other public entities and the market comply with constitutional rights and duties, necessitates a clearly defined structure, budget, and normative backing. Beyond the institutional framework, it is essential to assess whether the substantive and procedural laws enable effective action and to examine performance metrics to ascertain if there is a genuine alignment between the prescribed roles and actual practice, beyond mere legal provisions and theoretical doctrines.

Brazil still faces significant challenges, including recent attacks on the Constitutional Democratic state, such as the assault on the Praça dos Três Poderes and the Supreme Federal Court on 8 January 2023. Additionally, there have been changes to anti-corruption legislation, such as Law No. 14,230 of 25 October 2021, which have reduced the control by the Ministério Público. There is also a persistent conflict between the 'jeitinho' and legality, which still makes the statement true: 'Brazil's laws were among the most rigorous and complete in the world, but they lacked compliance.'[76] However, we are making progress, especially in areas related to the collective protection of rights.

Concrete cases could not be addressed in this text, just to give some recent examples where the action of the Ministério Público was essential are the Mariana (Rio Doce)[77] and Brumadinho[78] disasters, involving the two largest mining companies in the world, and the Brazilian version of the global case known as Diesel Gate, involving one of the largest vehicle manufacturers.[79]

In these contemporary times, the resilience of democracies depends on the interplay of various institutions, the checks and balances system, the active engagement of the people, and the critical stance of scholars.

[76] McAllister (n 18) 4.

[77] Zaneti Jr., (n 46) 361; DW Carvalho, 'The Ore Tailings Dam Rupture Disaster in Mariana' (2019) 59 *Natural Resources Journal* 281.

[78] E Vitorelli, 'Equal Justice in The Context of Disasters: The Brumadinho Multi-Layer Settlements Case' (2023) 338 *Revista de Processo* 209.

[79] For more data see Zaneti Jr. (n 46); H Zaneti Jr., 'The Brazilian Experience from over 40 Years of Collective Redress: Some Comments on the ERCP Collective Redress Rules from a Brazilian Perspective', in A Stadler, E Jeuland and V Smith (eds), *Collective and Mass Litigation in Europe. Model Rules for Effective Dispute Resolution* (Cheltenham, Edward Elgar, 2020) 346.

20

Financing Collective Actions and Strategic Litigation in Europe: The Role of Third-Party Funders in the Shadow of the Procedure

ADRIANI DORI AND XANDRA KRAMER*

I. Introduction

Third-party litigation funding (TPLF) has been one of the 'hot potatoes' in European civil justice in recent years. While funding of litigation by commercial parties is not a new phenomenon and has found its way to commercial arbitration and different types of commercial or non-commercial court litigation, its use has expanded in Europe. Litigation is notoriously expensive, while public funding is often limited or may not be available at all. In Europe, discussions on third-party litigation funding have intensified as a result of the Representative Action Directive (RAD) for consumer cases, which became applicable on 25 June 2023.[1] In some countries, this has also led to an increase in what is considered strategic litigation or public interest litigation, with climate litigation being one of the prominent examples. This type of litigation also benefits from private donations, for instance, the *Shell* litigation in the Netherlands,[2] but also a number of cases

* This chapter is made possible by the funding of the VICI project 'Affordable Access to Justice: towards sustainable cost and funding mechanisms for civil litigation in Europe' (project no VI.C.191.082), financed by the Dutch Research Council (NWO). See www.euciviljustice.eu. The Italian regulation on academic evaluation requires some form of identification of each author's individual contribution to a joint paper. Exclusively for this purpose, we mention that sections I, II, and V were written by Xandra Kramer and III and IV by Adriani Dori.

[1] Directive (EU) 2020/1828 of the European Parliament and of the Council of 25 November 2020 on representative actions for the protection of the collective interests of consumers and repealing Directive 2009/22/EC [2020] OJ L 409/1 ('RAD').

[2] District Court The Hague, 26 May 2021, ECLI:NL:RBDHA:2021:5337 (*Milieudefensie cs v Shell*); Court of Appeal The Hague 12 November 2024, ECLI:NL:GHDHA:2024:2100 (*Shell v Milieudefensie cs*).

following the Diesel emission scandal have benefitted from commercial funding.[3] The same goes for other idealistically-driven cases or collective actions, for instance in the area of privacy protection.[4]

A crucial element of TPLF, as is also evident from the RAD, is that a conflict of interest should be avoided, and commercial funders should thus refrain from interfering in the procedure. Nevertheless, funders play an important part in the shadow of the procedure, as without funding, the bringing of these actions is often not feasible. Apart from providing the necessary funding, commercial litigation funders often also have a lot of expertise in litigation, relying on an experienced team of lawyers, which may also support strategic decisions and shaping the procedure.

This chapter discusses the role of commercial funders in light of the development and regulation of TPLF in Europe, in particular in collective actions and strategic litigation. In this context, it will also address the concerns about TPLF, including those voiced by the European Parliament (EP) that adopted a Resolution on 'Responsible Private Litigation Funding' in 2022, urging the European Commission to propose a directive, implementing regulation for third-party funders as regards governance, oversight and transparency, and capping of the fees.[5] After setting the scene for collective and strategic actions, and the rise and regulation of third-party litigation funding (section II), the chapter delves into the role of funders (section III), and discusses their role at the forefront and in the shadow of the procedure (section IV). It closes with concluding remarks by way of assessment of the role of funders (section V).

The chapter relies on relevant legislation, including the RAD and national (implementing) legislation, case law, literature, and interview findings. Considering that the Netherlands is one of the few EU Member States with an effective collective action scheme and where third-party litigation has been used, the chapter will often rely on examples derived from Dutch legal practice. Interestingly, in 2023, a report was published commissioned by the Dutch Ministry of Justice on financing of collective actions,[6] followed by an English book in 2024,[7] which also provides a source of inspiration.

[3] See, eg, District Court Amsterdam, 30 March 2022, ECLI:NL:RBAMS:2022:1541 (*Stichting Diesel Emissions Justice v Volkswagen*) (interim judgment, appeal pending). See also K van Elten and B Rehder, 'Dieselgate and Eurolegalism: How a Scandal Fosters the Americanization of European Law' (2022) 29 *Journal of European Public Policy* 281; DR Hensler and others, 'The Globalization of Mass Civil Litigation: Lessons from the Volkswagen "Clean Diesel" Case', RAND Corporation 2021 www.rand.org/t/RRA917-1 (accessed 15 August 2024).

[4] See, eg, three interim judgments in the *TikTok* case in the Netherlands: District Court Amsterdam 9 November 2022, ECLI:NL:RBAMS:2022:6488; 25 October 2023, ECLI:NL:RBAMS:2023:6694 and 10 January 2024, ECLI:NL:RBAMS:2024:83 ('*TikTok cs*').

[5] European Parliament resolution of 13 September 2022 with recommendations to the Commission on responsible private funding of litigation (2020/2130(INL)).

[6] X Kramer and others, *Nut, Noodzaak, Vormgeving en Kosten van een (Revolverend) Processenfonds voor Collectieve Acties: Report for the Research and Data Centre* (WODC) (September 2023) repository.wodc.nl/handle/20.500.12832/3294 (accessed 15 August 2024).

[7] X Kramer and others, *Financing Collective Actions in the Netherlands: Towards a Litigation Fund?* (The Hague, Eleven International Publishing, 2024).

For the purpose of this chapter, three interviews were conducted with commercial funders that are important market players in three different EU Member States.[8] These served to obtain more insights into the role of funders in civil litigation in practice; they are not intended as a representative sample. The semi-structured interviews evolved around a number of questions, asking the interviewees how they see or would describe the role of funders; how in their experience parties in need of funding and funders get into contact; what their role is in the preparatory stages of the procedure, in their relation to the attorneys; whether there is a difference in this regard between collective actions and other cases; what the role of funders is, if any, during the procedures; what their role is in reaching a settlement; and whether recent developments have changed or may change the funding industry and the role of funders.

II. Setting the Scene: Collective Actions, Strategic Litigation and Third-Party Funding

An important trigger for the rise of and subsequent debates around third-party litigation funding results from the increase of and new legislation on collective actions in Europe. Due to the high costs of collective actions and limited possibilities of other types of funding – for instance, public legal aid – in particular, more high-profile collective actions benefit from funding by commercial funders.[9] Against this background, the present section first outlines EU developments in the area of collective actions and strategic litigation before discussing the rise and legislative framework of third-party litigation funding.

A. Developments in Collective Actions and Strategic Litigation

The resolution of mass damage cases has received a lot of attention in Europe in the past 15 years, both at the national level and in the EU. At the EU level, this has been triggered primarily by the desire to further develop an area of freedom, security, and justice,[10] in particular by facilitating access to justice and securing a high level of consumer protection. This is also expressed by the Commission Recommendation on Collective Redress that was adopted in 2013, which aimed at increasing access to justice in relation to violations of EU law by recommending

[8] The semi-structured interviews were conducted by the second author of this chapter and processed anonymously. All three interviews took place in May 2024 and lasted 40–60 minutes. The interviewees all have extensive experience in litigation funding. In one interview two interviewees participated. The interviews were recorded and auto-transcribed.

[9] See for an analysis from a Dutch perspective: Kramer and others (n 7) 40ff.

[10] Arts 67–89 Treaty of the Functioning of the European Union (TFEU).

Member States to adopt basic principles for collective redress.[11] A wide variety of existing collective redress mechanisms and the absence of (effective) collective action systems in about half of the Member States necessitated action at the EU level.[12] In view of this disparity between legal systems, the adoption of a binding EU horizontal instrument proved impossible.

Considering that the non-binding Recommendation had little effect, the Commission's efforts shifted towards developing sectorial instruments focusing on consumer law. A proposal for collective actions for the protection of EU consumer law was put forward as part of the 2018 'New Deal for Consumers'.[13] After intense negotiations, the Representative Actions Directive for consumer cases (RAD) was adopted at the end of 2020 and became effective on 25 June 2023.[14] The RAD provides a legal framework for so-called 'Qualified Entities' that fulfil the Directive's requirements to bring injunctive and redress (compensatory) collective actions.[15] In addition, it provides a number of rules on costs and funding of collective actions, including TPLF. The RAD does not prohibit TPLF but does include a few rules aiming at, in particular, avoiding possible conflict of interest. This legislative framework will be discussed in greater detail in subsection C of the present Section.

In the different European countries, legislative activities and legal practice have evolved at different speeds.[16] At present, relying on the data from the CMS report of 2024, the most significant jurisdictions for collective actions and strategic litigation are the UK, the Netherlands, Portugal, and Germany. But other Member States, including Slovenia, France, Spain, Italy, and Poland, have also experienced a growth in the number of collective actions.[17] In England and Wales, several types

[11] Commission Recommendation 2013/396/EU of 11 June 2013 on common principles for injunctive and compensatory collective redress mechanisms in the Member States concerning violations of rights granted under Union Law [2023] OJ L201/60, particularly Recital 10.

[12] ibid Recital 12.

[13] Communication from the Commission to the European Parliament, the Council and the European Economic and Social Committee, 'A New Deal for Consumers' COM (2018) 183 final; A Biard and X Kramer, 'The EU Directive on Representative Actions for Consumers: A Milestone or Another Missed Opportunity?' [2019] *ZEuP* 249.

[14] For an overview, see, inter alia, A Biard and S Voet, 'Collective Redress in the EU: Will It Finally Come True' in A Uzelac and S Voet (eds), *Class Actions in Europe: Holy Grail or a Wrong Trail?* (Cham, Springer, 2021) 287; B Gsell, 'The New European Directive on Representative Actions for the Protection of the Collective Interests of Consumers: A Huge, but Blurry Step Forward' (2021) 58 *Common Market Law Review* 1365.

[15] See Art 4 RAD; the requirements include that the entity had to be publicly active in consumer protection for at least twelve months, that is non-profit and that it is independent. The different types of collective actions are laid down in Arts 6–9 RAD.

[16] More recent edited volumes discussing different jurisdictions include: A Uzelac and S Voet (eds), *Class Actions in Europe: Holy Grail or a Wrong Trail?* (Cham, Springer, 2021); A Stadler, E Jeuland and V Smith (eds), *Collective and Mass Litigation in Europe: Model Rules for Effective Dispute Resolution* (Cheltenham, Edward Elgar, 2020).

[17] See, eg, CMS, 'European Class Actions Report 2024' 16 ('CMS Report 2024') that quantifies the jurisdictional distribution of class actions filed in the last 5 years across Europe as follows: England and Wales (46%), Netherlands (12%), Portugal (11%), Germany (9%), Slovenia (4%). Italy, France, Spain and Poland (each 2%).

of collective and group action regimes are in place that operate primarily on an opt-in basis and are regulated in the Civil Procedure Rules (CPR). In addition, specific rules are in place mostly geared to competition claims, which have also enabled opt-out actions since 2015.[18] In recent years, in particular competition class actions have been on the rise.[19]

In the EU Member States, a plurality of systems exists, though the implementation of the RAD has brought a certain – limited – degree of harmonisation regarding consumer claims. As in England and Wales, some Member States have different regimes for different types of claims or only for specific claims, for instance, the opt-in consumer group action in Belgium[20] and the various forms of (public) class actions and group litigation in the Nordic countries.[21] Also in Germany, different regimes have been put in place, in particular for investment cases and cartel damages, while also assignment models are an important means of bundling claims.[22] As a result of the need to implement the RAD, the existing Injunctions Act (*Underlassungsklagengesetz*) was amended and a new Consumer Rights Enforcement Act (*Verbraucherrechtedurchsetzungsgesetz*) was adopted.[23]

Along with, among others, France, Slovenia, and Portugal,[24] the Netherlands has a more general collective action regime, though there are a few variations depending on the type of claim. After introducing a collective action mechanism for injunctions in 1994 and a collective settlement mechanism ('WCAM') in 2005,[25] as of 1 January 2020, the collective action regime was extended to collective actions for compensation ('WAMCA').[26] Contrary to Germany, only a few minor amendments were made to implement the RAD – and only for cases in

[18] CPR, Part 19 includes two specific procedures for collective actions; Part 3 contains rules on consolidation of claims. Specific rules are laid down in the Competition Act 1998 and Consumer Rights Act 2015, with the Competition Appeal Tribunal (CAT) as a special tribunal. See, eg, R Mulheron, 'Further Impetus for a Statutory Class Action, Post-Lloyd v Google' (2023) 42 *Civil Justice Quarterly* 10.

[19] CMS Report 2024 (n 17) 15f.

[20] S Voet, 'Class Actions in Belgium: Evaluation and the Way Forward', in A Uzelac and S Voet (eds), *Class Actions in Europe: Holy Grail or a Wrong Trail?* (Cham, Springer, 2021) 131.

[21] MA Hjort, 'Class Actions and Group Litigation: A Norwegian Perspective', in A Uzelac and S Voet (eds), *Class Actions in Europe: Holy Grail or a Wrong Trail?* (Cham, Springer, 2021) 165; L Ervo, 'Group Actions in East-Nordic Legal Culture', in A Uzelac and S Voet (eds), *Class Actions in Europe: Holy Grail or a Wrong Trail?* (Cham, Springer, 2021) 177.

[22] A Stadler, 'German Collective Actions: Is Litigation Funding in a Dead End?', in X Kramer and others (eds), *Frontiers in Civil Justice: Privatisation, Monetisation and Digitisation* (Cheltenham, Edward Elgar, 2022) 259; B Gsell, C Meller-Hannich and A Stadler, 'Prozessfinanzierung in Deutschland vor dem Hintergrund Europäischer Regelungsinitiativen' (2023) 78 *JuristenZeitung* 989.

[23] P Rott, 'The New German Representative Action: A Mixed Bag' [2024] *European Journal of Consumer Law* 154.

[24] CMS Report 2024 (n 17).

[25] See, eg, B Krans, 'The Dutch Act on Collective Settlement of Mass Damages' (2014) 27 *Pacific McGeorge Global Business & Development Law Journal* 281; H van Lith, 'The Dutch Collective Settlements Act and Private International Law' (Antwerp, Maklu, 2011).

[26] I Tzankova and X Kramer, 'From Injunction and Settlement to Action: Collective Redress and Funding in the Netherlands', in A Uzelac and S Voet (eds), *Class Actions in Europe: Holy Grail or a Wrong Trail?* (Cham, Springer, 2021) 97.

which the RAD applies – as the existing legislative framework was considered to be largely in compliance with the Directive.[27]

Along with the rise of collective actions, strategic litigation has also gained importance in Europe. Collective actions cover a broad range of cases, including cases dealing with consumer law, labour law, cartel damage cases, product liability, and privacy law. Not all of these come under the umbrella of 'strategic litigation' – those intended to promote a broader societal or political change[28] – but some cases, particularly in the area of consumer law (for instance in the Dieselgate scandal) or labour law, go beyond the mere purpose of enforcing private rights and obtaining compensation. The two most notable areas in which strategic or public interest litigation has gained importance in Europe are human rights law and – in part overlapping with that – environmental law.[29]

The Dutch WAMCA has a slightly different regime for 'idealistic' collective claims; in such cases, not all – rather strict – requirements for representative organisations apply.[30] This regime only applies when the case has an idealistic purpose and the financial interests involved are limited, or the nature of the claim of the foundation or the individuals whose interests are at stake require so. This provision doesn't seem to lend itself to being applied, for instance, in environmental cases or privacy cases where substantial compensation is requested. However, it has been applied in a copyright case where societal interests were considered to be at stake[31] and in a claim against a pharmaceutical company.[32]

B. The Rise of Third-Party Litigation Funding

As mentioned above, one of the triggers of the rise of TPLF and the ensuing discussions on the merits and risks of commercial funding is the development of collective actions requiring appropriate funding.

A clear example of this can be seen in the Netherlands, where the enactment of the WAMCA in 2020 enabled collective actions for compensation and has resulted in a growing market for TPLF.[33] The 2023 Study commissioned by the Dutch Ministry of Justice found that all compensatory collective actions filed so

[27] Kramer and others (n 7) 39f; X Kramer, 'The Quest for Funding Under the Dutch WAMCA: Third Party Funding and the Viability of a Procedural Fund' (2024) 38 *Emory International Law Review* 101, 109.

[28] See, eg, A Maglica, 'Public End through Private Means: A Comparative Study on Public Interest Litigation in Europe' [2023] *Erasmus Law Review* 71; J Setzer and C Higham, 'Global Trends in Climate Change Litigation: 2024 Snapshot' (Grantham Research Institute on Climate Change and the Environment, LSE – June 2024); J Barrett and H Lau, 'Trends in Public Law Climate Litigation: A Comparative Analysis of the UK and Australia' [2023] *Judicial Review* 28(3) 178.

[29] ibid.

[30] Art 3:305a para 6 Dutch Civil Code (DCC); see, Kramer and others (n 7) 38f.

[31] District Court Midden-Nederland, 2 June 2021, ECLI:NL:RBMNE:2021:2142 ('*Brein v YISP*').

[32] District Court Amsterdam, 17 July 2024, ECLI:NL:RBAMS:2024:4255 ('*Farma v AbbVie*').

[33] See Introduction; Kramer and others (n 7) 63ff.

far have been financed by commercial funders.[34] This trend may be explained by the lack of alternative funding options, such as public legal aid, a litigation fund as is available in Canadian jurisdictions, or contingency fees, which are permitted, for instance, in England and the United States but not in the Netherlands.[35] It also suggests that (certain) high-value collective actions are seen as attractive investments by commercial litigation funders.[36] It is important to note that the total number of collective actions in the Netherlands remains limited. In the first four and a half years following the enactment of the WAMCA, a total of 94 collective actions have been brought, with only about one-quarter involving claims for damages.[37]

Despite the recent hype in regulatory and academic circles across Europe about the funding of collective actions, TPLF has a much longer history and has long been well-established in other areas, such as arbitration, commercial litigation, and personal liability cases across various regions. In Scandinavia, particularly in Sweden, TPLF has significantly developed in commercial litigation but hardly plays a role in collective actions, which are uncommon in practice. Similarly, in Germany, commercial funding for collective actions has been limited, even if TPLF has gained traction in other sectors. Additionally, in jurisdictions like Germany, Austria, or Italy, bundling claims through assignment models and debt collection services have functioned as a cost- and time-efficient alternative to traditional collective actions.[38] Further historical and regional factors have led to varying degrees of TPLF integration across different European legal systems and have influenced how TPLF is applied in collective actions and consumer claims. These factors include litigation cultures, the degree of privatisation of dispute resolution, strong reliance on public enforcement, allowance of contingency fees, availability of litigation insurance, and investment conditions.

While the TPLF market has developed unevenly across jurisdictions, it has seen a remarkable growth in recent years, evolving into a global industry valued at billions of dollars.[39] According to data from 2021, the United States dominates, holding over 50 per cent of the market value, but Europe has rapidly gained

[34] ibid 167f.

[35] ibid.

[36] For more on that see also subsection IV.C.

[37] All collective actions are registered in the WAMCA Register www.rechtspraak.nl/Registers/centraal-register-voor-collectieve-vorderingen (accessed 15 August 2024). See for data analyses Kramer and others (n 7) 81ff; Deminor & Finch, 'Four Years of WAMCA: A Third Quantitative Analysis' (2024) www.deminor.com/en/news-insights/four-years-of-wamca-a-third-quantitative-analysis/.

[38] D Markworth, 'The German Litigation Funding Market's Black Swan Event: Take-Aways from a New World of Litigation Funding and Legal Services Provision', in X Kramer and others (eds), *Sustaining Access to Justice: New Avenues for Costs and Funding* (Oxford, Hart Publishing, forthcoming); G Afferni, 'Bundling of Claims by Way of Assignment in Italy' (2022) 2 *Mass Claims* 30.

[39] For more quantitative data and further sources, see: European Parliamentary Research Service (EPRS), 'Responsible Private Funding of Litigation' (March 2021) 3ff, 49ff ('EPRS Studies'); S Augenhofer and A Dori, 'The Proposed Regulation of Third Party Litigation Funding: Much Ado About Nothing? [2023] *Zeitschrift für das Privatrecht der Europäischen Union* 198.

momentum.[40] The TPLF market in the EU-27 accounted for about 15 per cent of the global market in 2021, with projections suggesting significant further increases in the future.[41] This growth has been fuelled by regulatory changes, a rising demand for access to justice, and the appeal of high-stake litigation. Germany, the Netherlands, and Portugal are emerging as key jurisdictions due to legal reforms and an uptick in collective actions, particularly in consumer and competition law.[42] The United Kingdom remains Europe's most advanced TPLF market, primarily driven by complex commercial disputes but also collective consumer actions.[43] Overall, commercial litigation is the largest segment of TPLF investments across Europe, followed by arbitration and bankruptcy claims, with antitrust funding especially prevalent in Germany, Italy, the Netherlands, the UK, and Spain. The expansion of the EU TPLF market reflects the strategic interests of commercial funders in investing in EU-related litigation and the growing acceptance of TPLF as a legitimate funding mechanism.

This trend is also supported by the establishment of funders associations. Most importantly for present purposes is the European Litigation Funders Association (ELFA), which is modelled after the successful self-regulatory body of the Association of Litigation Funders in England & Wales (ALF),[44] and was established in June 2022 to promote the interests of the TPLF market in Europe and advance best practices within the industry.[45]

C. The Legal Framework for Third-Party Litigation Funding

Despite its growing relevance, the TPLF market in the EU operates within a largely unregulated legal landscape. The RAD was the first to provide a European framework addressing both specific aspects of TPLF and the general funding questions of qualified entities which may also intersect with TPLF.[46] Article 10 of the RAD allows funding by a commercial party, as far as allowed under national law, provided that conflicts of interests are prevented, and funders do not unduly influence litigation. Additionally, qualified entities must disclose their funding sources to courts or administrative authorities, which may take necessary measures to ensure compliance, such as modifying funding arrangements or rejecting the entity's standing. The RAD general provisions on funding, potentially affecting TPLF too, include a list of requirements for qualified entities (Article 4),

[40] T Holzheu and others, 'U.S. litigation Funding and Social Inflation: The Rising Costs of Legal Liability' (Swiss Re Institute, 9 December 2021) 3.

[41] ibid; EPRS Studies (n 39) 4.

[42] CMS Report 2024 (n 17) 12, 15.

[43] R Mulheron, 'A Review of Litigation Funding in England and Wales: A Legal Literature and Empirical Study' (Legal Services Board 28 March 2024) 23 ff.

[44] For more on ALF see ibid 49ff.

[45] See elfassociation.eu/ (accessed 15 August 2024).

[46] For an overview see Kramer and others (n 7) 71ff; Kramer (n 27) 111f; Augenhofer and Dori (n 39) 202ff (with further references).

such as being non-profit, independent from external economic interests, and transparent about their funding sources. Article 20 requires Member States to ensure that the costs of proceedings do not prevent qualified entities from bringing claims, mandating that Member States secure appropriate funding through measures like limiting administrative fees, providing public funding, and offering structural support. Whether awarding a percentage of damages to third-party funders aligns with Article 20 (as it may affect the damages awarded to consumers) has been questioned in the literature.[47]

Beyond the RAD provisions, the EU lacks a cohesive legal framework governing TPLF, leaving regulation largely to individual Member States. While most EU Member States, except for Greece and Ireland, have permitted TPLF when implementing the RAD,[48] some have imposed stricter requirements. Germany, in particular, stands out for its stringent approach to TPLF in the context of collective actions, capping funders' profits at 10 per cent of the awarded compensation.[49]

Most of the regulation of TPLF has relied on self-regulation through codes of conduct, best practices, and ethical guidelines rather than formal legislation. In the United Kingdom, the Association of Litigation Funders (ALF) has established a Code of Conduct as a primary guideline for its members.[50] Similarly, a self-regulatory instrument has long been utilised in the Netherlands ('ClaimCode') and was amended in 2019 to include a new principle governing TPLF.[51] In 2022, the European Litigation Funding Association (ELFA) also introduced its Code of Conduct.[52] Recognising the significance of costs and funding, and more importantly the need for harmonised solutions, the ELI-UNIDROIT Model European Rules of Civil Procedure provided guidance on how modern dispute resolution frameworks should approach TPLF and issues of transparency and conflicts of interest (Articles 237 and 245).[53] Similarly, the European Law Institute (ELI) has engaged in a two-year-long project to develop guiding principles for TPLF, which were adopted in October 2024.[54]

Triggered by the rise of TPLF and its implications for collective actions within the EU, the European Parliament (EP) has stepped in, urging for regulating TPLF.

[47] Gsell (n 14), 1397ff; *cf.* Kramer (n 27) 112.

[48] See CMS, 'Class Actions Report 2023' 20.

[49] Rott (n 23) 272f; Markworth (n 38).

[50] Association of Litigation Funders of England and Wales (ALF), 'Code of Conduct for Litigation Funders' (January 2018) associationoflitigationfunders.com/wp-content/uploads/2018/03/Code-Of-Conduct-for-Litigation-Funders-at-Jan-2018-FINAL.pdf (accessed 15 August 2024); see also Mulheron (n 43) 49ff.

[51] Commissie Claimcode, Claimcode 2019 (Boom juridisch 2019); see also Kramer and others (n 7) 70ff.

[52] Available at elfassociation.eu/about/code-of-conduct (accessed 15 August 2024).

[53] See further X Kramer, 'The ELI-Unidroit Model European Rules of Civil Procedure: Key Features and Prospects of Costs and Funding of Collective Redress', in S Amrani-Mekki and T Clay (eds), *Mélanges en l'honneur du Professeur Loïc Cadiet* (Paris, LexisNexis, 2023) 823.

[54] See www.europeanlawinstitute.eu/projects-publications/current-projects/current-projects/eli-third-party-funding-of-litigation/ (accessed 30 October 2024).

In June 2021, a draft report, commonly referred to as the 'Voss Report' after its rapporteur, German MEP Axel Voss, was introduced into the political debate.[55] Supported by two EPRS studies,[56] the Voss Report advocated for a cautious approach to mitigate the potential risks associated with the commercialisation of justice and conflicts of interest between litigation funders and claimants, particularly the risk of funders exerting excessive control over legal proceedings and claiming disproportionate shares of the proceeds. In September 2022, the EP adopted a resolution on the responsible funding of litigation, calling for a directive to comprehensively regulate TPLF operations.[57] Its draft directive includes rules on governance, oversight, and transparency, proposing measures such as fee caps, fiduciary duties to claimants, and a system for the approval of TPLF activities similar to those in financial services. The EP's resolution has sparked a lively academic and policy debate, with some scholars questioning the need and motives for such stringent measures and practitioners criticising the potential impact on the litigation funding industry.[58]

In response, the European Commission chose not to instantly align with the EP's vision. Instead, it initiated a study to map the regulation and practice of TPLF across EU Member States, seeking to gain a clearer understanding of the current landscape before taking possible further action.[59]

In conclusion, while the TPLF market in the EU is gaining prominence, it still operates within a largely unregulated legal landscape. The discretion left to the Member States has resulted in a patchwork of regulations, with some Member States adopting stricter measures or at least a more cautious approach emphasising transparency, avoidance of conflicts of interest, and – from a broader perspective – the pitfalls of 'ambulance chasing', a practice where funders may aggressively seek out potential litigants to profit from their claims.

III. Funders at the Forefront and in the Shadow of the Procedure

Following the exploration of the procedural context and the rise and regulation of TPLF in Europe, this section will focus on to how TPLF operates. It will outline the

[55] See European Parliament, Draft Report with recommendations to the Commission on Responsible Private Funding of Litigation 2020/2130(INL) ('Voss Report').

[56] See EPRS Studies (n 39).

[57] See European Parliament resolution (n 5).

[58] See Augenhofer and Dori (n 39) 204ff (with further references). See, generally, A Cordina, 'Is It All That Fishy? A Critical Review of the Concerns Surrounding Third Party Litigation Funding in Europe' [2021] *Erasmus Law Review* 270.

[59] The Study with the title 'Mapping Third-Party Litigation Funding in the European Union' is conducted by the British Institute of International and Comparative Law (BIICL) in collaboration with Civic Consulting, the Asser Institute, and Risk & Policy Analysts (RPA). No public information has been published yet.

complexities and diversity surrounding the provision of litigation funding before proposing a classification that we believe highlights the various roles funders play within the legal and justice system.

A. The Ambiguities in Litigation Funding Operations

A typical litigation funding agreement involves a commercial funder providing financial support to a litigant in exchange for a portion of the award or settlement if the case is successful. This core business model of TPLF constitutes a breakthrough in the legal sector. However, subject as it is to varying regulatory perspectives, litigation funding has encountered challenges and restrictions across jurisdictions.[60]

In response to such regulatory pressures, the TPLF industry has undergone significant adaptations,[61] demonstrating remarkable creativity and innovation.[62] New economic paradigms among funders, clients, and lawyers have emerged, and new funding structures,[63] such as the aforementioned assignment of claims,[64] have blurred traditional boundaries,[65] particularly when claims are transferred without accompanying procedural rights or legal standing.[66] Complex funding arrangements often make it difficult to trace the origins and scope of funding,[67] while triangular relationships involving intermediaries, brokers, consultants, legal advisors, or Special-Purpose-Vehicles (SPVs),[68] and the development of a secondary market for trading litigation finance investments[69]

[60] See above subsection II.C.

[61] M DeStefano, 'Nonlawyers Influencing Lawyers: Too Many Cooks in the Kitchen or Stone Soup?' (2012) 80 *Fordham Law Review* 2791, 2843ff, who (drawing on the work of S Johnson, *Where Good Ideas Come From: The Natural History of Innovation* (London, Penguin, 2010) 145f) applies concepts such as adaptation and mutations to discuss evolutionary models in legal financing.

[62] M Steinitz, 'The Litigation Finance Contract' (2012) 54 *William & Mary Law Review* 455, 461; R Avraham and A Sebok, 'An Empirical Investigation of Third Party Consumer Litigant Funding' (2019) 104 *Cornell Law Review* 1133; M MacSweeney, 'Litigation Finance Spurs Innovation by Moving Past Single Cases', *Bloomberg Law* (16 March 2023) news.bloomberglaw.com/us-law-week/litigation-finance-spurs-innovation-by-moving-past-single-cases (accessed 15 August 2024).

[63] A Sebok, 'The Inauthentic Claim' (2011) 64 *Vanderbilt Law Review* 61, 66ff; T Healey, MB McDonald and TS Haley, 'Litigation Finance Investing: Alternative Investment Returns in the Presence of Information Asymmetry' (2022) 24 *Journal of Alternative Investments* 110, 111, 115.

[64] See also above subsection II.A.

[65] D Markworth, 'Coding a Collective Consumer Redress Vehicle in Germany' (2023) 12 *Journal of European Consumer and Market Law* 89; G Afferni, 'Bundling of Claims by Way of Assignment in Italy' (2022) 2 *Mass Claims* 30.

[66] Stadler (n 22) 268ff.

[67] AJ Sebok, 'The Rules of Professional Responsibility and Legal Finance: A Status Update' (2022) 57 *Wake Forest Law Review* 777, 779ff.

[68] Stadler (n 22) 265.

[69] J Freund, 'Secondary' Investing in Litigation Finance: Why, Why Now, and How to Approach Investing in Lit Fin Secondaries' *Litigation Funding Journal* (1 March 2022) legalfundingjournal.com/secondary-investing-in-litigation-finance-why-why-now-and-how-to-approach-investing-in-lit-fin-secondaries/ (accessed 15 August 2024).

add further layers of complexity to the already complicated legal and economic landscape of the litigation finance industry.[70] Such complexities, in turn, make the provision of litigation funding notably fluid and resistant to categorisation within traditional legal frameworks and conceptual boxes.

Diversification also characterises the approaches across jurisdictions regarding whether commercial litigation funding should be classified as banking or financial services. This is the case, for instance, in Italy,[71] while similar, albeit unsuccessful, attempts have been made in Australia.[72] The understanding of TPLF as a banking or financial service (and consequently the characterisation of the provision of the funding as a form of credit, investment, or insurance service) becomes crucial because it triggers stricter authorisation requirements and prudential supervision by public authorities.[73]

B. The Funders' Role in Civil Procedure

Despite the fluid structure of litigation funding agreements and the ambiguities surrounding the regulation of litigation financing, it is crucial to acknowledge the multifaceted role funders play.

Even the strongest advocates of TPLF would agree that, at the core, commercial funders are driven by egoistic motives – their main incentive is to achieve profitable returns. However, this pursuit of profit does not preclude their actions from having broader implications. In fact, their self-interest can often align with public benefits, positively impacting the legal system.

In view of the complex functions that TPLF performs, and the undeniable profit motives involved, we propose a classification that sketches and highlights the various positive roles funders can assume within the legal and justice system. These roles can be distinguished as follows: (a) identifying violations and breaches

[70] M Steinitz, 'Whose Claim Is This Anyway – Third Party Litigation Funding' (2011) 95 *Minnesota Law Review* 1269, 1276, 1282ff.

[71] In Italy, there are currently no rules or official interpretations as to whether TPLF should have a licence under the existing financial law framework and, if so, which one. However, some hints on the financial authorities' position can be drawn by looking at the main (and, to our knowledge, only) market participant: Be Cause Sicaf Spa. This is an entity that qualifies as a collective investment undertaking, shaped in the form of an investment company with fixed share capital. As its authorisation specifies, Be Cause carries out collective management of credits (data on the authorisation can be found at www.bancaditalia.it/). In turn, one can infer that TPLF performed by an investment company (and more broadly by assets managers) qualifies as collective asset management, regardless of its non-recourse nature and of whether it takes the form of claim assignment (monetisation), the two forms of TPLF Be Cause performs (www.because.law/).

[72] For more see M Legg, 'The Rise and Regulation of Litigation Funding in Australian Class Actions' [2021-4] *Erasmus Law Review* 221; J Geisker and D Luff, 'The Third Party Litigation Funding Law Review: Australia', The Law Reviews (8 December 2022) thelawreviews.co.uk/title/the-third-party-litigation-funding-law-review/australia (accessed 15 August 2024).

[73] See also VS Sahani, 'Global Laboratories of Third-Party Funding Regulation' (2021) 115 *AJIL Unbound* 34, 37f; VS Sahani, '"Keep to the Code:" A Global Ethics Code for Third-Party Funders, (2022) 102 *Boston University Law Review* 2331, 2366ff.

of legal rights; (b) empowering claimants by facilitating access to justice and mitigating associated risks; and (c) contributing to the development of case law.

This subsection will analyse each of these functions in detail, incorporating insights from the three interviews with funders conducted for the purpose of this chapter.[74] While the interviews express the views of funders, the findings have been critically assessed by the authors to ensure a thorough analysis.

i. Detecting Violations and Breaches

Litigation funders play a pivotal role in identifying rights infringements, often on a large scale. In this capacity, they can act as detectors of legal violations, uncovering breaches that might otherwise go unnoticed, especially in complex and opaque legal landscapes where financial constraints hinder claimants. By leveraging their expertise and resources, funders can provide additional oversight and enable that more instances of wrongdoing are addressed through legal channels. This role is crucial across all legal systems, whether they rely primarily on public or on private enforcement.

The involvement of litigation funders as detectors of violations typically begins with a lawyer (or a specialised law firm) representing individual claimants, groups of claimants, or consumer associations approaching a funder. The interviews revealed that this practice is particularly prevalent in Europe, where portfolio funding and external ownership of law firms by investors remain largely unknown or restricted[75] compared to other legal systems.[76] Contact between the party requiring funding and the funder is usually initiated by a legal representative. Legal representatives have their own reasons for initiating contacts with funders. In all legal systems, attorneys must advise their clients about all financial risks of litigation, including legal fees and court costs. When clients cannot afford such expenses and risks, lawyers consider it impractical to proceed. As was clear from the interviews, this financial challenge explains the growing interest among lawyers in connecting with funders. When approached with potential cases, factors such as the reputation of lawyers give funders initial confidence in the validity of a case, and the assurance that it will be handled with the highest level of expertise and professionalism. High-reputation lawyers are more likely to present well-prepared and meritorious cases, thereby increasing the likelihood of a favourable outcome and hence helping funders managing financial risks effectively. Therefore, trust and credibility, play a pivotal role for funders when deciding to invest in a case.

[74] See Introduction.

[75] The question whether a German prohibition of outside equity investments (shareholders) in law firms violated fundamental freedoms of EU law is currently pending at the CJEU; see Case C-295/23 *Halmer Rechtsanwaltsgesellschaft*, Opinion of AG Campos Sánchez-Bordona, ECLI:EU:C:2024:581; See also Markworth (n 38); Augenhofer and Dori (n 39) 200.

[76] See A Pona, 'Trending: Non-Lawyer Ownership of Law Firms' (2022) 36 *Commercial Law World* 24, 27.

It is submitted that labelling litigation funders as mere ambulance chasers is a misleading portrayal and simplification of their role. In reality, funders in Europe are not pursuing ambulances but are invited to join the litigation journey, working alongside reputable lawyers to help realise legal remedies. This intermediary role of lawyers must not be disregarded. It shows that, at least in Europe, professional funders are not typically the ones initiating contact with potential claimants, nor do claimants usually approach funders directly. Instead, it is common for potential claimants to reach out to funders through their legal representatives. This practice ensures that claimants receive proper legal counsel before engaging with funders and remain guided by their lawyers throughout the process.

In addition, it appears that funders actively cultivate strong relationships with reputable law firms.[77] This practice facilitates a steady flow of high-quality cases and streamlines the evaluation process. While these collaborations enhance efficiency and provide funders with valuable initial assessments, they do not eliminate the need for independent case screening. The interviewees emphasised that the initial reports from claimants' lawyers, while insightful, are insufficient due to potential misalignments of interests between lawyers and funders. Therefore, funders must conduct their own due diligence,[78] often seeking input from external legal experts for an unbiased perspective. Regardless of the involvement of independent legal experts, the critical role of lawyers in connecting funders with cases – hence with potential claimants – underlines the need for regulation of the TPLF market to be closely tied to the regulation of legal professionals. Effective oversight of TPLF requires acknowledging the pivotal role of lawyers in the entire process and ensuring adherence to ethical and professional standards.

Establishing initial contact with funders is just the start of their role as detectors of legal violations. To manage the complexity of modern collective actions, funders – whether operating independently or in collaboration with the claimant's lawyers – increasingly rely on information technology (IT) solutions, particularly during the book-building phase, to streamline case-building, evaluation, and funding processes.[79] This approach is especially relevant within collective opt-in systems, which are most common in European jurisdictions and in which the funders often lead in managing communication with clients and aggregating claims. In such cases, technology plays a crucial role in mobilising potential claimants to join collective efforts, enhancing participation and coordination, which in turn improves the detection of large-scale violations. However, technology has a dual nature. While it facilitates the engagement of victims in opt-in mechanisms, it can also be used by defendants to dissuade participation in opt-out collective

[77] For similar US trends see Avraham and Sebok (n 62) 1164ff.

[78] See also below subsection IV.C.

[79] See, eg, Stadler (n 22) 260; For TPLF and the intersections in the case of *Dieselgate* see van Elten and Rehder (n 3); Hensler and others (n 3).

actions. For example, in a Dutch labour case initiated by labour unions against an online work platform, around a quarter of the workers making use of this platform opted out as a result of (possibly misleading) campaigning by the platform to opt out, which was enabled by simply clicking a button. This resulted in the claim being partially declared inadmissible.[80] Although this example is not related to a commercially funded case, it illustrates the potentially disruptive effect of technology and social media on collective litigation, depending on the model adopted during the book-building phase.

ii. Empowering Claimants

The TPLF market addresses a critical financial disparity in litigation, particularly in 'David vs. Goliath' scenarios, where victims lack the resources to pursue legal action against powerful defendants.[81] TPLF steps in and provides essential financial support, levelling the playing field and enabling claimants to seek justice and hold wrongdoers accountable. It is precisely the funder's interest in matching the claimant's demand by funding the legal claim that gave rise to the TPLF market, as, if such claims succeed, have the potential to generate revenues for investors. For these reasons, the TPLF market has predominantly evolved to serve claimants, ensuring their access to justice, although a developing market also caters to defendants.[82]

Therefore, a fundamental role of third-party litigation funders, or at least the result of the availability of TPLF, is empowering potential claimants by providing the necessary financial support to all associated costs, thereby enabling individuals to seek redress in court. This democratisation of legal resources ensures that justice is not exclusively reserved for those with substantial financial means but is accessible to a broader and more vulnerable segment of society.[83] We submit that funders can play a critical role in promoting fairness and equity within the judicial system by lowering the financial barriers to litigation, especially in times of economic austerity and governmental constraints.[84]

[80] District Court Amsterdam, 11 October 2023, ECLI:NL:RBAMS:2023:6389 (*FNV and CNV v Temper*); Kramer (n 27) 107.

[81] P Beasley and B Summerfield, 'The Users of Litigation Finance: Who, Where, When and Why?', in S Friel (ed), *The Law and Business of Litigation Finance* (London, Bloomsbury Professional, 2020) 319, 335.

[82] E Samra, 'The Business of Defense: Defense-Side Litigation Financing' (2016) 83 *University of Chicago Law Review* 2299; L Pollard, 'Is Funding Defendants the Future of Disputes?' Fivehundred Magazine (June 2019) 93 www.legal500.com/fivehundred-magazine/editors-views/is-funding-defendants-the-future-of-disputes/ (accessed 15 August 2024).

[83] See also C Ucin, 'How Can Business Best Approach Human Rights in Third-Party Litigation Funding?' [2023-2] *Erasmus Law Review* 102.

[84] See X Kramer, C Ucin and A Dori, 'Challenges to Access to Civil Justice in the European Context', in M Woo and R van Rhee (eds), *Handbook of Comparative Civil Procedure Law* (Cheltenham, Edward Elgar, forthcoming).

While TPLF traditionally focused on aiding those unable to afford legal expenses, there is a shift towards funders being used to mitigate litigation risks even for wealthier litigants, who, while capable of bearing legal costs, prefer to minimise their financial exposure. This trend can be observed in business-to-business (B2B) scenarios, where funders are increasingly engaged in managing the financial uncertainties of litigation. Unlike legal expense insurance, which is typically arranged before any legal issue arises, funders step in to cover legal expenses after the event. The interviews reveal that this shift is especially relevant in the Nordic markets, where legal expense insurance often provides limited coverage for large commercial claims, making TPLF an attractive option for managing substantial legal costs.

iii. Enriching Case Law

While critically viewed by some, the availability of TPLF can also play a role in advancing and enriching case law. It can bridge financial gaps, enabling legal issues to reach the courts that might otherwise be neglected. Funders support a wide range of cases: from straightforward contractual, tort, and competition disputes to complex high-profile constitutional or societal matters, recognising that every case, regardless of complexity, can influence legal precedent while also offering viable returns on investment. By backing these cases, it can be ensured that even 'David vs. Goliath' scenarios and cases with smaller, widespread damages have their day in court. This facilitates the enforcement of rights and the evolution of legal doctrine. As funded cases progress, they contribute to new legal applications, clarifications, and the development of jurisprudence. Additionally, funders may enhance the quality of legal arguments by enabling claimants to secure top-tier legal representation and expert witnesses; well-prepared cases lead to more thorough examinations of issues and more precise judicial rulings.

The active role of experienced funders in shaping the legal landscape not only drives the ongoing assessment and refinement of the law. It can drive the adaptation of law to societal changes, contemporary challenges, and technological advancements. For example, in the Netherlands, funders have been crucial in supporting lawsuits on privacy, climate litigation, and other strategic (collective) actions.[85] The fact that under the new Dutch WAMCA regime, all compensatory collective actions have been backed by funders[86] demonstrates that without TPLF, the WAMCA compensatory scheme might have remained a theoretical framework – a law in the books studied primarily by students – rather than a practical tool applied by courts and actively shaping real-world legal outcomes. Thus, funders are instrumental in advancing collective litigation and ensuring that these legal innovations translate into effective practice for litigants and courts.

[85] Kramer (n 27) 104ff.
[86] Kramer and others (n 7) 65, 85; see also subsection II.B.

Historically, litigation funders have focused on specific legal areas where pattern recognition based on established precedents allows for more accurate outcome predictions, such as collective actions following cartel damages claims after binding competition authority decisions.[87] Conversely, they have often avoided novel, high-risk cases lacking such predictability, like climate litigation, due to concerns about the viability of TPLF investments.[88]

However, the litigation funding market has recently shifted, particularly with the rapid growth of Environmental, Social, and Corporate Governance (ESG) litigation, centred on climate-related cases.[89] Studies indicate that the number of climate-related cases globally is on the rise.[90] By the end of 2022, around 2,200 climate cases had been filed across 65 jurisdictions and various adjudicatory bodies,[91] with over 1,500 in the US and 650 elsewhere.[92] This number is expected to increase.[93] While methodological challenges and pending cases complicate the data on judicial outcomes, evidence suggests a success rate with over 50 per cent of decisions favouring climate actions.[94] In areas like climate-washing litigation, this rate exceeds 70 per cent, presenting significant market opportunities for funders.[95]

Recent trends show a growing focus on ESG litigation among funders, who increasingly view certain subsets of climate-related disputes, especially those with clear social and environmental stakes, as fundable.[96] The interviews confirm this trend, showing well-established funders' willingness to support high-risk, lower-margin cases with significant ESG impacts, including those related to climate change, environmental damage, and social justice. NGOs play a crucial role, seeking both commercial returns and positive ESG outcomes. The intersection of TPLF with ESG and NGO efforts is driving meaningful change, with some funders allocating now ethically oriented capital (according to the interviews up to 20 per cent of their resources) to cases with important social and environmental benefits, despite lower financial returns. However, challenges remain. The interviews revealed internal tensions within funding institutions, as profit motives may clash with social responsibility, with institutional investors often favouring more

[87] See, eg, T Kohlmeier and M Wegmüller, 'ESG and Litigation Funding – Tied at the Hip? A Practitioners View', in X Kramer and others (eds), *Sustaining Access to Justice: New Avenues for Costs and Funding* (Oxford, Hart Publishing, forthcoming).

[88] ibid.

[89] ibid.

[90] Setzer and Higham (n 28); the Sabin Center for Climate Change Law provides two comprehensive databases with climate change caselaw; see climatecasechart.com/ (accessed 15 August 2024).

[91] United Nations Environment Programme, 'Global Climate Litigation Report: 2023 Status Review' (2023) 9.

[92] ibid.

[93] ibid 63ff.

[94] Setzer and Higham (n 28) 28.

[95] ibid 38; see also L Rogerson, 'Majority of Climate-washing Litigation Succeeds in Producing Positive Outcomes but Prompts Companies to Proceed Cautiously' *Thompson Reuters* (19 July 2024) www.thomsonreuters.com/en-us/posts/esg/climate-washing-litigation/ (accessed 15 August 2024).

[96] Kohlmeier and Wegmüller (n 87).

financially rewarding cases. This tension can limit involvement in socially impactful matters outside their financial mandates.

Amidst ongoing regulatory debates, at present especially in Europe, funders are faced with evolving expectations. Policymakers and regulatory bodies are increasingly scrutinising TPLF practices, emphasising transparency, ethical conduct, and stricter standards.[97] As funders and their employees express a growing desire to contribute meaningfully to ESG issues, balancing profit with societal purpose becomes crucial. Whether driven by a genuine commitment to social change, the pursuit of profit, or the need to enhance their reputation amid intensifying calls for regulatory oversight, the intersection of ESG and TPLF is (potentially) highly impactful. It brings more cases into the legal system, allowing critical ESG issues to reach courts, set legal precedents, and influence governmental decisions. Thus, funders can play a key role in advancing ESG litigation, shaping the legal landscape, and meeting societal demands for accountability and sustainability.

IV. Debating the Funders' Role

A. The Polarised Views: Greed or Good?

The previous section highlights the tripartite role of TPLF in the legal system: funders can help detect legal violations, empower claimants, and contribute to enriching case law. While these functions are valuable, they raise concerns about entrusting such pivotal roles to profit-motivated private actors. Yet, while the profit incentive is undeniable, the positive impact of funders in all the functions mentioned above cannot be disregarded. This leads to a crucial question: Should the potential risks of privatising these functions outweigh the benefits funders can bring to the legal landscape?

In a Manichaean world, where everything is perceived in stark terms of absolute good versus absolute evil, funders could be seen in extremes. Unfortunately, the political and policy debate surrounding the future regulation of the TPLF market, particularly in Europe, influenced as it is by varying motivations and interests, often falls prey to such polarised views. Some critics argue against litigation funders using rhetoric that resembles the portrayal of *Gordon Gekko*, the character from the movie 'Wall Street' who embodies the mantra 'Greed is good'. From this perspective, litigation funders are presented as ruthless profiteers exploiting others' misfortunes, leading to the commodification of justice, distortions of the legal process, an increase in unmeritorious lawsuits, and even risks

[97] See, eg, Voss Report (n 55); EP Resolution (n 5); for an overview analysis see Augenhofer and Dori (n 39).

to national security.[98] Conversely, funders can also be depicted as champions of justice, providing access to those who cannot afford it and strengthening the rule of law.[99] The truth, however, likely lies somewhere in the middle of these two extremes, reflecting the complexity of the funders' role.

Regardless of the regulatory perspective, one point is clear: from a purely economic perspective, TPLF offers an alternative means to pursue legal claims. The question, therefore, is not whether TPLF enables access to justice in certain cases – this should be uncontested – but whether the 'justice' accessed through TPLF is equivalent to the 'justice' that would have been available without such funding. To understand the broader implications of TPLF and the potential need for regulation, it is crucial to examine fundamental objections raised concerning the 'justice' offered by funders. These include the argument of the increase of litigation volume, particularly frivolous lawsuits (IV.B); the role of due diligence in selecting and managing funded cases (IV.C); and the degree of funder involvement, in the shadows of the procedure including issues of control, case management, and conflicts of interest (IV.D). We will also explore whether funding contracts can offer solutions (IV.E) and whether and how existing legal frameworks can address TPLF-related challenges (IV.F).

B. The Funders' Impact on Litigation Volume

A key argument in the critical literature on TPLF is the claim that it increases the number of lawsuits, particularly through portfolio funding.[100] But is this really the case, in particular within the European context?[101]

First, third-party litigation funders are rational actors focused on returns. Empirical evidence shows that funders accept only a small percentage of cases, with acceptance rates ranging from an estimated 3 to 5 per cent in the United Kingdom[102] and 5 to 10 per cent in some EU Member States, depending on the

[98] See, eg, US Chamber of Commerce – Institute for Legal Reforms (ILR), 'ILR Briefly: A New Threat: The National Security Risk of Third Party Litigation Funding' (November 2022); *cf.* J Freund, 'Unsubstantiated Arguments against Third Party Litigation Funding by the U.S. Chamber of Commerce' *Legal Funding Journal* (24 March 2023) legalfundingjournal.com/unsubstantiated-arguments-against-third-party-litigation-funding-by-the-u-s-chamber-of-commerce/ (accessed 15 August 2024).

[99] See, eg, International Legal Finance Association (ILFA), 'Resourcing the Rule of Law in Europe' (June 2023).

[100] See, eg, EPRS Studies (n 39) 20; US Chamber of Commerce – ILR (n 98).

[101] See also S Antill and SR Grenadier, 'Financing the Litigation Arms Race' (2023) 149 *Journal of Financial Economics* 218; EPRS Studies (n 39) 78; I Tillema, 'Entrepreneurial Motives in Dutch Collective Redress', in WH van Boom (ed), *Litigation, Costs, Funding and Behaviour: Implications for the Law* (Abingdon, Routledge, 2017) 222; J Skog, 'Illusory Truths and Frivolous Claims: Critical Reflections on a Report on Litigation Funding by the European Parliamentary Research Service', in E Storskrubb (ed), *YSEC Yearbook of Socio-Economic Constitutions 2022: Funding Justice* (Cham, Springer, 2022) 87.

[102] Mulheron (n 43) 33.

type of cases and the funder.[103] This data highlights the rigorous criteria funders apply,[104] countering the notion that they indiscriminately support cases like 'ambulance chasers'. This selectivity is reflected in the industry's high success rates; for example, litigation finance-backed cases in the United States have a loss rate of only 10–15 per cent,[105] with similarly low rates in the United Kingdom.[106]

These findings suggest that funders' experience in evaluating case merits is crucial to their decision-making and success. The selection process involves a multi-layered filtering system. Initially, the claimant's lawyers assess the case before approaching funders.[107] Trust, credibility, professionalism, and reputation are key at this stage. Funders then conduct their own thorough screening, either internally or with external legal experts, resulting in a very low acceptance rate for funded cases. Those cases that do proceed to court tend to have a very high success rate. To put this in perspective, out of 100 cases presented, fewer than ten receive funding. This high level of selectivity ensures that only well-founded cases move forward. The high success rate of these funded cases validates the funders' rigorous criteria: of the ten cases funded, roughly only one is lost. It is hard to believe that nine out of ten funded lawsuits are frivolous or unmeritorious and that the justice system failed to recognise and dismiss them. Even if that were the case, such realisation would signify a failure of the justice system rather than a flaw in the TPLF market.

The interviews have also revealed a fascinating paradox: the high success rates of funded cases stand out even more when considering the significant challenges reported by litigation funders. Despite relying on trusted and reputable lawyers, funders face adverse selection risks, sometimes encountering higher-risk cases that can be more complex, may take longer, and can be less predictable. After all, the difficulty, duration, and uncertainty of these cases may often drive claimants and their lawyers to seek funding, thereby increasing the funders' risks. Additionally, there is a concern about moral hazards. Knowing that financial losses are cushioned by the funder may influence claimants' behaviour, potentially leading them to pursue riskier litigation strategies with less prudence. The delicate balance between risk and reward becomes a tightrope for all parties involved. Despite these challenges, funders maintain high success rates through rigorous selection and strategic management.

Given these dynamics, it is not surprising that funders see themselves as 'gatekeepers' of the justice system. As one interviewee stated: 'We are probably saving the courts a lot of resources and time'. While this perspective is subject to change

[103] Estimates deriving from the interviews conducted in some Member States for this chapter and corroborated by information obtained through seminar presentations and earlier informal talks with funders.

[104] More on these criteria in subsection IV.C.

[105] Holzheu and others (n 40) 18.

[106] Mulheron (n 43) 96f.

[107] See above in text subsection III.B.i.

with new evidence, current data on the acceptance and success rates of funded cases supports rather than contradicts the funders' role as gatekeepers who reduce the burden on courts and benefit the justice system.

C. Due Diligence

Funders' rigorous approach to due diligence is evident in the types of cases they reject. Notably, cases that funders decline are not necessarily deemed frivolous but are assessed based on various factors.

The interviewees highlighted that the legal domain is a critical consideration in funders' initial assessments. Some areas, like follow-on competition damages claims, offer safer and more predictable investments and are therefore preferred due to their straightforward nature, clear evidence, and binding competition authority decisions. For example, the European Commission's record fines in the infamous 2016 European Truck Cartel[108] led to numerous follow-on actions and attracted significant third-party funding across multiple jurisdictions, eg, the United Kindom, the Netherlands, Spain, Portugal, and Germany. Funded European Truck Cartel cases have also spurred legal developments, including the long-awaited and well-discussed UK's *PACCAR* ruling of July 2023, addressing the enforceability of litigation funding agreements.[109] By contrast, funders are generally cautious about certain types of cases that present high-risk profiles, particularly in complex sectors. One such example, mentioned by one of the interviewees, are construction disputes which are avoided by some funders due to the need for local expertise and the difficulty in remotely assessing facts. These cases involve complex issues and heavy reliance on expert testimonies, increasing unpredictability and risk. Procedural factors, such as the reliability of evidence, are also pivotal. Cases hinging on uncertain or difficult-to-assess evidence, like single-witness testimonies, are typically excluded as their outcome often depends on the witness's ability to recall and convey critical details convincingly. According to one interviewee, this level of unpredictability renders those cases akin to 'gambling', which is at odds with the funders' objectives of minimising risk and ensuring more predictable returns on investment.

Funders employ a multifaceted approach to case selection, thoroughly evaluating risk, potential success, exposure, and expected return on investment. Decisions are influenced by factual, economic, and legal factors, including well-established

[108] In July 2016 and September 2017, the European Commission imposed record fines totalling approximately €3.8 billion on six major European truck manufacturers; see European Commission, 'Antitrust: Commission Fines Truck Producers €2.93 Billion for Participating in a Cartel' Press Release (Brussels, 19 July 2016); European Commission, 'Antitrust: Commission Fines Scania €880 Million for Participating in Trucks Cartel' Press Release (Brussels, 27 September 2017).

[109] *PACCAR v CAT* [2023] UKSC 28; R Mulheron, 'Unpacking Paccar: Statutory Interpretation and Litigation Funding' (2024) 83 *The Cambridge Law Journal* 99.

precedents.[110] Emerging areas, such as ESG litigation, are also being explored despite higher risks, as they represent potential new markets within third-party funding.[111] Existing literature extensively documents the factors influencing funders' decisions.[112] Our findings align with this research, highlighting that the value of the claim is paramount, requiring substantial returns on investment. Other critical considerations include cost accuracy, case strength, duration, evidence availability, and the presence of potential counterclaims. A high likelihood of success is essential, which invariably includes a merits review,[113] with due diligence ensuring funders make informed decisions that minimise risk and maximise returns.

Minimising risk exposure involves more than conducting a merits review. Imagine a scenario where the claimant wins, but the defendant proves elusive when it comes to satisfying the judgment (or arbitral award). In such instances, securing a favourable judgment is only part of the battle. The ability to enforce that judgment is equally crucial, and funders are often exposed to various enforcement risks.[114] If the defendant lacks resources, the chances of recovering the investment diminish. Some defendants may resist compliance, leading to prolonged satellite litigation. They might also attempt to transfer or hide assets during litigation. For all these reasons, the interviewees emphasised the importance of assessing the defendant's solvency and financial stability, the willingness to comply, and the location of their assets, particularly in cross-border cases, where different jurisdictions present varying enforcement challenges. From the literature it is clear that, for instance, in personal injury claims in the United States, funders and lawyers closely examine the defendant's insurance coverage.[115] Overall, as the interviewees emphasised, reliable defendants, such as banks or insurance companies, secure a higher probability of successful enforcement. Failure to enforce judgments undermines legal proceedings' effectiveness, serving no one's interests.

In conclusion, the high success rate of funded cases is not a mere game of playing the odds. It results from rigorous due diligence, balancing potential rewards against a spectrum of risks, including legal domains, precedents, evidentiary strength, financial considerations, and enforcement challenges. While fewer than ten out of 100 cases pass this stringent selection process and gain access to the courts,[116] those selected have a significantly higher chance of success, with

[110] See also above in text subsection III.B.c.

[111] ibid.

[112] For an overview see Mulheron (n 102) 33ff; EPRS Studies (n 39) 57ff; Avraham and Sebok (n 62); R Avraham and A Wickelgren, 'Third-Party Litigation Funding: A Signaling Model' (2014) 63 *DePaul Law Review* 233.

[113] EPRS Studies (n 39) 74.

[114] See also in detail A Hickson, 'High Risk, High Return', in S Friel (ed) *The Law and Business of Litigation Finance* (London, Bloomsbury Professional, 2020) 365, 381ff.

[115] Avraham and Sebok (n 62) 1148.

[116] See above nn 102–103.

an estimated nine out of ten likely to prevail.[117] This approach, while extremely selective, ultimately ensures that strong, well-supported cases advance, thereby enhancing the overall effectiveness and efficiency of the legal system.

However, the funders' selectivity raises important questions. One may ask: What about the 90 per cent of cases that funders reject? As one interviewee noted, cases that are denied funding may still be monitored, and experience shows that typically they do not progress and are abandoned. Do these cases not deserve their day in court? More critically, should this choice rest solely with funders? It is impossible to determine whether rejected cases lack merit or simply fail to promise the financial returns needed to justify the investment. In a perfect world – one with unlimited resources – every case would be heard in court regardless of its financial implications. Unfortunately, we do not live in such a perfect world. In our second-best reality – one with financial constraints that often prevent victims from seeking redress – funders provide solutions. The fact that ten out of 100 cases do proceed, thanks to TPLF, should not be overlooked. These aren't mere statistics; they represent access to justice for meritorious lawsuits. And while many cases do not reach court, the success of those that do highlights the essential role funders play in enabling access to justice.

The issue, therefore, is not that over 90 per cent of the cases suggested to funders do not move forward but that there are no viable alternatives for these cases. Instead of critiquing the selectivity of funders, who enable meritorious cases to go to court, the focus should be on understanding why so many others are left behind. The challenge lies not in the selectivity of funders but in the broader system that appears to leave so many potential claimants without viable alternatives and a path to justice.

D. Influence in the Shadows: Control, Case Management, and Conflicts of Interest

The degree of funders' involvement in litigation proceedings raises important issues regarding control, case management, and potential conflicts of interest. A common universal criticism of litigation funding is that funders can influence strategic decisions, such as lawyer selection, legal arguments, litigation expenses, or settlement choices. This influence can create tensions, particularly when funders' financial interests may not fully align with those of the claimants. It is precisely this potential influence on the course of the proceedings and conflict of interests that has been brought up by critiques and that has also been addressed by policymakers and legislators.[118]

[117] See above nn 105–106.

[118] See, eg, Voss Report (n 55) paras 5ff; European Parliament resolution (n 5) para 7; Art 10 RAD; Art 305a, paras 2 and 3 Dutch Civil Code (DCC).

i. Contextual Dynamics

Before making an attempt to provide a more nuanced analysis, two preliminary points must be made clear to understand the debate on the funders' influence.

First, context is critical. Legal systems are shaped by cultural, historical, and economic factors, which may also influence their approach to TPLF, among them how questions regarding the funders' involvement and control are handled. For example, a strong tradition of individual rights and autonomy underpins the US legal system that primarily relies on private enforcement and focuses heavily on commercial litigation, class actions, and punitive damages.[119] In such systems, concerns about funders' control would be typically viewed through the lens of contractual autonomy, with an emphasis on the freedom of litigants to engage with funders.

In contrast, in the EU, the legal system prioritises collective rights and public interest and often relies on public enforcement.[120] The focus is primarily on collective actions in issues crucial for the Internal Market, such as consumer rights, antitrust violations, and more recently, privacy and environment.[121] As litigation funding of compensatory collective actions becomes more important in these areas, the intersections between private and public enforcement intensify and blur further the lines,[122] creating a unique legal environment where concerns about funders' undue influence are heightened.[123] The RAD exemplifies this, raising fears of funders exerting control in cases involving significant societal and political interests, such as enforcing EU consumer law and, by extension, the safeguarding of the Internal Market. The contrast between the US and EU approaches shows how the debate on the funders' control and the severity of those issues may shift depending on the type of case and the interplay between collective rights, individual autonomy, and public interest considerations in a legal system.

The second point that requires attention concerns systemic parallels across legal contexts. Importantly, the influence of funders on legal proceedings may find resonance beyond the mere context of litigation funding, reflecting established patterns observed across various procedural scenarios.[124] For example, the

[119] See in general F Cafaggi and H-W Micklitz, 'Administrative and Judicial Collective Enforcement of Consumer Law in the US and the European Community' EUI LAW Working Paper No. 2007/22.

[120] See, eg, G Howells, 'European Consumer Law', in C Barnard and S Peers (eds), *European Union Law*, 2nd edn (Oxford, OUP, 2017) 686, 705ff.

[121] See subsection II.A.

[122] For the blurred lines between public and private enforcement in the EU see T Tridimas, 'Rights, Remedies, and Access to Justice in Consumer-Related Litigation: Is Union Law Fit for Purpose? [2023] *European Journal of Consumer Law* 513; A Jones and C Townley, 'Competition Law', in C Barnard and S Peers (eds), *European Union Law*, 2nd edn (Oxford, OUP, 2017) 509, 514.

[123] See, eg, Voss Report (n 55) paras 5ff; European Parliament resolution (n 5) para 7.

[124] See, eg, from the US literature: WB Wendel, 'Controlling the Delegation of Control' (2024) 25 *Theoretical Inquiries in Law*, available at SSRN: ssrn.com/abstract=4566351; T Baker, 'What Litigation Funders Can Learn About Settlement Rights from the Law of Liability Insurance' University of Pennsylvania, Institute for Law and Economics Research Paper No 23-41; A Sebok, 'Should the

typical relationships between insurers and policyholders or defendants/claimants and guarantors involved in third-party proceedings reveal similar dynamics, as the added third party is often granted the power to intervene in the litigation and influence defences, litigation strategies, counterclaims, and crossclaims.[125] Similarly, creditors and others with financial interests can influence disputes involving those interests as the law often permits non-owners to manage claims, potentially sidelining the actual owner. This is seen, for instance, in derivative actions, where shareholders assert company rights, and in indirect actions (often referred to as 'oblique actions') where creditors exercise the rights in the debtors' name and for their benefit. Both derivative and indirect actions are widely recognised legal mechanisms across jurisdictions.

The purpose of drawing these parallels is not to equate the role of funders with third-party proceedings or derivative and indirect actions, but to offer reflections as to whether the challenges posed by funders' control can be seen as part of a larger legal landscape.[126] Procedural laws are not entirely unfamiliar with granting or conferring power to a third party that may affect the course of legal proceedings. Rather than overemphasising the risks of potential power transfers to funders – a concern often highlighted by critics of the TPLF market – a more balanced approach could be beneficial. It might be worth exploring, particularly in the EU context, how existing solutions and case law that have effectively addressed similar conflicts and balanced diverse interests could provide guidance for the challenges arising from TPLF.

ii. Control and Oversight in Practice

In the literature, a distinction is often made between passive and active funding.[127] In passive funding, the funder plays a minimal role after the initial case vetting, primarily receiving updates on key developments. In contrast, active funding involves a more hands-on approach, with the funder selecting lawyers, influencing legal strategies, and controlling settlement decisions. The United States and Australia are typically cited as examples of active funding systems, while Canada and the United Kingdom are noted for their passive approaches, influenced by prohibitions on champerty and maintenance.[128]

Law Preserve Party Control? Litigation Investment, Insurance Law, and Double Standards' (2015) 56 *William & Mary Law Review* 833; AJ Sebok, 'What Do We Talk About When We Talk About Control?' (2014) 82 *Fordham Law Review* 2939, 2955ff; JT Molot, 'A Market in Litigation Risk' (2009) 76 *University of Chicago Law Review* 367, 380.

[125] ibid.

[126] This argument is also further developed in subsection IV.F.

[127] See, eg, C Veljanovski, 'Third Party Litigation Funding in Europe' (2012) 8 *Journal of Law, Economics & Policy* 405, 442f; M Steinitz, 'Follow the Money? A Proposed approach for Disclosure of Litigation Finance Agreements' (2019) 53 *UC Davis Law Review* 1073, 1108ff; I Tillema, *Entrepreneurial Mass Litigation: Balancing the Building Blocks* (Rotterdam, Erasmus University, 2019) 58, 177ff.

[128] Eg, J Kalajdzic, P Cashman, and A Longmoore, 'Justice for Profit: A Comparative Analysis of Australian, Canadian and U.S. Third Party' (2013) 61 *The American Journal of Comparative Law* 121; Veljanovski (n 127) 408.

However, such binary distinctions and categorisations often only scratch the surface of a more complex reality. The differences across jurisdictions can be subtle, especially considering the international nature of many TPLF entities and their cross-border engagement. Funders may adjust their involvement based on specific cases and national rules. For instance, in the Netherlands, the WAMCA prescribes as an admissibility requirement that control over the action remains with the claimant.[129] Consequently, there is a common understanding among practitioners of the funders' role to be an advisory one, focusing on financial oversight without interfering substantially in legal decisions.[130]

Moreover, the true extent of funder involvement is difficult to ascertain since many TPLF agreements are not publicly disclosed.[131] Therefore, our understanding relies on literature, case law, and self-reported information from funders, their clients, or their opponents, with anecdotal evidence often cited in policy documents but also contested.[132] Conflicts between funders and clients in high-profile cases occasionally generate sensational legal headlines and may influence public opinion.

A notable example is a US case between Burford Capital, one of the largest global litigation funders, and Sysco Corporation, the world's global foodservice leader, that hit the news in 2023.[133] Burford, having invested over $140 million in Sysco's antitrust claims, exercised its contractual veto when Sysco attempted to settle for an amount Burford deemed too low, alleging that Sysco breached the TPLF agreement by failing to obtain consent. This led to multiple legal actions, including Sysco's attempt to nullify an arbitration order that blocked the settlement.[134] The case drew significant attention, with the US Chamber of Commerce joining as amicus curiae to express its concerns about the TPLF industry's practices.[135]

Burford and Sysco ultimately resolved their dispute quickly through a settlement;[136] Burford created a subsidiary to purchase Sysco's claims and substitute Sysco in the proceedings.[137] Despite this win-win outcome, the case served

[129] Art 3:305a(2) DCC requires that claim organisations have sufficient resources and maintain control over the action. Excessive decision-making power by the funder would also conflict with the requirement to safeguard the interests of the constituency. Therefore, Dutch courts can review the claim organisation's financial structure and request the TPLF agreement.

[130] D Horeman and M de Monchy (eds), *Unlocking the WAMCA: A Practical Guide to the New Collective Action Regime in the Netherlands*, 3rd edn (De Brauw Blackstone Westbroek, 2024) 55f.

[131] Steinitz (n 62) 461.

[132] Eg, Voss Report (n 55) paras 5ff; European Parliament resolution (n 5) paras 7ff; EPRS Studies (n 39) 29. *cf.* Skog (n 101).

[133] See, eg A Frankel, 'Sysco Sues Litigation Funder Burford, Blasts Boies Schiller over $140 million Soured Deal' *Reuters* (10 March 2023).

[134] For an overview see Baker (n 124).

[135] C Symons, 'US Chamber Backs Sysco In Litigation Funding Dispute' (28 March 2023) www.law360.com/articles/1590762/us-chamber-backs-sysco-in-litigation-funding-dispute (accessed 15 August 2024).

[136] A Frankel, 'Sysco Cedes Antitrust Claims to Litigation Funder Burford as Two Sides Drop Cases' *Reuters* (29 June 2023).

[137] M Scarcella, 'Litigation Funder Burford Wins Bid to Take Over Sysco Chicken Antitrust Cases' *Reuters* (22 March 2024).

as a vivid illustration of the potential perils of the TPLF market. For this reason, it was also repetitively instrumentalised by the strongest opponents of TPLF, most notably the US Chamber of Commerce.[138] Overall, the *Sysco/Burford* case raises key issues about control over the litigation, the enforceability of TPLF agreements, and the consequences of their breaches.[139] It also brings to the forefront questions regarding the need for stricter oversight, including potential judicial or administrative interventions, to balance contractual autonomy with necessary safeguards in the TPLF industry.[140]

The examples from various jurisdictions, including the *Burford/Sysco* case, ultimately reveal how funder involvement can influence both litigation outcomes and public perception. They also highlight the need for clear and enforceable boundaries in TPLF agreements (see also immediately below), ensuring that funders' roles remain properly defined and aligned with the principles of fairness and legal autonomy.

E. Balancing Control and Interests in Funding Agreements

Balancing funders' influence with litigants' procedural autonomy is complex. Funders that provide substantial financial support, naturally seek to protect their investments, ensuring that their resources are utilised effectively. Fully excluding funders from any control reduces their incentives to fund a case or increase funders' fees due to enhanced risks.

Additionally, as the interviewees emphasised, funders are legally and contractually required to inform their investors about the risks associated with funded cases. This reporting duty is not intended to interfere with the litigation. It is mandated by financial authorities, subject to sanctions, and it is crucial for funders to meet their obligations to investors, such as pension funds. To comply, funders must stay updated on case management and strategy. Therefore, funding agreements typically include reporting obligations for the funded party, ensuring transparency while protecting the confidentiality essential to the litigation.[141]

[138] US Chamber of Commerce – Institute for Legal Reforms (ILR), 'Grim Realities: Debunking Myths in Third-Party Litigation Funding' (August 2024) 6ff; US Chamber of Commerce – Institute for Legal Reforms (ILR), 'Lawsuit Against Burford Gives a Peek Into the Secretive World of Litigation Funding' (2 August 2023) instituteforlegalreform.com/blog/lawsuit-against-burford-gives-a-peak-into-the-secretive-world-of-litigation-funding/ (accessed 15 August 2024); US Chamber of Commerce – Institute for Legal Reforms (ILR), 'Control Litigation, Maximize Profits: The Real Stories of TPLF' (21 February 2024) instituteforlegalreform.com/blog/control-litigation-maximize-profits-the-real-stories-of-tplf/ (accessed 15 August 2024).

[139] DWC Feman, 'Breaching a Litigation Funding Agreement – The Sysco/Burford Story' *Bloomberg Law* (29 March 2023) news.bloomberglaw.com/us-law-week/breaching-a-litigation-funding-agreement-the-sysco-burford-story (accessed 15 August 2024).

[140] See also below subsection IV.F with examples from the NL (n 154).

[141] See EPRS Studies (n 39) 66f; A Lempiner and J Barnes, 'The Litigation Funding Agreement', in S Friel (ed), *The Law and Business of Litigation Finance* (London, Bloomsbury Professional, 2020) 143, 154.

Balancing investor interests with case management in TPLF agreements is typically handled through detailed contractual provisions. The interviewees have also emphasised that when disagreements arise, such as over settlement terms, the funding contracts often include clauses that require neutral third-party involvement to ensure impartial resolution, binding both parties by the outcome.[142] Arbitration or mediation proceedings are often part of this process.[143] The validity of such clauses, however, is jurisdiction-specific and depends on the governing law to the TPLF agreement. While such formal dispute resolution mechanisms are standard, the interviews revealed that funders often rely on informal consultations with experienced litigators, legal advisors, retired judges, and other experts. This approach allows funders to seek expert opinions on strategic decisions, such as settlements, without strictly adhering to formal procedures, highlighting the practical aspects of their decision-making process.

Some final considerations are necessary to complete the picture. The debate on control and conflicts of interest in TPLF arrangements is often shaped by the US and UK contexts, but the situation in the EU differs significantly. In the EU, unlike in other parts of the world, contractual relationships between funders and lawyers representing the funded party are uncommon. This is due to the widespread restrictions or prohibitions on non-lawyers holding ownership stakes in law firms, though the question of the compatibility with EU law of such prohibition is pending at the CJEU.[144] Tripartite relationships between the funder, lawyer, and client are also uncommon, meaning that lawyers are primarily accountable to their clients, with a duty to protect and serve their interests exclusively. The interviews confirmed that European funders generally view settlements as a risk management tool rather than a hindrance, contrasting with the more adversarial approach in the United States, where punitive damages can significantly increase financial stakes. Given these differences, it is questionable whether concerns about funders' control observed in other regions apply directly to the EU.

It is also unrealistic to assume that issues of control and decision-making will not be explicitly detailed in TPLF agreements. These contractual terms are rooted in the principles of freedom of contract and private autonomy, though their limits vary by jurisdiction. In the EU, the Unfair Contract Terms Directive (UCTD)[145] applies but only if a funder contracts directly with consumers, which is highly unlikely as discussed above.[146] In this scenario, the funding contract would be subject to the stricter transparency and fairness requirements of the UCTD. Arbitration clauses in these cases would be considered unfair and not have a binding effect, at least if not individually negotiated. If, however, a claim organisation or consumer association the party to the TPLF agreement, as is usually the case in

[142] See also Lempiner and Barnes (n 141) 158.
[143] ibid.
[144] See above n 75.
[145] Council Directive 93/13/EEC of 5 April 1993 on unfair terms in consumer contracts [1995] OJ L95/29 (as amended by subsequent Directive 2011/83/EU and Directive (EU) 2019/2161).
[146] See subsection III.B.i.

the EU, the UCTD does not apply. In this scenario, the content of the clauses will be governed by general contract law or specific laws such as those implementing the RAD, like the WAMCA, which for instance includes maintaining control over the action to the claimant as an admissibility requirement.[147]

Breaches of contractual obligations under TPLF agreements could lead to satellite litigation, as seen in the *Sysco/Burford* case.[148] However, both parties typically seek to avoid such disputes, as evidenced by the mutually beneficial resolution of the *Sysco/Burford* conflict.

F. Unique Challenges or Common Struggles?

The multifaceted role of litigation funders[149] introduces complex dynamics and raises concerns about their influence, both at the forefront and in the shadow of procedure.[150] However, these challenges are not unique to litigation funding. As previously analysed,[151] third parties' control over litigation strategies can also be seen in other procedural contexts, such as third-party proceedings or derivative and indirect actions. The same dynamics are also evident in banking contracts,[152] where covenants, such as negative pledges, often restrict borrowers' behaviour for protecting lenders' interests. Likewise, litigation funding agreements often limit the flexibility of the counterparty to protect the funders' anticipated returns, for example by requiring the funder's consent for settlements or claim assignment.[153]

Thus, concerns over funders' control should be viewed in a broader procedural and financial context of analogous dynamics. Recognising these parallels suggests that the challenges posed are not as novel as perceived. Moreover, if current frameworks fall short to provide solutions, it is essential to articulate and assess the broader interests that set funding agreements apart, especially given the funders' support of private enforcement of rights – typically contract or tort claims – even in public interest litigation and collective actions. So, for instance, covenants in banking and funding contracts impose similar constraints on contractual freedom, which is why both types of contracts are governed by the same protective laws (eg, the UCTD in the EU). However, the need for prudential regulation of banks stems not from the content of their contractual activities, but from the necessity to protect depositors and ensure financial stability. Likewise, funders that qualify as 'investment funds' under EU law (eg, pension funds), are already regulated accordingly to ensure appropriate oversight of their function vis-à-vis their investors.

[147] Art 3:305a(2) Dutch Civil Code; Horeman and De Monchy (n 129) 55f.

[148] See above n 129.

[149] See above subsection III.B.

[150] See above subsection IV.D.i.

[151] ibid.

[152] For corresponding clauses and similarities between litigation funding agreements and bank credits agreement see, eg, Lempiner and Barnes (n 141) 147f.

[153] ibid 153ff.

While many control issues echo common patterns seen in other legal and financial contexts, criticism against funders often arises from misconceptions about their role in litigation. To clarify this, further analogies can be drawn. One such comes from competition law: Entities with significant market power are typically referred to as 'price makers' because they set prices and influence others' pricing strategies, unlike 'price takers', who lack this power and must accept the prices established by 'price makers'. By substituting 'price' with 'rule', this model helps explain much of the criticism against TPLF. While funders are often seen as 'rule makers' with substantial powers, they should actually be considered 'rule takers'. The ultimate authority in litigation resides with the judicial system: judges, not funders, are the 'rule makers', who determine the success or failure of funded claims, thus, holding the true 'market power' in the litigation funding landscape. It is, in the end, for the court to safeguard the proceedings and, where necessary, balance the rights of all parties involved, which may include reviewing TPLF agreements and the roles of funders and other participants in a particular case. And indeed, in recent WAMCA cases, Dutch courts have exercised this oversight by assessing the agreement and the factual independence of the claiming organisation from commercial funders.[154]

Nevertheless, opponents of TPLF tend to portray funders as the (unofficial) 'rule makers' and attribute various issues to the TPLF's modus operandi. Such concerns range from the price paid by litigants for accessing justice (eg, such as allegedly 'disproportionate' funders fees)[155] to fears of forum shopping (eg, when claimants, supported by funders, submit 'similar' claims to different tribunals in search of a favourable ruling).[156] Such or similar arguments often overlook a reality: many of the problems attributed to TPLF stem from deficiencies within the judicial procedures and broader justice system, rather than from the TPLF market itself. Funders merely identify such structural and procedural inefficiencies within the justice system and leverage these to their advantage. For instance, forum shopping in the case mentioned above is not driven by the availability of funding mechanisms, contrary to critics' suggestions, but by – what appears to be – an inconsistent application of doctrines like *res judicata*, which is intended to prevent the re-litigation of 'similar' matters. Strengthening the enforcement of this doctrine would more effectively address this issue than directing criticism at the existence of TPLF.

[154] See in particular District Court Amsterdam, 25 October 2023, ECLI:NL:RBAMS:2023:6683 (*St. Nuon-CLAIM v Vattenfall*); District Court Amsterdam, 10 January 2024, ECLI:NL:RBAMS:2024:83 (*TBYP/SMC/SOMI v TikTok*); District Court The Hague, 20 September 2023, ECLI:NL:RBDHA:2023:14036 (*St. Investor Loss Compensation v Airbus SE*). In the latter case, the claim was declared inadmissible as the claimant organisation (seemingly) depended too much on the expertise of the commercial funder; Kramer (n 27) 106, 113f.

[155] See, eg, European Parliament resolution (n 5) Preamble G; European Parliament Draft Directive, Recital 26; EPRS Studies (n 39) 65.

[156] See, eg, A Uzelac, 'Third-Party Litigation Funding as a Vehicle for Access to Justice: A Sustainable Avenue or a Dead End?', in X Kramer and others (eds), *Sustaining Access to Justice: New Avenues for Costs and Funding* (Oxford, Hart Publishing, forthcoming).

In light of these considerations, it is worth questioning whether these (or similar) concerns are truly rooted in TPLF itself. How unique are these issues, and do they justify the calls for stringent regulation that could render TPLF non-viable, such as one capping funders' fees to 10 per cent as is done in Germany?[157] Who would benefit from the underenforcement of rights? Certainly not the claimants in funder-supported cases. Moreover, even if risks exist, procedural mechanisms already could offer ways to address them. For instance, a legal framework could allow judges to impose cost sanctions on funders who engage in abusive or frivolous litigation, similar to how existing frameworks permit sanctions against litigants who fail to attempt ADR or mediation and lose in court. Such measures could curb the alleged risks of TPLF while preserving its benefits.

Unfortunately, the political and policy discussions surrounding TPLF, influenced as they are by various motivations, have not always been as constructive as one might expect. Criticisms directed at funders often overlook the deeper systemic issues contributing to these problems, with the most significant being the lack of alternative means to access justice. This broader concern highlights fundamental gaps in the justice system that drive reliance on litigation funding. For sure, there are limits to the costs that a publicly subsidised adjudication system can face. Once the limits of public funding are reached, however, restricting TPLF out of the fear that this can disrupt procedural autonomy and fairness would inevitably curb access to justice. Other alternatives likely exist that would avoid throwing the baby out with the bathwater.

V. Concluding Remarks

The rise of collective actions and different forms of strategic litigation has triggered the debate on TPLF and the role of funders in Europe. Although TPLF has a longer history, the evolving market and its increasing involvement in high-profile collective actions and public interest litigation – often aimed at addressing the conduct of businesses and governments – have changed the dynamics. The 2022 European Parliament Resolution reflects this shift, calling for stricter regulation that extends beyond the existing rules on conflicts of interest found in the RAD, national laws, and self-regulation instruments.

Based on literature, case law, legal practice, and information collected from interviews, this chapter has examined the role of funders, challenges, and attributed risks – which have also underpinned the scarcely substantiated calls for stricter regulation.[158]

[157] See above subsection II.C and n 23.

[158] A Stadler, 'Third-Party Funding in Collective Redress', in X Kramer, S Voet, L Ködderitzsch, M Tulibacka and B Hess (eds), *Delivering Justice: A Holistic and Multidisciplinary Approach* (Oxford,

It is evident that in certain cases the presence of TPLF is essential to ensure access to justice. Public legal aid is limited, litigation costs in complex cases are high, and individual claimants – or representative organisations like consumer associations in collective actions – cannot easily bear the inherent risks of litigation. In such instances, the financial resources and expertise provided by funders become indispensable. In this sense, funders help facilitate remedies for violations of EU law, including consumer law, privacy law, competition law, and environmental law, thereby empowering claimants and contributing to the development of case law. Research in the Netherlands, a leader in collective action systems in the EU, has shown that so far collective actions for compensation (need to) fully rely on commercial funding.[159]

While third-party litigation funders are not established to serve as noble knights or, as the title of this book suggests, 'heroes' of the legal procedure, it is equally unrealistic to depict them as greedy figures like *Gordon Gekko*, who will boost frivolous litigation and undermine justice in pursuit of maximising their return on investment. In reality, funders are typically approached by claimants/ claiming organisations or – more often – their lawyers. After an extensive legal and financial assessment, including due diligence by their support team, they accept only between 3 to 10 per cent of cases. Funders cannot afford to engage in 'ambulance chasing' or finance unmeritorious litigation, as their financial sustainability hinges on sound risk management, expertise, and a strong reputation. The high success rate of commercially funded cases – which represent only a small fraction of those brought to court – further contradicts the arguments of some critical voices.[160]

A downside of these qualities is, of course, that cases with low financial value or very high risks are generally not appealing to commercial funders. As a result, the TPLF market is only relevant for certain types of cases, and its role in that regard is limited. Entrusting private profit-driven actors with the decision of which cases can or cannot proceed to court may be undesirable. This alone highlights the enduring importance of a robust public legal aid system, coupled with a justice system that is equipped to efficiency and reduce costs and risks of litigation.

This overall positive assessment of the role of commercial litigation funders does not imply that monitoring the growth of the litigation finance market and maintaining oversight over TPLF is unnecessary. For the sake of transparency, ensuring procedural autonomy, and avoiding conflicts of interest, TPLF

Hart Publishing, 2022) 151; Gsell, Meller-Hannich and Stadler (n 22) Augenhofer and Dori (n 39); ILFA (n 99); See also the contributions to a seminar organised by Erasmus School of Law: A Cordina and E Storskrubb, 'The Future Regulation of Third-Party Funding in Europe, Conference Report' (2022) 26 Nederlands-Vlaams tijdschrift voor mediation en conflictmanagement (TDM) 38.

[159] See above subsection II.B.

[160] See above subsection III.B.c.

agreements must meet specific requirements and, where appropriate, be subject to judicial oversight. However, overly strict regulation and rigid caps on funders' fees will stifle the development of the TPLF market, raise transaction costs, and hinder the evolution of the European collective action system, especially for high-risk cases that are essential for the development of the law to reach the court.

INDEX

www.ingramcontent.com/pod-product-compliance
Ingram Content Group UK Ltd.
Pitfield, Milton Keynes, MK11 3LW, UK
UKHW020233290926
15470UKWH00002B/513

9 781509 980529